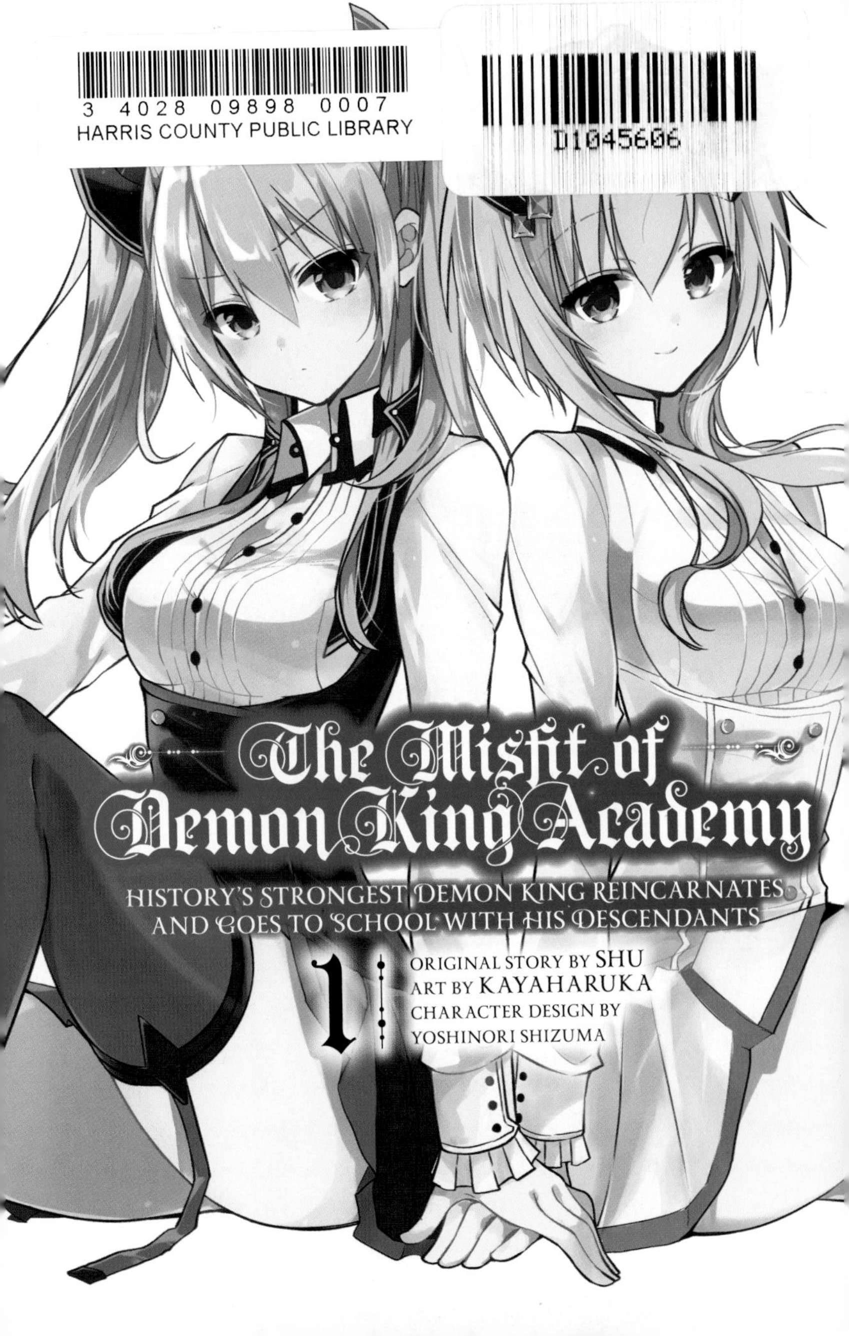
The Misfit of Demon King Academy
HISTORY'S STRONGEST DEMON KING REINCARNATES AND GOES TO SCHOOL WITH HIS DESCENDANTS
1
ORIGINAL STORY BY SHU
ART BY KAYAHARUKA
CHARACTER DESIGN BY
YOSHINORI SHIZUMA

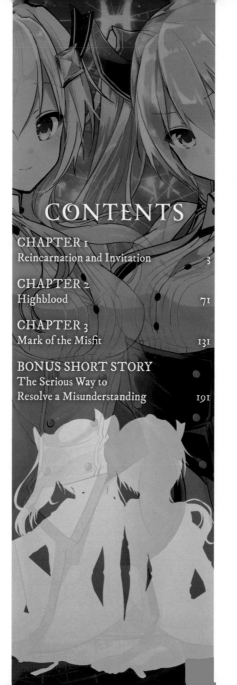

CONTENTS

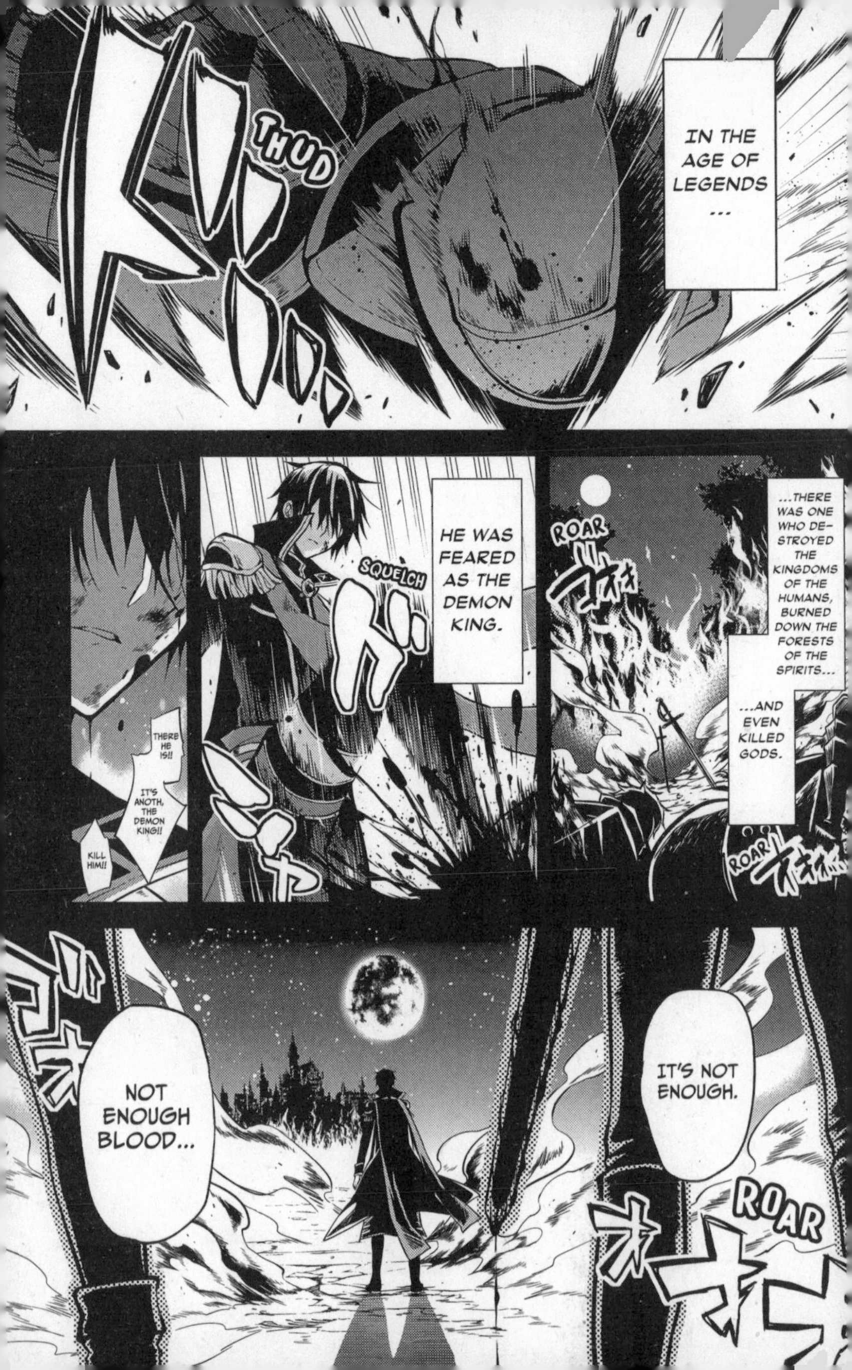
IN THE AGE OF LEGENDS ...
THUD
...THERE WAS ONE WHO DE-STROYED THE KINGDOMS OF THE HUMANS, BURNED DOWN THE FORESTS OF THE SPIRITS...
ROAR
...AND EVEN KILLED GODS.
ROAR
HE WAS FEARED AS THE DEMON KING.
SQUELCH
THERE HE IS!!
IT'S ANOTH, THE DEMON KING!!
KILL HIM!!
IT'S NOT ENOUGH.
ROAR
NOT ENOUGH BLOOD...

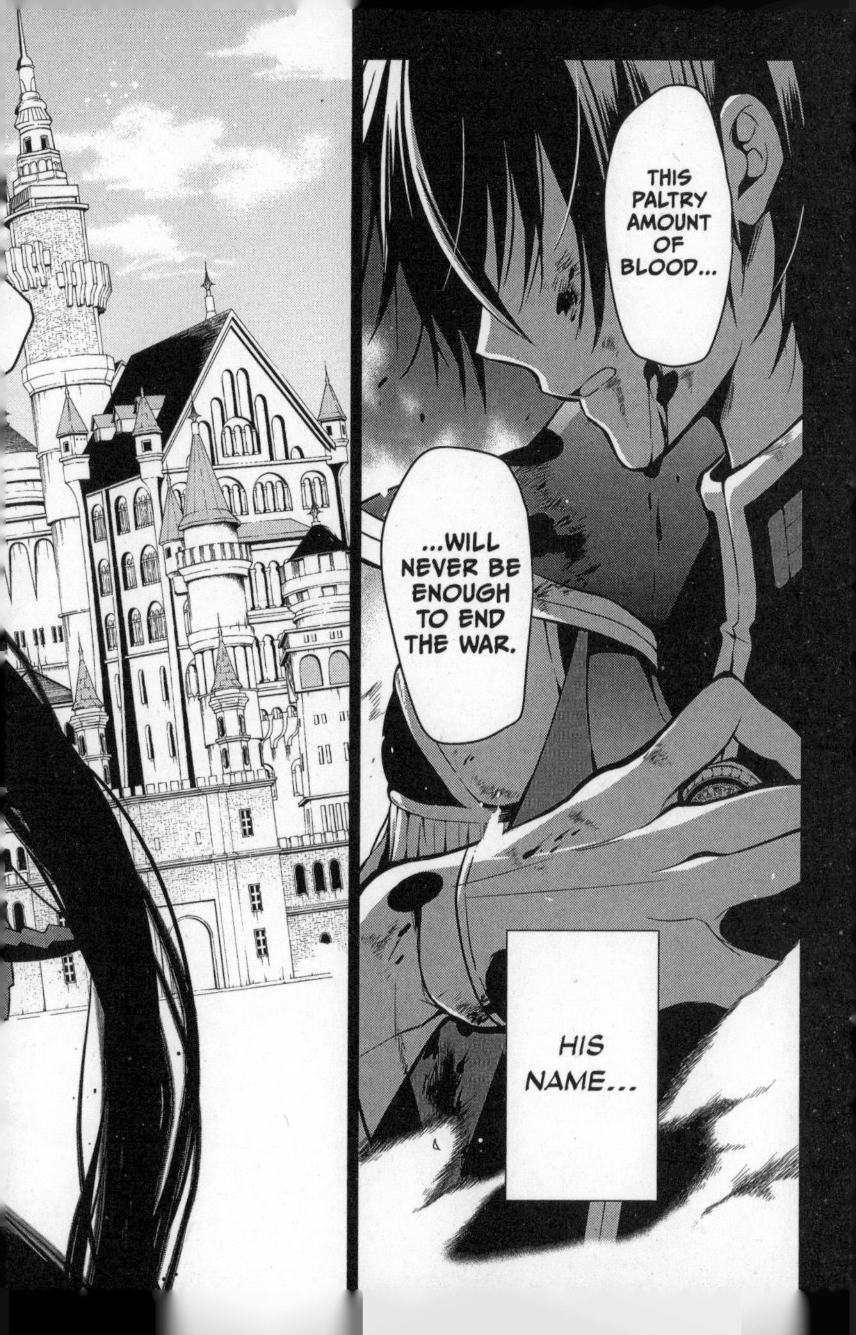
THIS PALTRY AMOUNT OF BLOOD...
...WILL NEVER BE ENOUGH TO END THE WAR.
HIS NAME...

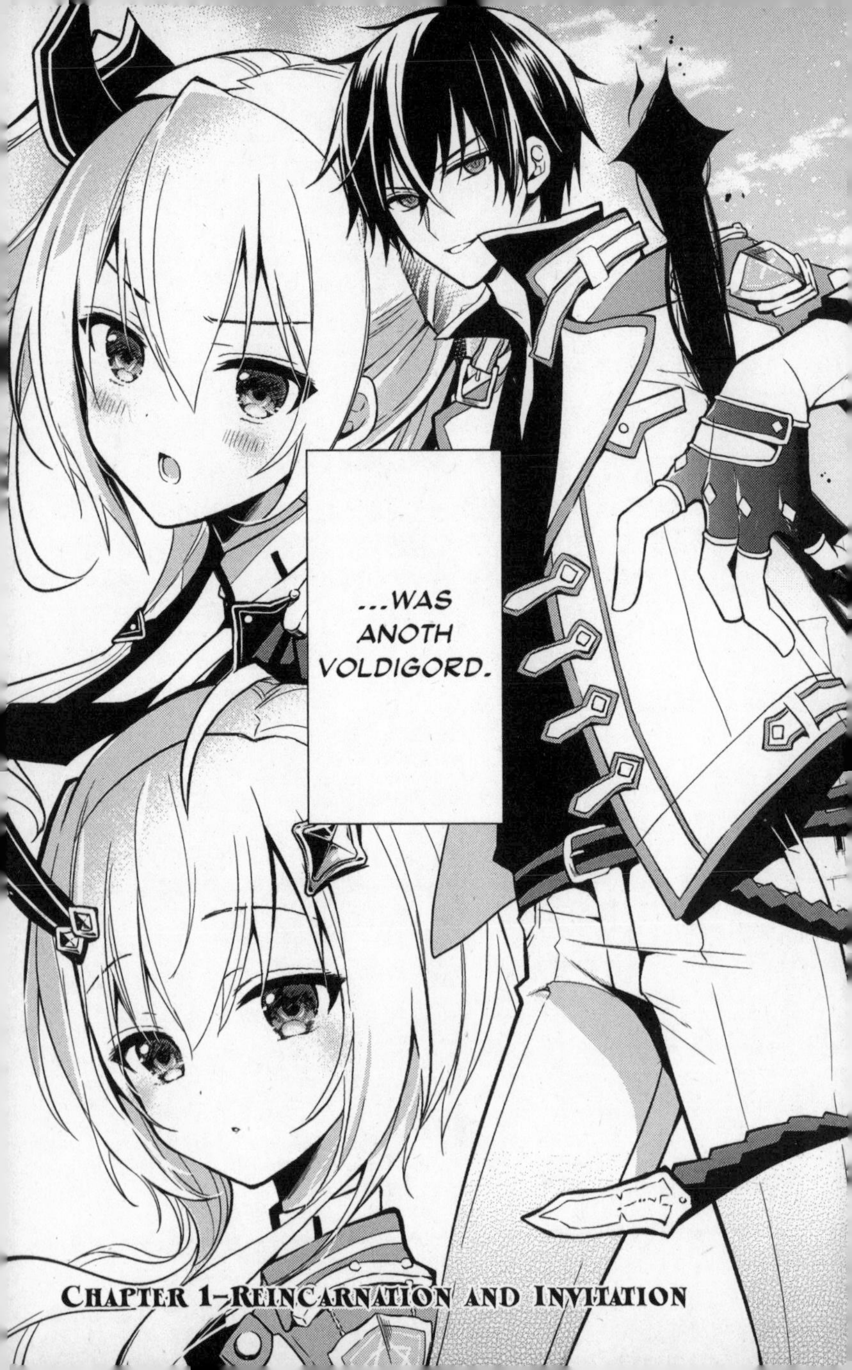
...WAS ANOTH VOLDIGORD.

Chapter 1—Reincarnation and Invitation

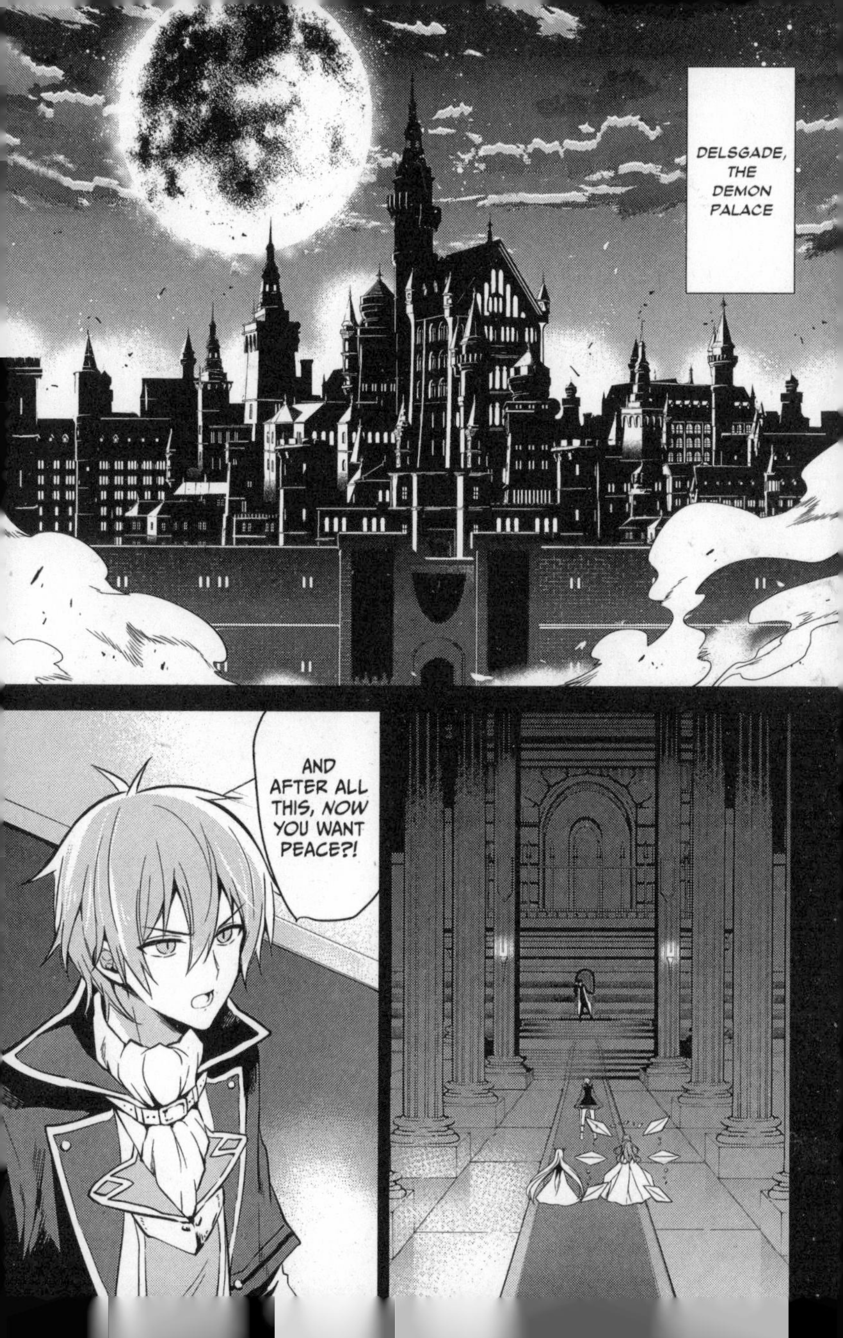
DELSGADE, THE DEMON PALACE
AND AFTER ALL THIS, *NOW* YOU WANT PEACE?!

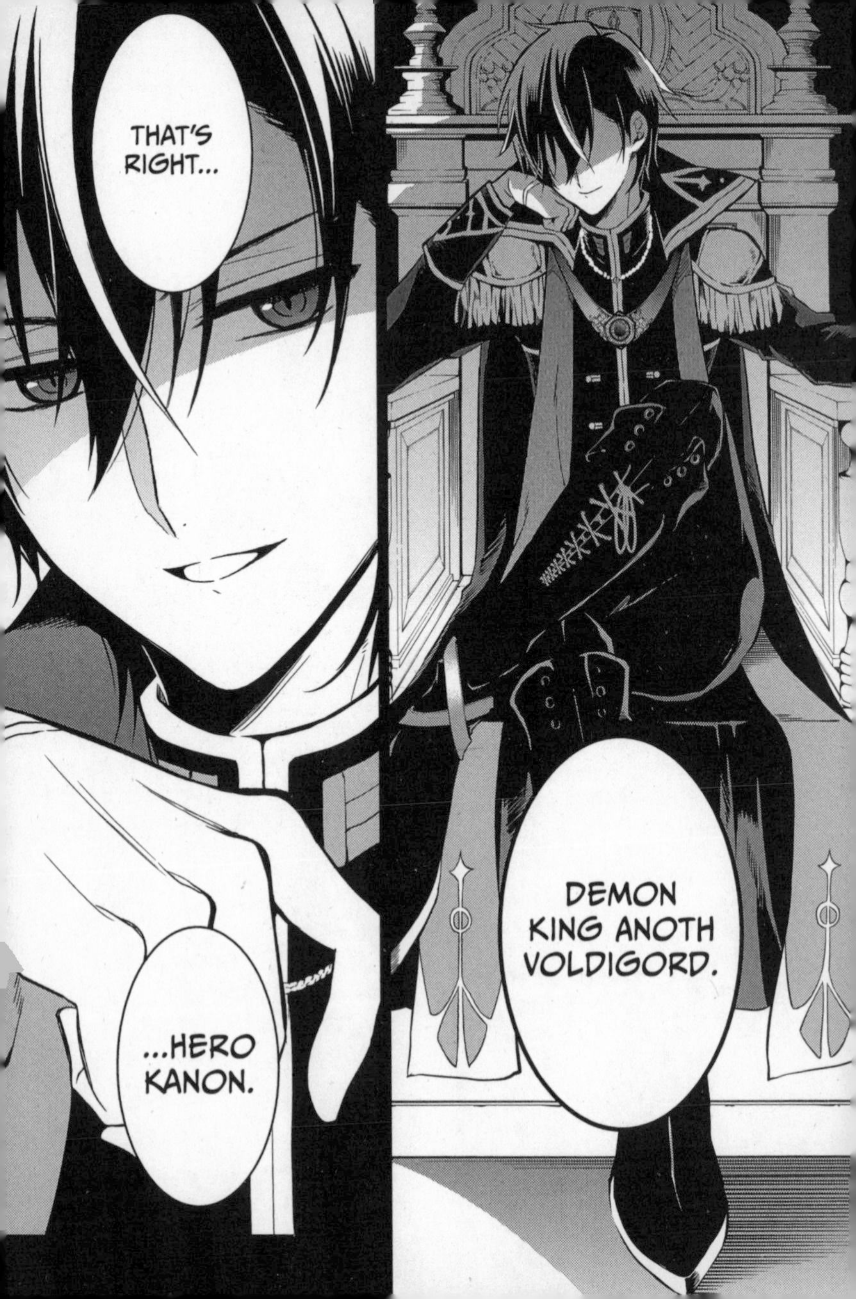
DEMON KING ANOTH VOLDIGORD.
THAT'S RIGHT...
...HERO KANON.

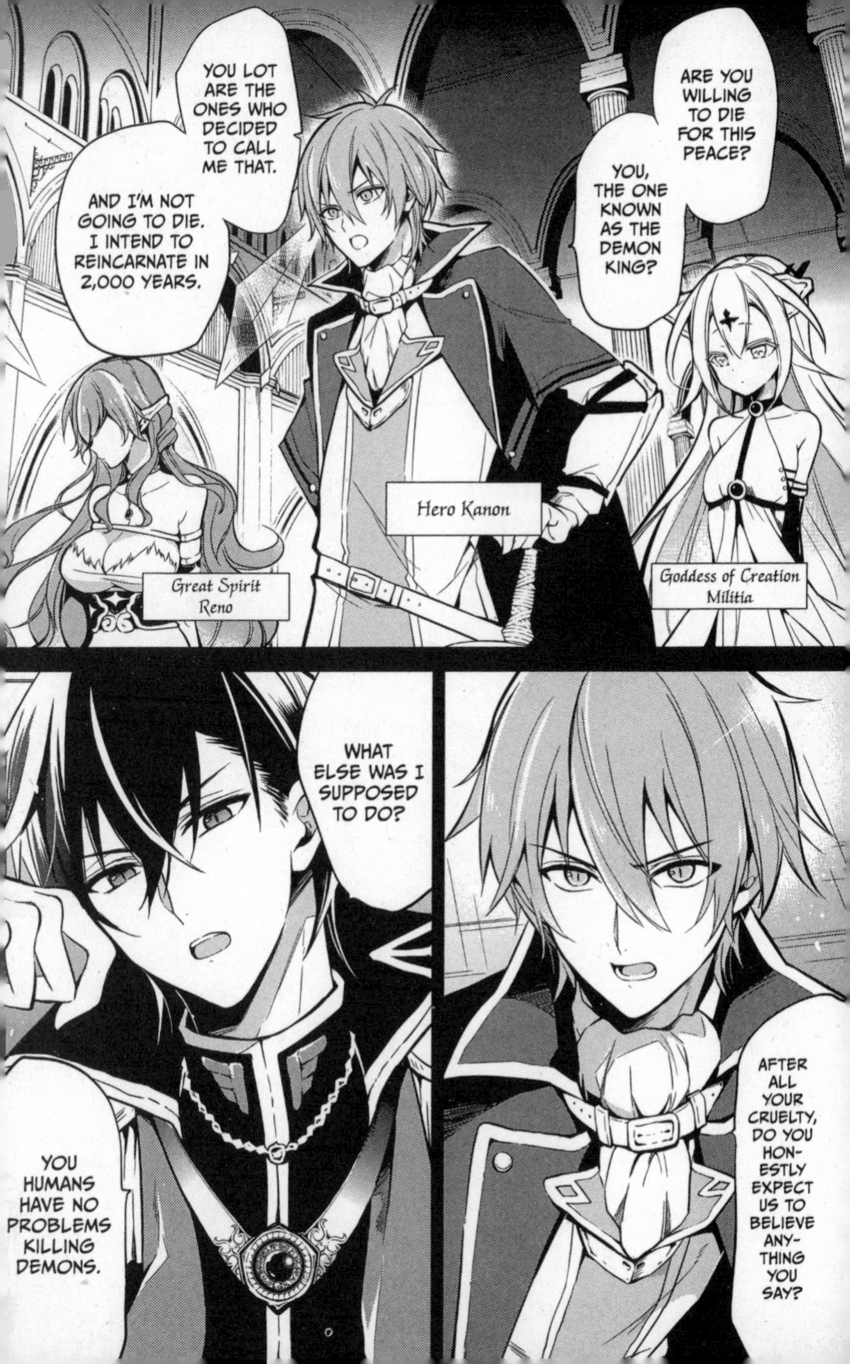
ARE YOU WILLING TO DIE FOR THIS PEACE?
YOU, THE ONE KNOWN AS THE DEMON KING?
YOU LOT ARE THE ONES WHO DECIDED TO CALL ME THAT.
AND I'M NOT GOING TO DIE. I INTEND TO REINCARNATE IN 2,000 YEARS.
Goddess of Creation Militia
Hero Kanon
Great Spirit Reno
AFTER ALL YOUR CRUELTY, DO YOU HON-ESTLY EXPECT US TO BELIEVE ANY-THING YOU SAY?
WHAT ELSE WAS I SUPPOSED TO DO?
YOU HUMANS HAVE NO PROBLEMS KILLING DEMONS.

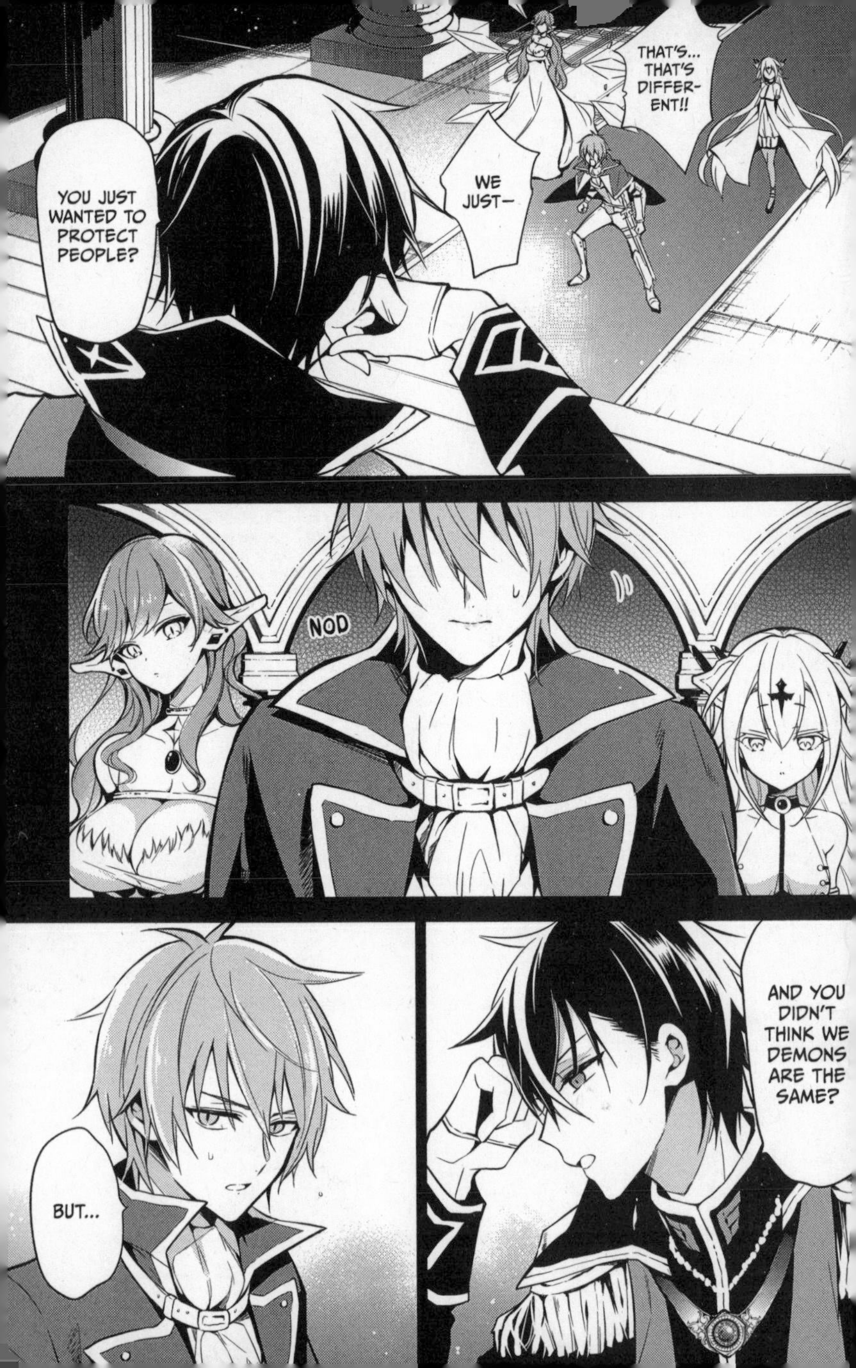
THAT'S... THAT'S DIFFERENT!!
WE JUST—
YOU JUST WANTED TO PROTECT PEOPLE?
NOD
AND YOU DIDN'T THINK WE DEMONS ARE THE SAME?
BUT...

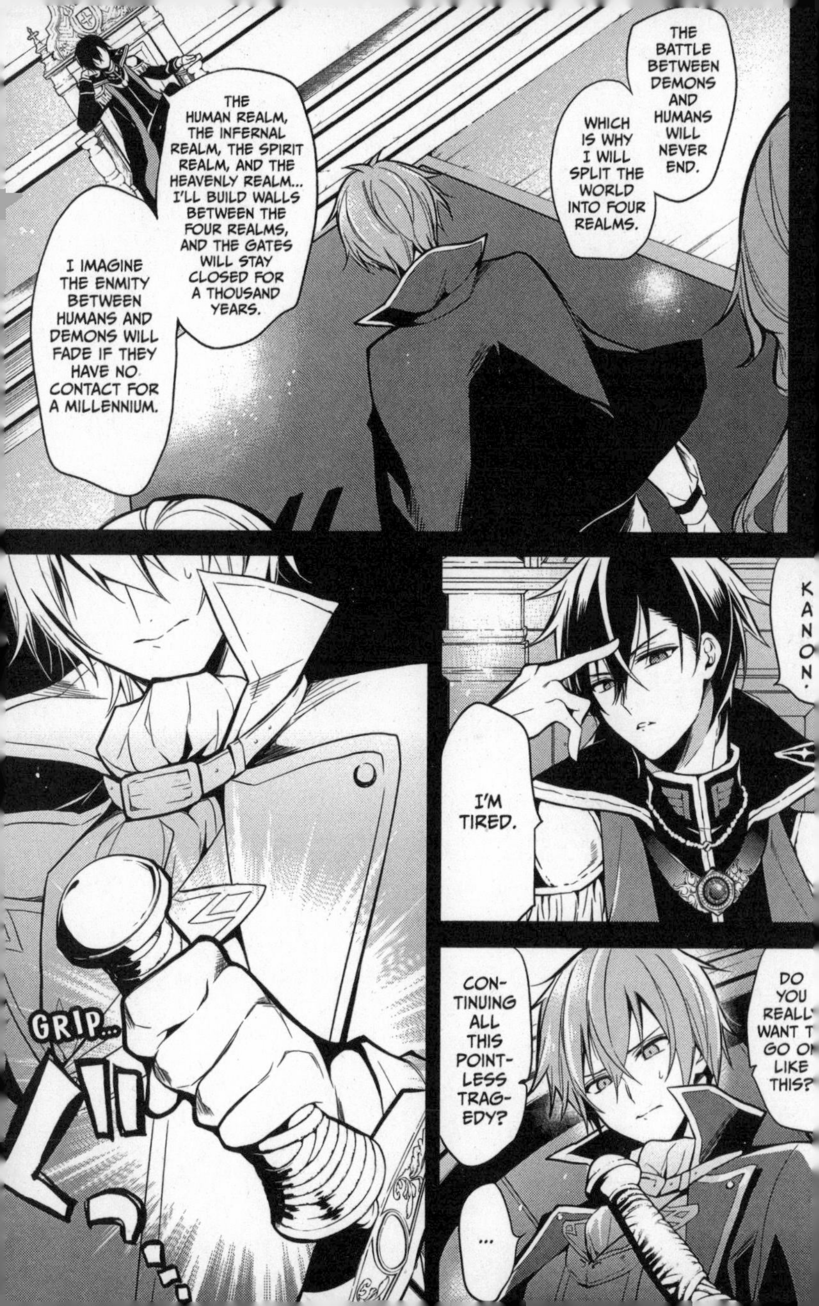
THE BATTLE BETWEEN DEMONS AND HUMANS WILL NEVER END.
WHICH IS WHY I WILL SPLIT THE WORLD INTO FOUR REALMS.
THE HUMAN REALM, THE INFERNAL REALM, THE SPIRIT REALM, AND THE HEAVENLY REALM... I'LL BUILD WALLS BETWEEN THE FOUR REALMS, AND THE GATES WILL STAY CLOSED FOR A THOUSAND YEARS.
I IMAGINE THE ENMITY BETWEEN HUMANS AND DEMONS WILL FADE IF THEY HAVE NO CONTACT FOR A MILLENNIUM.
KANON.
I'M TIRED.
DO YOU REALL WANT T GO O LIKE THIS?
CON-TINUING ALL THIS POINT-LESS TRAG-EDY?
...
GRIP...

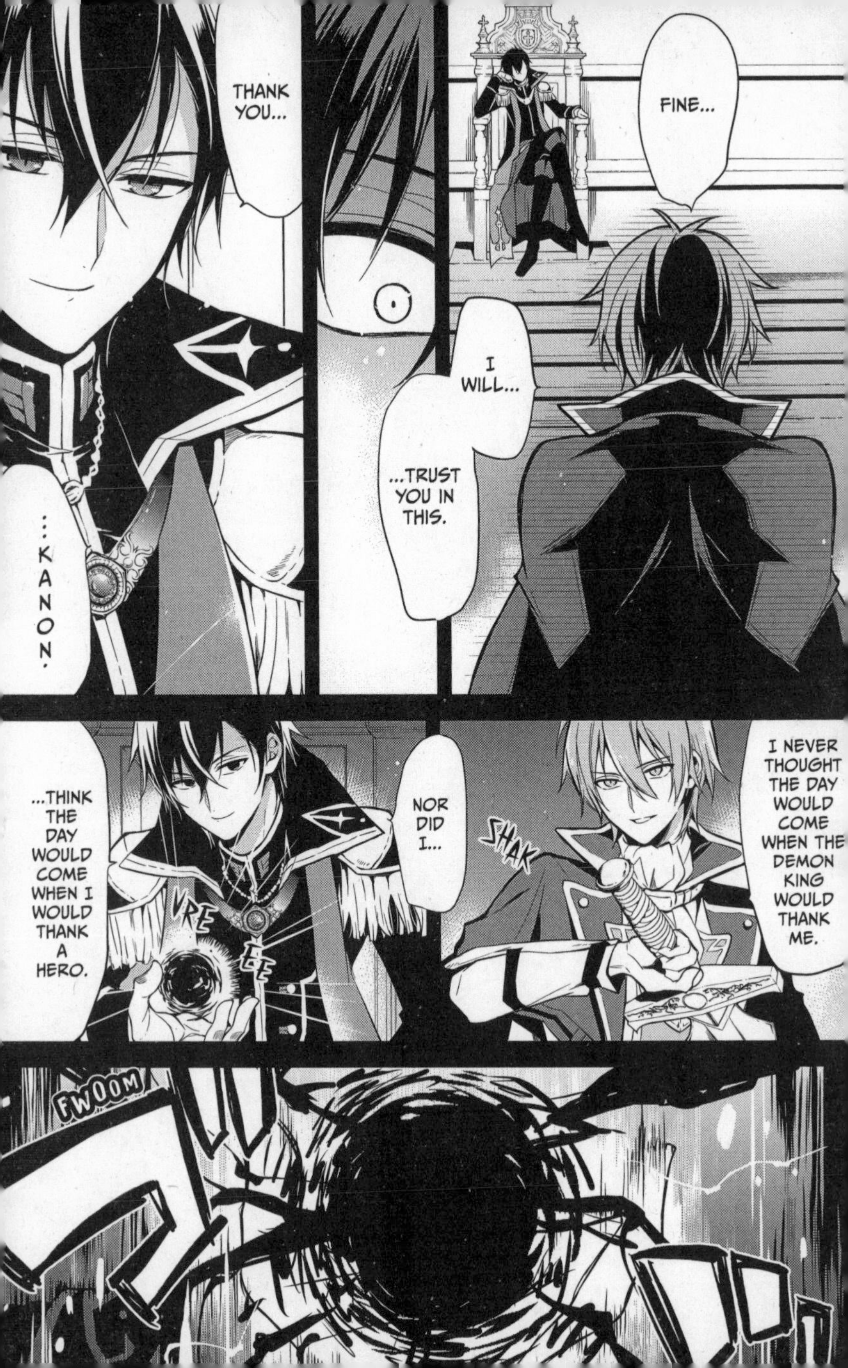
FINE...
I WILL...
...TRUST YOU IN THIS.
THANK YOU...
...KANON.
I NEVER THOUGHT THE DAY WOULD COME WHEN THE DEMON KING WOULD THANK ME.
SHAK
NOR DID I...
...THINK THE DAY WOULD COME WHEN I WOULD THANK A HERO.
VREEE
FWOOM

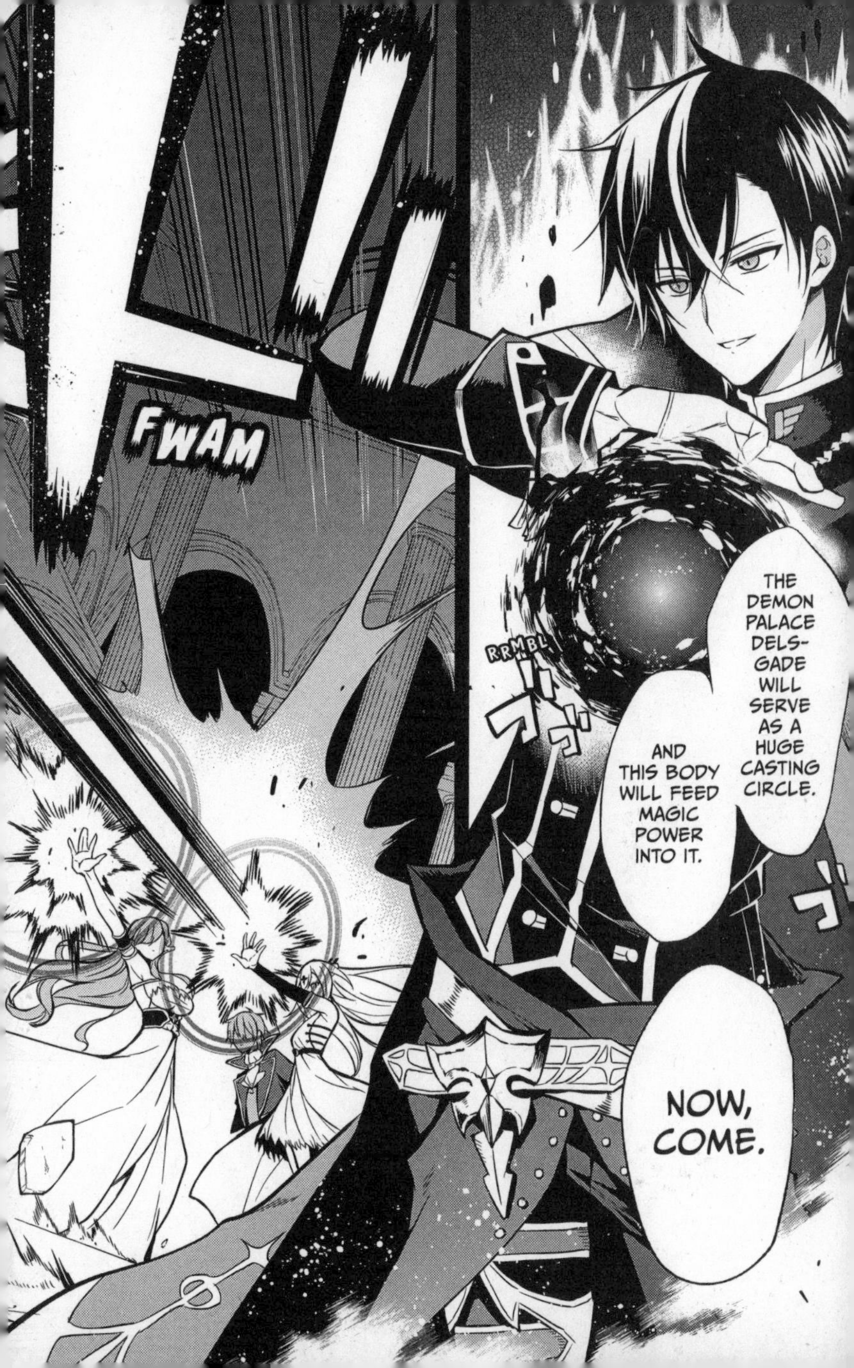
THE DEMON PALACE DELS-GADE WILL SERVE AS A HUGE CASTING CIRCLE.
AND THIS BODY WILL FEED MAGIC POWER INTO IT.
RRMBL
NOW, COME.
FWAM

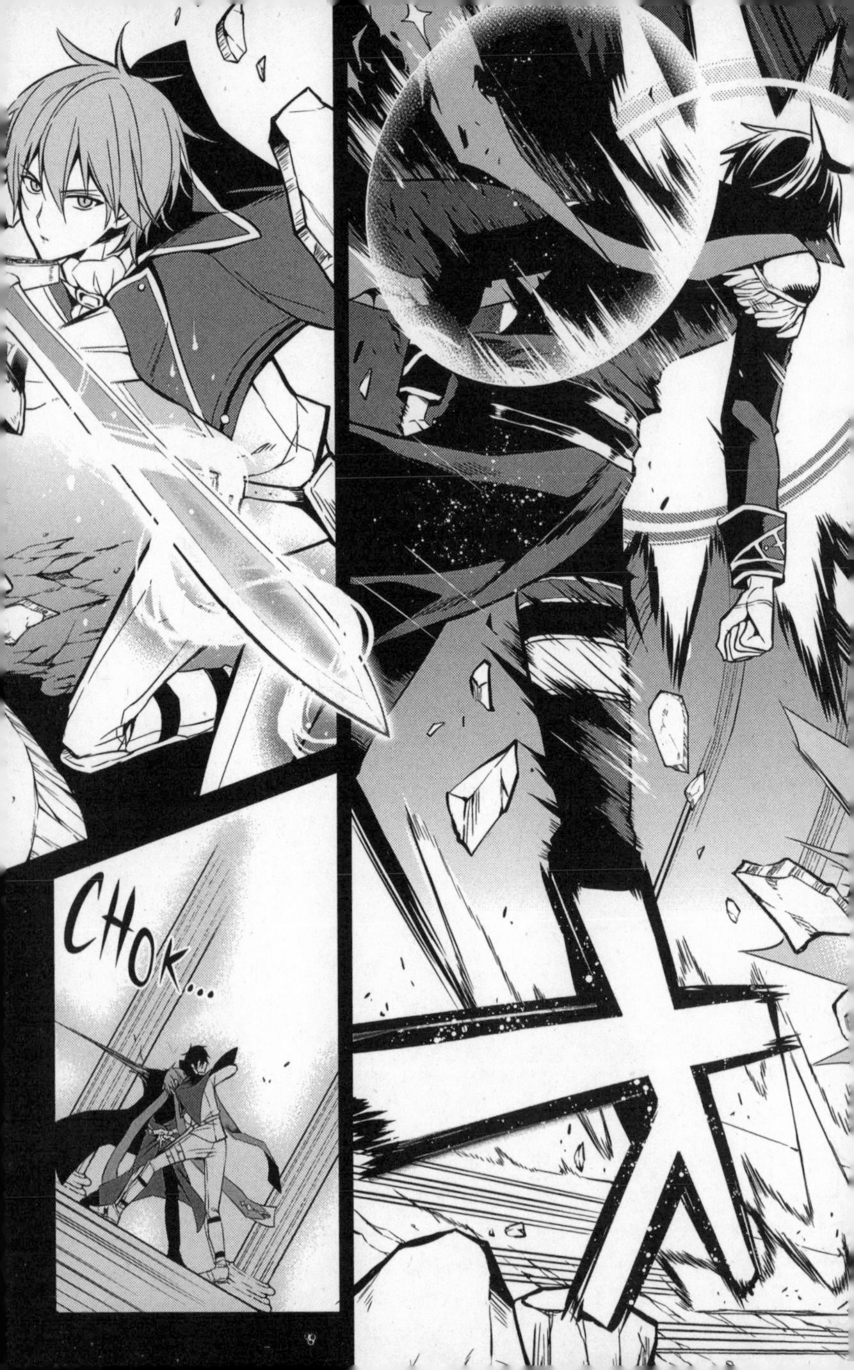
CHOK...

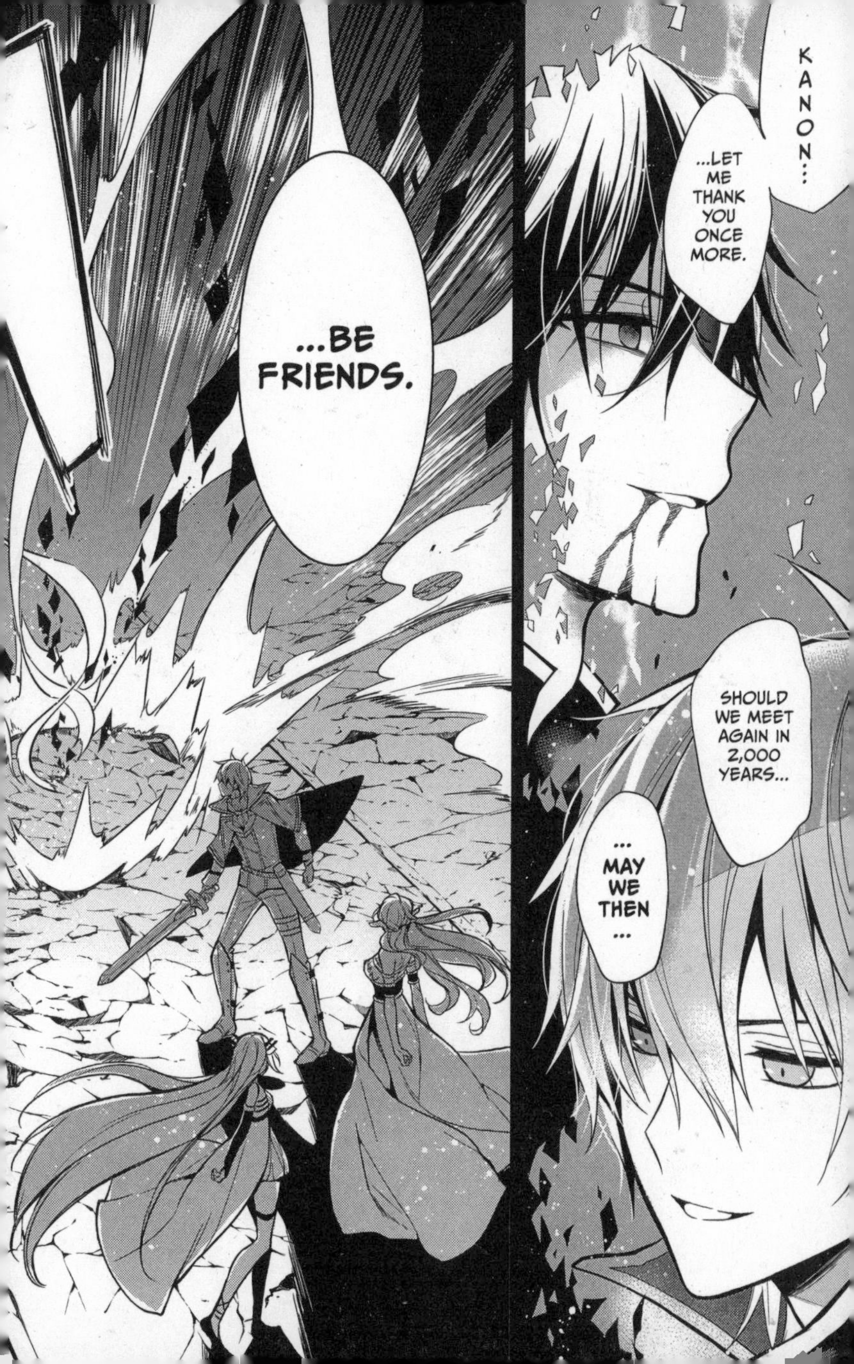
KANON...
...LET ME THANK YOU ONCE MORE.
SHOULD WE MEET AGAIN IN 2,000 YEARS...
...MAY WE THEN ...
...BE FRIENDS.

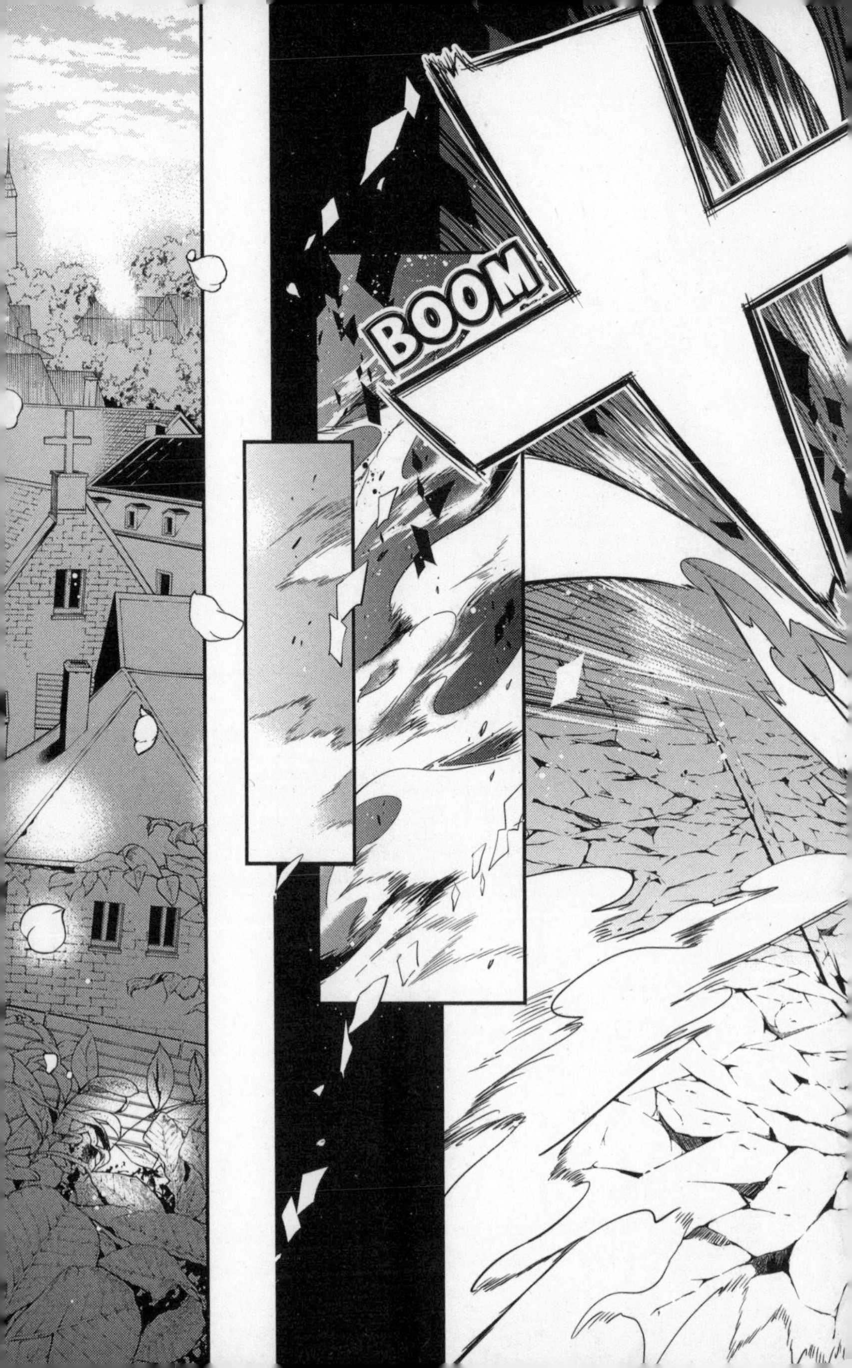
BOOM

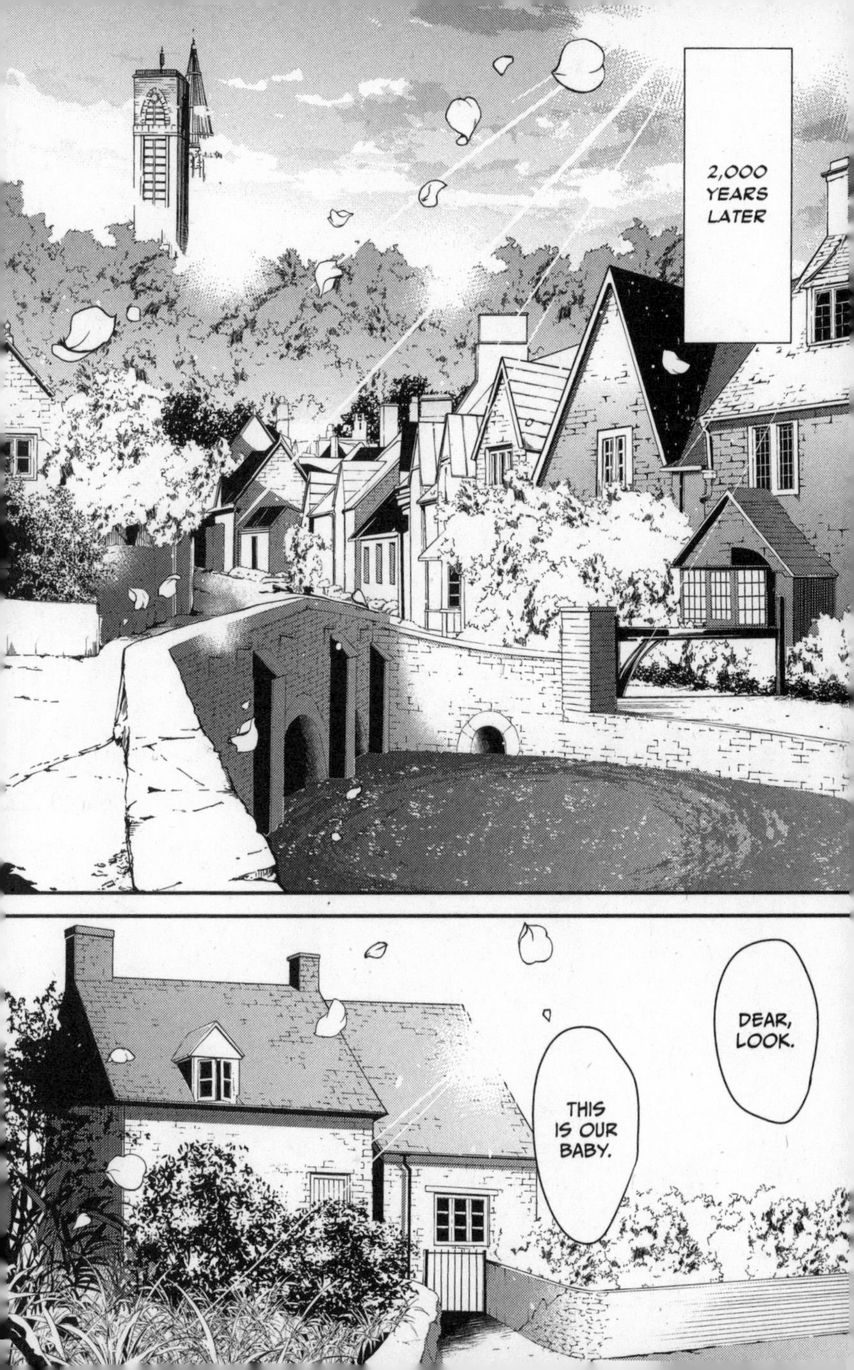
2,000 YEARS LATER
DEAR, LOOK.
THIS IS OUR BABY.

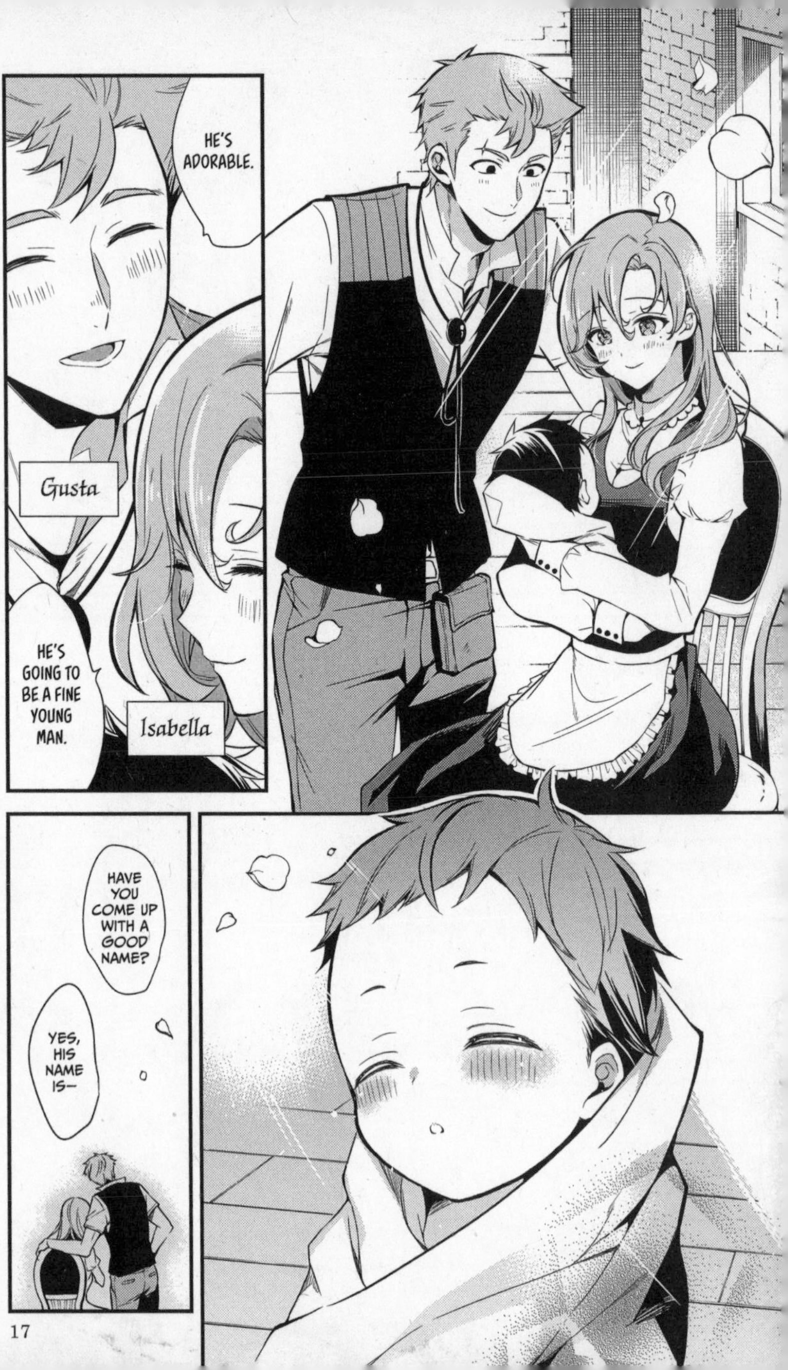
HE'S ADORABLE.
Gusta
HE'S GOING TO BE A FINE YOUNG MAN.
Isabella
HAVE YOU COME UP WITH A GOOD NAME?
YES, HIS NAME IS—

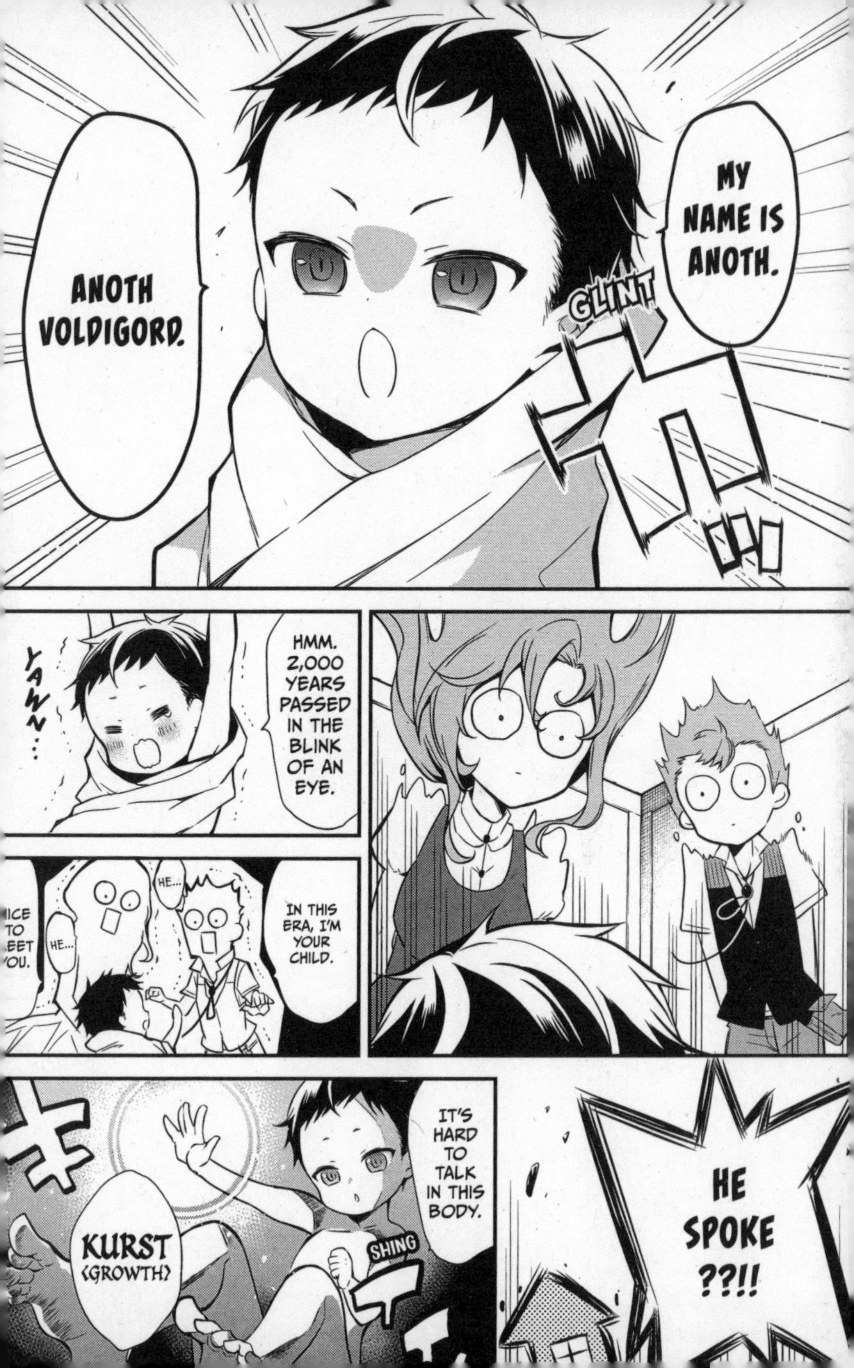
MY NAME IS ANOTH.
GLINT
ANOTH VOLDIGORD.
HMM. 2,000 YEARS PASSED IN THE BLINK OF AN EYE.
YAWN...
IN THIS ERA, I'M YOUR CHILD.
HE...
HE...
ICE TO EET YOU.
HE SPOKE ??!!
IT'S HARD TO TALK IN THIS BODY.
SHING
KURST ‹GROWTH›

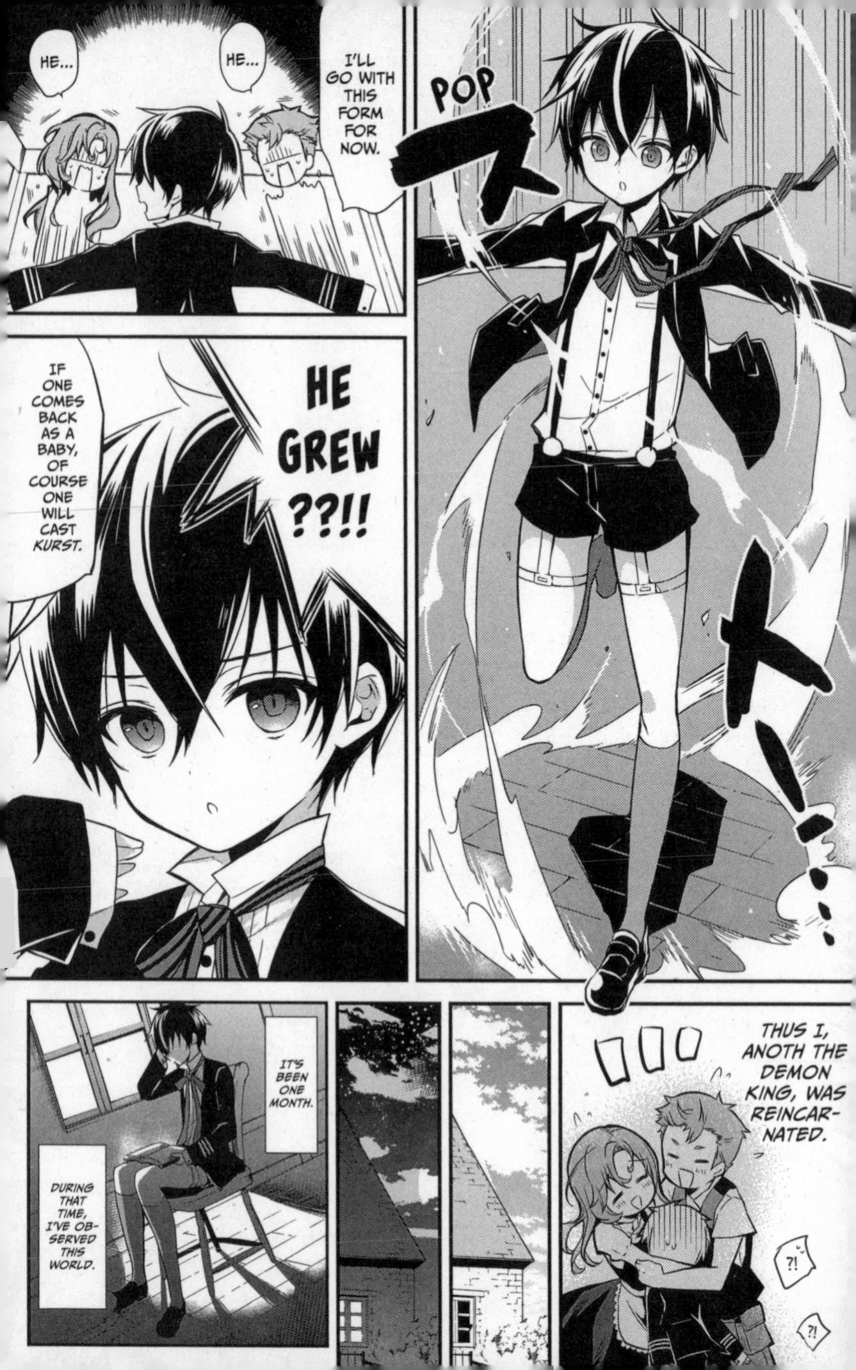
POP
!...
I'LL GO WITH THIS FORM FOR NOW.
HE...
HE...
HE GREW ??!!
IF ONE COMES BACK AS A BABY, OF COURSE ONE WILL CAST KURST.
THUS I, ANOTH THE DEMON KING, WAS REINCARNATED.
?!
?!
IT'S BEEN ONE MONTH.
DURING THAT TIME, I'VE OBSERVED THIS WORLD.

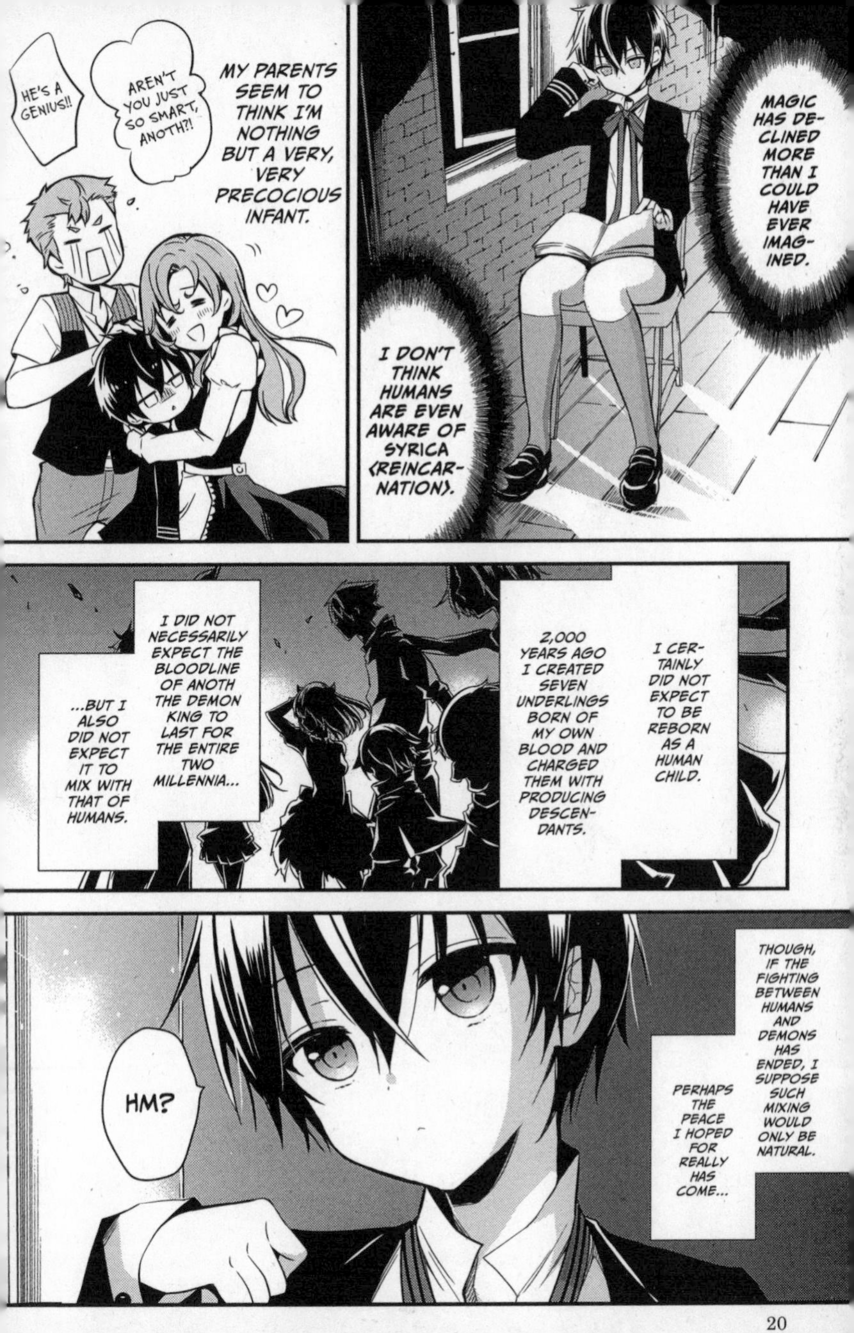
MAGIC HAS DECLINED MORE THAN I COULD HAVE EVER IMAGINED.
I DON'T THINK HUMANS ARE EVEN AWARE OF SYRICA ‹REINCARNATION›.
MY PARENTS SEEM TO THINK I'M NOTHING BUT A VERY, VERY PRECOCIOUS INFANT.
AREN'T YOU JUST SO SMART, ANOTH?!
HE'S A GENIUS!!
I CERTAINLY DID NOT EXPECT TO BE REBORN AS A HUMAN CHILD.
2,000 YEARS AGO I CREATED SEVEN UNDERLINGS BORN OF MY OWN BLOOD AND CHARGED THEM WITH PRODUCING DESCENDANTS.
I DID NOT NECESSARILY EXPECT THE BLOODLINE OF ANOTH THE DEMON KING TO LAST FOR THE ENTIRE TWO MILLENNIA...
...BUT I ALSO DID NOT EXPECT IT TO MIX WITH THAT OF HUMANS.
THOUGH, IF THE FIGHTING BETWEEN HUMANS AND DEMONS HAS ENDED, I SUPPOSE SUCH MIXING WOULD ONLY BE NATURAL.
PERHAPS THE PEACE I HOPED FOR REALLY HAS COME...
HM?

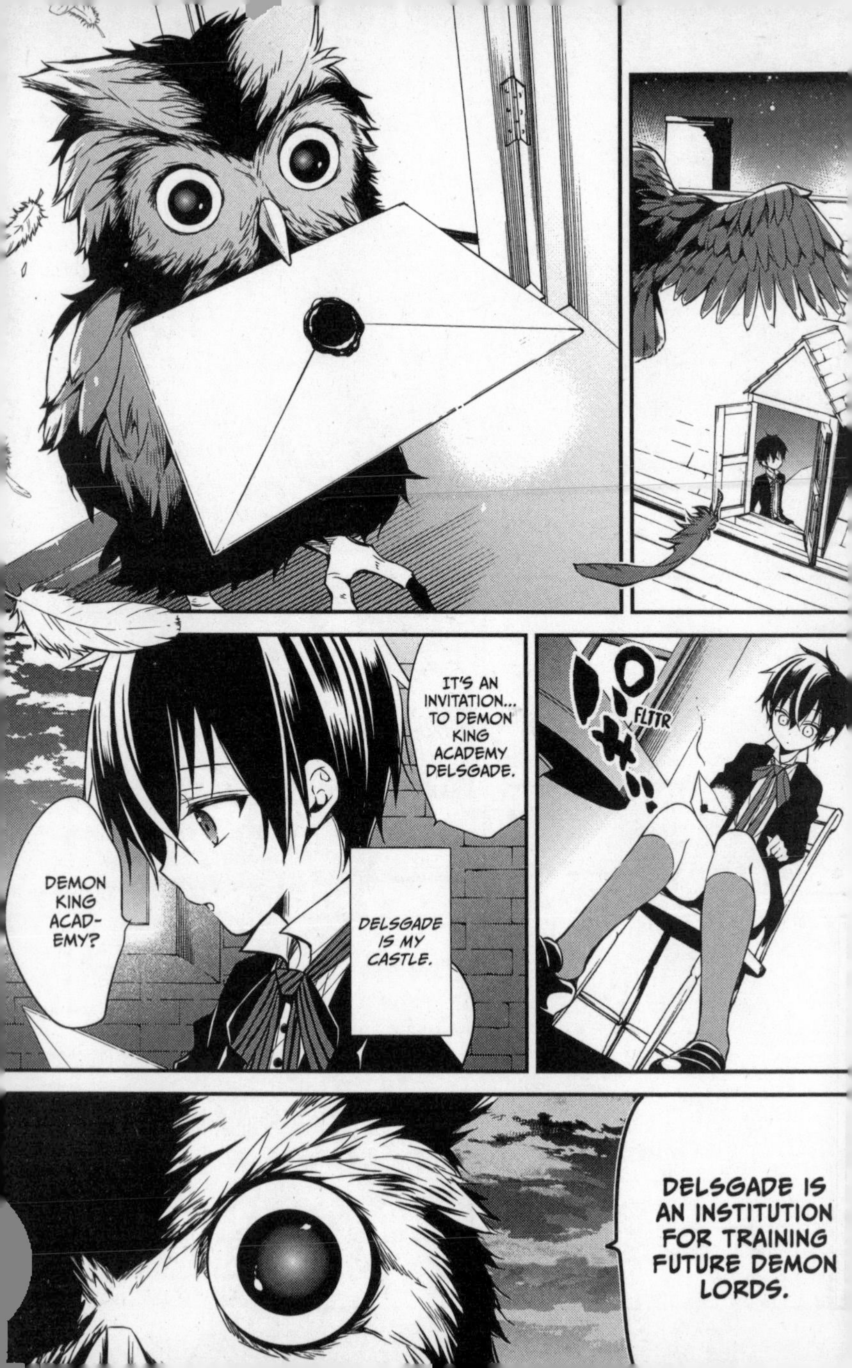
FLTTR
IT'S AN INVITATION... TO DEMON KING ACADEMY DELSGADE.
DEMON KING ACAD-EMY?
DELSGADE IS MY CASTLE.
DELSGADE IS AN INSTITUTION FOR TRAINING FUTURE DEMON LORDS.

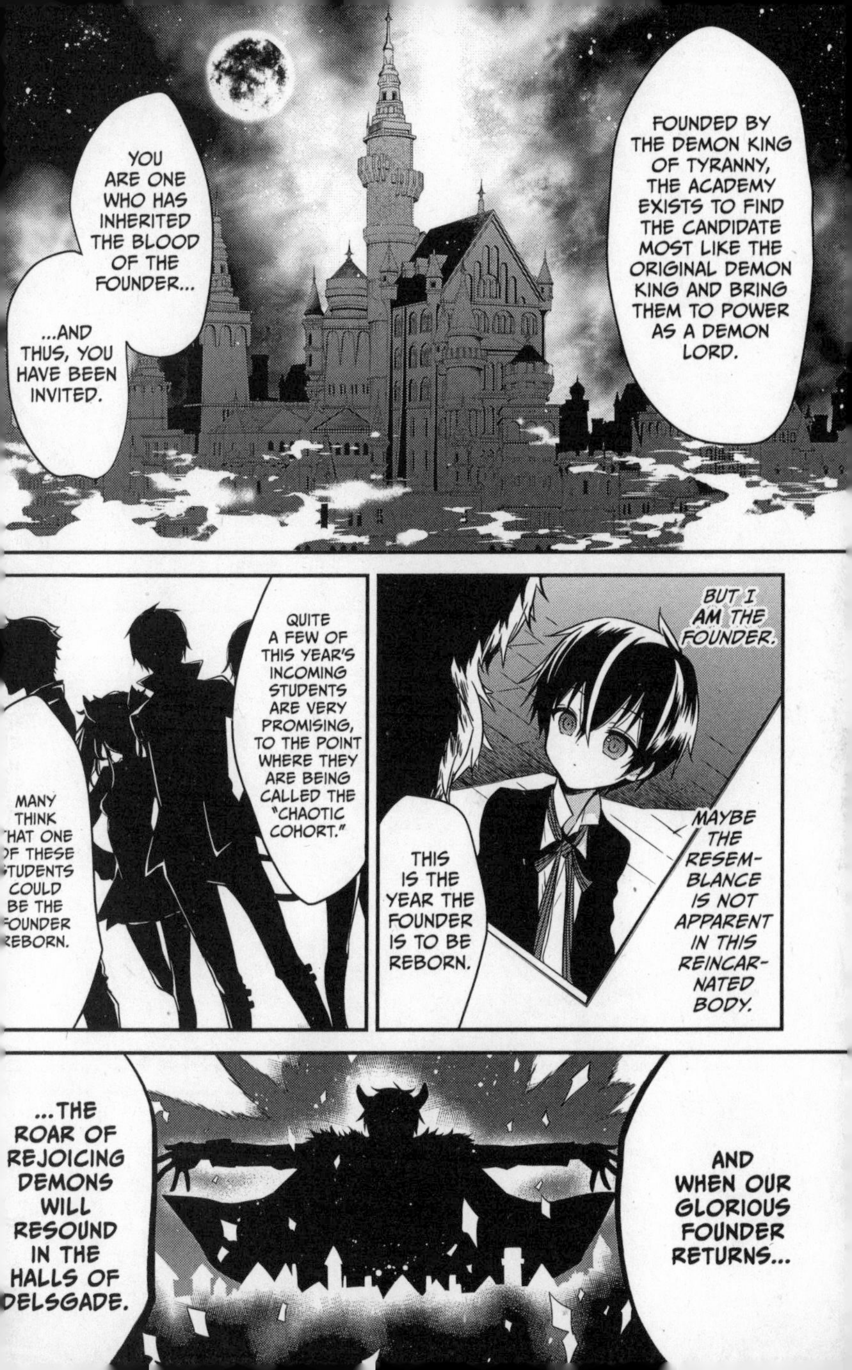
FOUNDED BY THE DEMON KING OF TYRANNY, THE ACADEMY EXISTS TO FIND THE CANDIDATE MOST LIKE THE ORIGINAL DEMON KING AND BRING THEM TO POWER AS A DEMON LORD.
YOU ARE ONE WHO HAS INHERITED THE BLOOD OF THE FOUNDER...
...AND THUS, YOU HAVE BEEN INVITED.
BUT I *AM* THE FOUNDER.
MAYBE THE RESEMBLANCE IS NOT APPARENT IN THIS REINCARNATED BODY.
THIS IS THE YEAR THE FOUNDER IS TO BE REBORN.
QUITE A FEW OF THIS YEAR'S INCOMING STUDENTS ARE VERY PROMISING, TO THE POINT WHERE THEY ARE BEING CALLED THE "CHAOTIC COHORT."
MANY THINK HAT ONE F THESE TUDENTS COULD BE THE OUNDER EBORN.
AND WHEN OUR GLORIOUS FOUNDER RETURNS...
...THE ROAR OF REJOICING DEMONS WILL RESOUND IN THE HALLS OF DELSGADE.

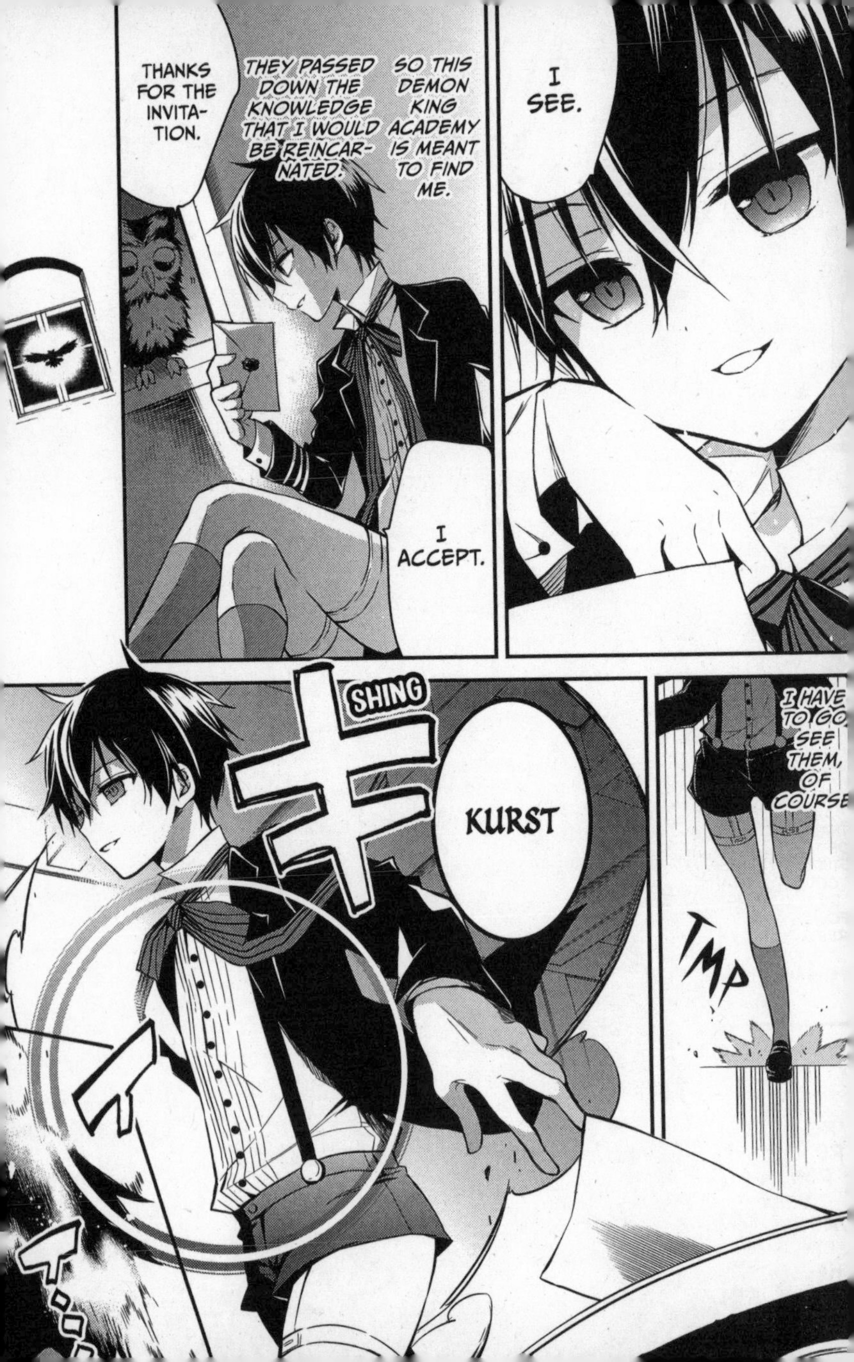
I SEE.
SO THIS DEMON KING ACADEMY IS MEANT TO FIND ME.
THEY PASSED DOWN THE KNOWLEDGE THAT I WOULD BE REINCAR-NATED.
THANKS FOR THE INVITA-TION.
I ACCEPT.
I HAVE TO GO SEE THEM, OF COURSE
TMP
SHING
KURST

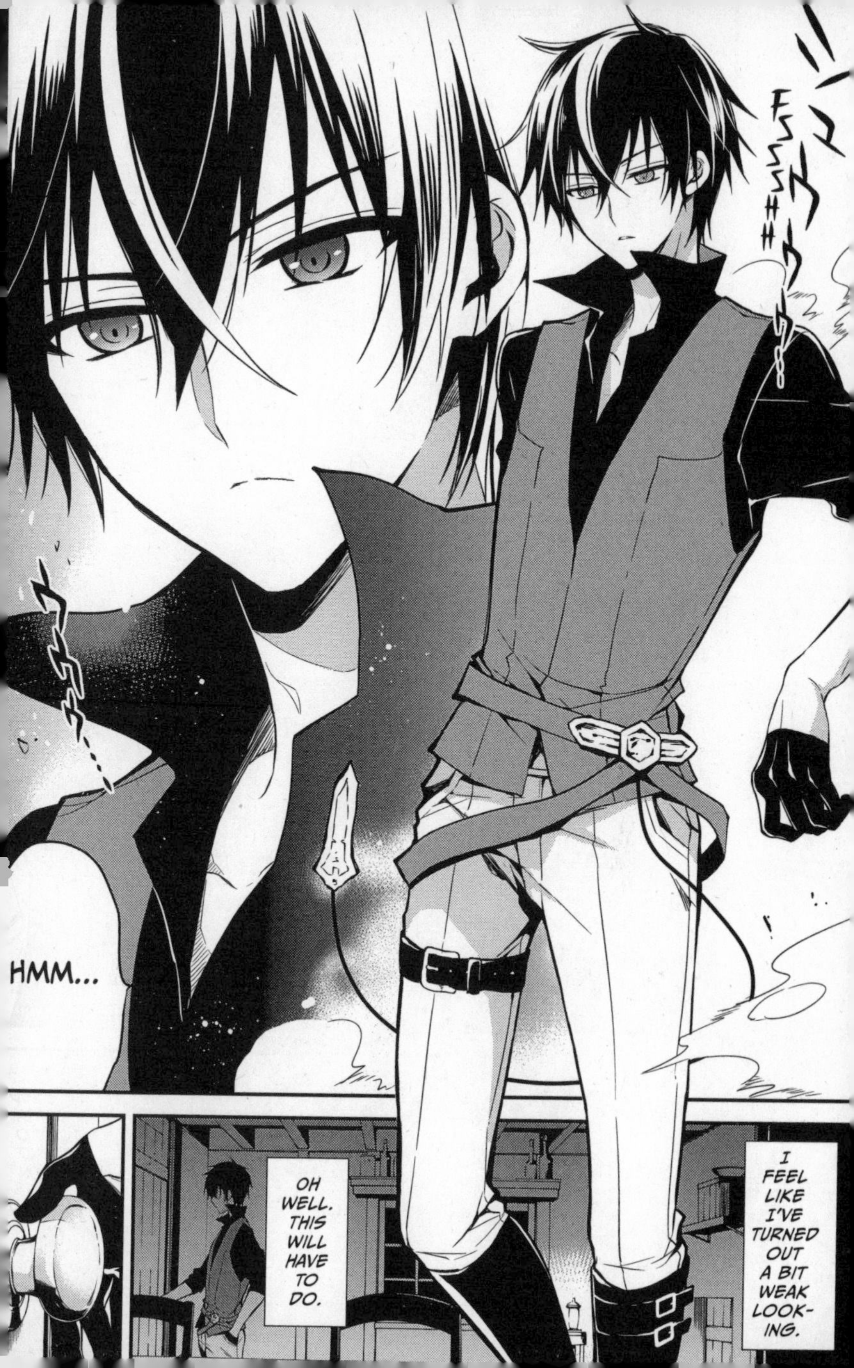
FSSHH
HMM...
I FEEL LIKE I'VE TURNED OUT A BIT WEAK LOOKING.
OH WELL. THIS WILL HAVE TO DO.

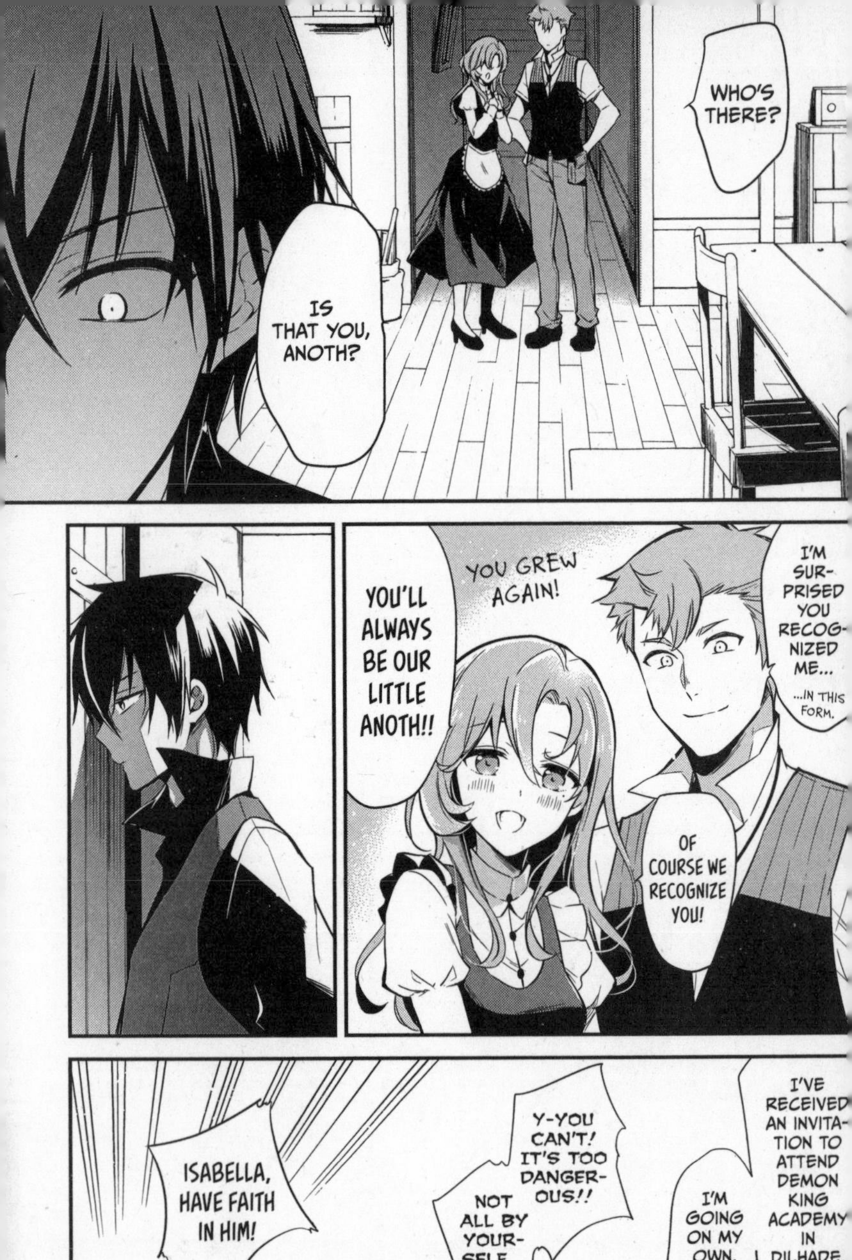
WHO'S THERE?
IS THAT YOU, ANOTH?
I'M SURPRISED YOU RECOGNIZED ME...
...IN THIS FORM.
OF COURSE WE RECOGNIZE YOU!
YOU GREW AGAIN!
YOU'LL ALWAYS BE OUR LITTLE ANOTH!!
I'VE RECEIVED AN INVITATION TO ATTEND DEMON KING ACADEMY IN DILHADE.
I'M GOING ON MY OWN.
Y-YOU CAN'T! IT'S TOO DANGEROUS!!
NOT ALL BY YOURSELF...
ISABELLA, HAVE FAITH IN HIM!

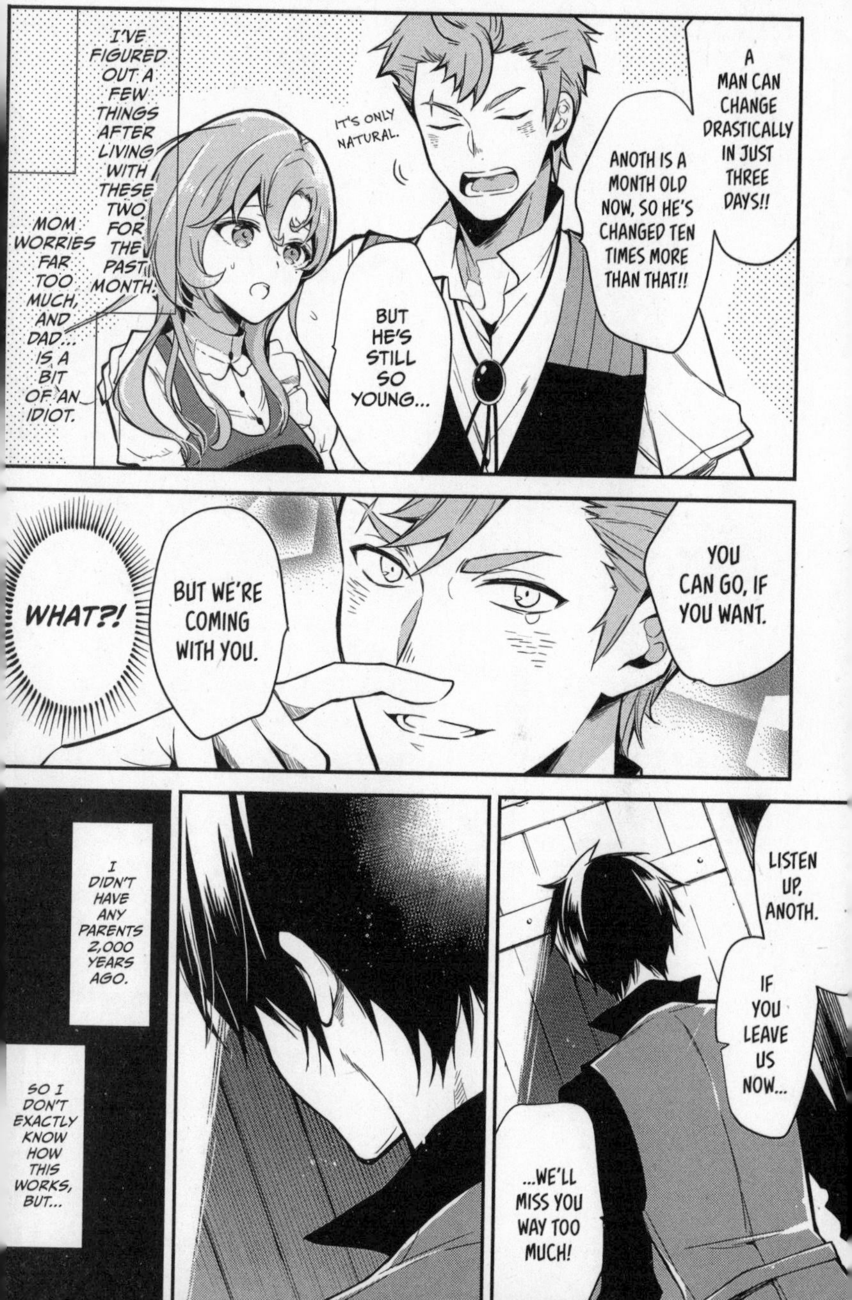
A MAN CAN CHANGE DRASTICALLY IN JUST THREE DAYS!!
ANOTH IS A MONTH OLD NOW, SO HE'S CHANGED TEN TIMES MORE THAN THAT!!
IT'S ONLY NATURAL.
BUT HE'S STILL SO YOUNG...
I'VE FIGURED OUT A FEW THINGS AFTER LIVING WITH THESE TWO FOR THE PAST MONTH.
MOM WORRIES FAR TOO MUCH, AND DAD... IS A BIT OF AN IDIOT.
YOU CAN GO, IF YOU WANT.
BUT WE'RE COMING WITH YOU.
WHAT?!
LISTEN UP, ANOTH.
IF YOU LEAVE US NOW...
...WE'LL MISS YOU WAY TOO MUCH!
I DIDN'T HAVE ANY PARENTS 2,000 YEARS AGO.
SO I DON'T EXACTLY KNOW HOW THIS WORKS, BUT...

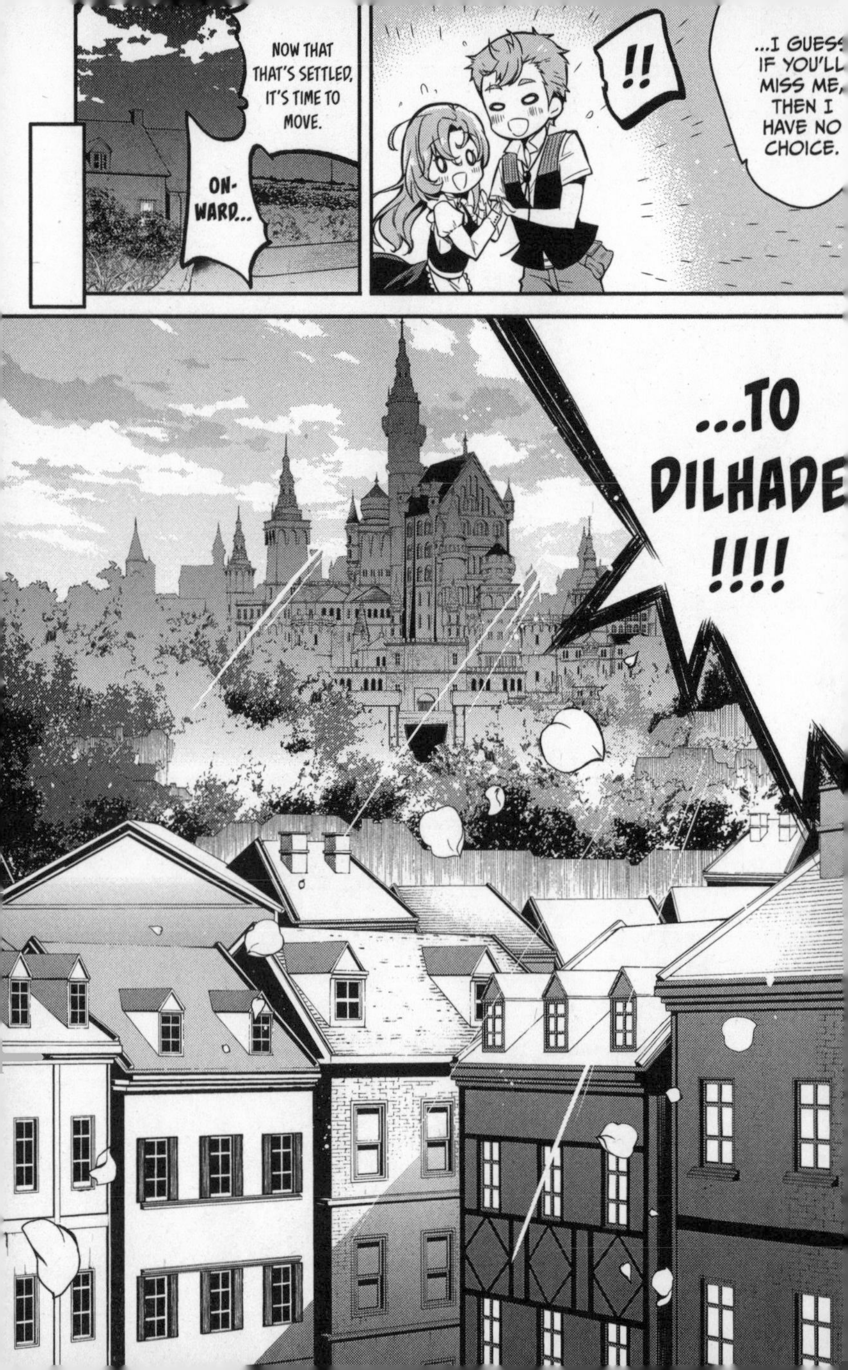
...I GUESS IF YOU'LL MISS ME, THEN I HAVE NO CHOICE.
!!
NOW THAT THAT'S SETTLED, IT'S TIME TO MOVE.
ON-WARD...
...TO DILHADE!!!!

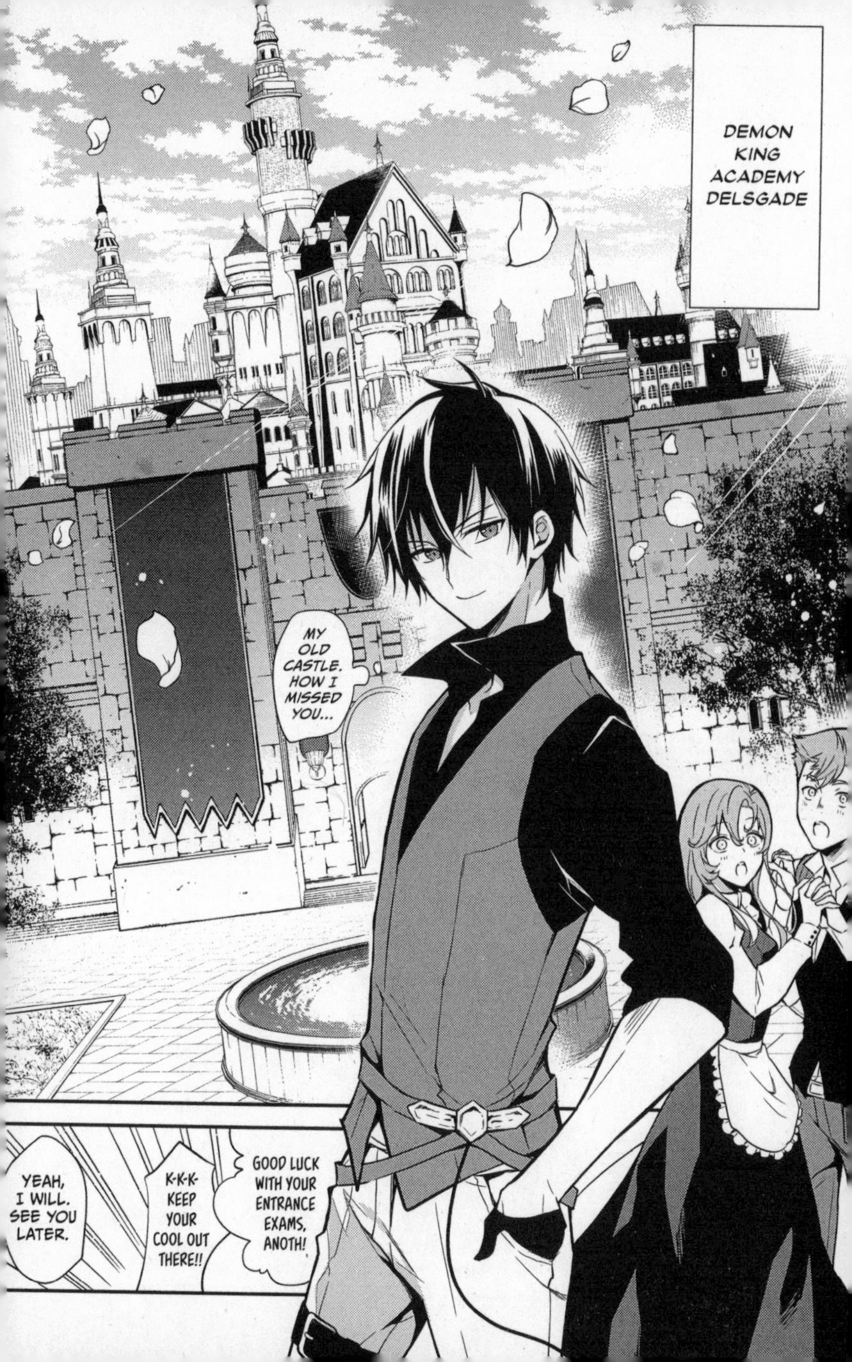
DEMON KING ACADEMY DELSGADE
MY OLD CASTLE. HOW I MISSED YOU...
GOOD LUCK WITH YOUR ENTRANCE EXAMS, ANOTH!
K-K-K-KEEP YOUR COOL OUT THERE!!
YEAH, I WILL. SEE YOU LATER.

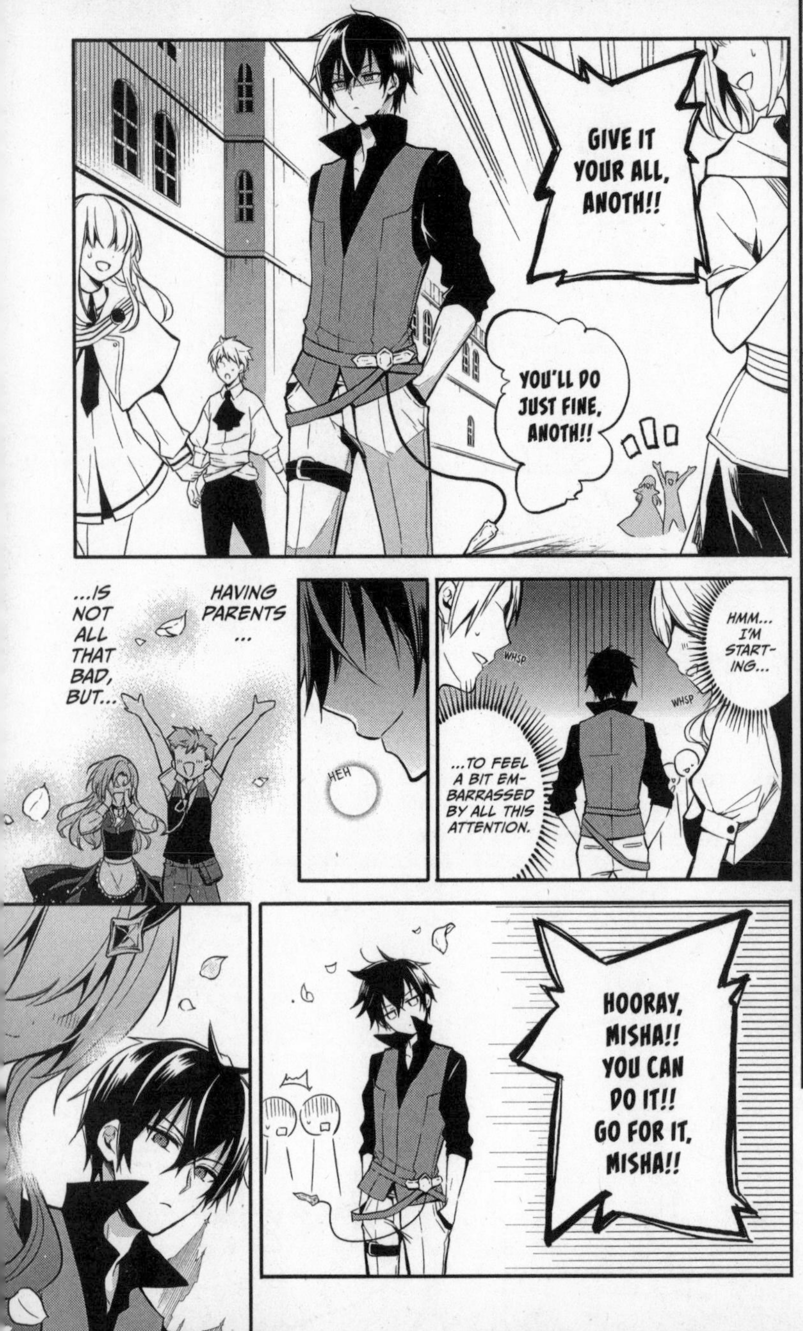
GIVE IT YOUR ALL, ANOTH!!
YOU'LL DO JUST FINE, ANOTH!!
HMM... I'M START-ING...
WHSP
WHSP
...TO FEEL A BIT EM-BARRASSED BY ALL THIS ATTENTION.
HEH
HAVING PARENTS...
...IS NOT ALL THAT BAD, BUT...
HOORAY, MISHA!! YOU CAN DO IT!! GO FOR IT, MISHA!!

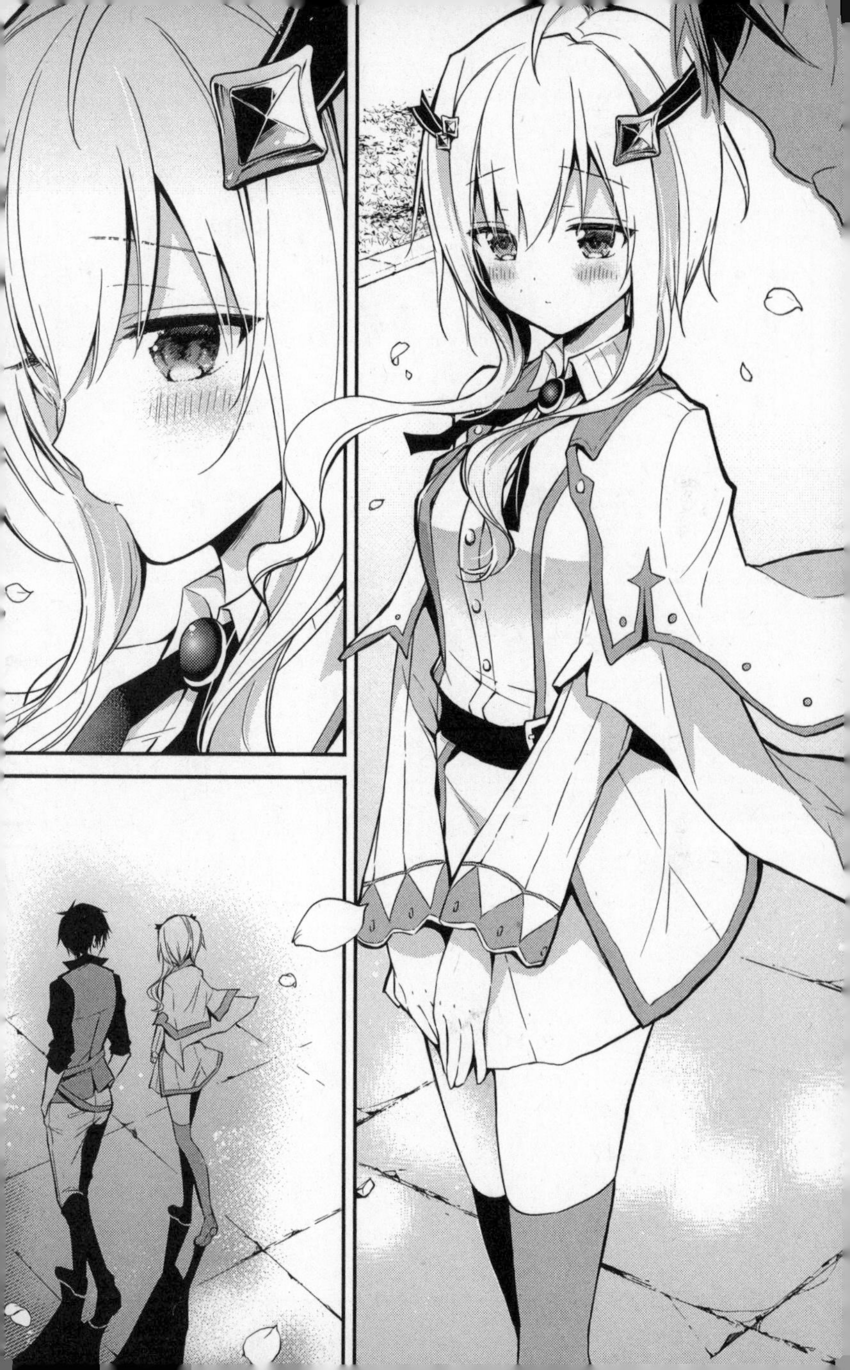

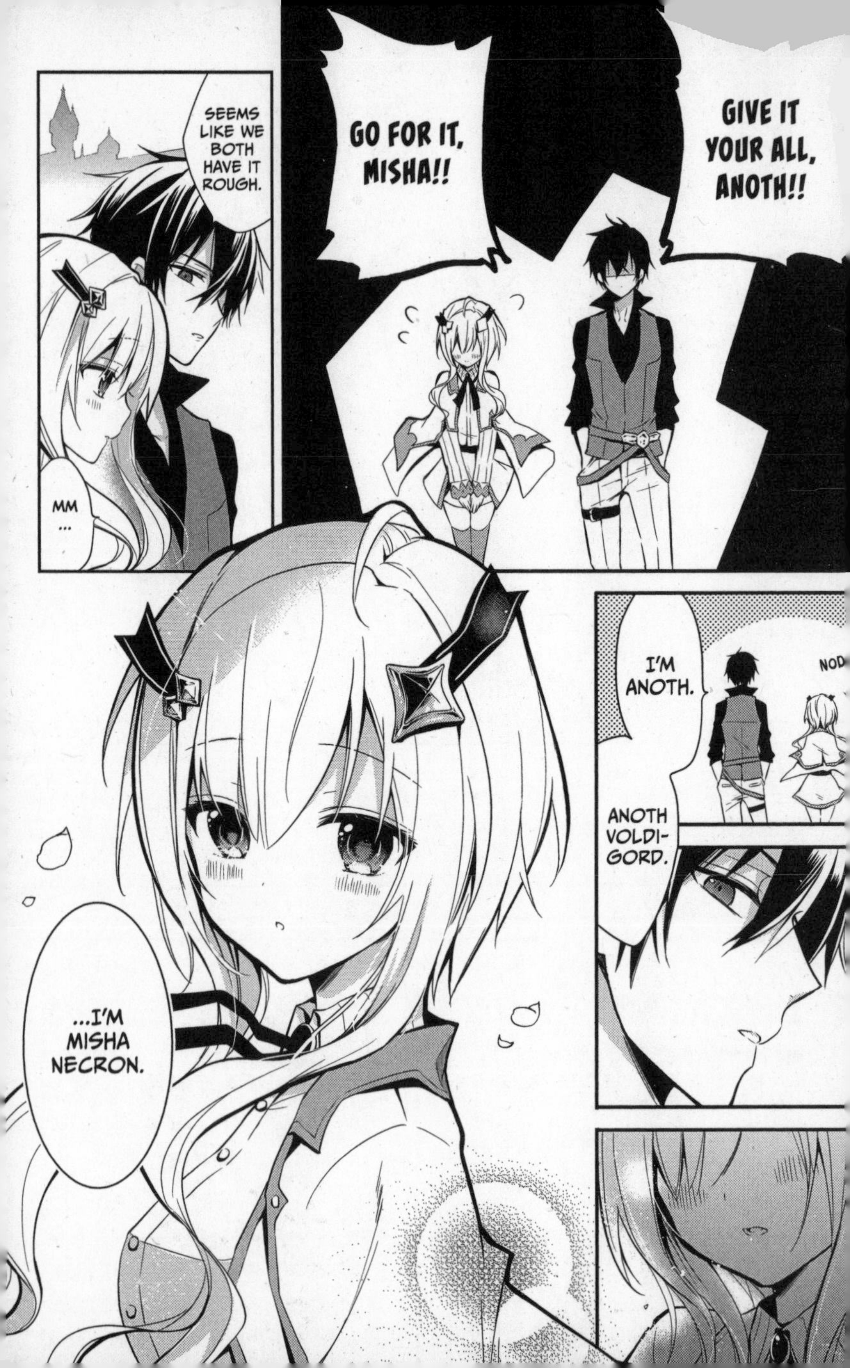
GIVE IT YOUR ALL, ANOTH!!
GO FOR IT, MISHA!!
SEEMS LIKE WE BOTH HAVE IT ROUGH.
MM...
I'M ANOTH.
NOD
ANOTH VOLDIGORD.
...I'M MISHA NECRON.

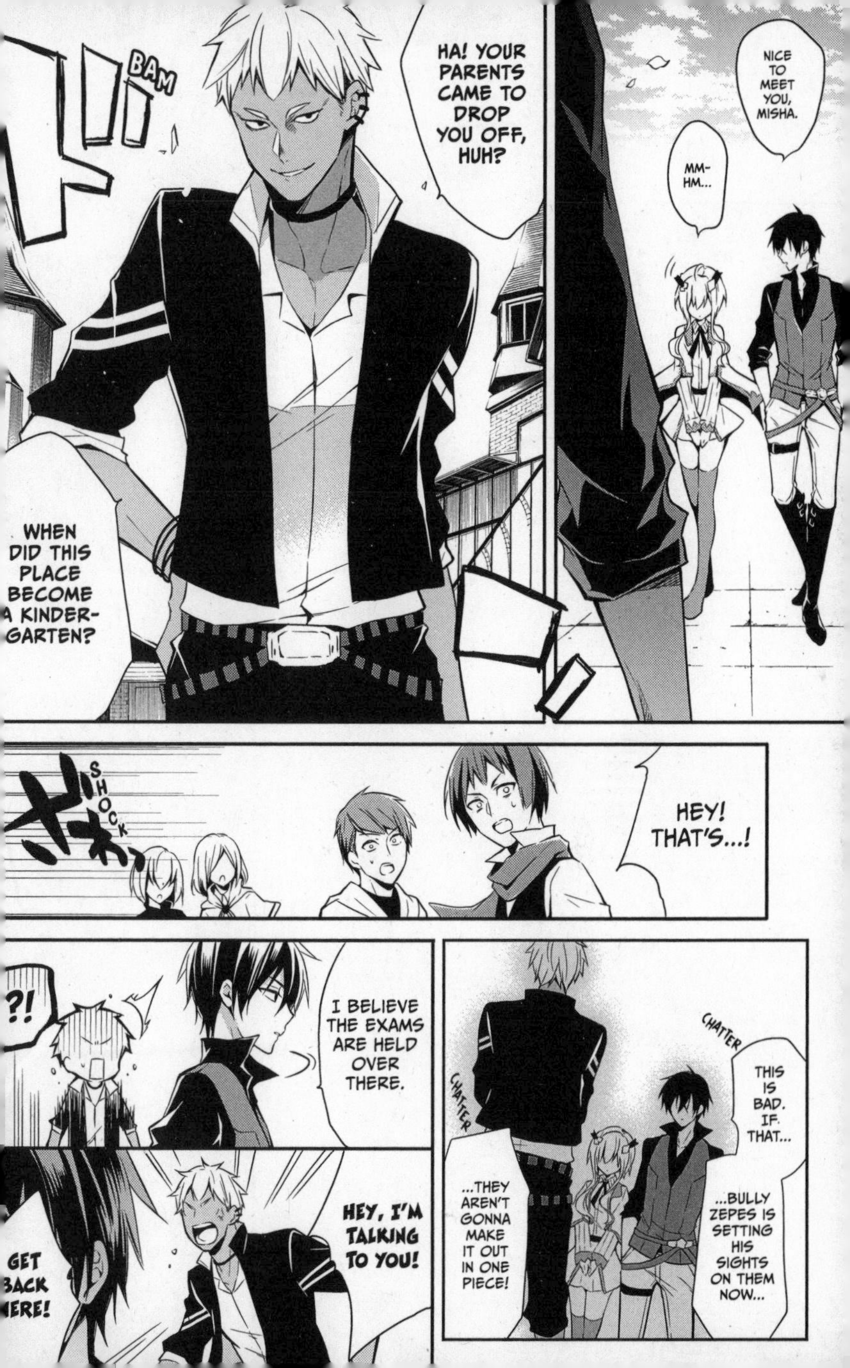
NICE TO MEET YOU, MISHA.
MM-HM...
BAM
HA! YOUR PARENTS CAME TO DROP YOU OFF, HUH?
WHEN DID THIS PLACE BECOME A KINDER-GARTEN?
HEY! THAT'S...!
SHOCK
CHATTER
THIS IS BAD. IF THAT...
...BULLY ZEPES IS SETTING HIS SIGHTS ON THEM NOW...
CHATTER
...THEY AREN'T GONNA MAKE IT OUT IN ONE PIECE!
I BELIEVE THE EXAMS ARE HELD OVER THERE.
?!
HEY, I'M TALKING TO YOU!
GET BACK HERE!

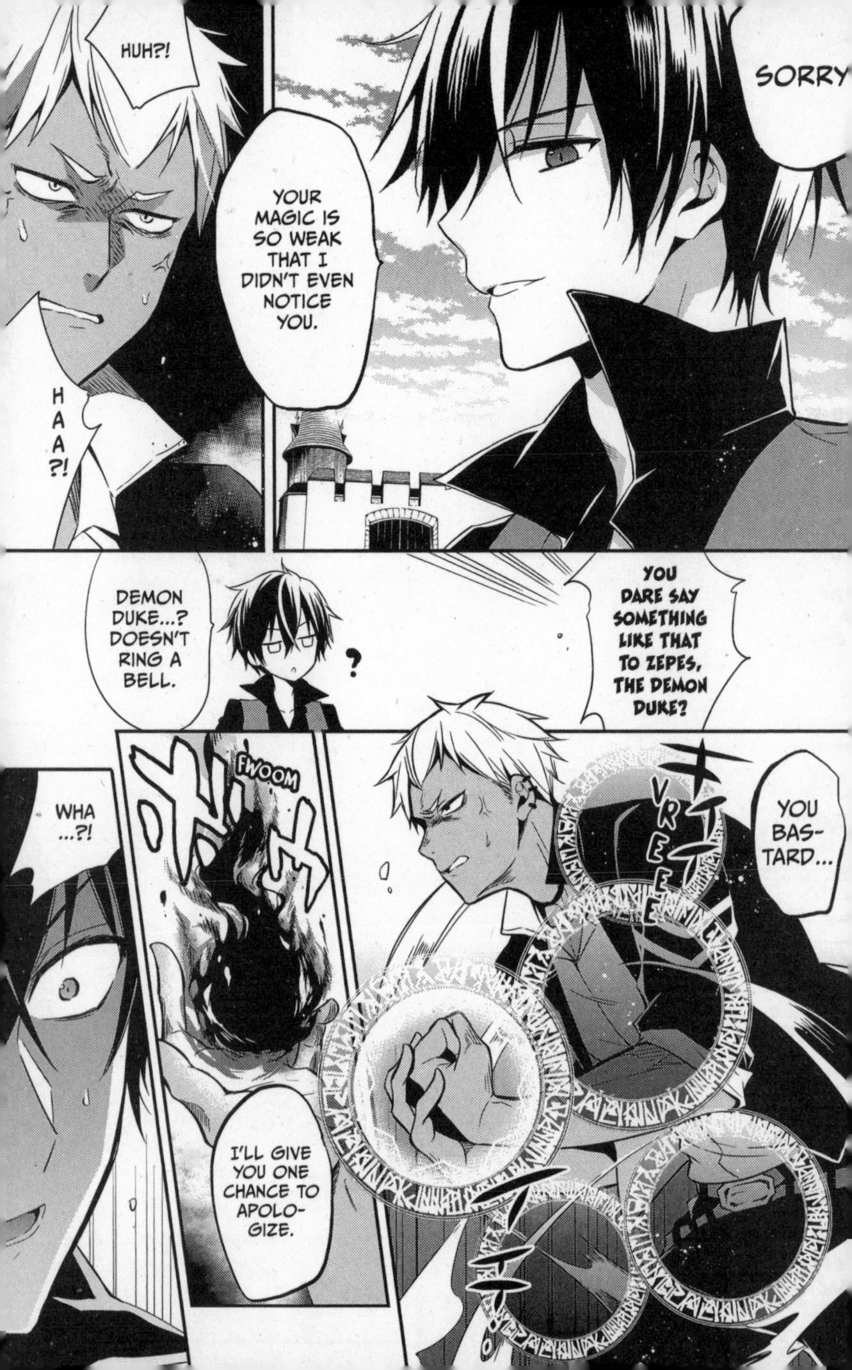
SORRY
YOUR MAGIC IS SO WEAK THAT I DIDN'T EVEN NOTICE YOU.
HUH?!
HAAA?!
YOU DARE SAY SOMETHING LIKE THAT TO ZEPES, THE DEMON DUKE?
DEMON DUKE...? DOESN'T RING A BELL.
?
YOU BAS-TARD...
VREEE
FWOOM
I'LL GIVE YOU ONE CHANCE TO APOLO-GIZE.
WHA...?!

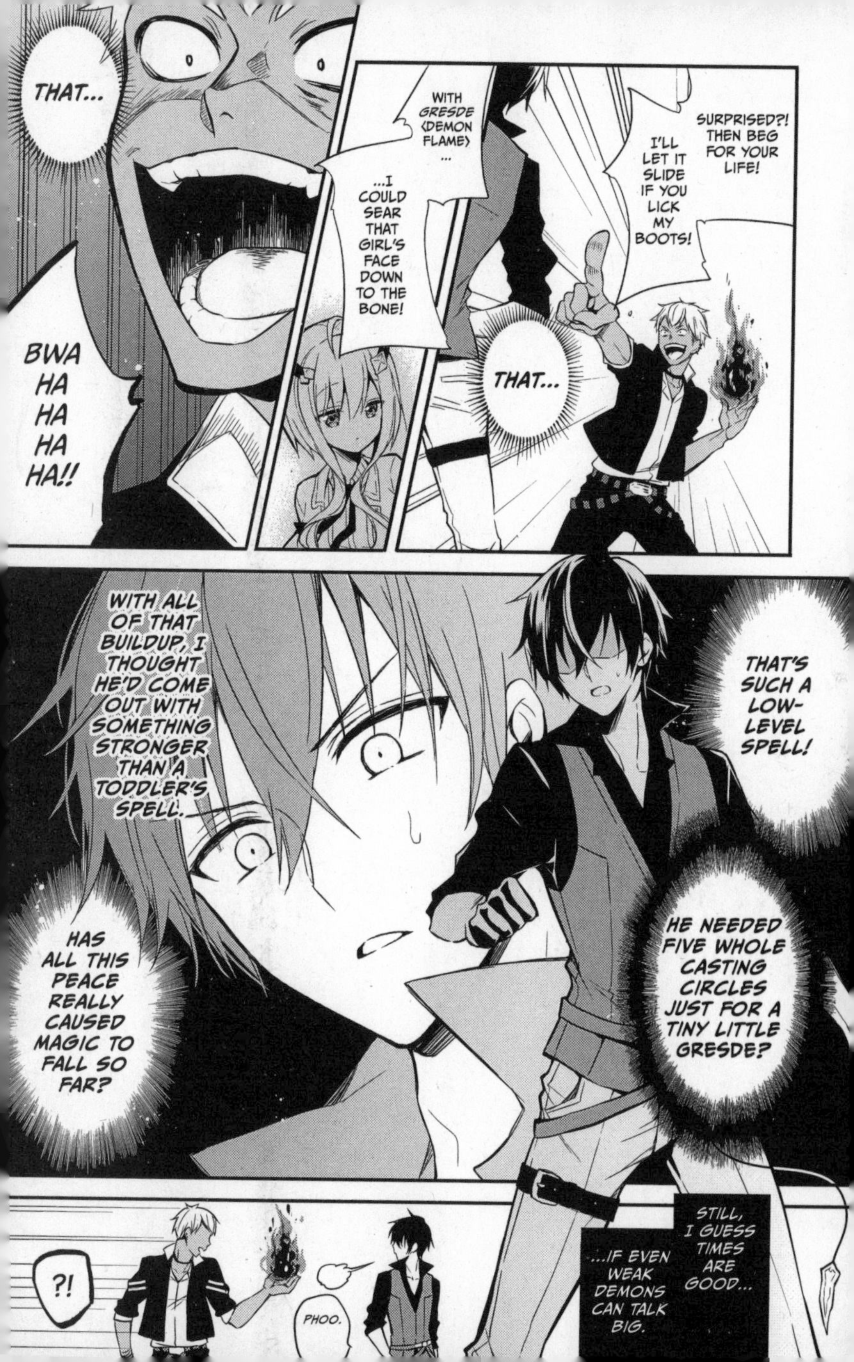

SURPRISED?! THEN BEG FOR YOUR LIFE!
I'LL LET IT SLIDE IF YOU LICK MY BOOTS!
WITH GRESDE ⟨DEMON FLAME⟩ ...
...I COULD SEAR THAT GIRL'S FACE DOWN TO THE BONE!
THAT...
THAT...
BWA HA HA HA HA!!
THAT'S SUCH A LOW-LEVEL SPELL!
WITH ALL OF THAT BUILDUP, I THOUGHT HE'D COME OUT WITH SOMETHING STRONGER THAN A TODDLER'S SPELL.
HE NEEDED FIVE WHOLE CASTING CIRCLES JUST FOR A TINY LITTLE GRESDE?
HAS ALL THIS PEACE REALLY CAUSED MAGIC TO FALL SO FAR?
STILL, I GUESS TIMES ARE GOOD...
...IF EVEN WEAK DEMONS CAN TALK BIG.
PHOO.
?!

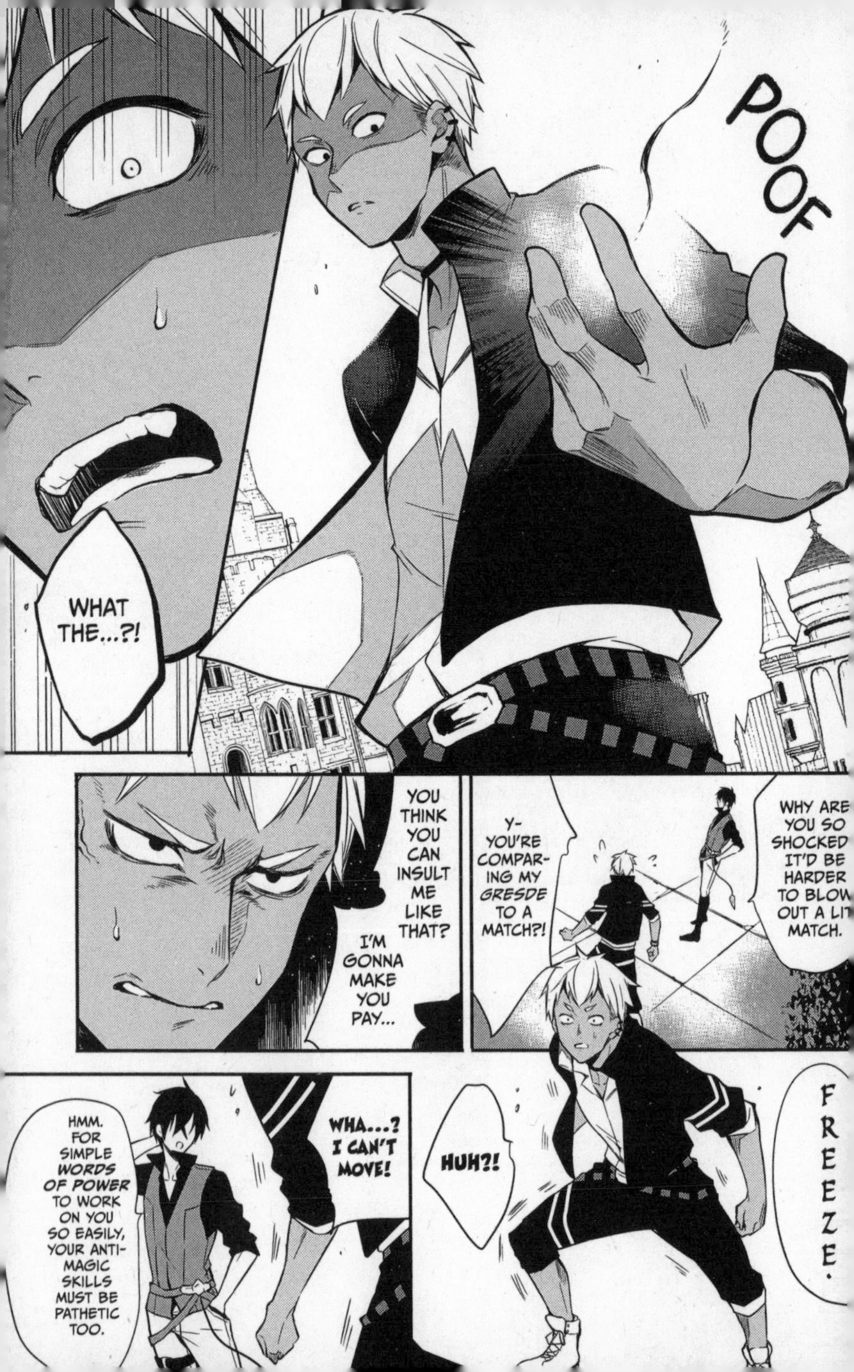
POOF
WHAT THE...?!
WHY ARE YOU SO SHOCKED IT'D BE HARDER TO BLOW OUT A LIT MATCH.
Y-YOU'RE COMPARING MY *GRESDE* TO A MATCH?!
YOU THINK YOU CAN INSULT ME LIKE THAT?
I'M GONNA MAKE YOU PAY...
FREEZE.
HUH?!
WHA...? I CAN'T MOVE!
HMM. FOR SIMPLE *WORDS OF POWER* TO WORK ON YOU SO EASILY, YOUR ANTI-MAGIC SKILLS MUST BE PATHETIC TOO.

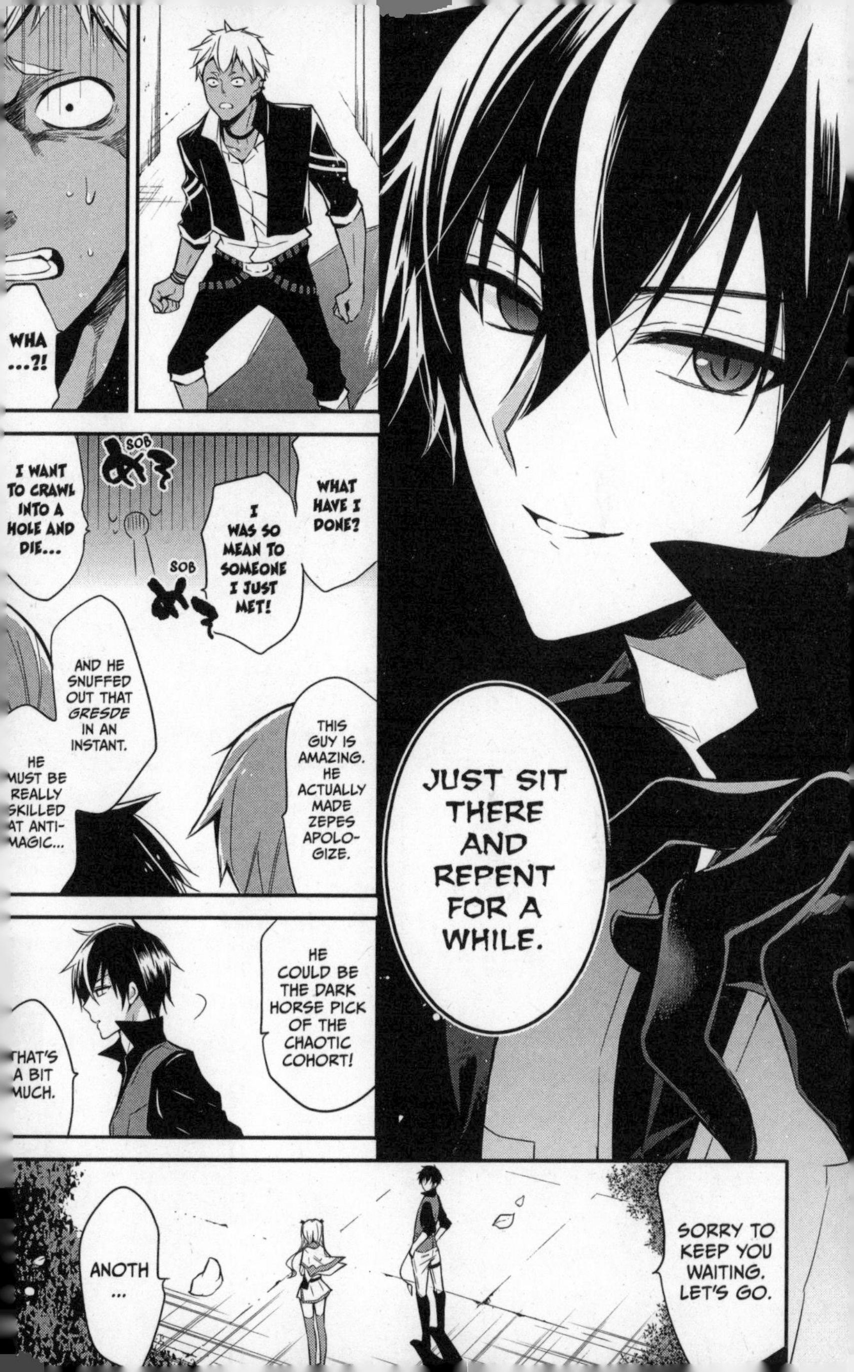
JUST SIT THERE AND REPENT FOR A WHILE.
WHA ...?!
WHAT HAVE I DONE?
I WAS SO MEAN TO SOMEONE I JUST MET!
SOB
I WANT TO CRAWL INTO A HOLE AND DIE...
SOB
THIS GUY IS AMAZING. HE ACTUALLY MADE ZEPES APOLOGIZE.
AND HE SNUFFED OUT THAT *GRESDE* IN AN INSTANT.
HE MUST BE REALLY SKILLED AT ANTI-MAGIC...
HE COULD BE THE DARK HORSE PICK OF THE CHAOTIC COHORT!
THAT'S A BIT MUCH.
SORRY TO KEEP YOU WAITING. LET'S GO.
ANOTH ...

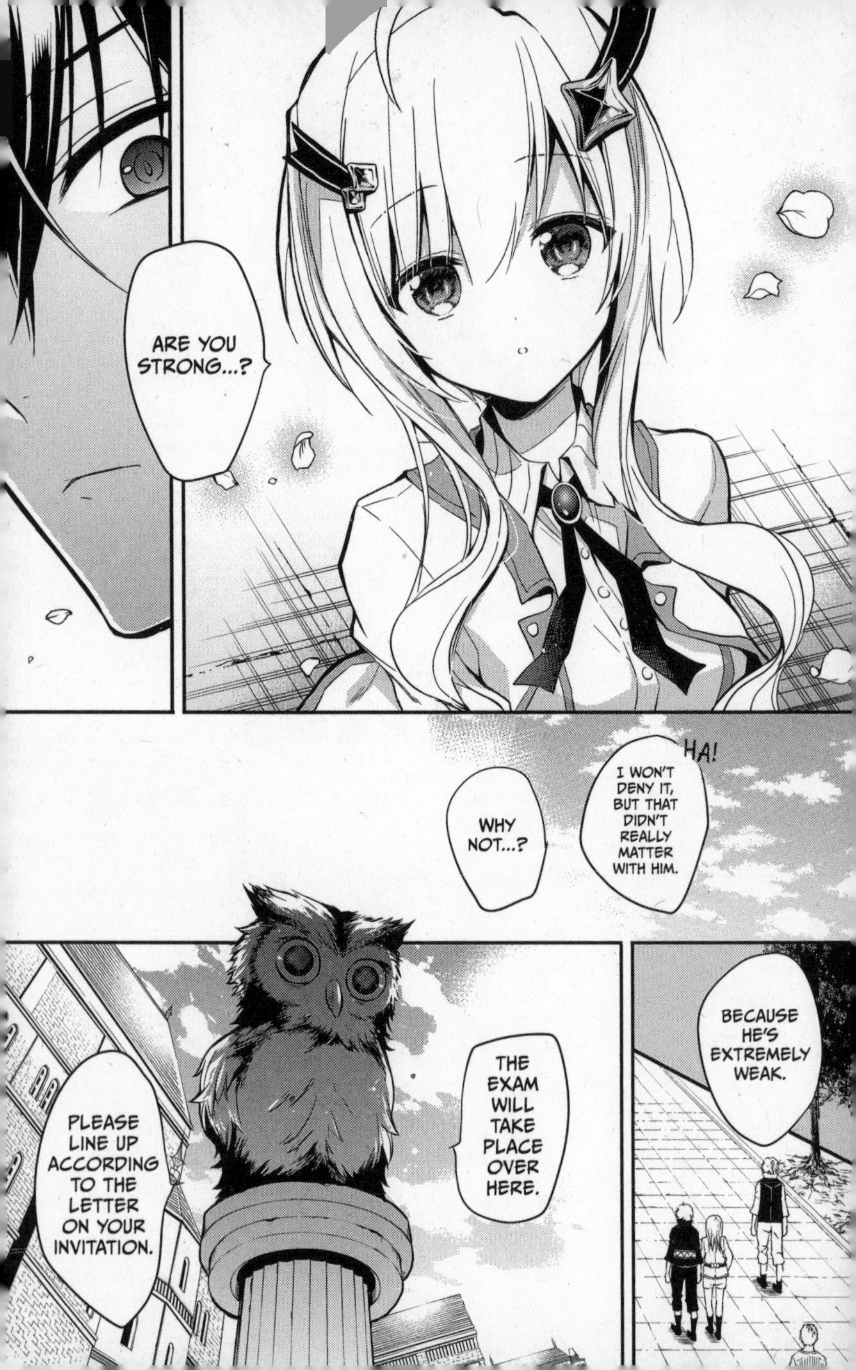
ARE YOU STRONG...?
HA!
I WON'T DENY IT, BUT THAT DIDN'T REALLY MATTER WITH HIM.
WHY NOT...?
BECAUSE HE'S EXTREMELY WEAK.
THE EXAM WILL TAKE PLACE OVER HERE.
PLEASE LINE UP ACCORDING TO THE LETTER ON YOUR INVITATION.

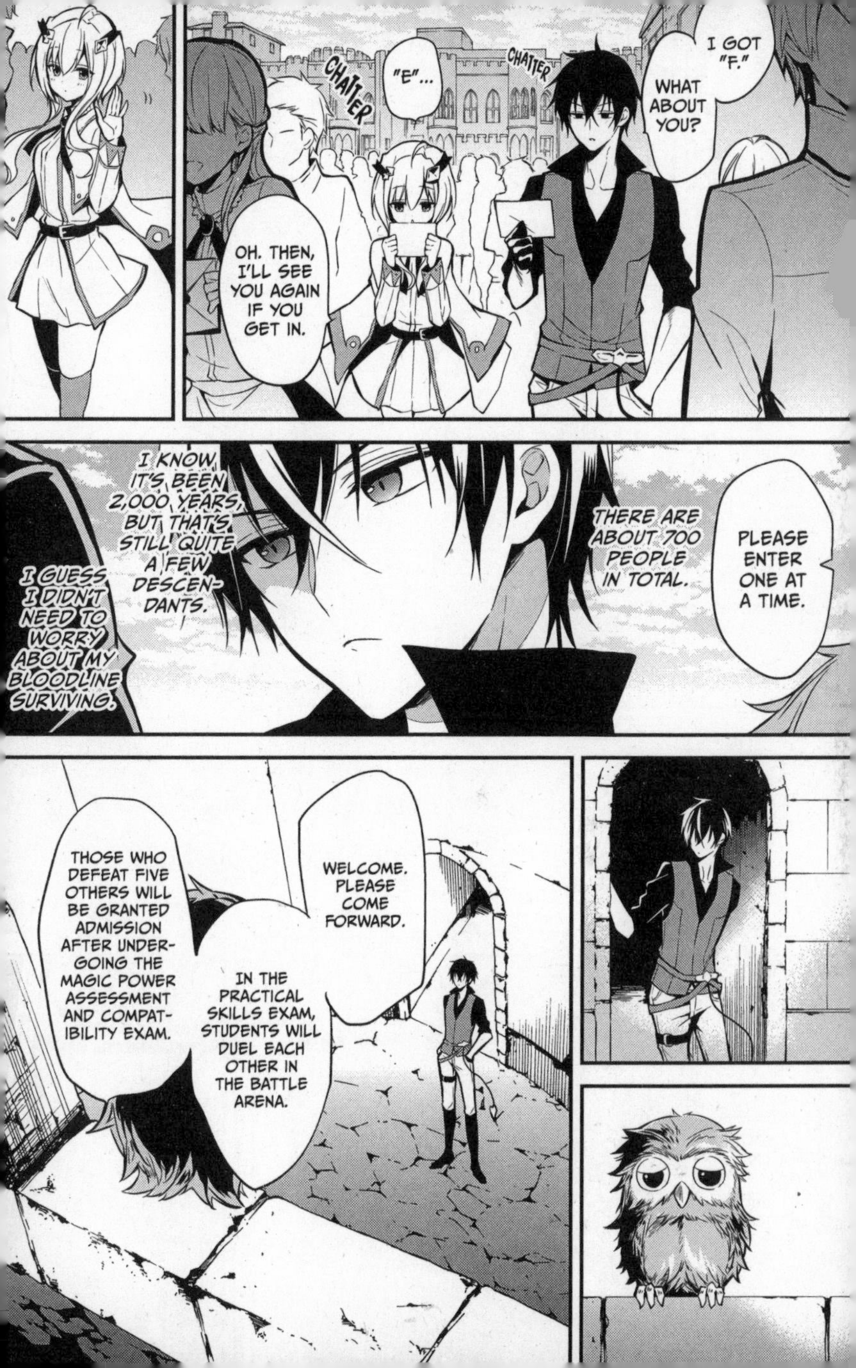
I GOT "F." WHAT ABOUT YOU?
CHATTER
"E"...
CHATTER
OH. THEN, I'LL SEE YOU AGAIN IF YOU GET IN.
PLEASE ENTER ONE AT A TIME.
THERE ARE ABOUT 700 PEOPLE IN TOTAL.
I KNOW IT'S BEEN 2,000 YEARS, BUT THAT'S STILL QUITE A FEW DESCENDANTS.
I GUESS I DIDN'T NEED TO WORRY ABOUT MY BLOODLINE SURVIVING.
WELCOME. PLEASE COME FORWARD.
IN THE PRACTICAL SKILLS EXAM, STUDENTS WILL DUEL EACH OTHER IN THE BATTLE ARENA.
THOSE WHO DEFEAT FIVE OTHERS WILL BE GRANTED ADMISSION AFTER UNDERGOING THE MAGIC POWER ASSESSMENT AND COMPATIBILITY EXAM.

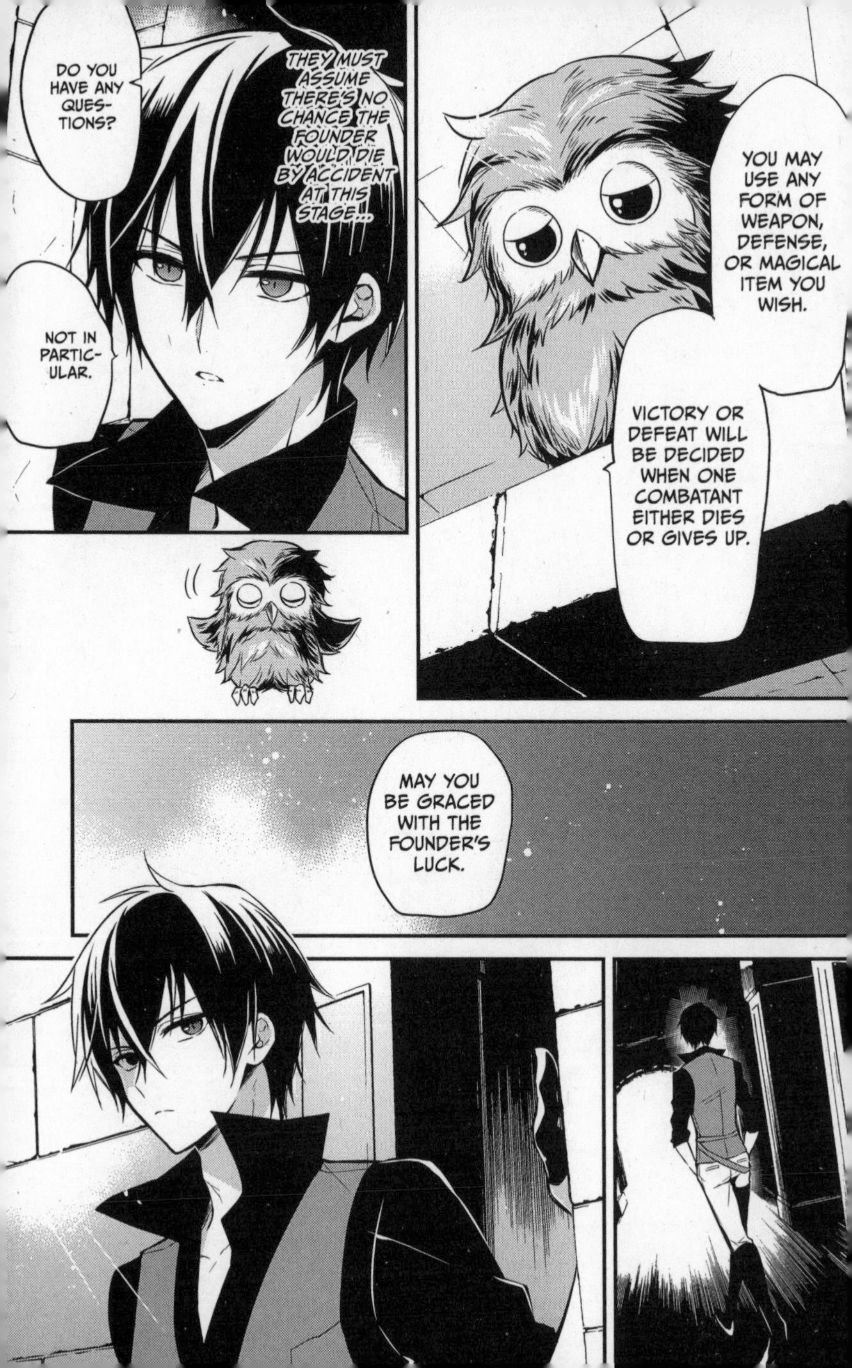
YOU MAY USE ANY FORM OF WEAPON, DEFENSE, OR MAGICAL ITEM YOU WISH.
VICTORY OR DEFEAT WILL BE DECIDED WHEN ONE COMBATANT EITHER DIES OR GIVES UP.
THEY MUST ASSUME THERE'S NO CHANCE THE FOUNDER WOULD DIE BY ACCIDENT AT THIS STAGE...
DO YOU HAVE ANY QUES-TIONS?
NOT IN PARTIC-ULAR.
MAY YOU BE GRACED WITH THE FOUNDER'S LUCK.

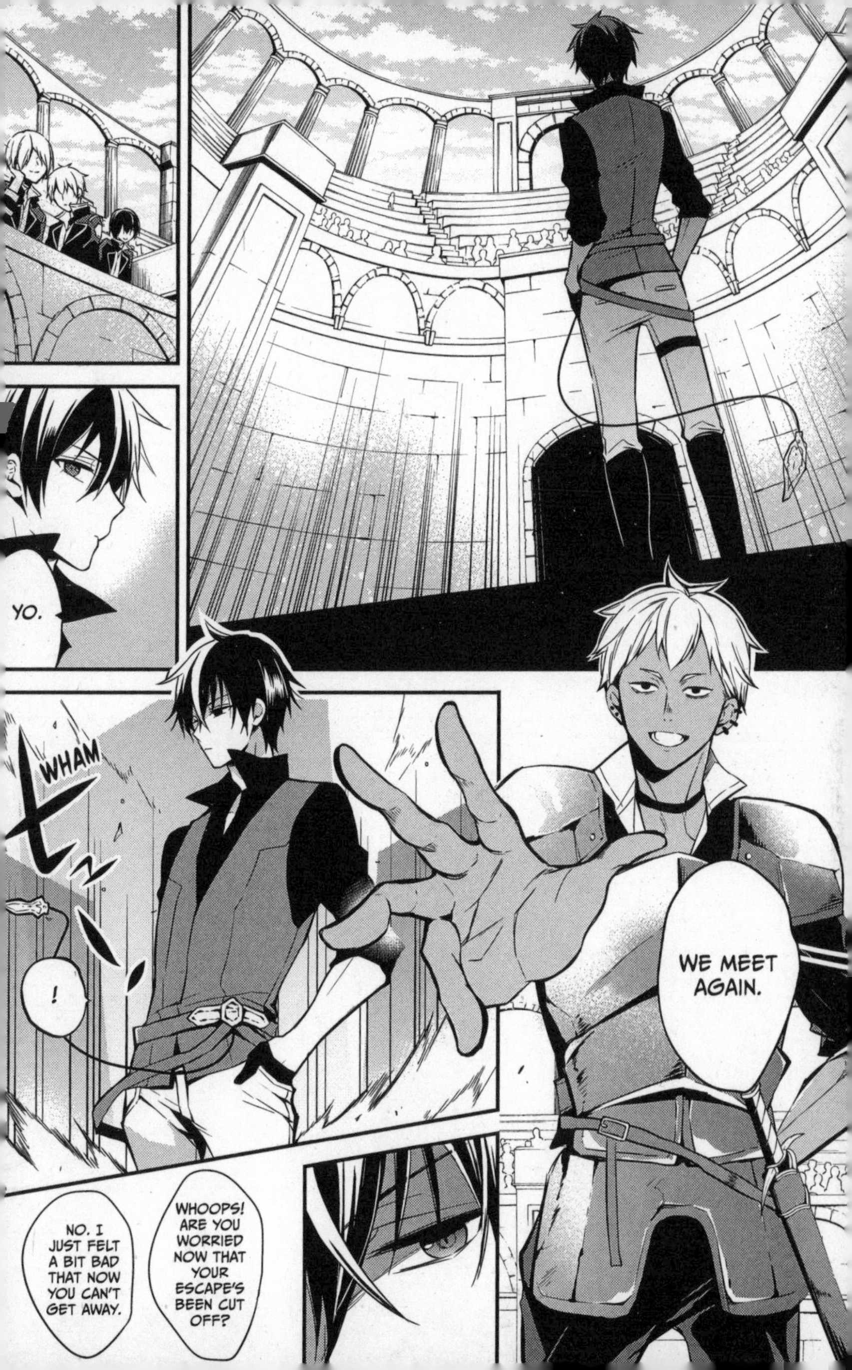
YO.
WE MEET AGAIN.
WHAM
!
WHOOPS! ARE YOU WORRIED NOW THAT YOUR ESCAPE'S BEEN CUT OFF?
NO. I JUST FELT A BIT BAD THAT NOW YOU CAN'T GET AWAY.

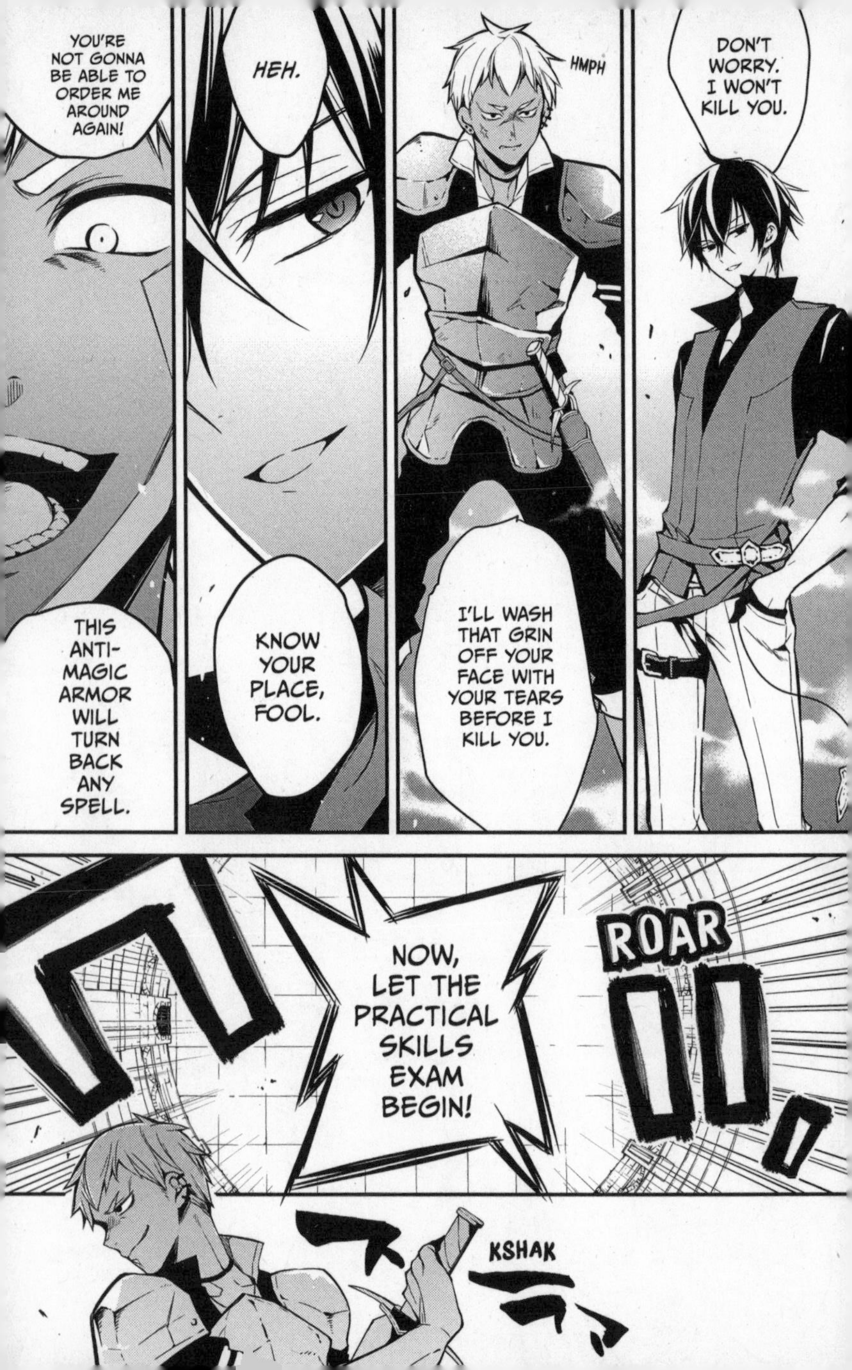
DON'T WORRY. I WON'T KILL YOU.
HMPH
I'LL WASH THAT GRIN OFF YOUR FACE WITH YOUR TEARS BEFORE I KILL YOU.
HEH.
KNOW YOUR PLACE, FOOL.
YOU'RE NOT GONNA BE ABLE TO ORDER ME AROUND AGAIN!
THIS ANTI-MAGIC ARMOR WILL TURN BACK ANY SPELL.
ROAR
NOW, LET THE PRACTICAL SKILLS EXAM BEGIN!
KSHAK

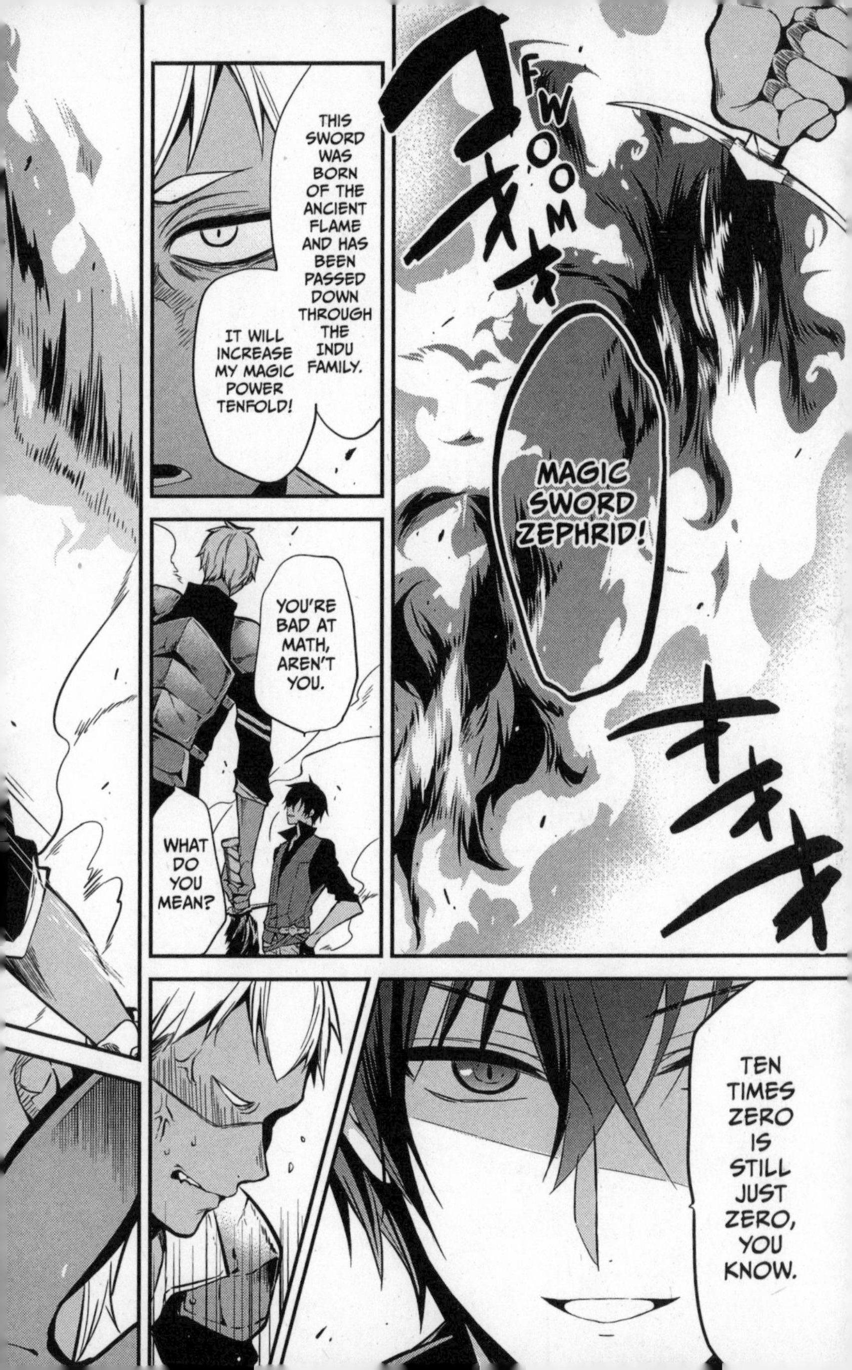
FWOOM
MAGIC SWORD ZEPHRID!
THIS SWORD WAS BORN OF THE ANCIENT FLAME AND HAS BEEN PASSED DOWN THROUGH THE INDU FAMILY.
IT WILL INCREASE MY MAGIC POWER TENFOLD!
YOU'RE BAD AT MATH, AREN'T YOU.
WHAT DO YOU MEAN?
TEN TIMES ZERO IS STILL JUST ZERO, YOU KNOW.

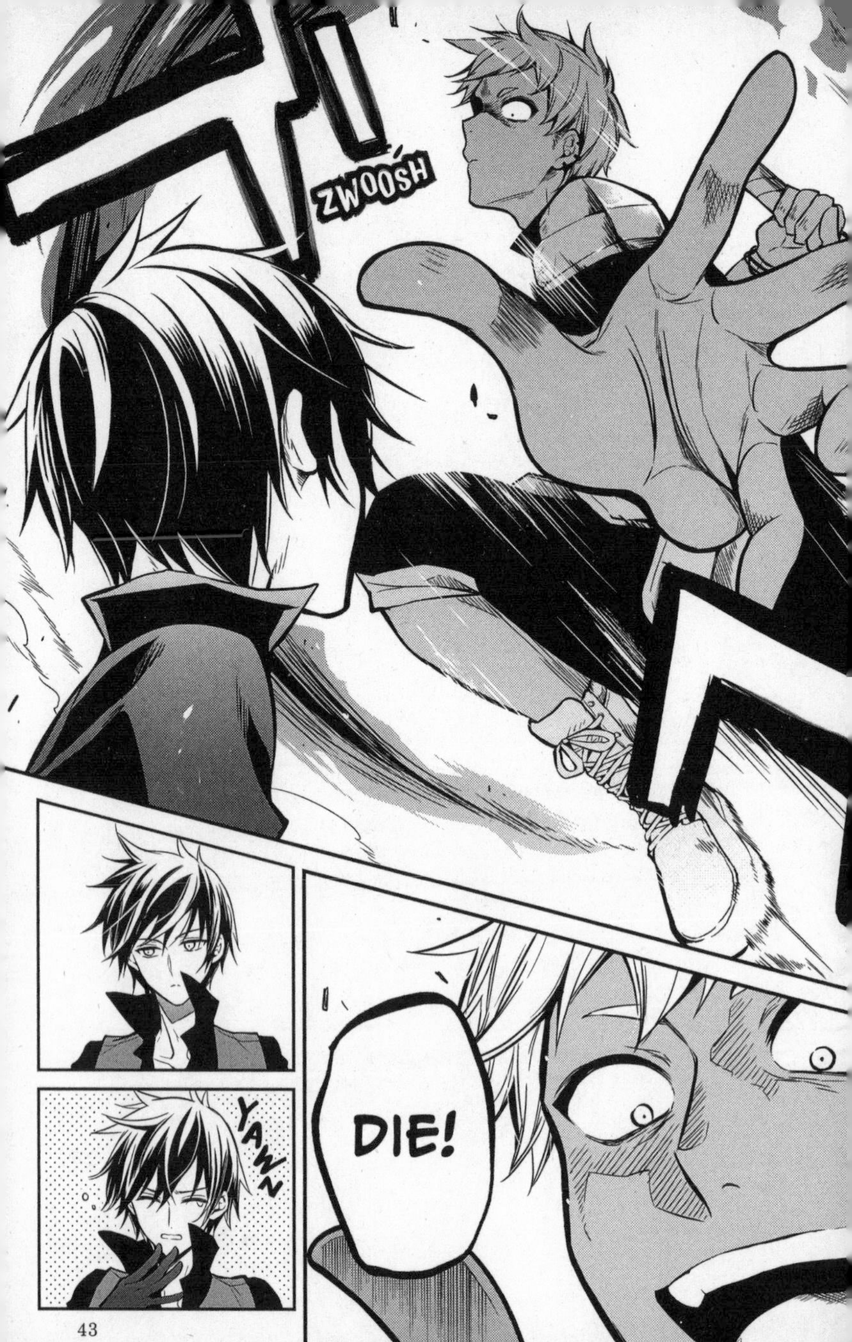
ZWOOSH
DIE!
YAWN

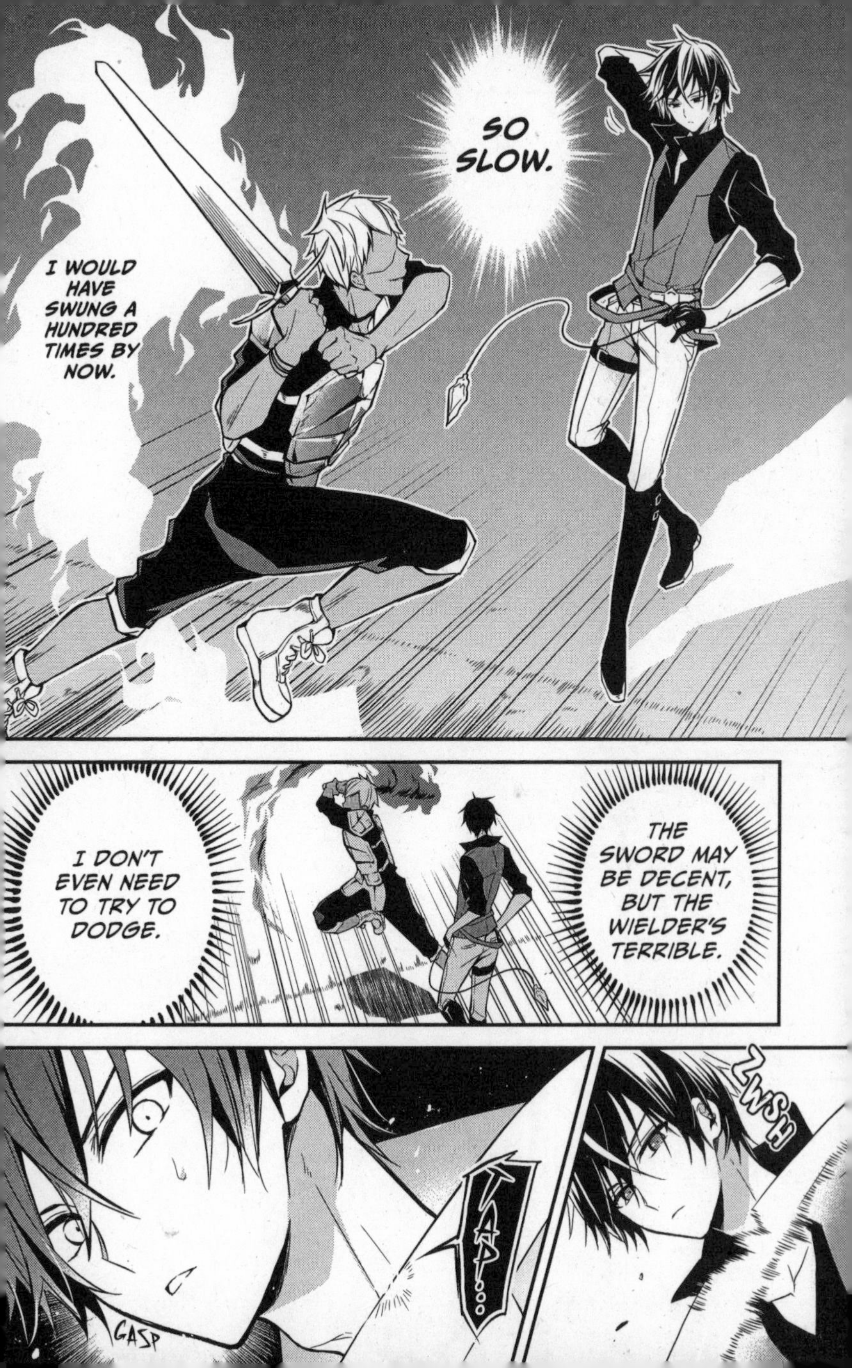
SO SLOW.
I WOULD HAVE SWUNG A HUNDRED TIMES BY NOW.
THE SWORD MAY BE DECENT, BUT THE WIELDER'S TERRIBLE.
I DON'T EVEN NEED TO TRY TO DODGE.
ZWSH
TAP...
GASP

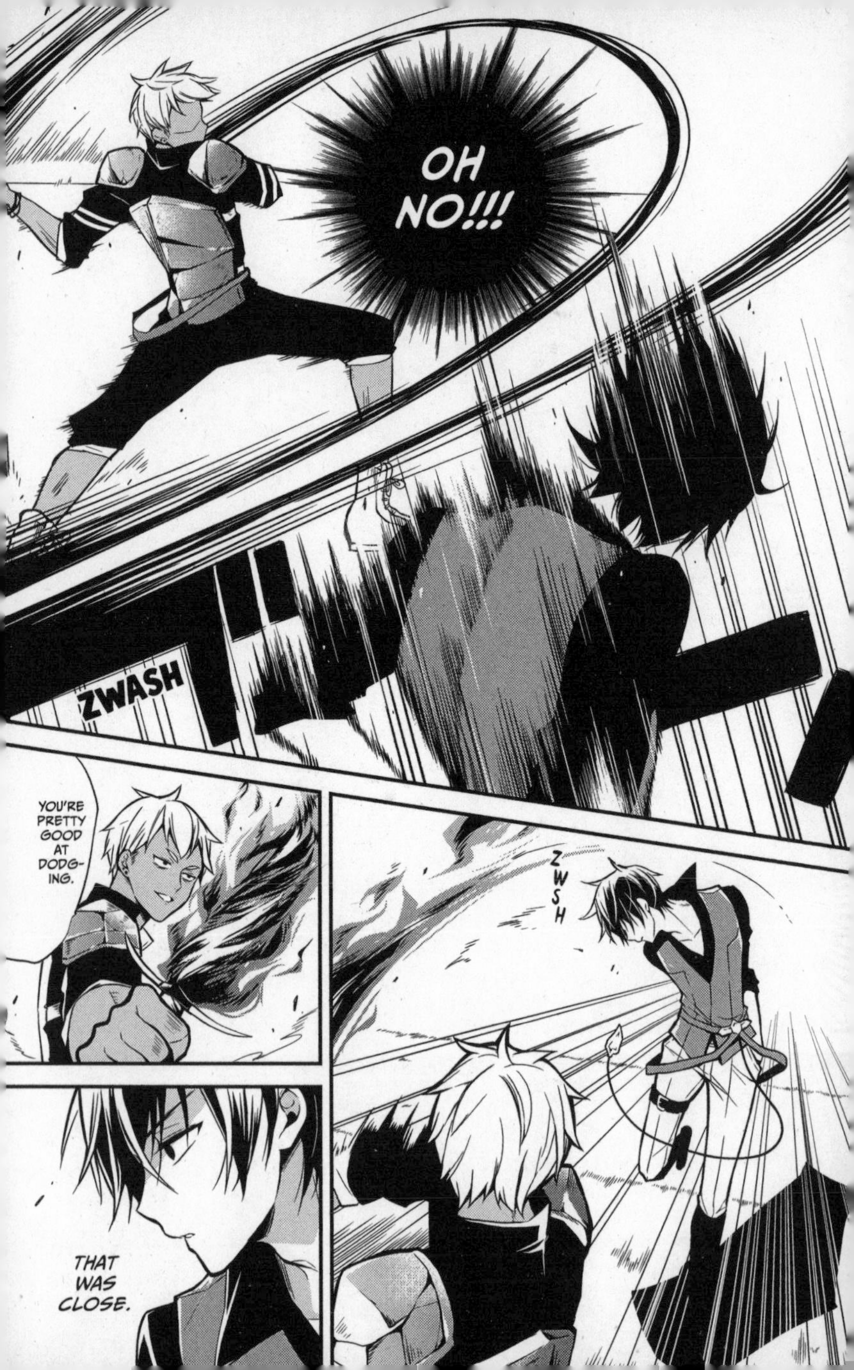
OH NO!!!
ZWASH
ZWSH
YOU'RE PRETTY GOOD AT DODG-ING.
THAT WAS CLOSE.

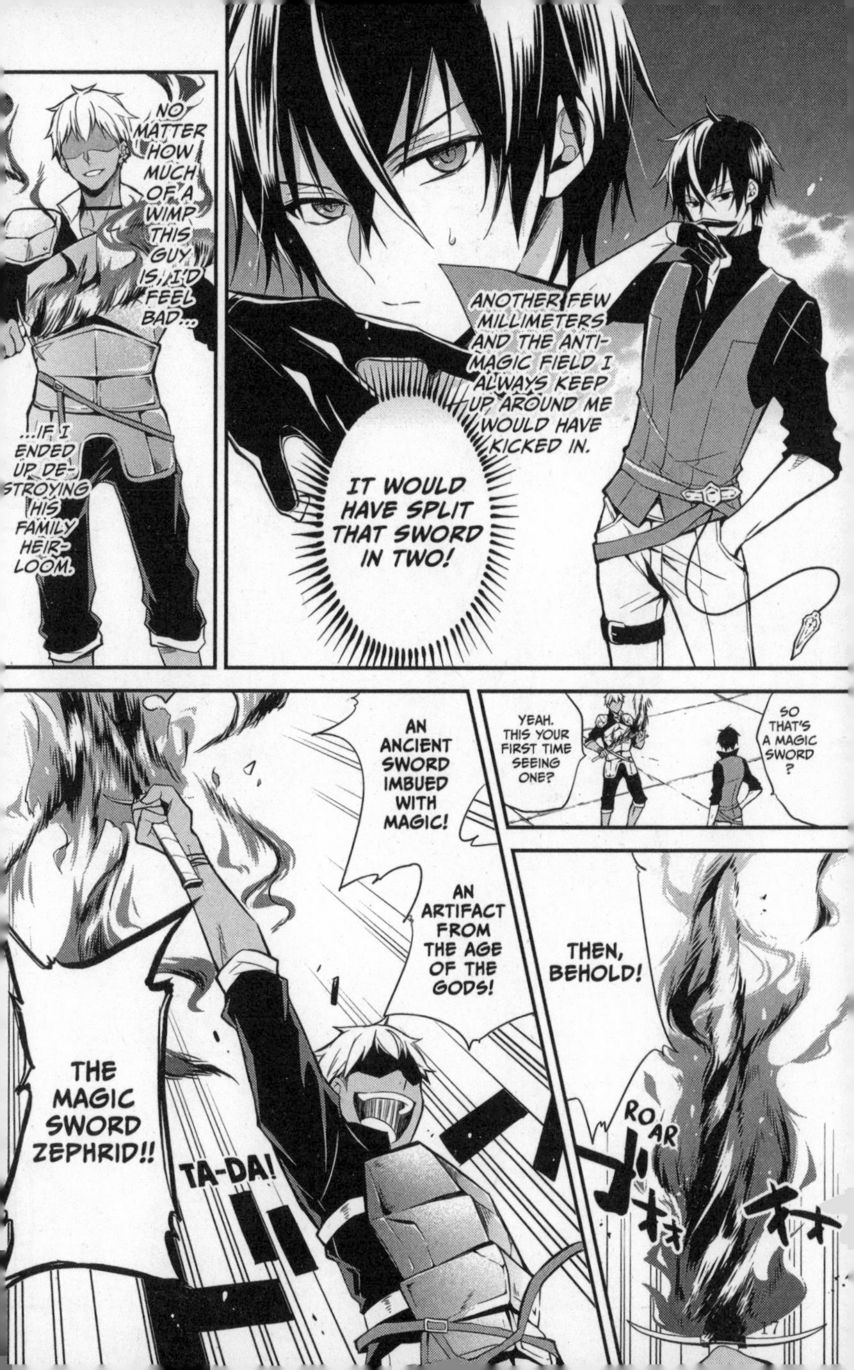
ANOTHER FEW MILLIMETERS AND THE ANTI-MAGIC FIELD I ALWAYS KEEP UP AROUND ME WOULD HAVE KICKED IN.
IT WOULD HAVE SPLIT THAT SWORD IN TWO!
NO MATTER HOW MUCH OF A WIMP THIS GUY IS, I'D FEEL BAD...
...IF I ENDED UP DE-STROYING HIS FAMILY HEIR-LOOM.
SO THAT'S A MAGIC SWORD?
YEAH. THIS YOUR FIRST TIME SEEING ONE?
THEN, BEHOLD!
ROAR
AN ANCIENT SWORD IMBUED WITH MAGIC!
AN ARTIFACT FROM THE AGE OF THE GODS!
THE MAGIC SWORD ZEPHRID!!
TA-DA!

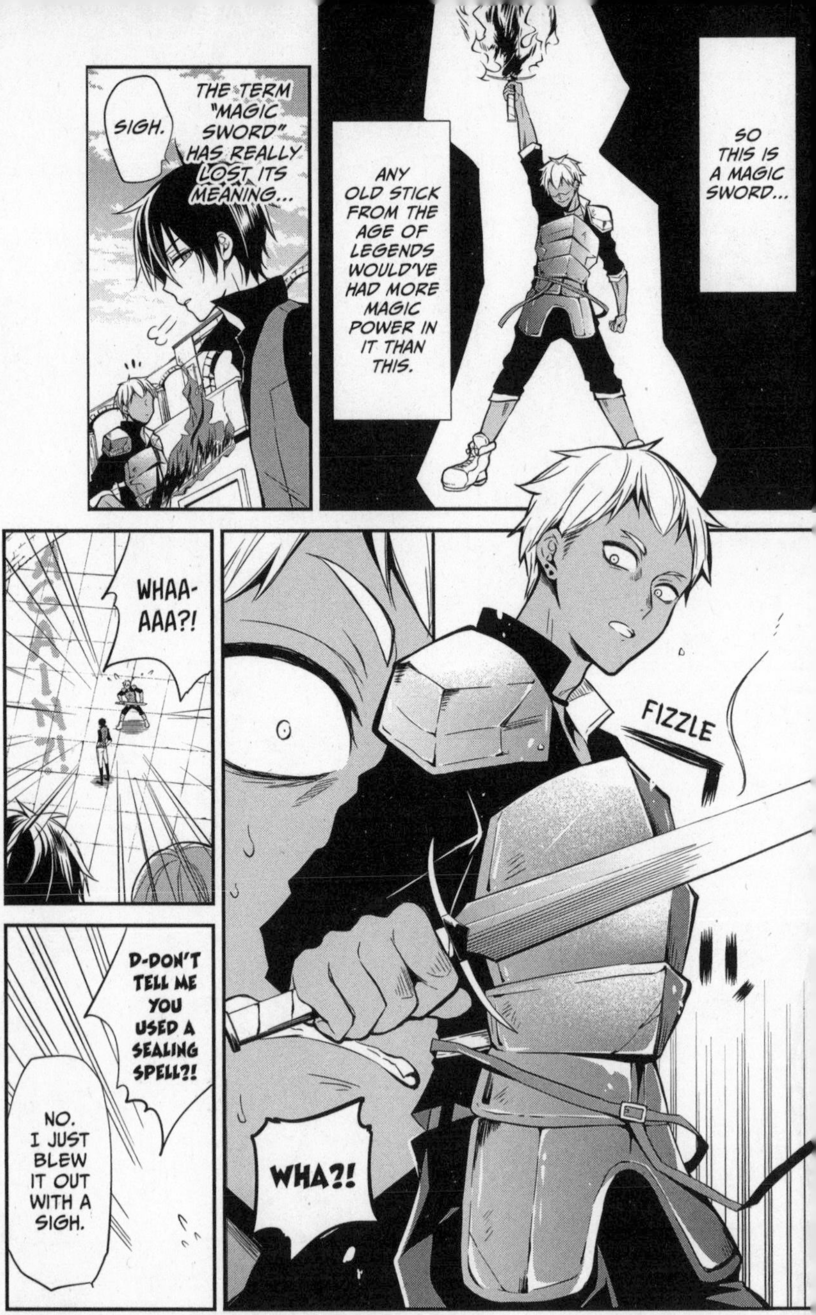
SO THIS IS A MAGIC SWORD...
ANY OLD STICK FROM THE AGE OF LEGENDS WOULD'VE HAD MORE MAGIC POWER IN IT THAN THIS.
THE TERM "MAGIC SWORD" HAS REALLY LOST ITS MEANING...
SIGH.
FIZZLE
WHA?!
WHAA-AAA?!
D-DON'T TELL ME YOU USED A SEALING SPELL?!
NO. I JUST BLEW IT OUT WITH A SIGH.

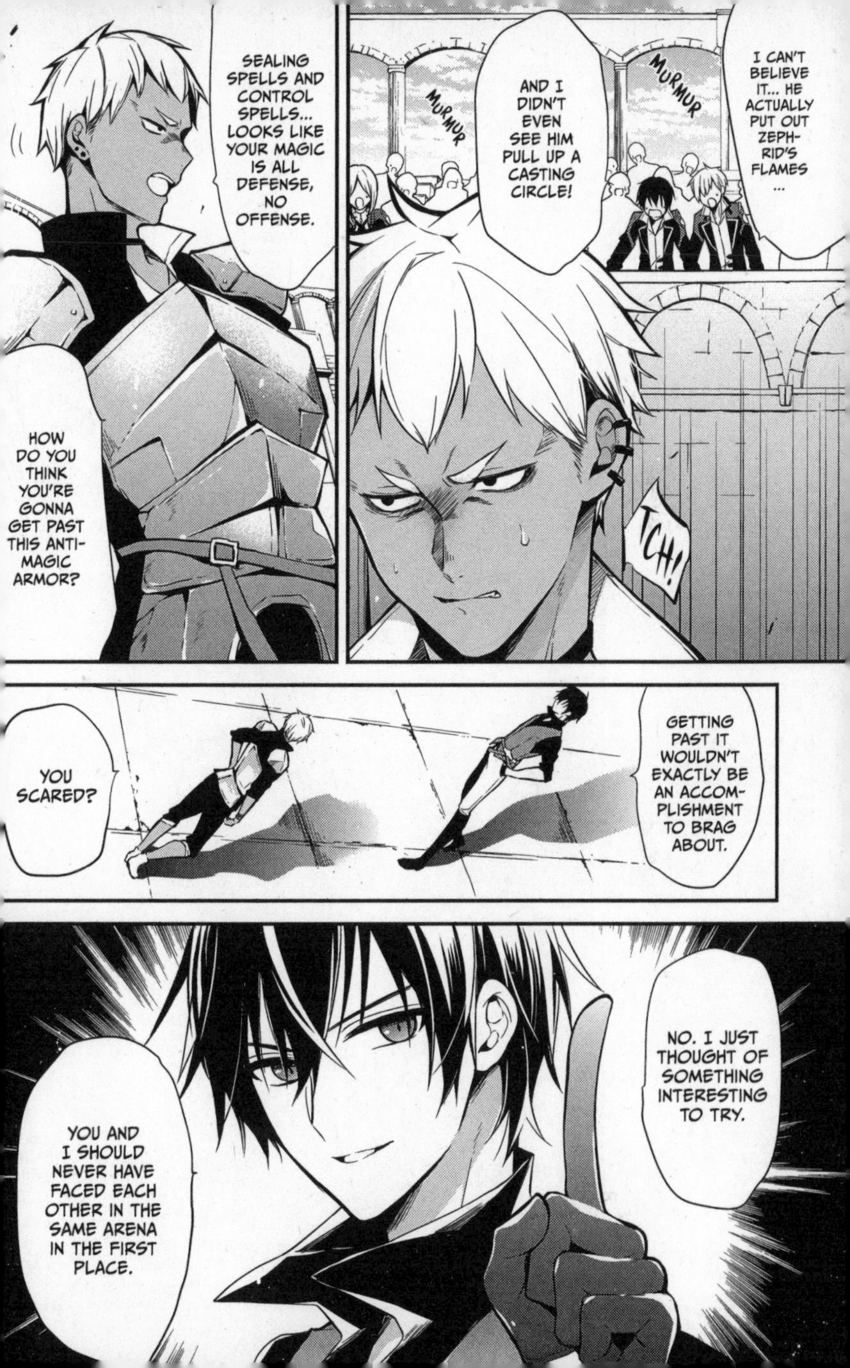
I CAN'T BELIEVE IT... HE ACTUALLY PUT OUT ZEPH-RID'S FLAMES...
MURMUR
AND I DIDN'T EVEN SEE HIM PULL UP A CASTING CIRCLE!
MURMUR
TCH!
SEALING SPELLS AND CONTROL SPELLS... LOOKS LIKE YOUR MAGIC IS ALL DEFENSE, NO OFFENSE.
HOW DO YOU THINK YOU'RE GONNA GET PAST THIS ANTI-MAGIC ARMOR?
GETTING PAST IT WOULDN'T EXACTLY BE AN ACCOM-PLISHMENT TO BRAG ABOUT.
YOU SCARED?
NO. I JUST THOUGHT OF SOMETHING INTERESTING TO TRY.
YOU AND I SHOULD NEVER HAVE FACED EACH OTHER IN THE SAME ARENA IN THE FIRST PLACE.

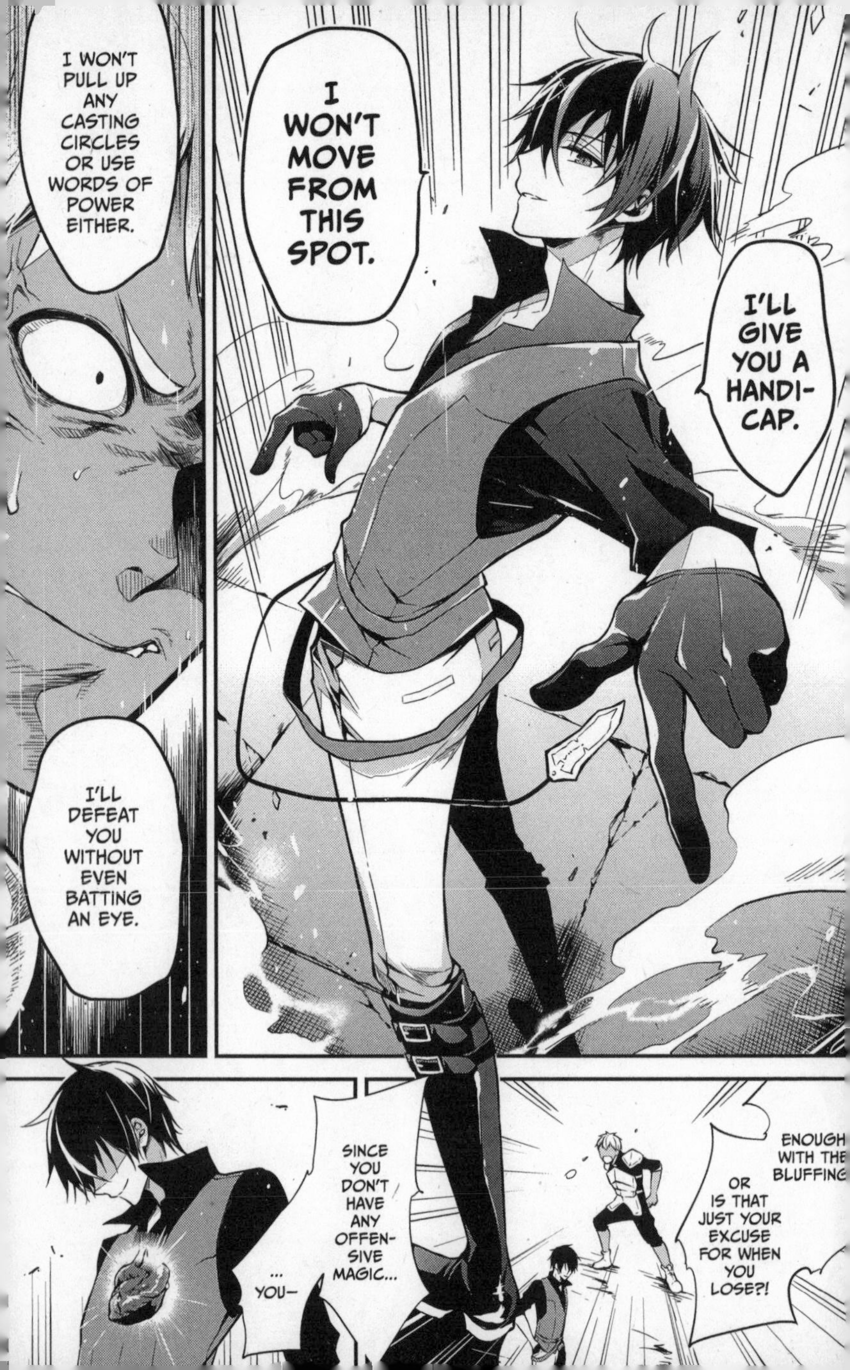
I'LL GIVE YOU A HANDI- CAP.
I WON'T MOVE FROM THIS SPOT.
I WON'T PULL UP ANY CASTING CIRCLES OR USE WORDS OF POWER EITHER.
I'LL DEFEAT YOU WITHOUT EVEN BATTING AN EYE.
ENOUGH WITH THE BLUFFING
OR IS THAT JUST YOUR EXCUSE FOR WHEN YOU LOSE?!
SINCE YOU DON'T HAVE ANY OFFEN- SIVE MAGIC...
... YOU—

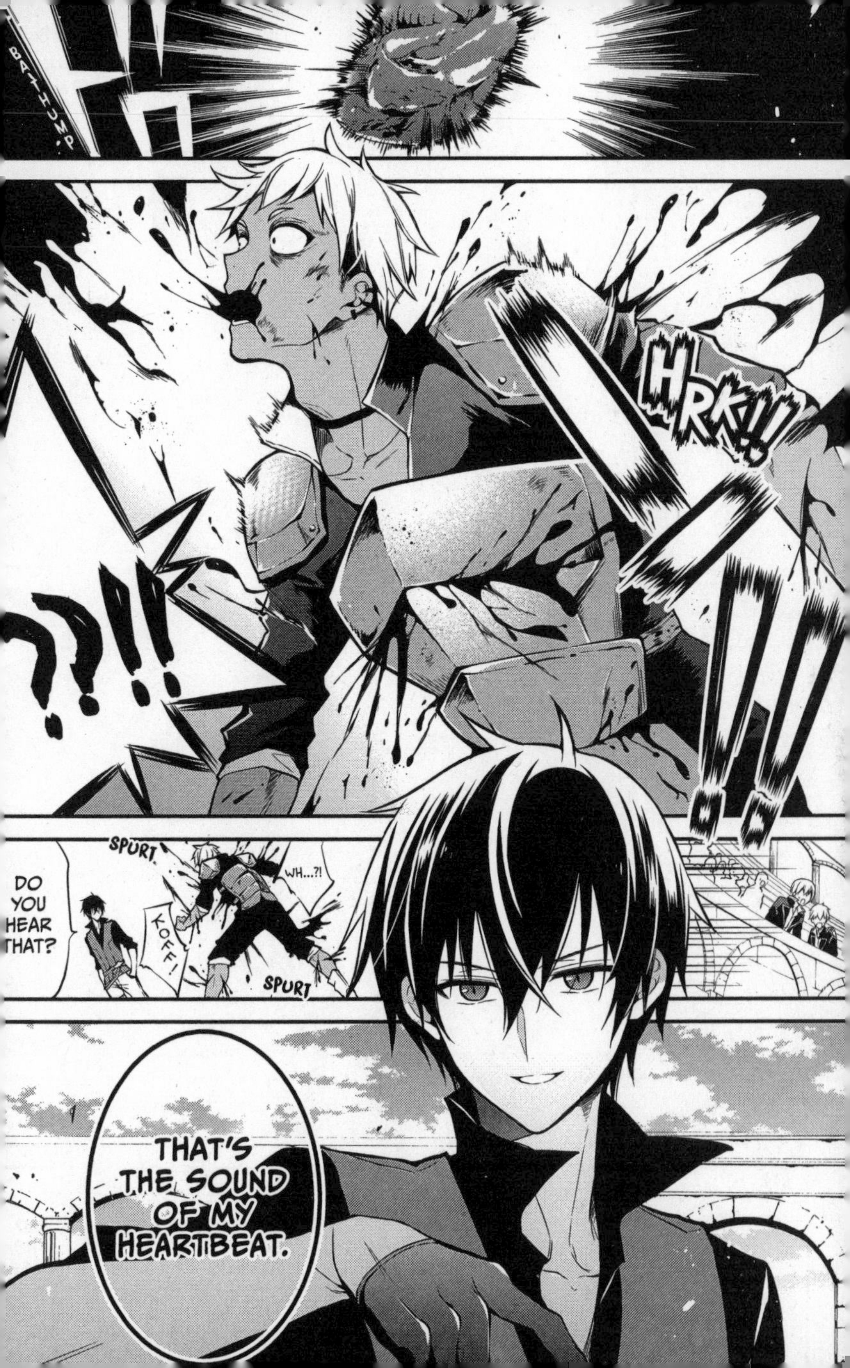
BATHUMP
HRK!!
!!
?!!
SPURT
WH...?!
KOFF!
SPURT
DO YOU HEAR THAT?
THAT'S THE SOUND OF MY HEARTBEAT.

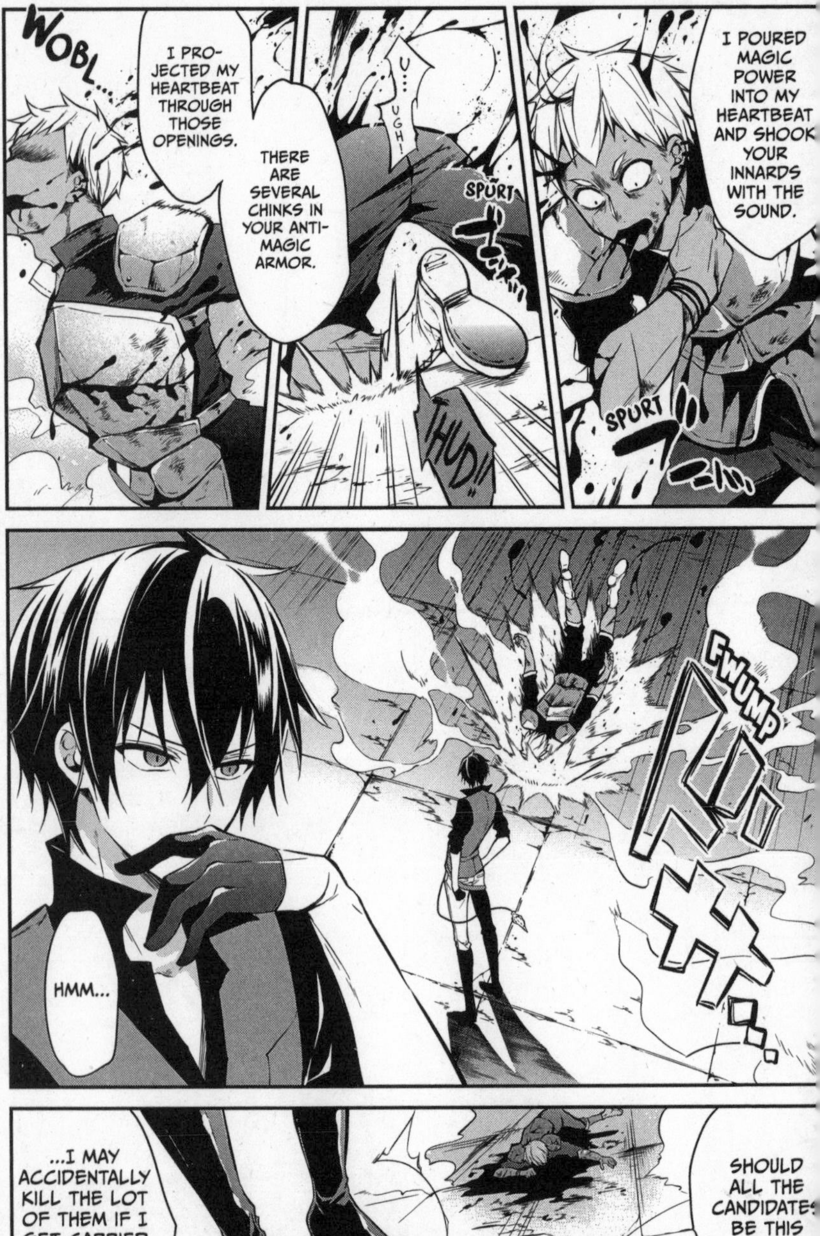
I POURED MAGIC POWER INTO MY HEARTBEAT AND SHOOK YOUR INNARDS WITH THE SOUND.
SPURT
U... UGH!
SPURT
THERE ARE SEVERAL CHINKS IN YOUR ANTI-MAGIC ARMOR.
THUD!!
WOBL...
I PRO-JECTED MY HEARTBEAT THROUGH THOSE OPENINGS.
FWUMP
HMM...
SHOULD ALL THE CANDIDATES BE THIS WEAK...
...I MAY ACCIDENTALLY KILL THE LOT OF THEM IF I GET CARRIED AWAY.

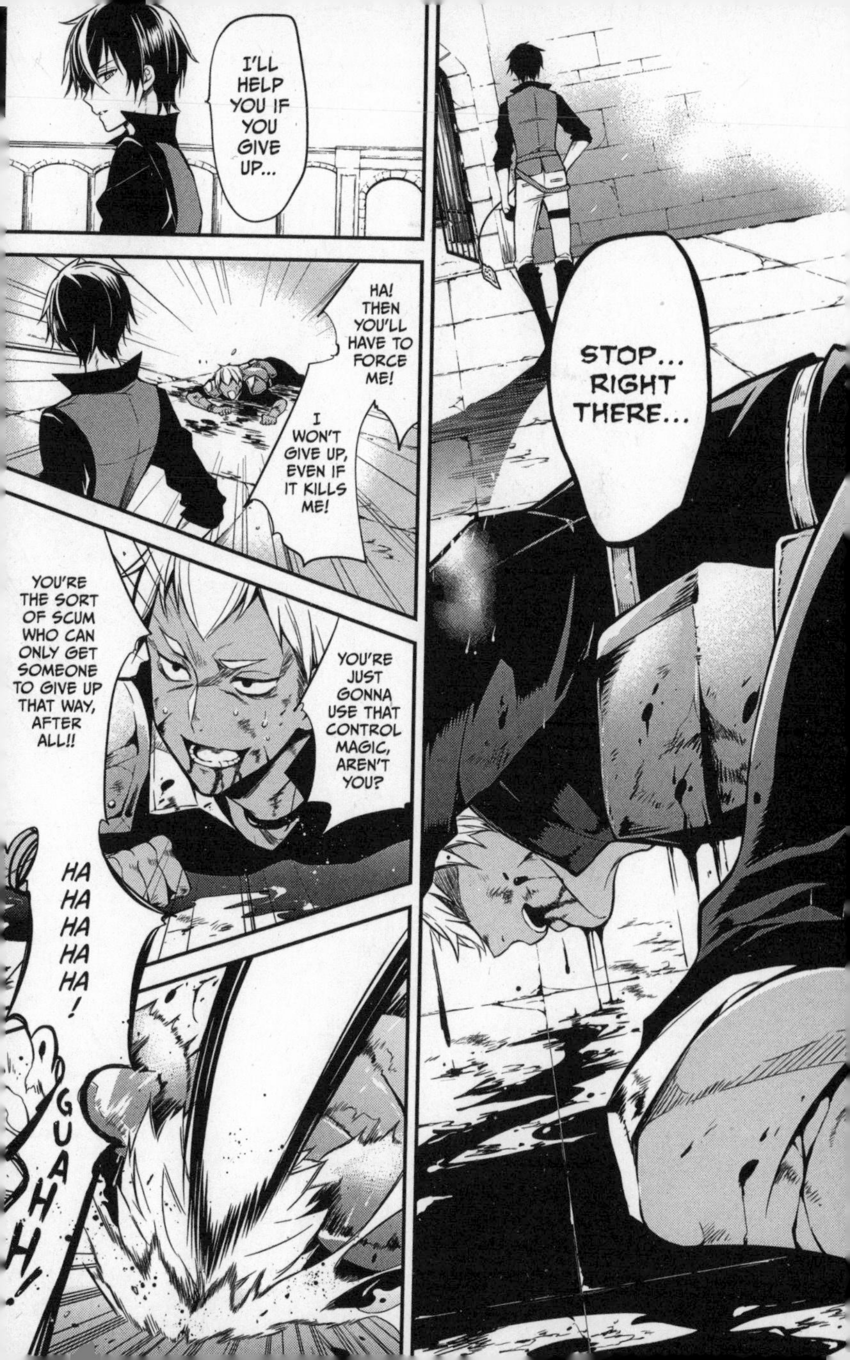
STOP... RIGHT THERE...
I'LL HELP YOU IF YOU GIVE UP...
HA! THEN YOU'LL HAVE TO FORCE ME!
I WON'T GIVE UP, EVEN IF IT KILLS ME!
YOU'RE JUST GONNA USE THAT CONTROL MAGIC, AREN'T YOU?
YOU'RE THE SORT OF SCUM WHO CAN ONLY GET SOMEONE TO GIVE UP THAT WAY, AFTER ALL!!
HA HA HA HA HA HA!
GUAHH!

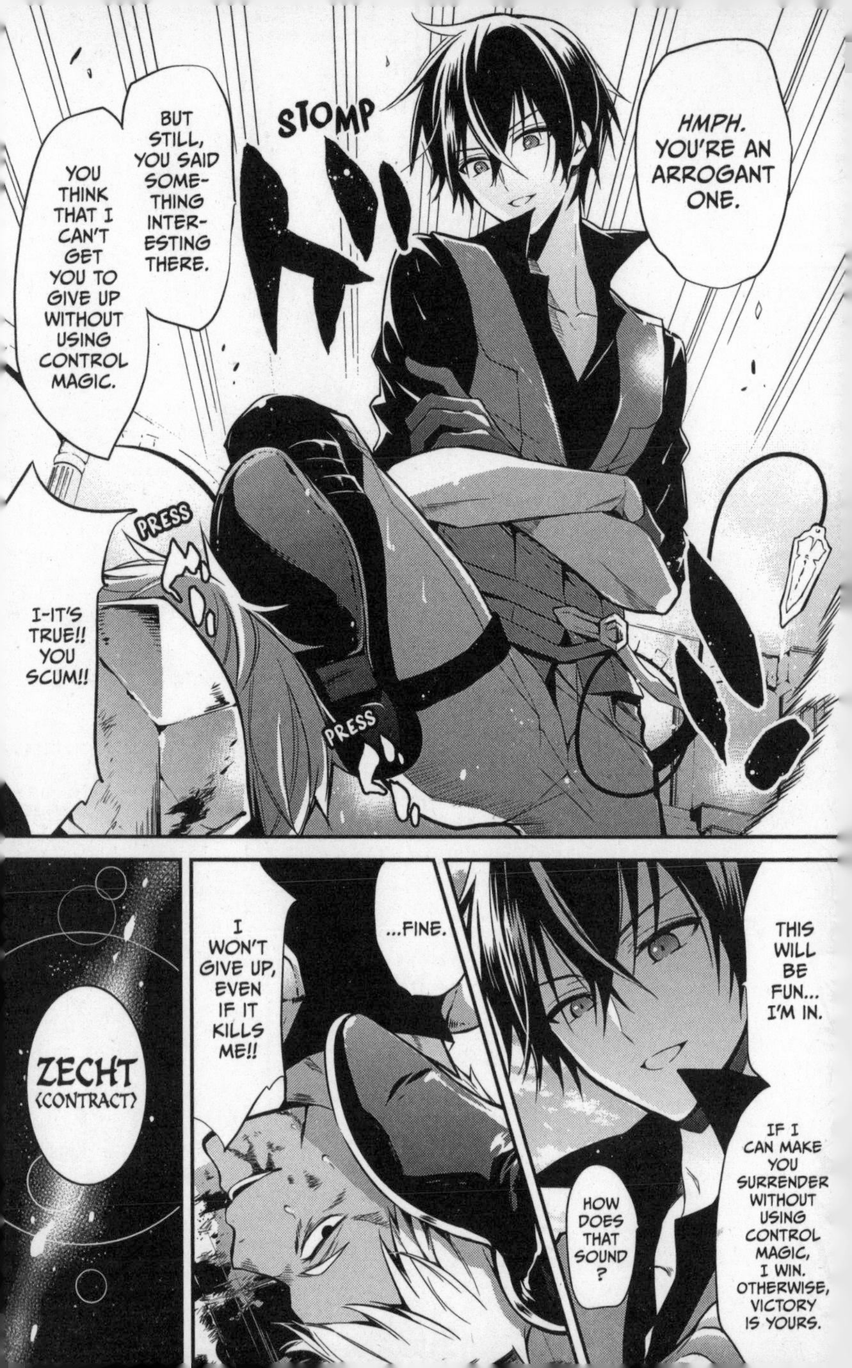
HMPH. YOU'RE AN ARROGANT ONE.
STOMP
BUT STILL, YOU SAID SOME-THING INTER-ESTING THERE.
YOU THINK THAT I CAN'T GET YOU TO GIVE UP WITHOUT USING CONTROL MAGIC.
PRESS
PRESS
I-IT'S TRUE!! YOU SCUM!!
THIS WILL BE FUN... I'M IN.
IF I CAN MAKE YOU SURRENDER WITHOUT USING CONTROL MAGIC, I WIN. OTHERWISE, VICTORY IS YOURS.
HOW DOES THAT SOUND?
...FINE.
I WON'T GIVE UP, EVEN IF IT KILLS ME!!
ZECHT
〈CONTRACT〉

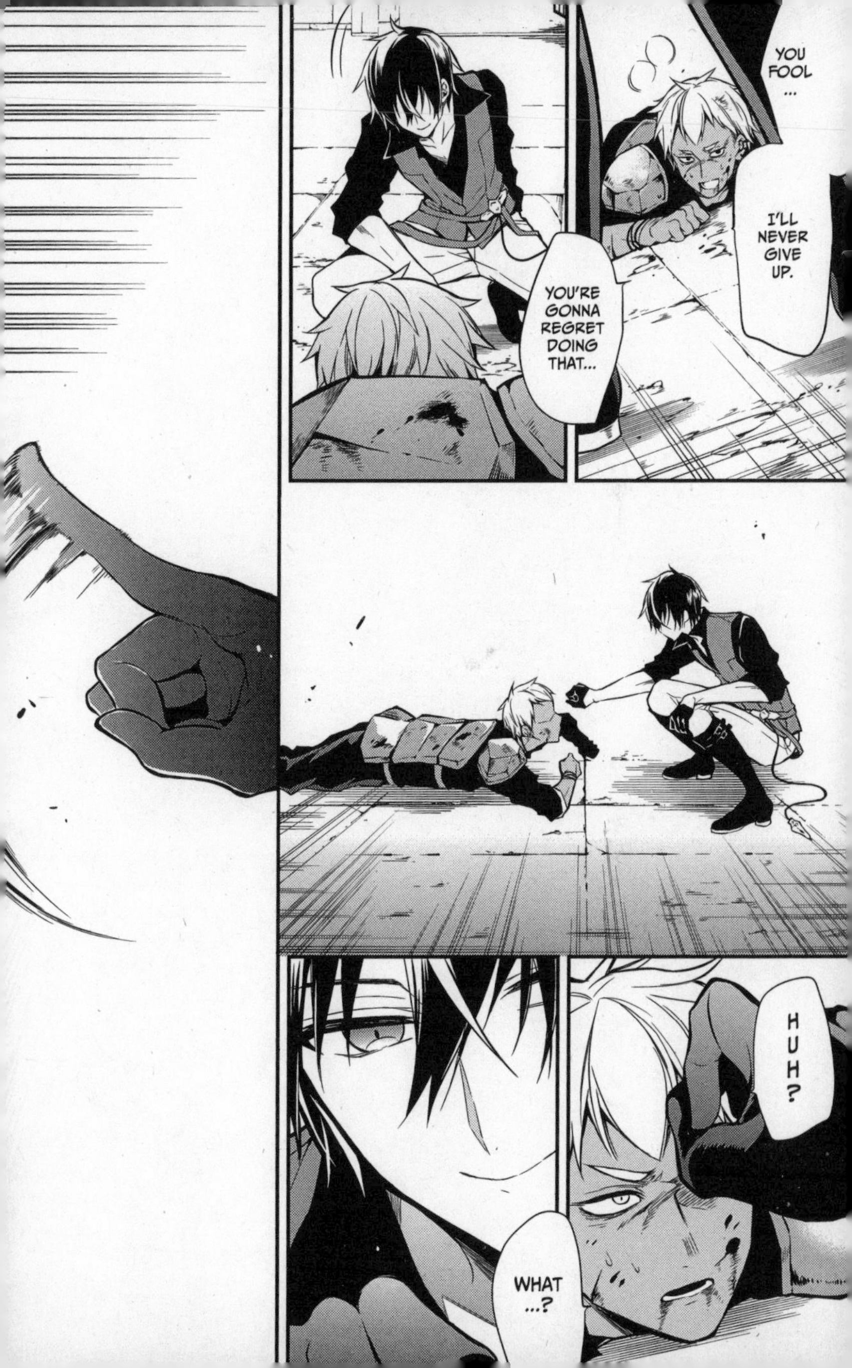
YOU FOOL ...
I'LL NEVER GIVE UP.
YOU'RE GONNA REGRET DOING THAT...
HUH?
WHAT ...?

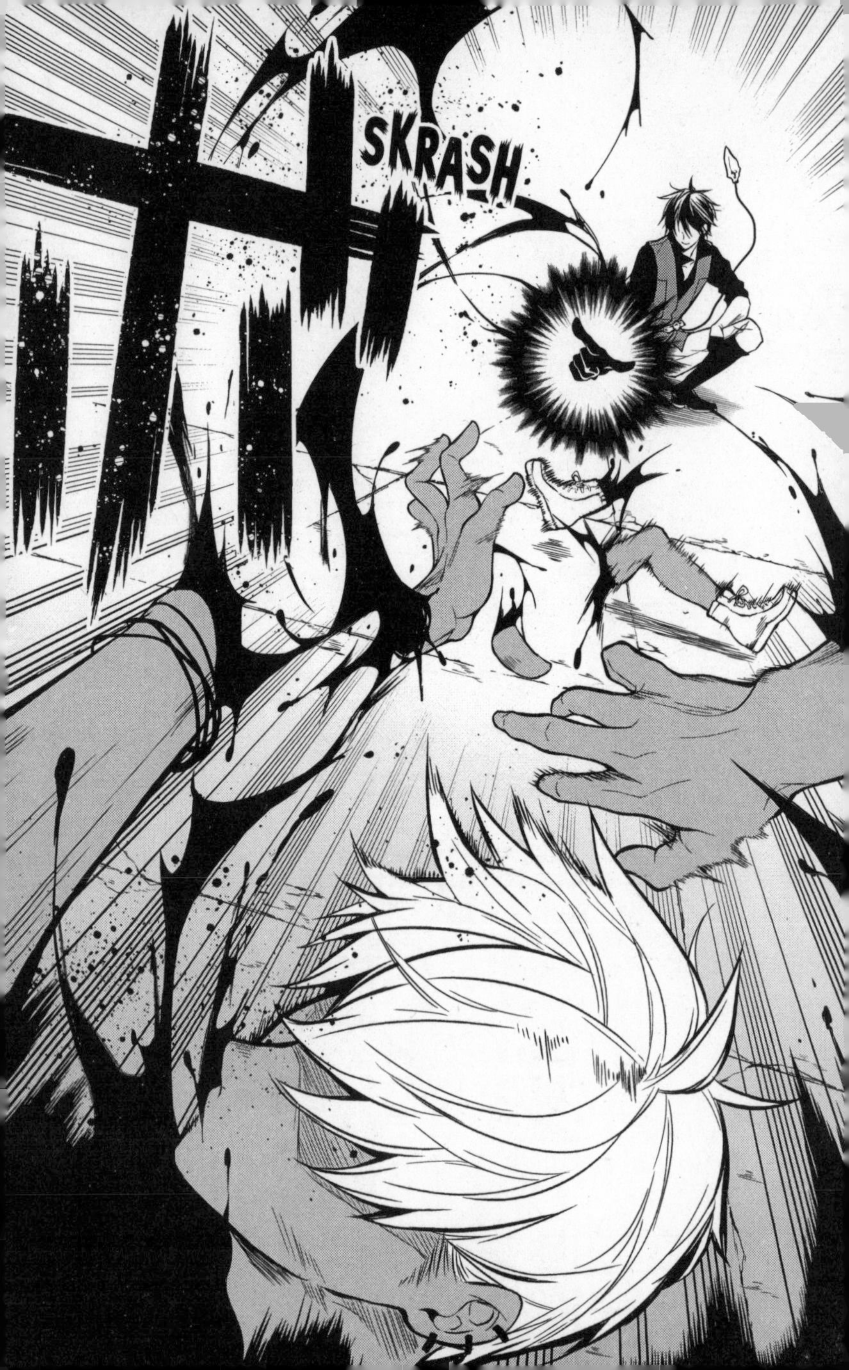
SKRASH

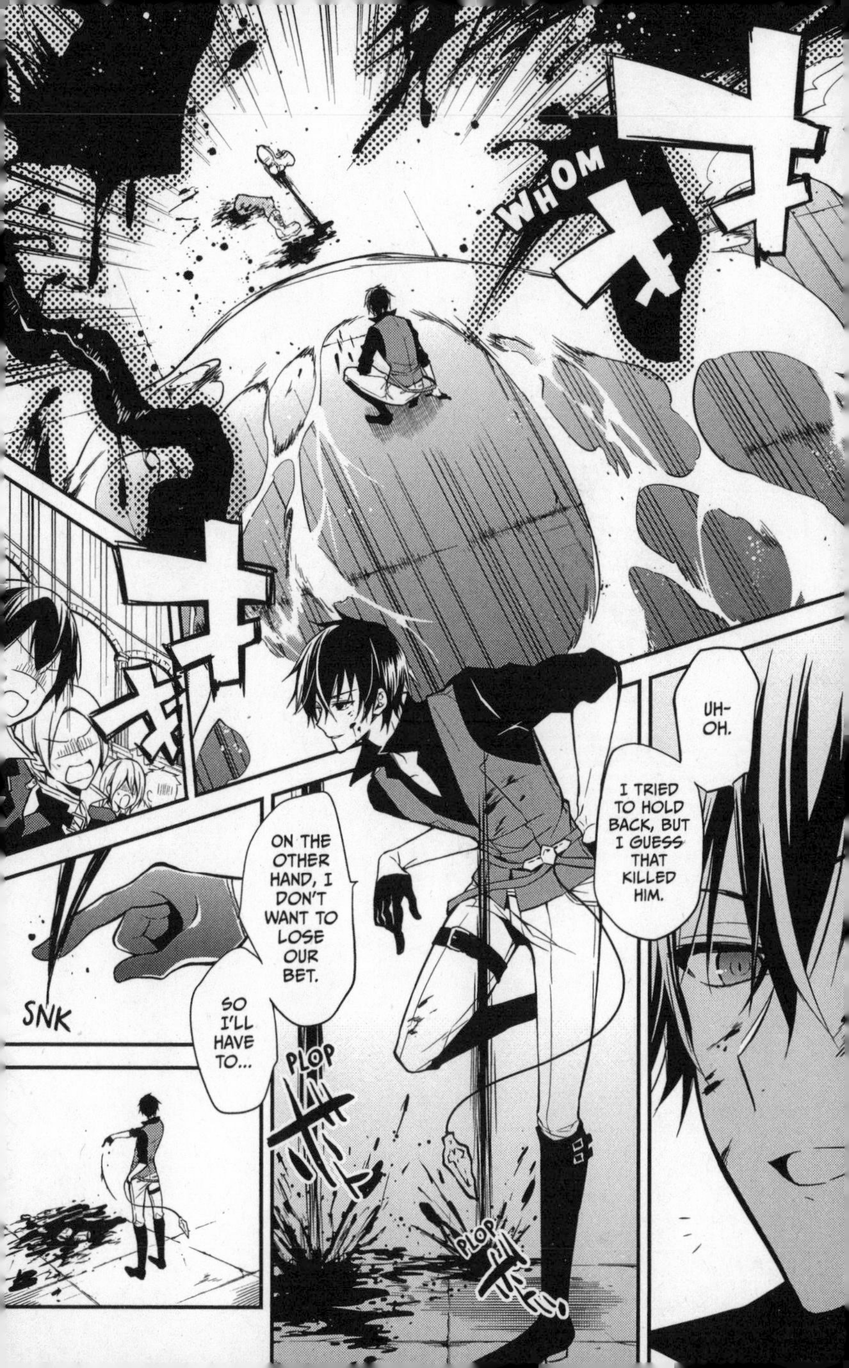
WHOM
UH-OH.
I TRIED TO HOLD BACK, BUT I GUESS THAT KILLED HIM.
ON THE OTHER HAND, I DON'T WANT TO LOSE OUR BET.
SO I'LL HAVE TO...
PLOP
PLOP
SNK

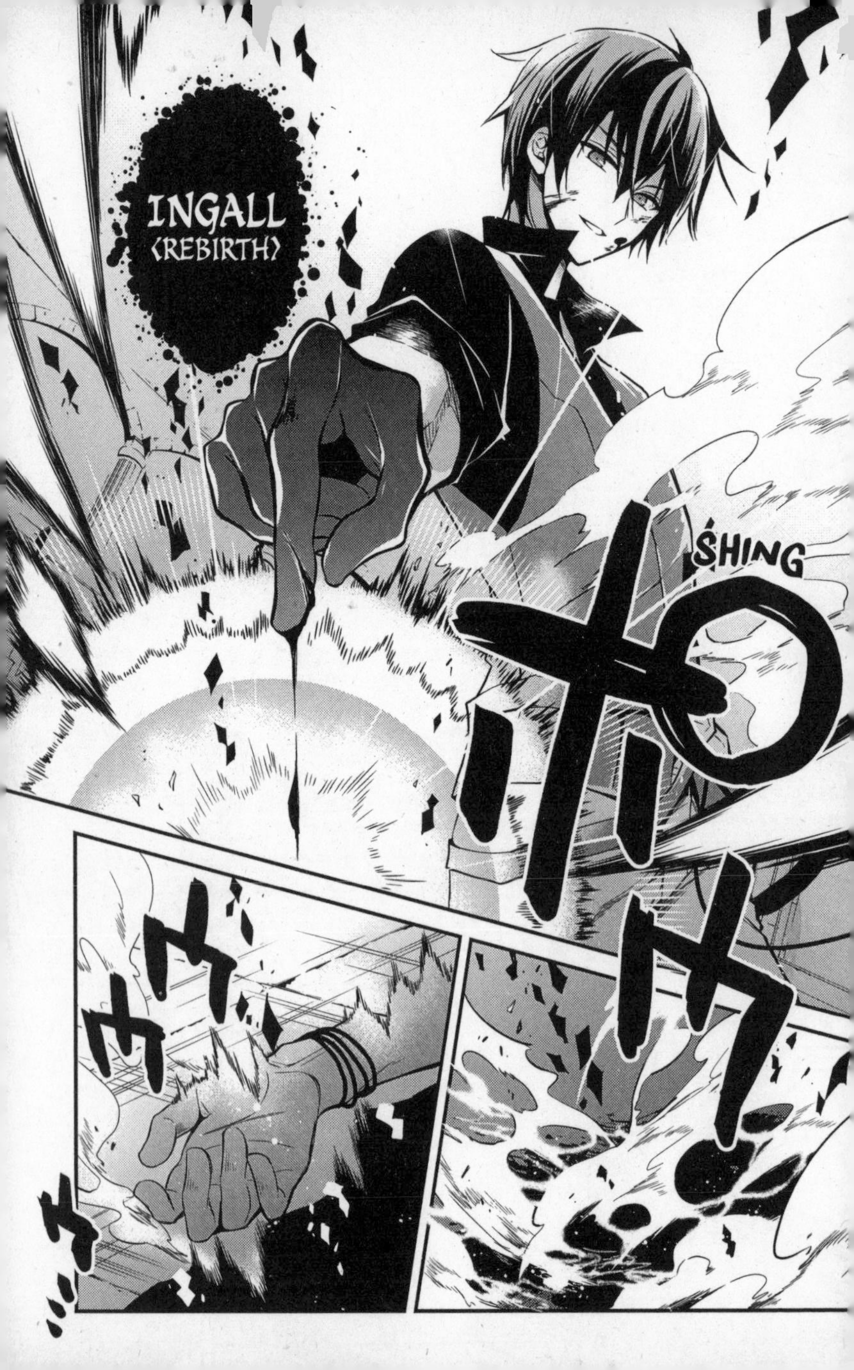
INGALL
<REBIRTH>
SHING

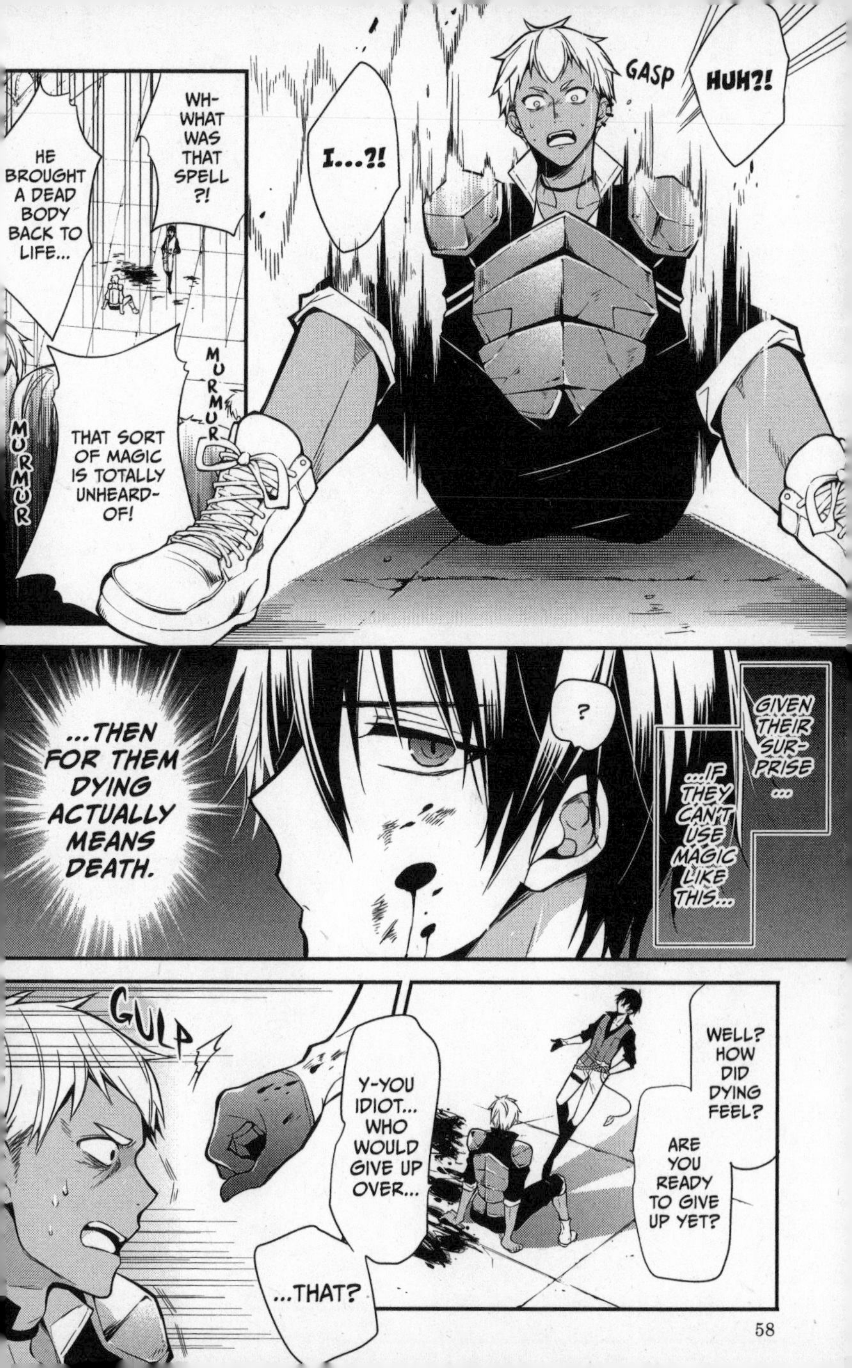
HUH?!
GASP
I...?!
WH-WHAT WAS THAT SPELL ?!
HE BROUGHT A DEAD BODY BACK TO LIFE...
MURMUR
THAT SORT OF MAGIC IS TOTALLY UNHEARD-OF!
MURMUR
GIVEN THEIR SURPRISE...
...IF THEY CAN'T USE MAGIC LIKE THIS...
?
...THEN FOR THEM DYING ACTUALLY MEANS DEATH.
WELL? HOW DID DYING FEEL?
ARE YOU READY TO GIVE UP YET?
Y-YOU IDIOT... WHO WOULD GIVE UP OVER...
...THAT?
GULP

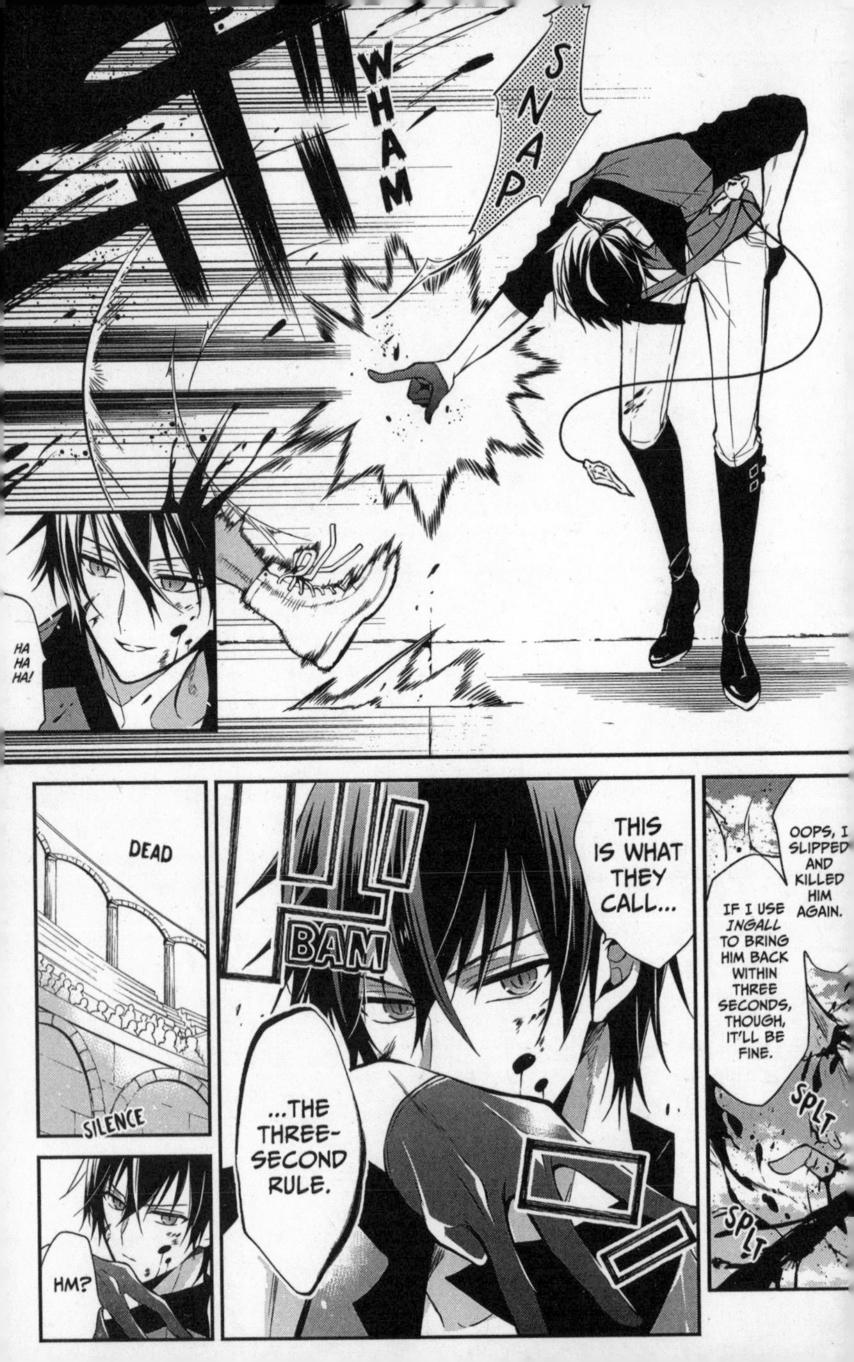
SNAP
WHAM
HA HA HA!
OOPS, I SLIPPED AND KILLED HIM AGAIN.
IF I USE *INGALL* TO BRING HIM BACK WITHIN THREE SECONDS, THOUGH, IT'LL BE FINE.
SPLT
SPLT
THIS IS WHAT THEY CALL...
BAM
...THE THREE-SECOND RULE.
DEAD
SILENCE
HM?

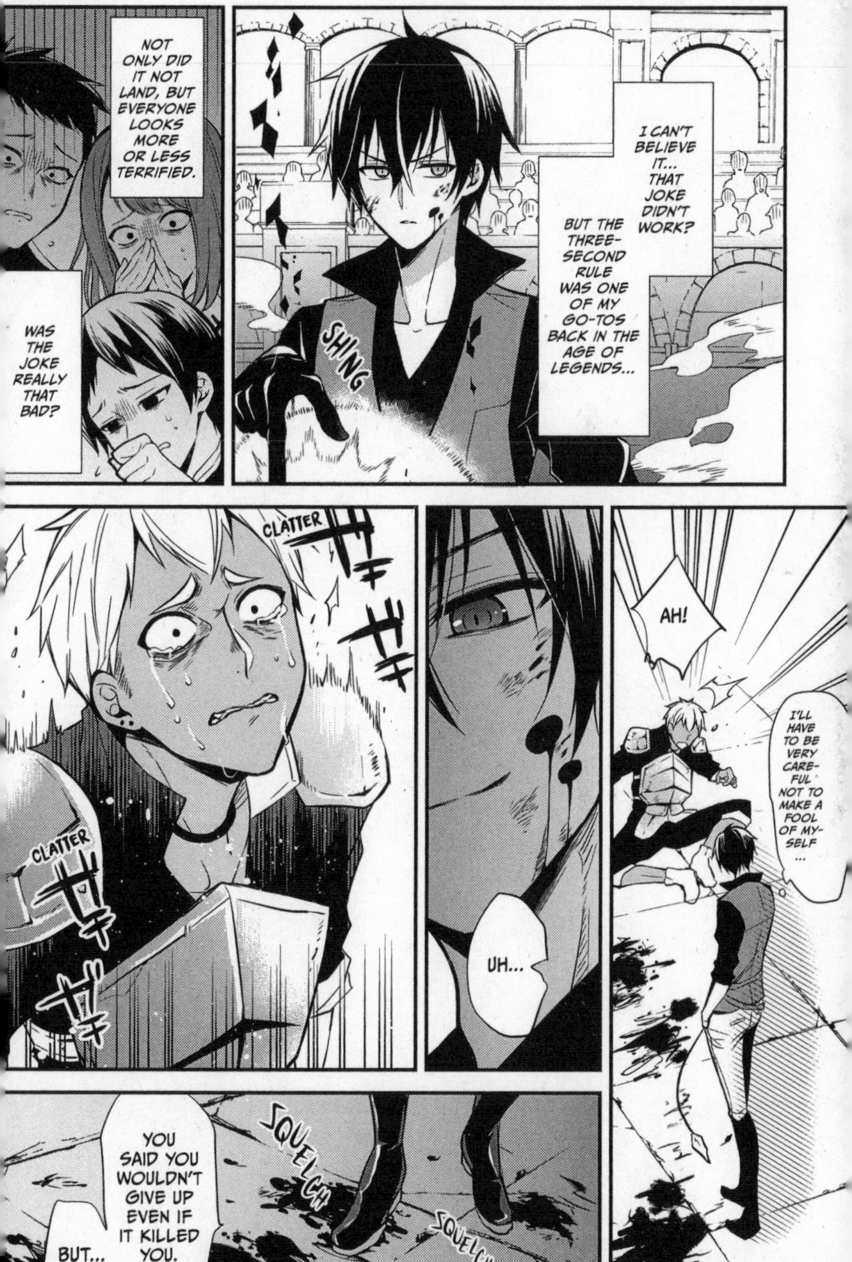
I CAN'T BELIEVE IT... THAT JOKE DIDN'T WORK?
BUT THE THREE-SECOND RULE WAS ONE OF MY GO-TOS BACK IN THE AGE OF LEGENDS...
SHING
NOT ONLY DID IT NOT LAND, BUT EVERYONE LOOKS MORE OR LESS TERRIFIED.
WAS THE JOKE REALLY THAT BAD?
AH!
I'LL HAVE TO BE VERY CARE-FUL NOT TO MAKE A FOOL OF MY-SELF...
UH...
CLATTER
CLATTER
SQUELCH
SQUELCH
YOU SAID YOU WOULDN'T GIVE UP EVEN IF IT KILLED YOU.
BUT...

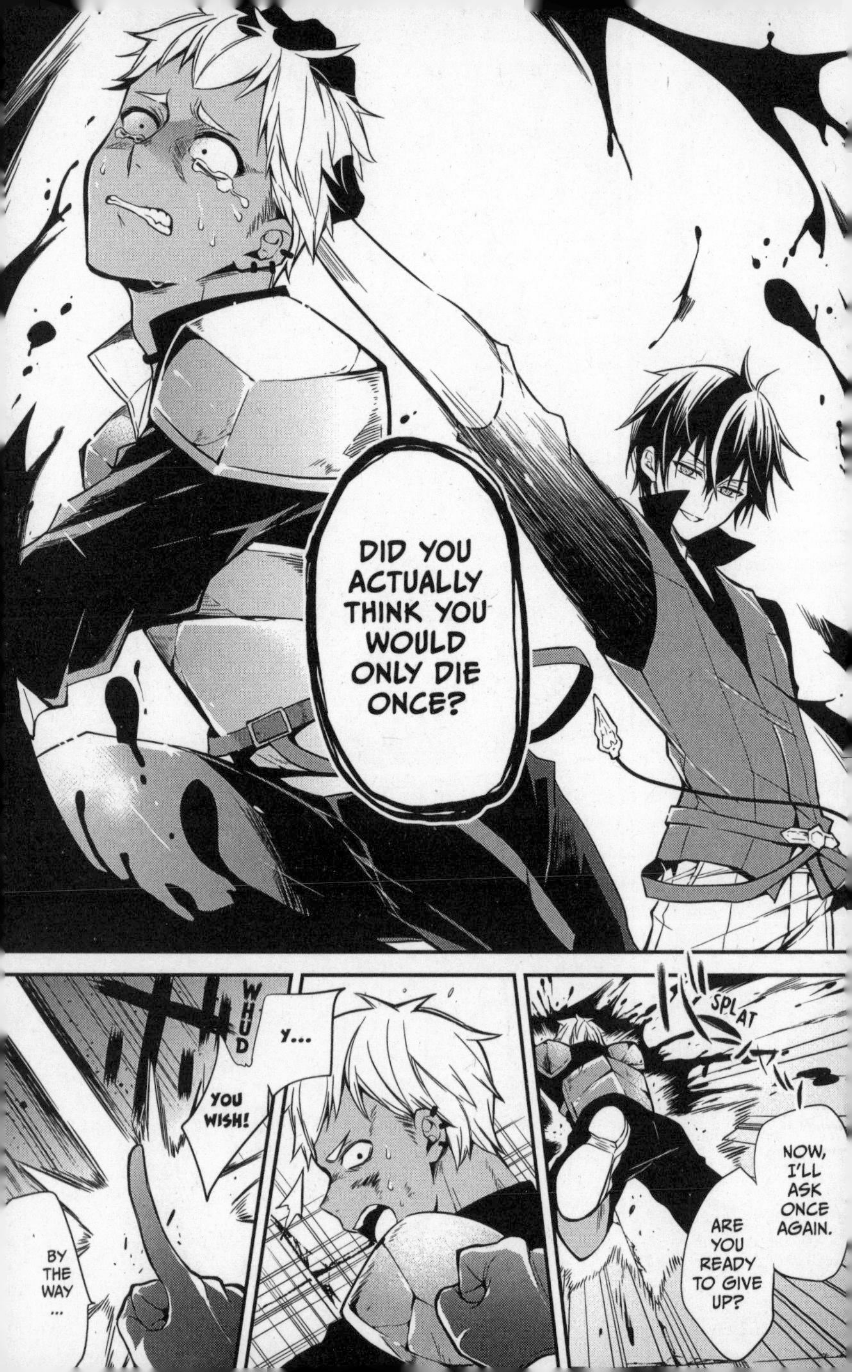
DID YOU ACTUALLY THINK YOU WOULD ONLY DIE ONCE?
SPLAT
NOW, I'LL ASK ONCE AGAIN.
ARE YOU READY TO GIVE UP?
Y...
WHUD
YOU WISH!
BY THE WAY ...

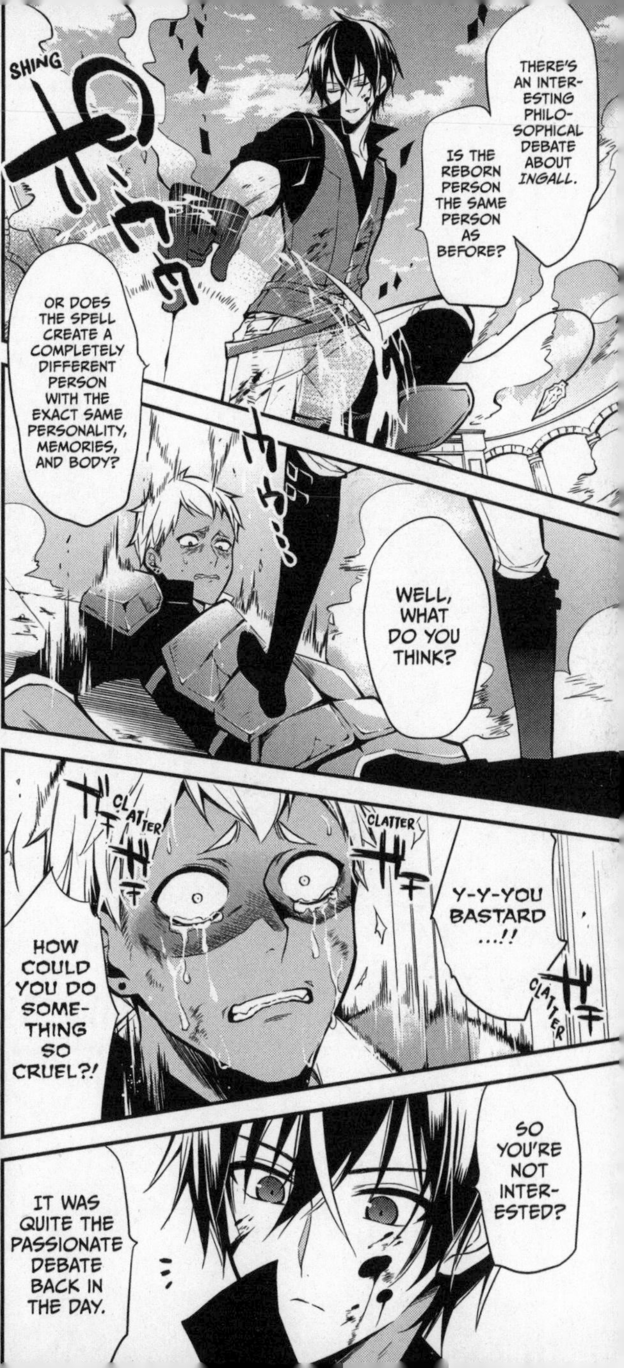
SHING
THERE'S AN INTERESTING PHILOSOPHICAL DEBATE ABOUT INGALL.
IS THE REBORN PERSON THE SAME PERSON AS BEFORE?
OR DOES THE SPELL CREATE A COMPLETELY DIFFERENT PERSON WITH THE EXACT SAME PERSONALITY, MEMORIES, AND BODY?
WELL, WHAT DO YOU THINK?
CLATTER
CLATTER
CLATTER
Y-Y-YOU BASTARD ...!!
HOW COULD YOU DO SOMETHING SO CRUEL?!
SO YOU'RE NOT INTERESTED?
IT WAS QUITE THE PASSIONATE DEBATE BACK IN THE DAY.
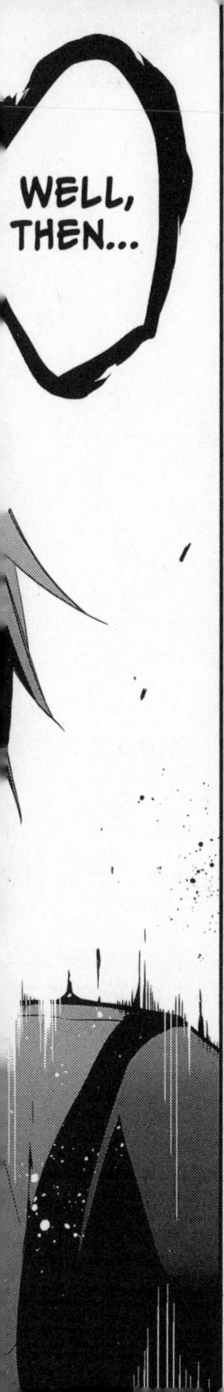
WELL, THEN...

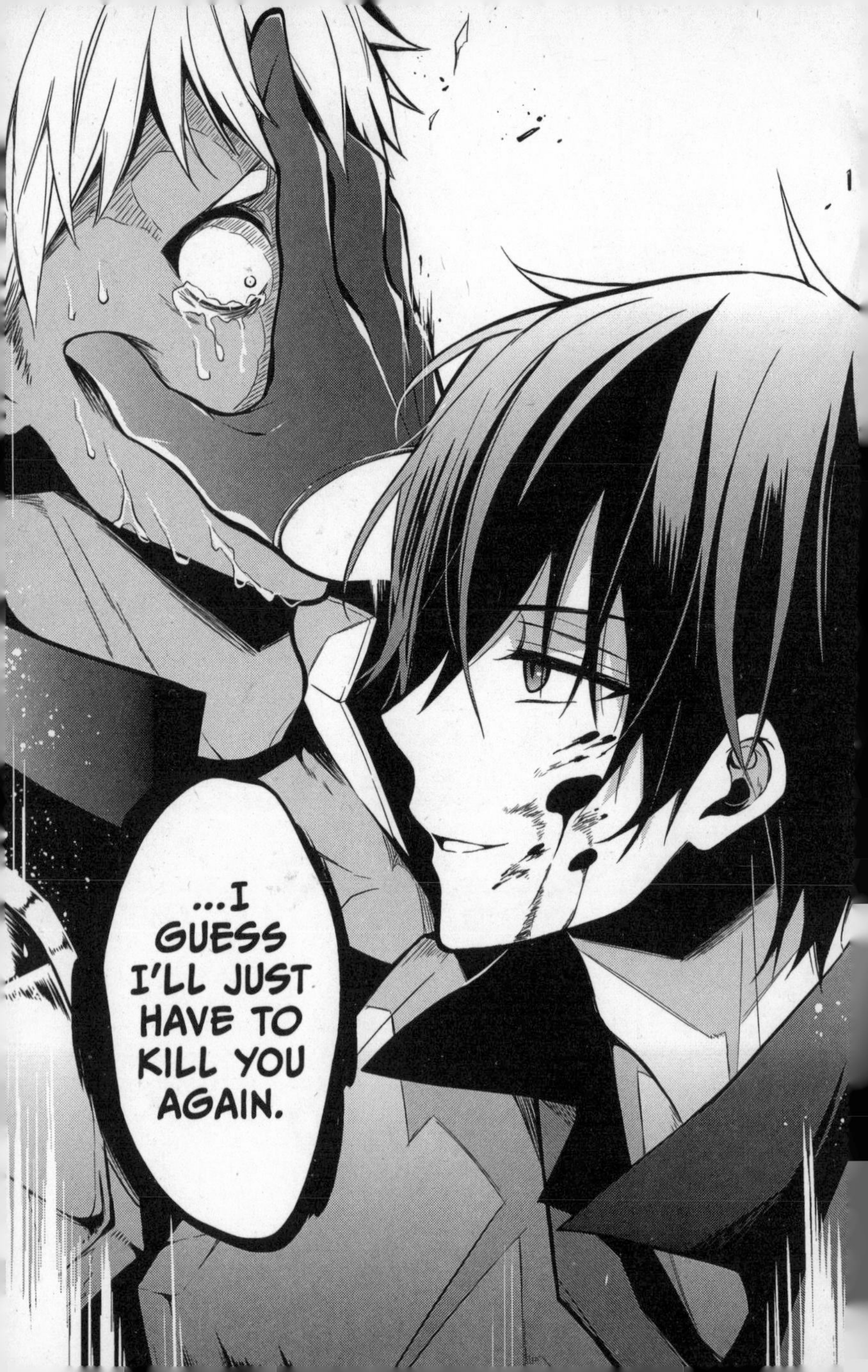
...I GUESS I'LL JUST HAVE TO KILL YOU AGAIN.

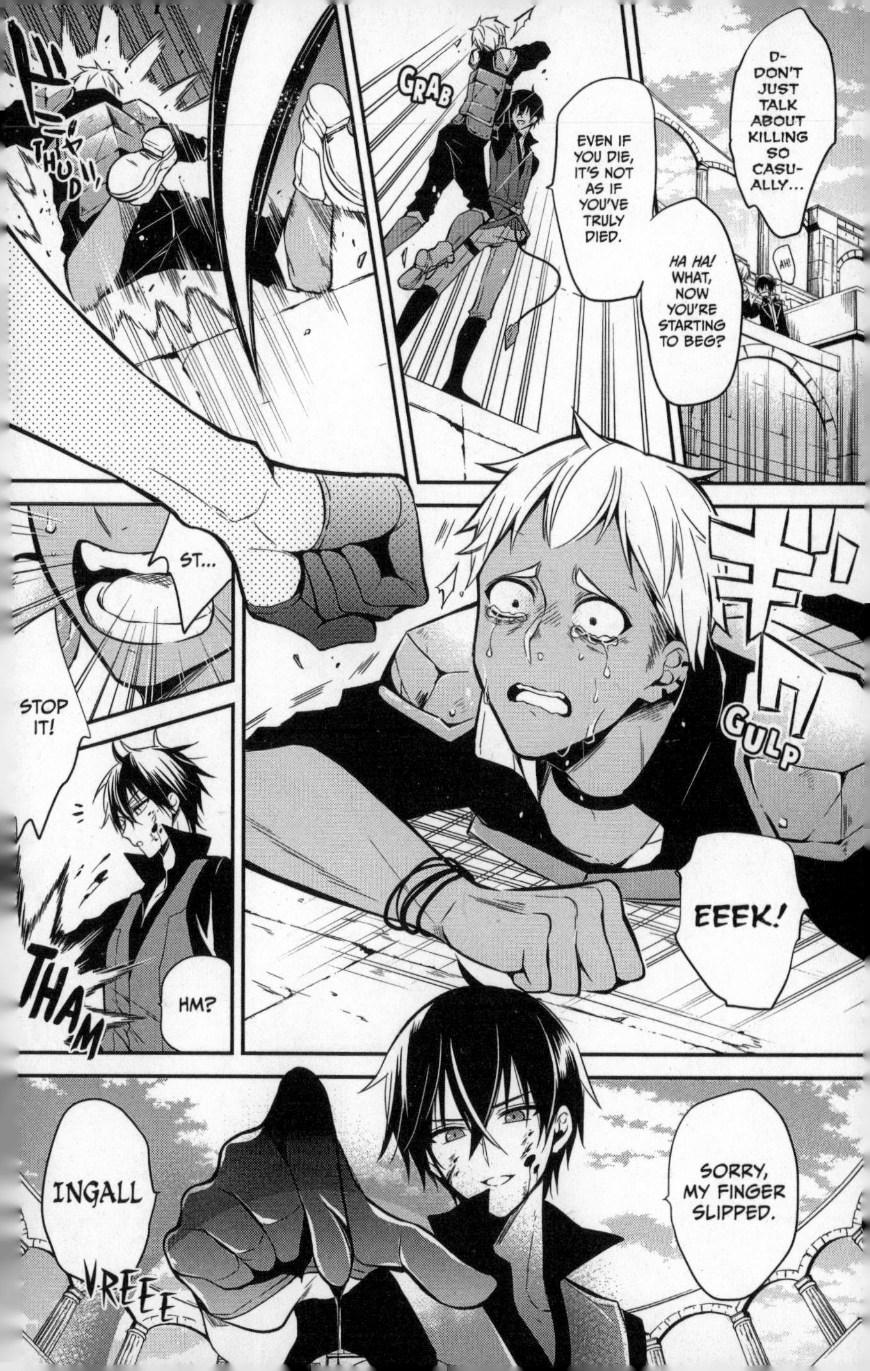
AH!
D-DON'T JUST TALK ABOUT KILLING SO CASU-ALLY...
EVEN IF YOU DIE, IT'S NOT AS IF YOU'VE TRULY DIED.
HA HA! WHAT, NOW YOU'RE STARTING TO BEG?
GRAB
THUD!!
GULP
EEEK!
ST...
STOP IT!
HM?
THAM
SORRY, MY FINGER SLIPPED.
INGALL
VREEE

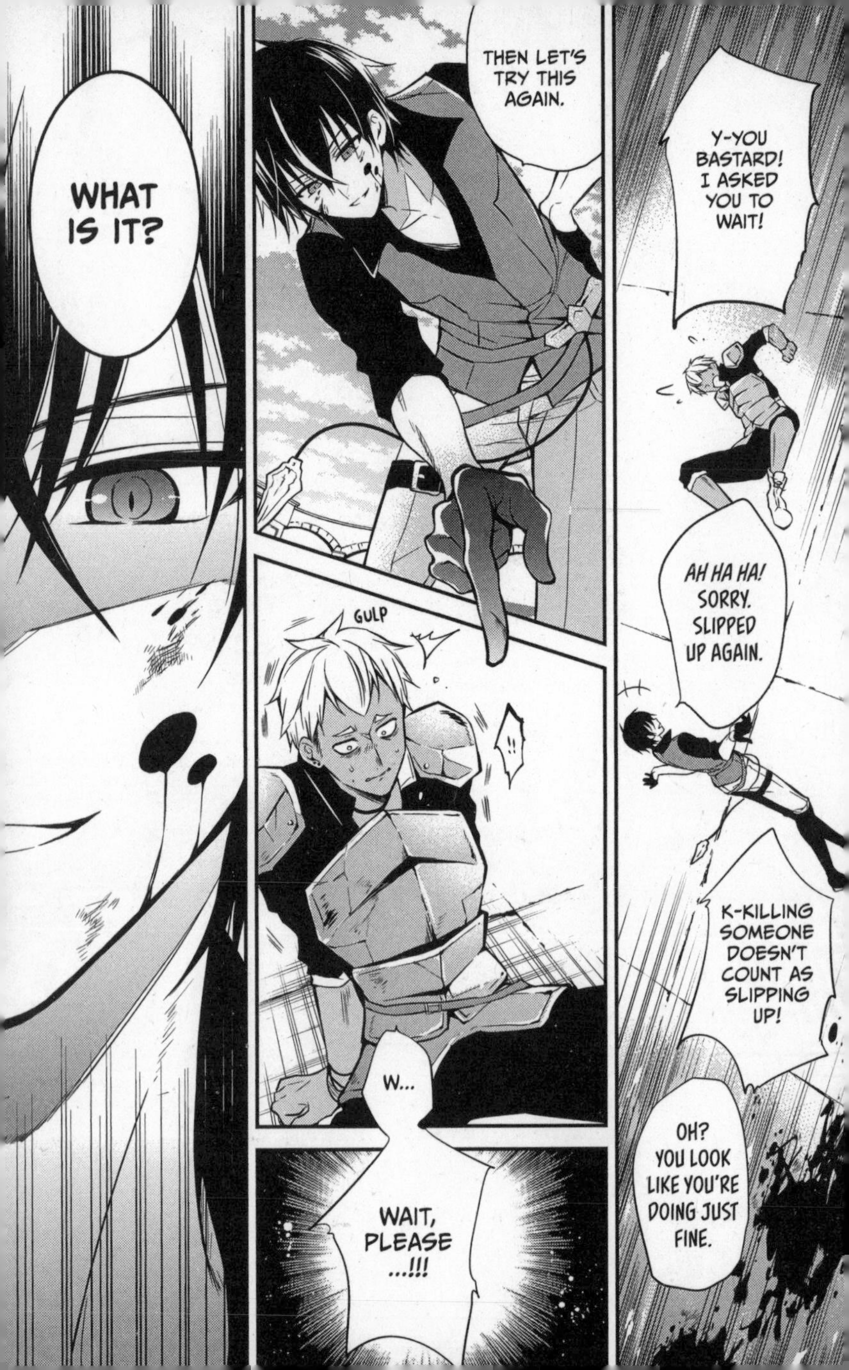
Y-YOU BASTARD! I ASKED YOU TO WAIT!
AH HA HA! SORRY. SLIPPED UP AGAIN.
K-KILLING SOMEONE DOESN'T COUNT AS SLIPPING UP!
OH? YOU LOOK LIKE YOU'RE DOING JUST FINE.
THEN LET'S TRY THIS AGAIN.
GULP
!!
W...
WAIT, PLEASE ...!!!
WHAT IS IT?

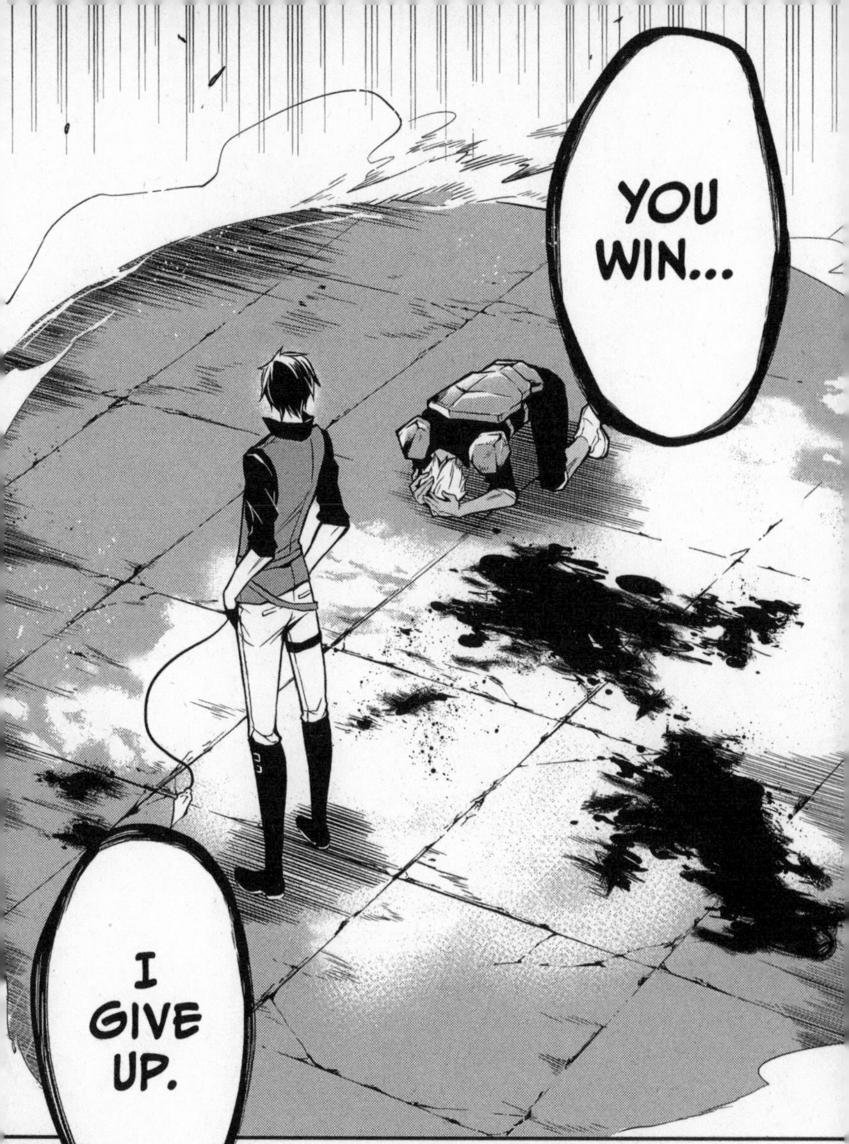
YOU WIN...
I GIVE UP.

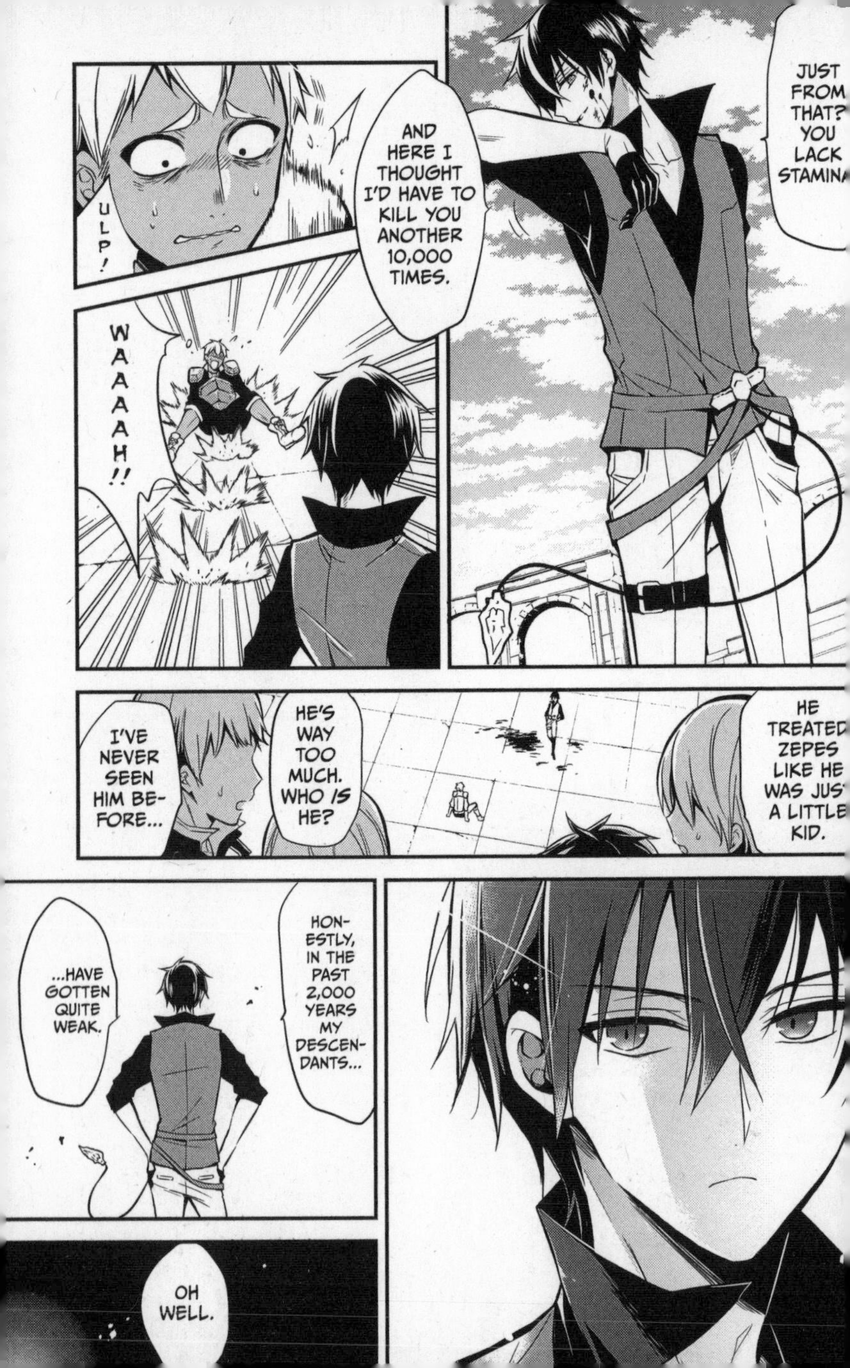
JUST FROM THAT? YOU LACK STAMIN
AND HERE I THOUGHT I'D HAVE TO KILL YOU ANOTHER 10,000 TIMES.
ULP!
WAAAAAH!!
HE TREATED ZEPES LIKE HE WAS JUS A LITTLE KID.
HE'S WAY TOO MUCH. WHO *IS* HE?
I'VE NEVER SEEN HIM BE-FORE...
HON-ESTLY, IN THE PAST 2,000 YEARS MY DESCEN-DANTS...
...HAVE GOTTEN QUITE WEAK.
OH WELL.

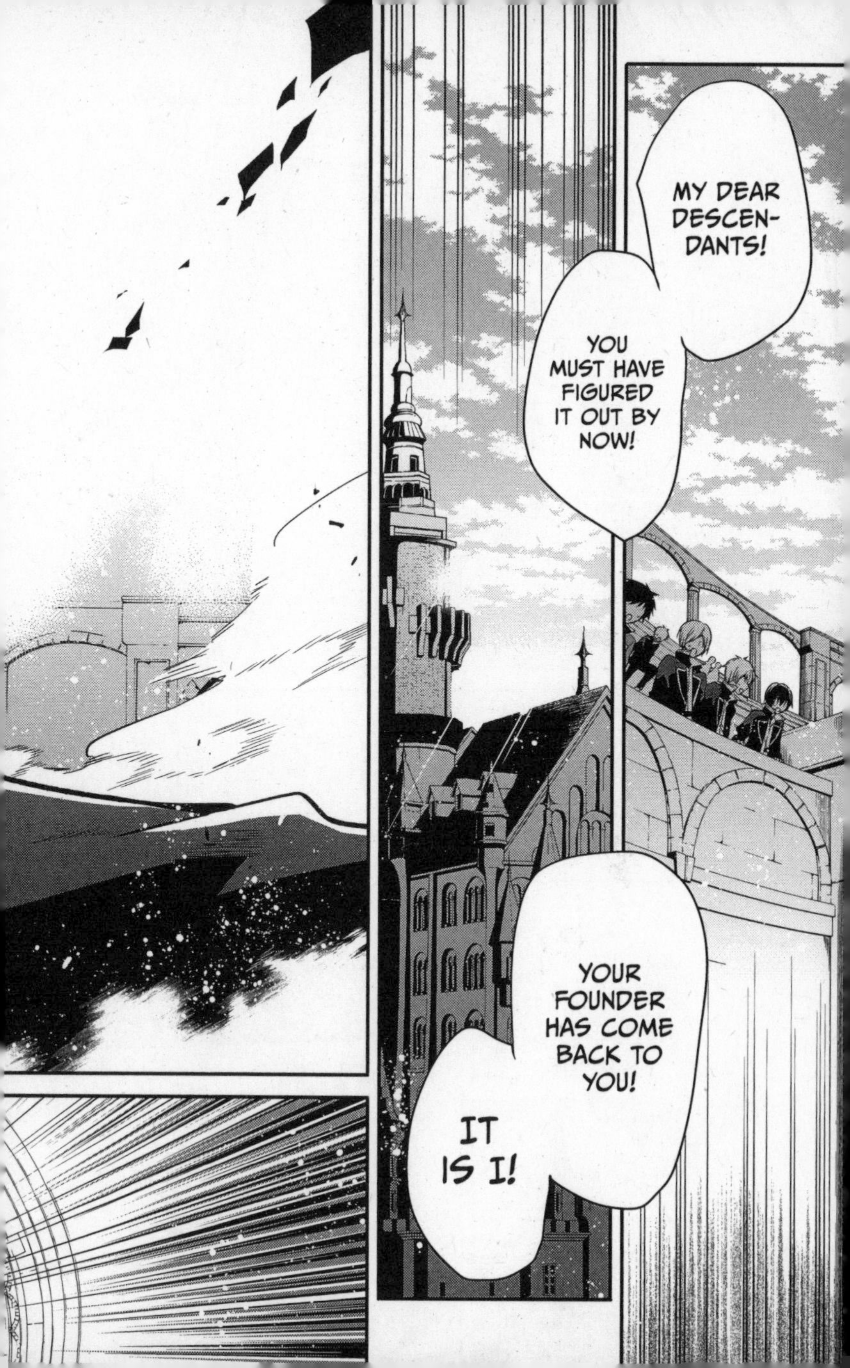
MY DEAR DESCENDANTS!
YOU MUST HAVE FIGURED IT OUT BY NOW!
YOUR FOUNDER HAS COME BACK TO YOU!
IT IS I!

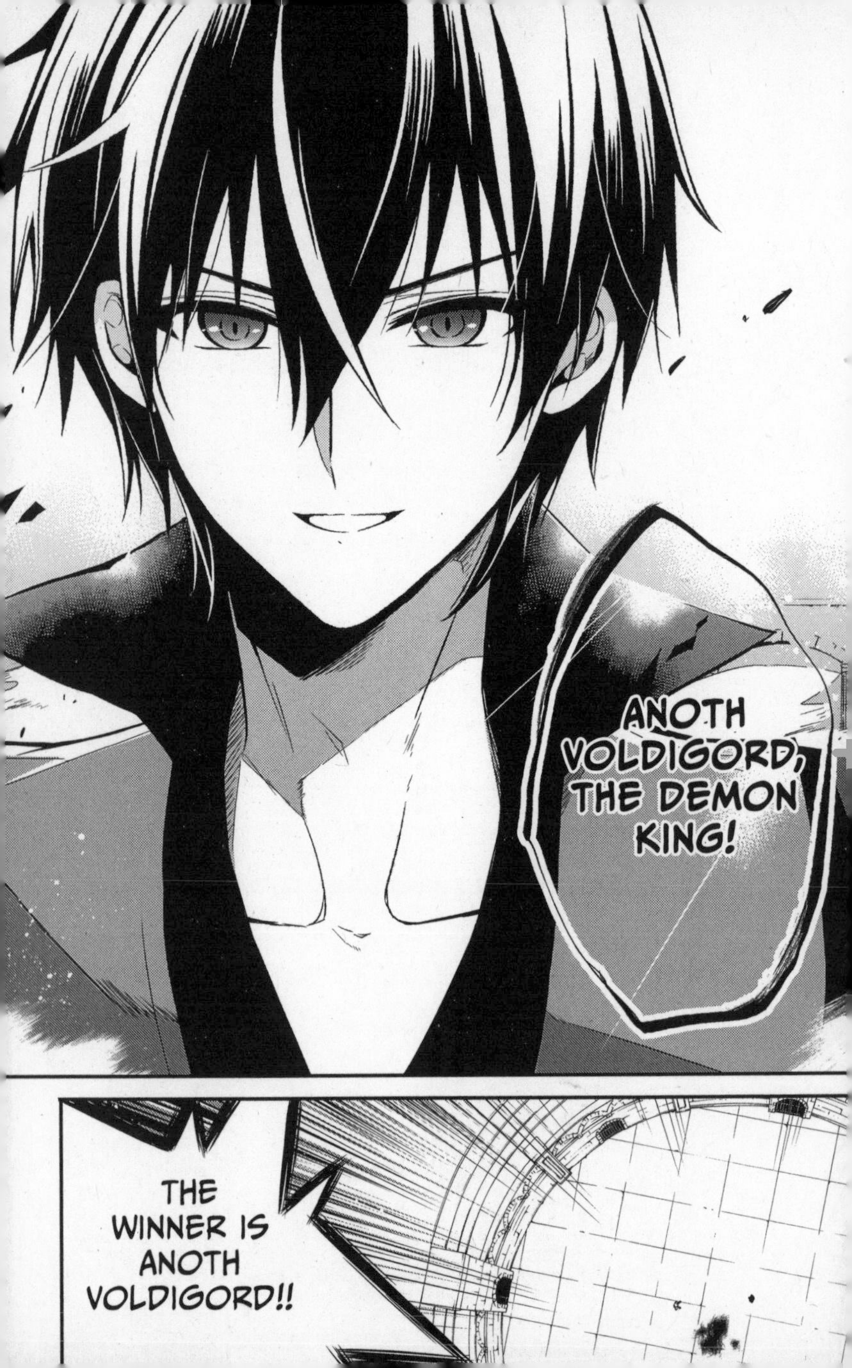
ANOTH VOLDIGORD, THE DEMON KING!
THE WINNER IS ANOTH VOLDIGORD!!

The Misfit of Demon King Academy

HISTORY'S STRONGEST DEMON KING REINCARNATES AND GOES TO SCHOOL WITH HIS DESCENDANTS

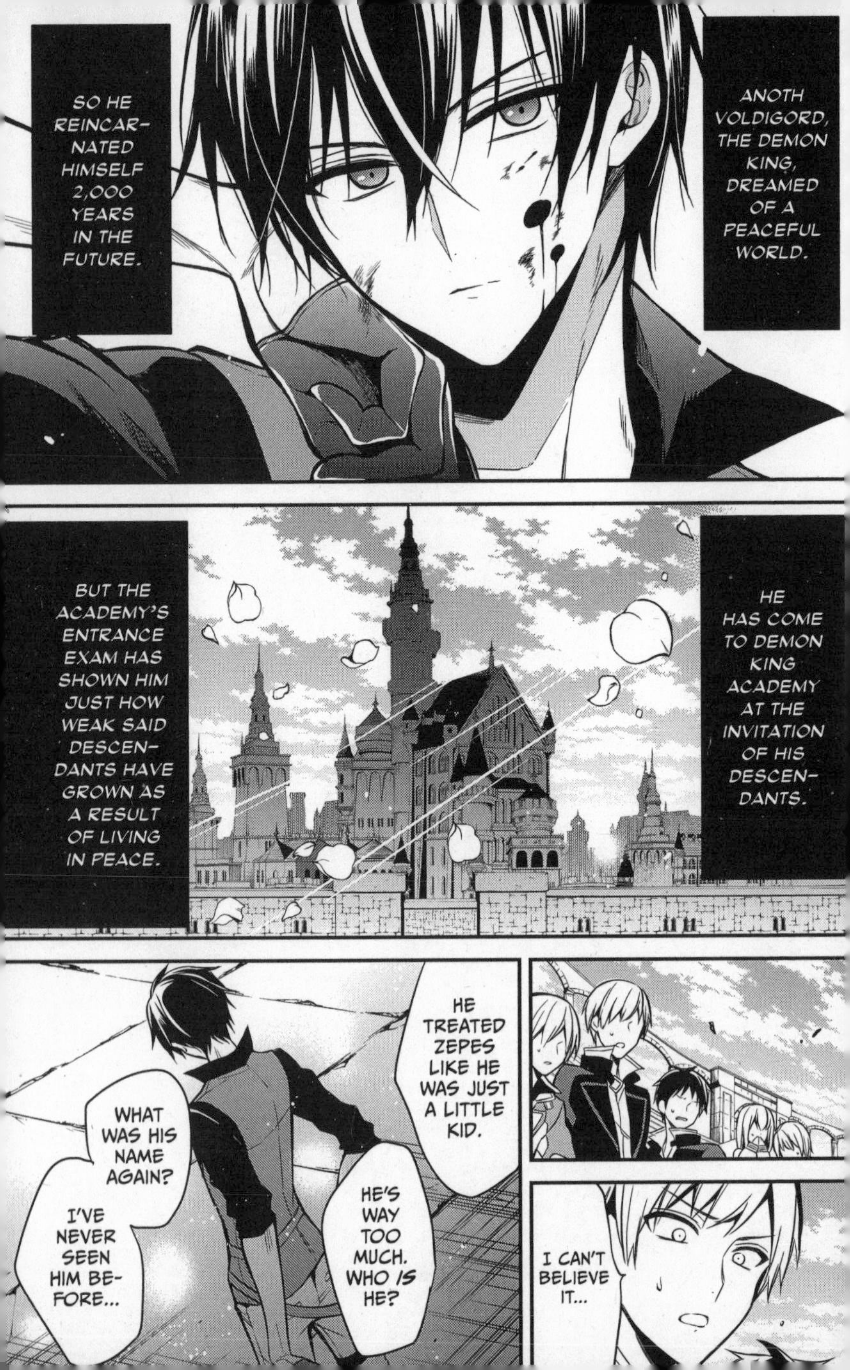
ANOTH VOLDIGORD, THE DEMON KING, DREAMED OF A PEACEFUL WORLD.
SO HE REINCARNATED HIMSELF 2,000 YEARS IN THE FUTURE.
HE HAS COME TO DEMON KING ACADEMY AT THE INVITATION OF HIS DESCENDANTS.
BUT THE ACADEMY'S ENTRANCE EXAM HAS SHOWN HIM JUST HOW WEAK SAID DESCENDANTS HAVE GROWN AS A RESULT OF LIVING IN PEACE.
I CAN'T BELIEVE IT...
HE TREATED ZEPES LIKE HE WAS JUST A LITTLE KID.
WHAT WAS HIS NAME AGAIN?
HE'S WAY TOO MUCH. WHO *IS* HE?
I'VE NEVER SEEN HIM BEFORE...

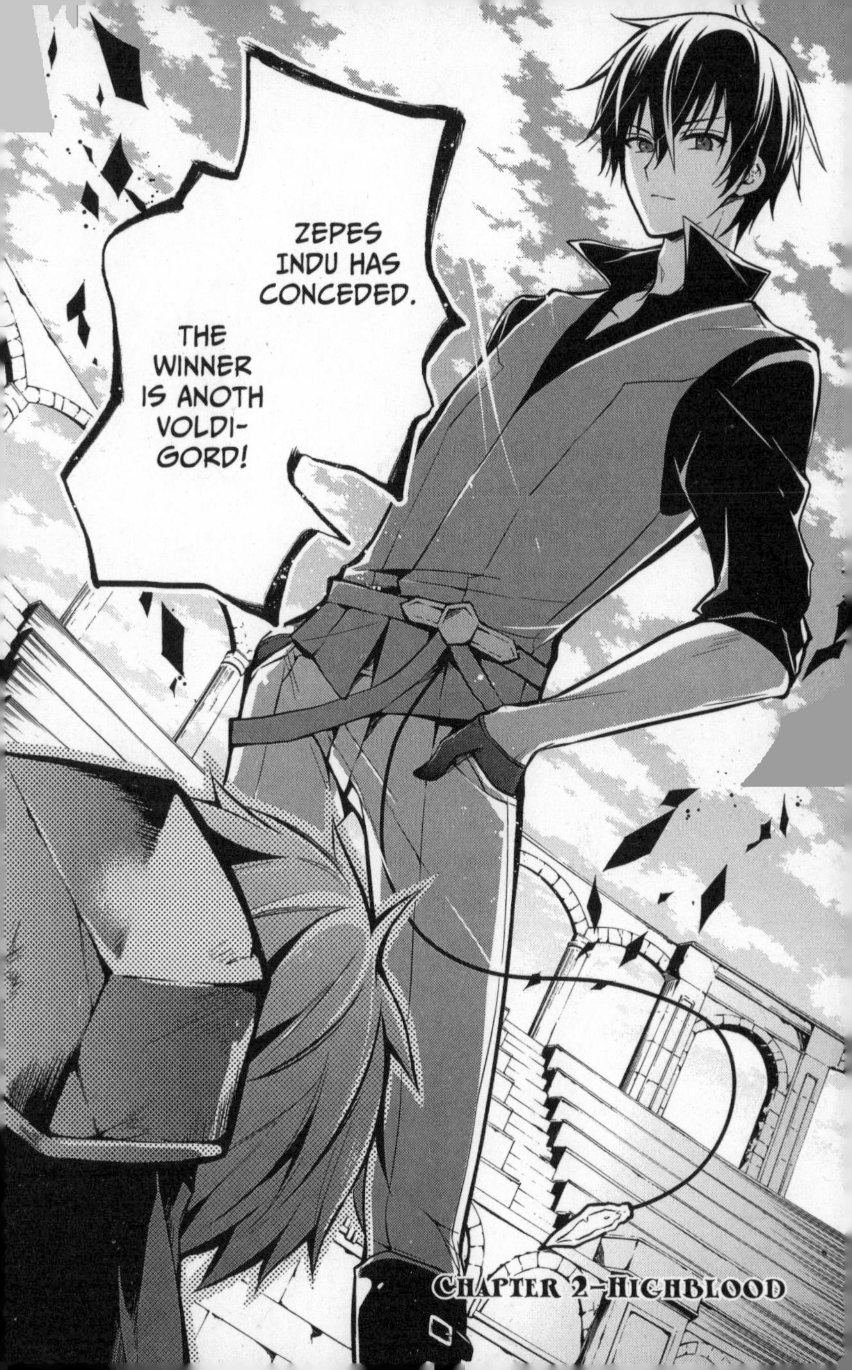
ZEPES INDU HAS CONCEDED.
THE WINNER IS ANOTH VOLDI-GORD!
CHAPTER 2—HIGHBLOOD

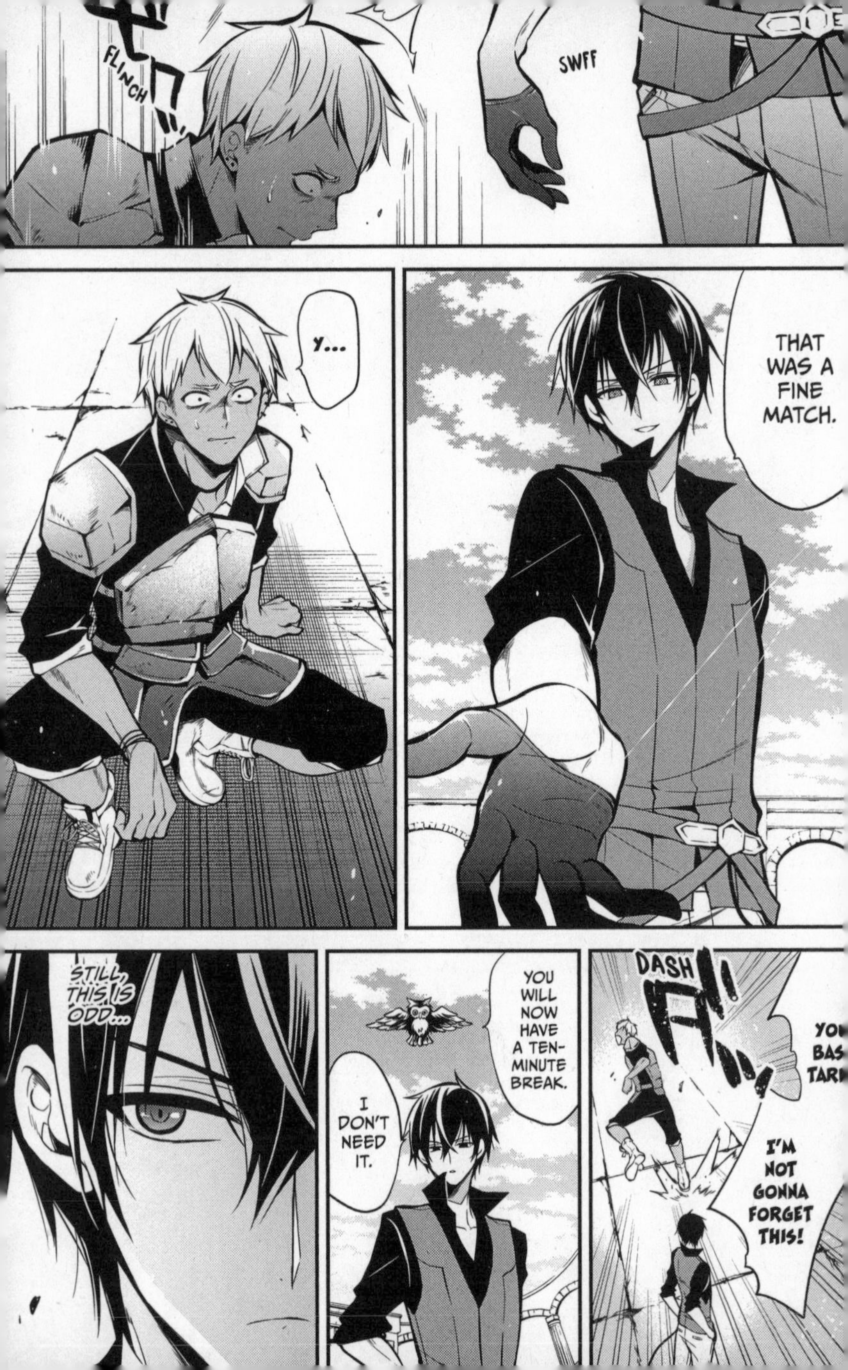
SWFF
FLINCH
THAT WAS A FINE MATCH.
Y...
DASH
YOU BAS TAR
I'M NOT GONNA FORGET THIS!
YOU WILL NOW HAVE A TEN-MINUTE BREAK.
I DON'T NEED IT.
STILL, THIS IS ODD...

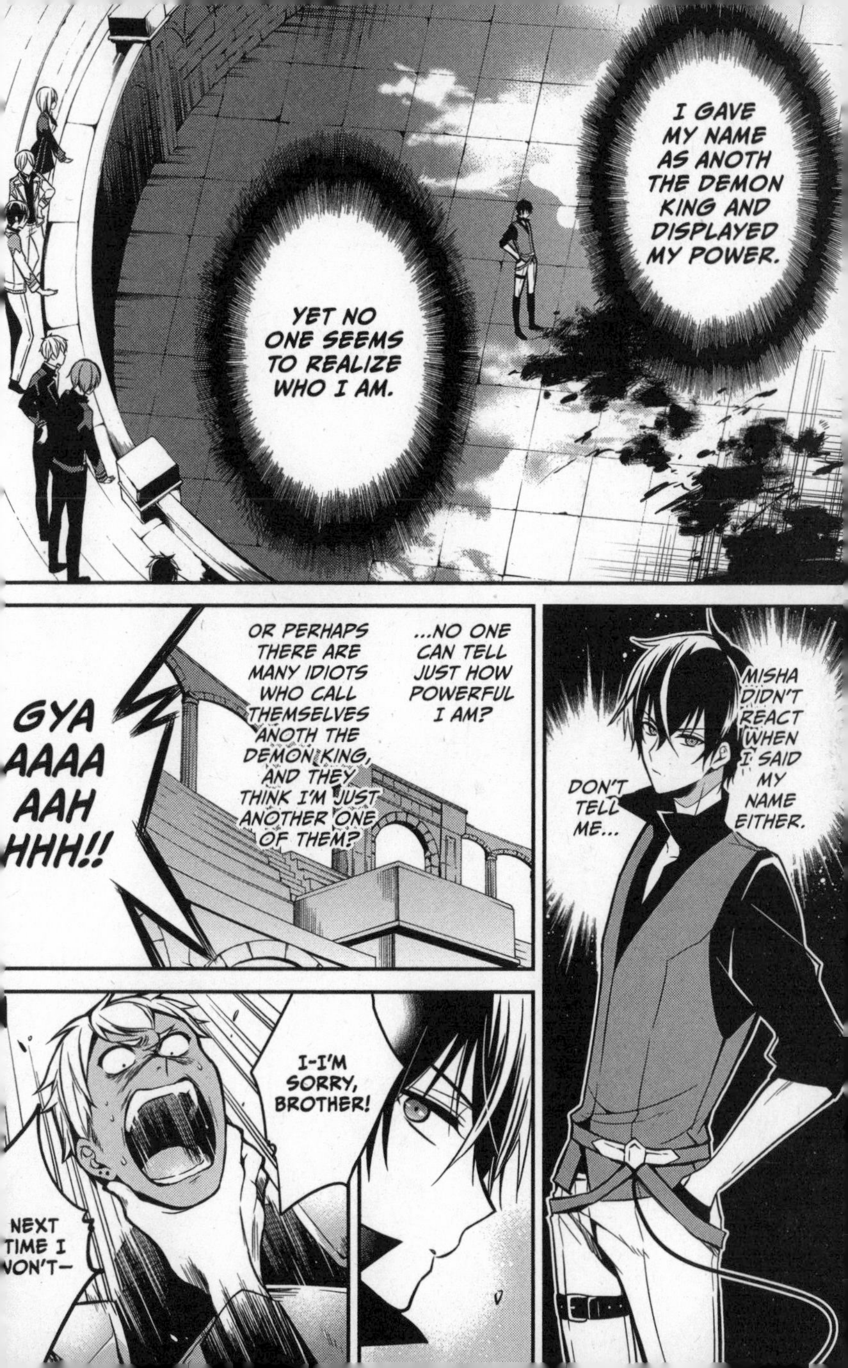
I GAVE MY NAME AS ANOTH THE DEMON KING AND DISPLAYED MY POWER.
YET NO ONE SEEMS TO REALIZE WHO I AM.
MISHA DIDN'T REACT WHEN I SAID MY NAME EITHER.
DON'T TELL ME...
...NO ONE CAN TELL JUST HOW POWERFUL I AM?
OR PERHAPS THERE ARE MANY IDIOTS WHO CALL THEMSELVES ANOTH THE DEMON KING, AND THEY THINK I'M JUST ANOTHER ONE OF THEM?
GYA AAAA AAH HHH!!
I-I'M SORRY, BROTHER!
NEXT TIME I WON'T—

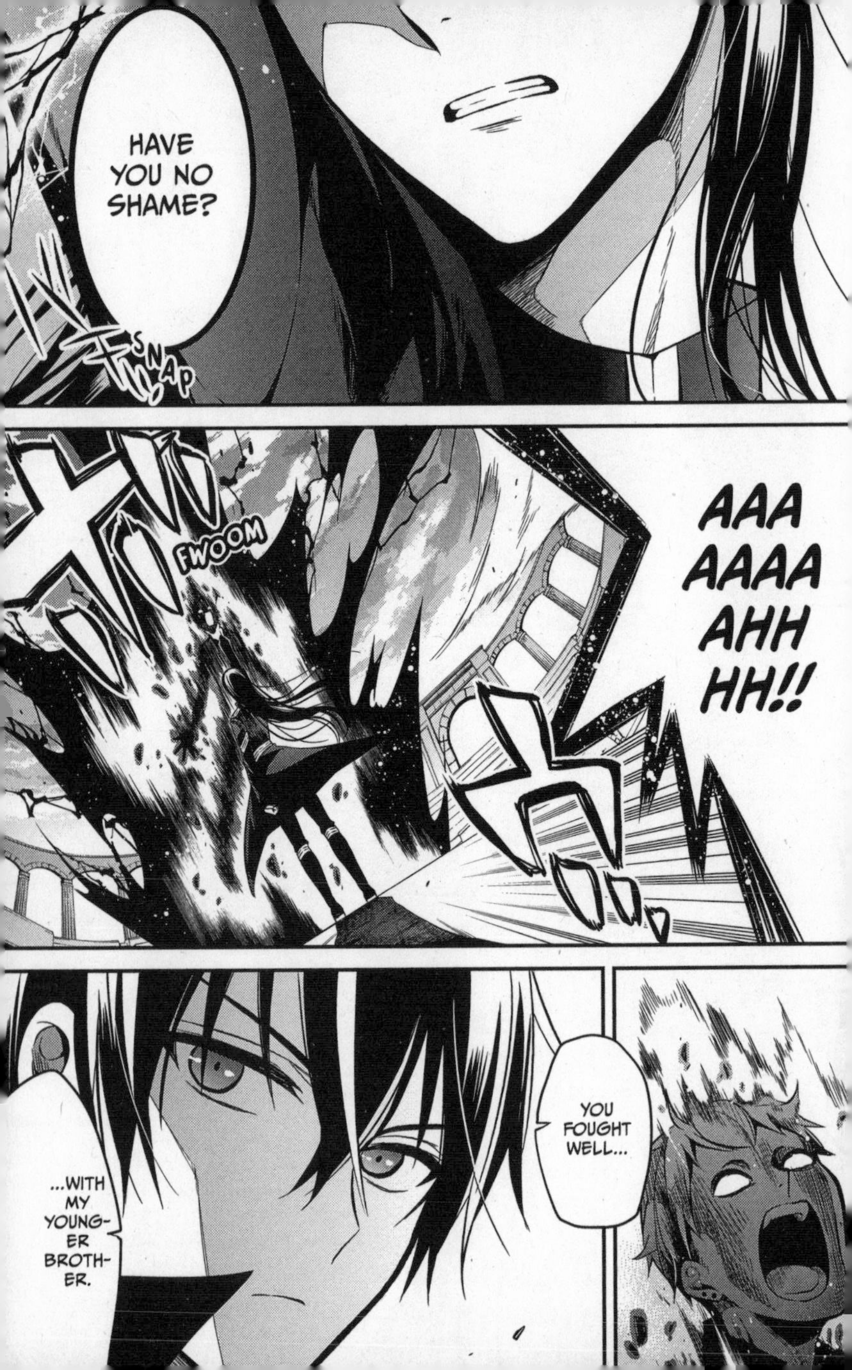
HAVE YOU NO SHAME?
SNAP
AAAAAAAAHHHH!!
FWOOM
YOU FOUGHT WELL...
...WITH MY YOUNGER BROTHER.

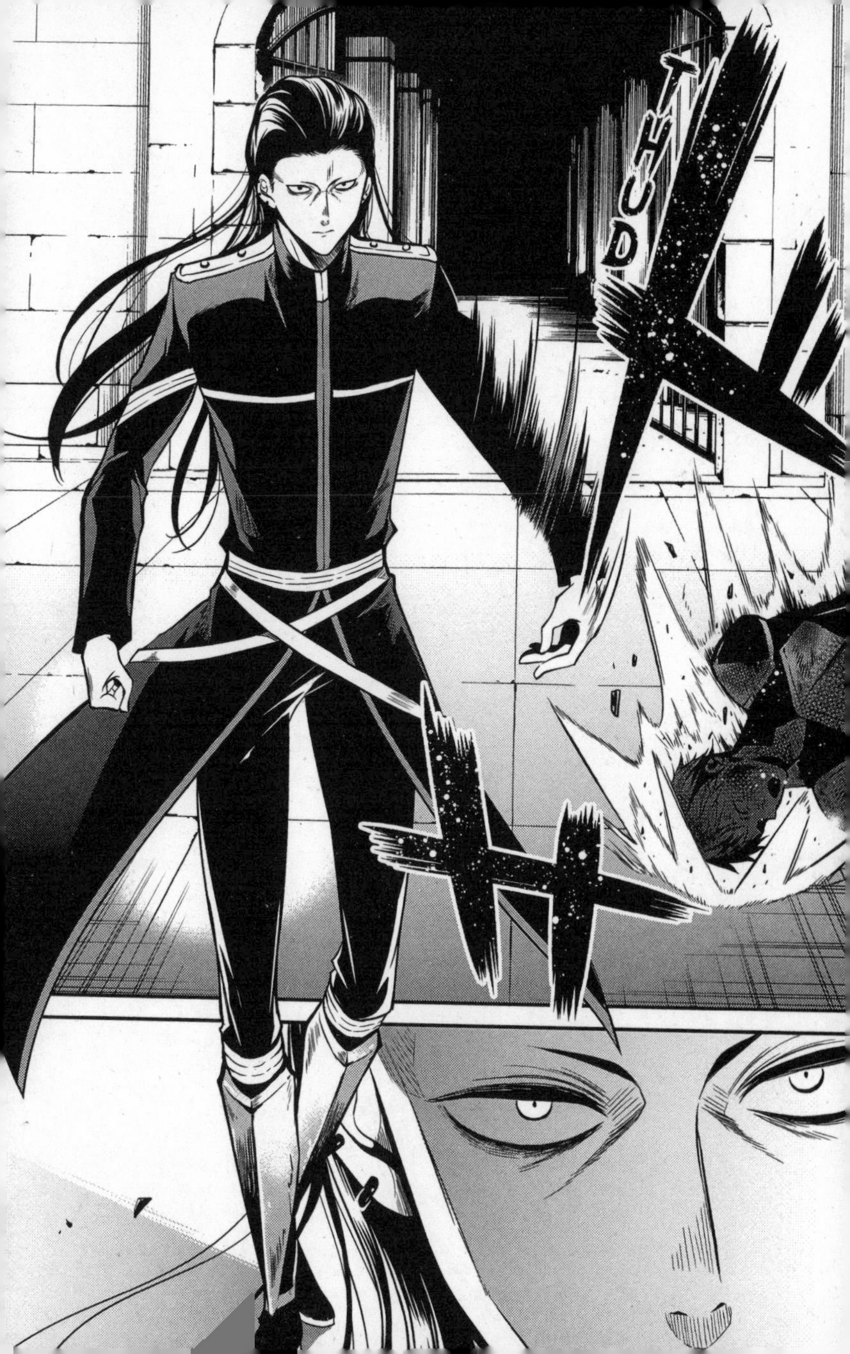
THUD

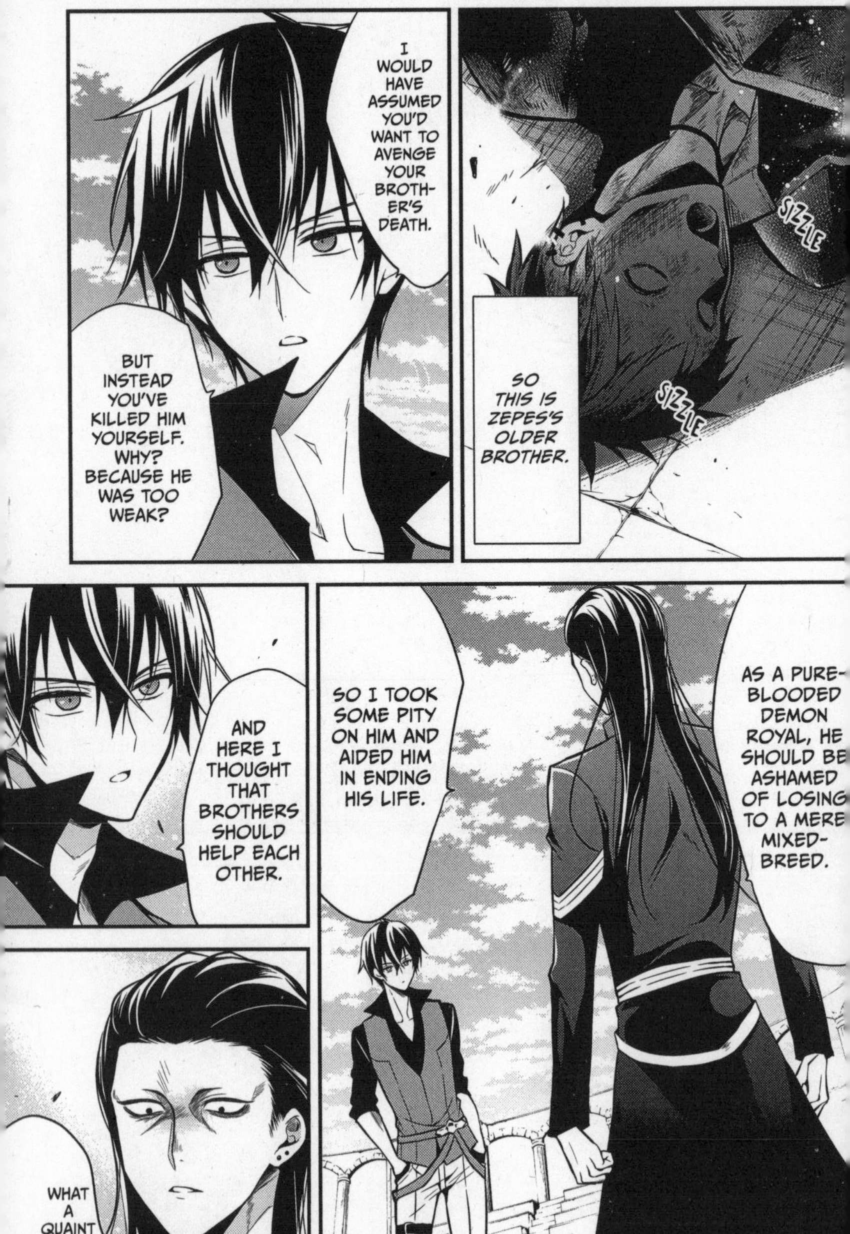
SIZZLE
SO THIS IS ZEPES'S OLDER BROTHER.
SIZZLE
I WOULD HAVE ASSUMED YOU'D WANT TO AVENGE YOUR BROTHER'S DEATH.
BUT INSTEAD YOU'VE KILLED HIM YOURSELF. WHY? BECAUSE HE WAS TOO WEAK?
AS A PURE-BLOODED DEMON ROYAL, HE SHOULD BE ASHAMED OF LOSING TO A MERE MIXED-BREED.
SO I TOOK SOME PITY ON HIM AND AIDED HIM IN ENDING HIS LIFE.
AND HERE I THOUGHT THAT BROTHERS SHOULD HELP EACH OTHER.
WHAT A QUAINT SENTIMENT.

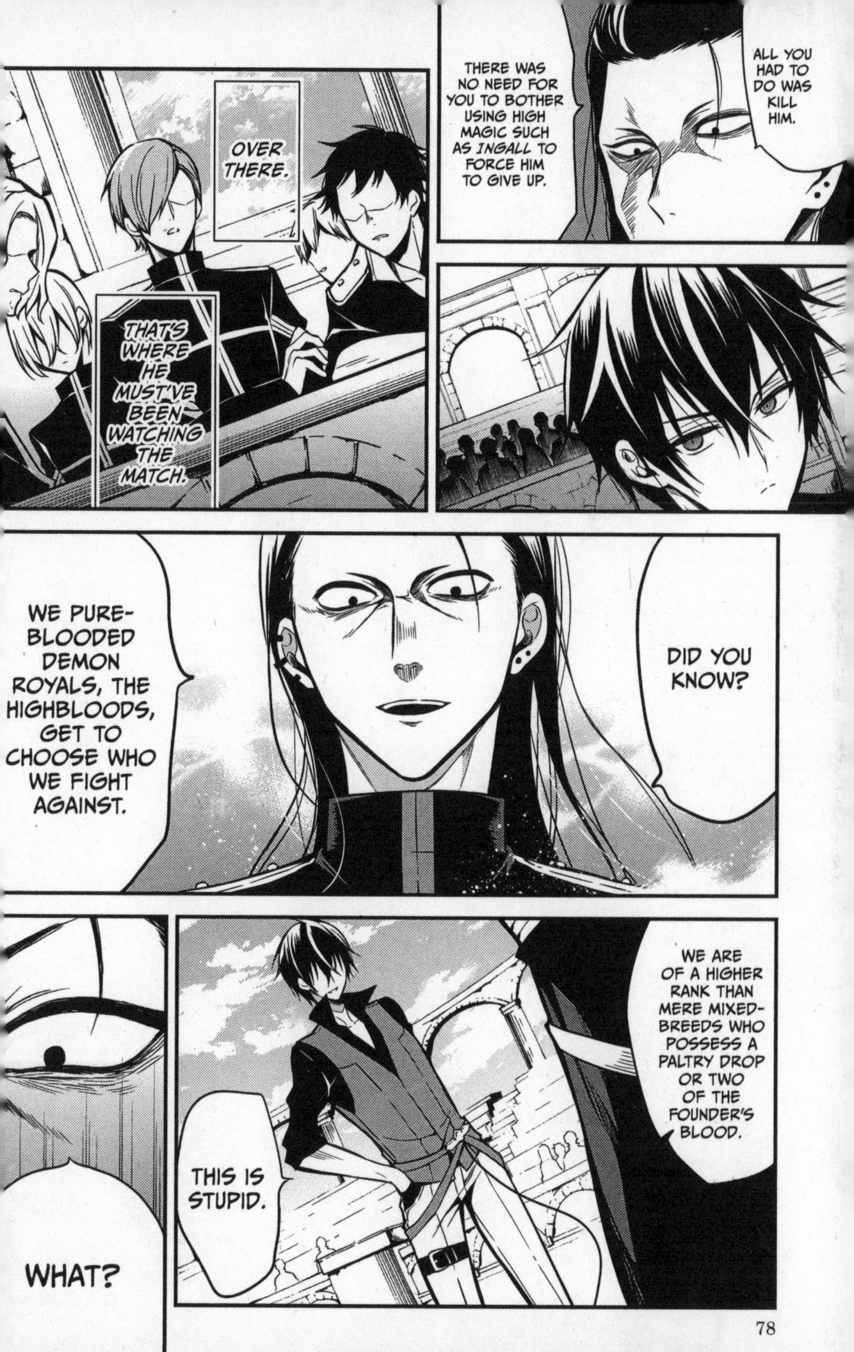
ALL YOU HAD TO DO WAS KILL HIM.
THERE WAS NO NEED FOR YOU TO BOTHER USING HIGH MAGIC SUCH AS INGALL TO FORCE HIM TO GIVE UP.
OVER THERE.
THAT'S WHERE HE MUST'VE BEEN WATCHING THE MATCH.
DID YOU KNOW?
WE PURE-BLOODED DEMON ROYALS, THE HIGHBLOODS, GET TO CHOOSE WHO WE FIGHT AGAINST.
WE ARE OF A HIGHER RANK THAN MERE MIXED-BREEDS WHO POSSESS A PALTRY DROP OR TWO OF THE FOUNDER'S BLOOD.
THIS IS STUPID.
WHAT?

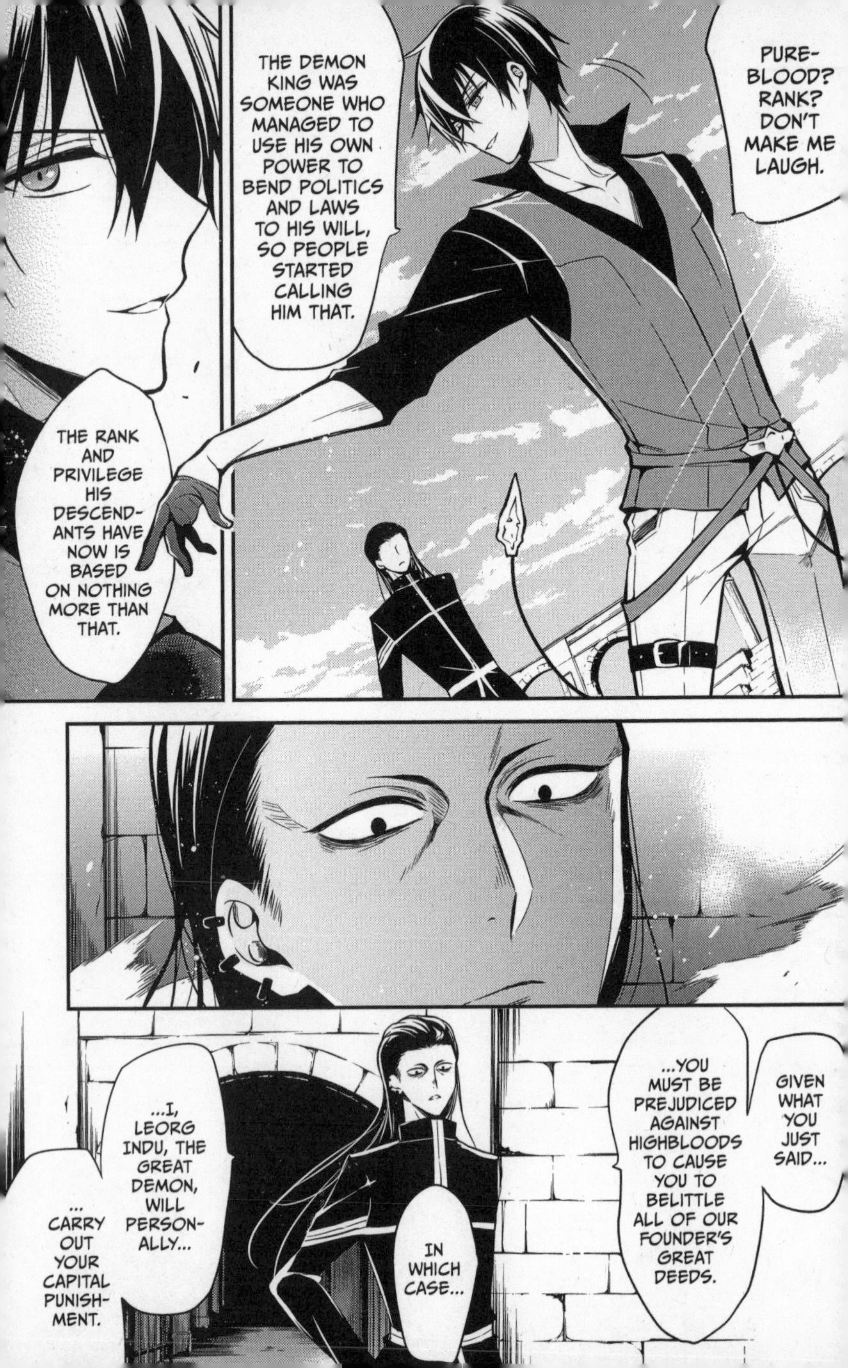
PURE-BLOOD? RANK? DON'T MAKE ME LAUGH.
THE DEMON KING WAS SOMEONE WHO MANAGED TO USE HIS OWN POWER TO BEND POLITICS AND LAWS TO HIS WILL, SO PEOPLE STARTED CALLING HIM THAT.
THE RANK AND PRIVILEGE HIS DESCENDANTS HAVE NOW IS BASED ON NOTHING MORE THAN THAT.
GIVEN WHAT YOU JUST SAID...
...YOU MUST BE PREJUDICED AGAINST HIGHBLOODS TO CAUSE YOU TO BELITTLE ALL OF OUR FOUNDER'S GREAT DEEDS.
IN WHICH CASE...
...I, LEORG INDU, THE GREAT DEMON, WILL PERSONALLY...
...CARRY OUT YOUR CAPITAL PUNISHMENT.

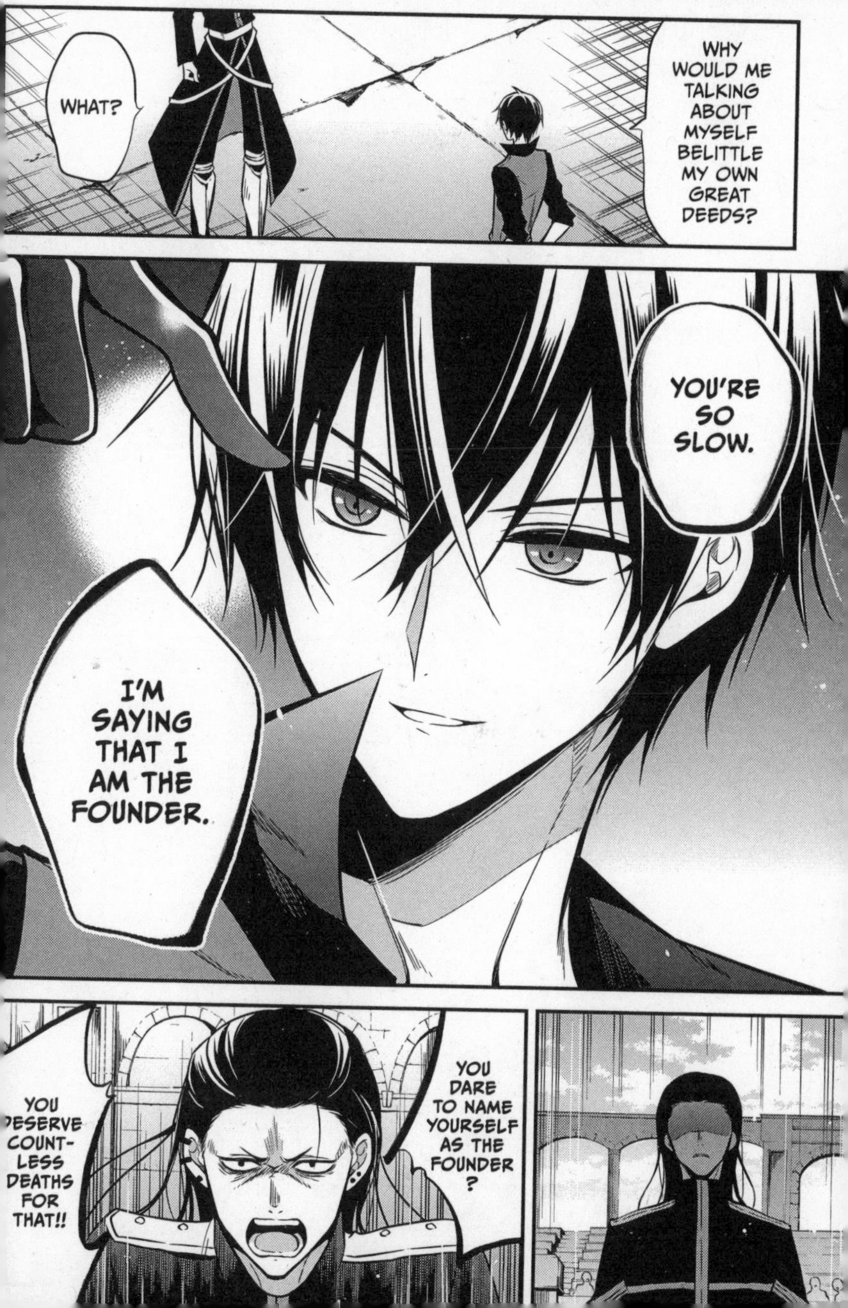
WHY WOULD ME TALKING ABOUT MYSELF BELITTLE MY OWN GREAT DEEDS?
WHAT?
YOU'RE SO SLOW.
I'M SAYING THAT I AM THE FOUNDER.
YOU DARE TO NAME YOURSELF AS THE FOUNDER?
YOU DESERVE COUNT-LESS DEATHS FOR THAT!!

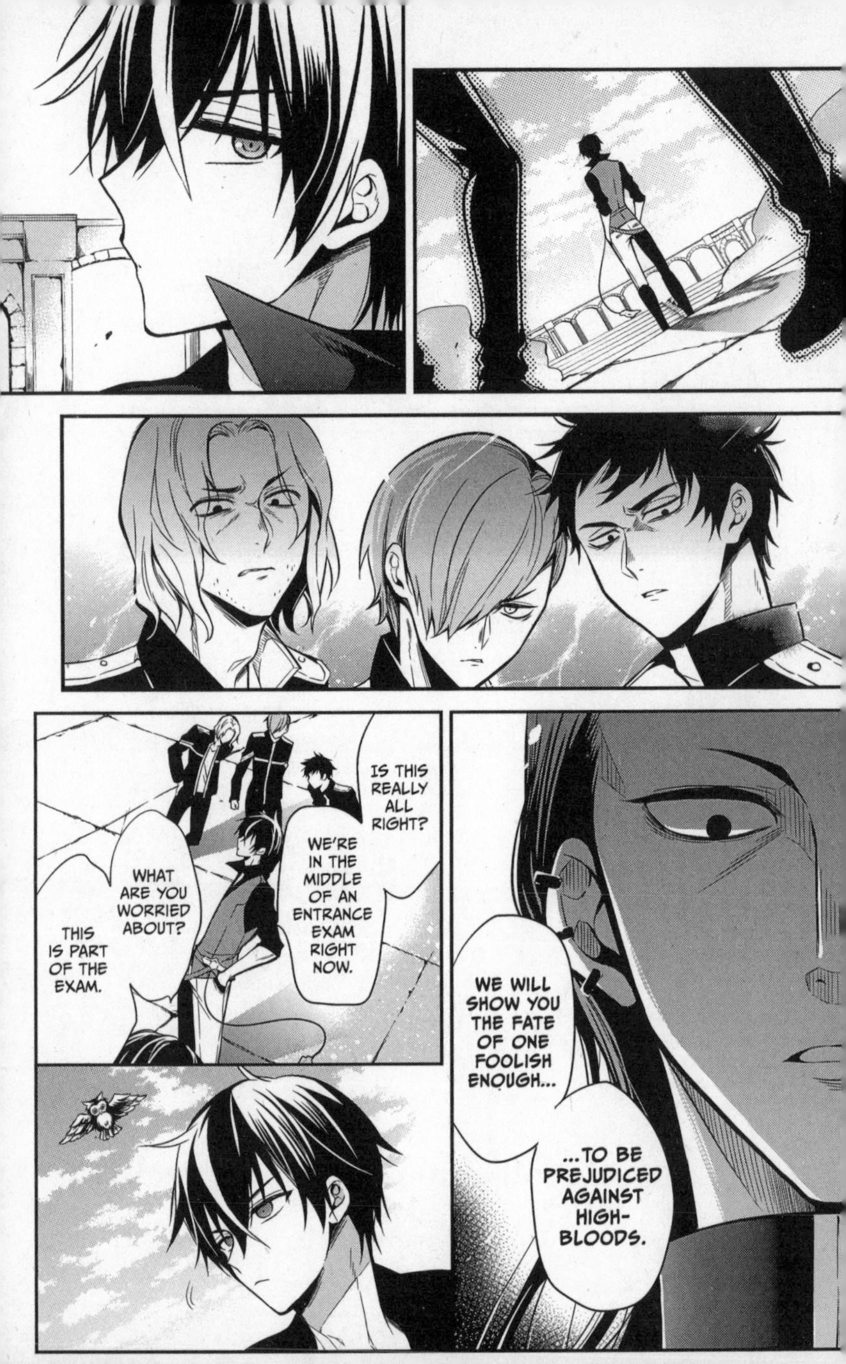
WE WILL SHOW YOU THE FATE OF ONE FOOLISH ENOUGH...
...TO BE PREJUDICED AGAINST HIGH-BLOODS.
IS THIS REALLY ALL RIGHT?
WE'RE IN THE MIDDLE OF AN ENTRANCE EXAM RIGHT NOW.
WHAT ARE YOU WORRIED ABOUT?
THIS IS PART OF THE EXAM.

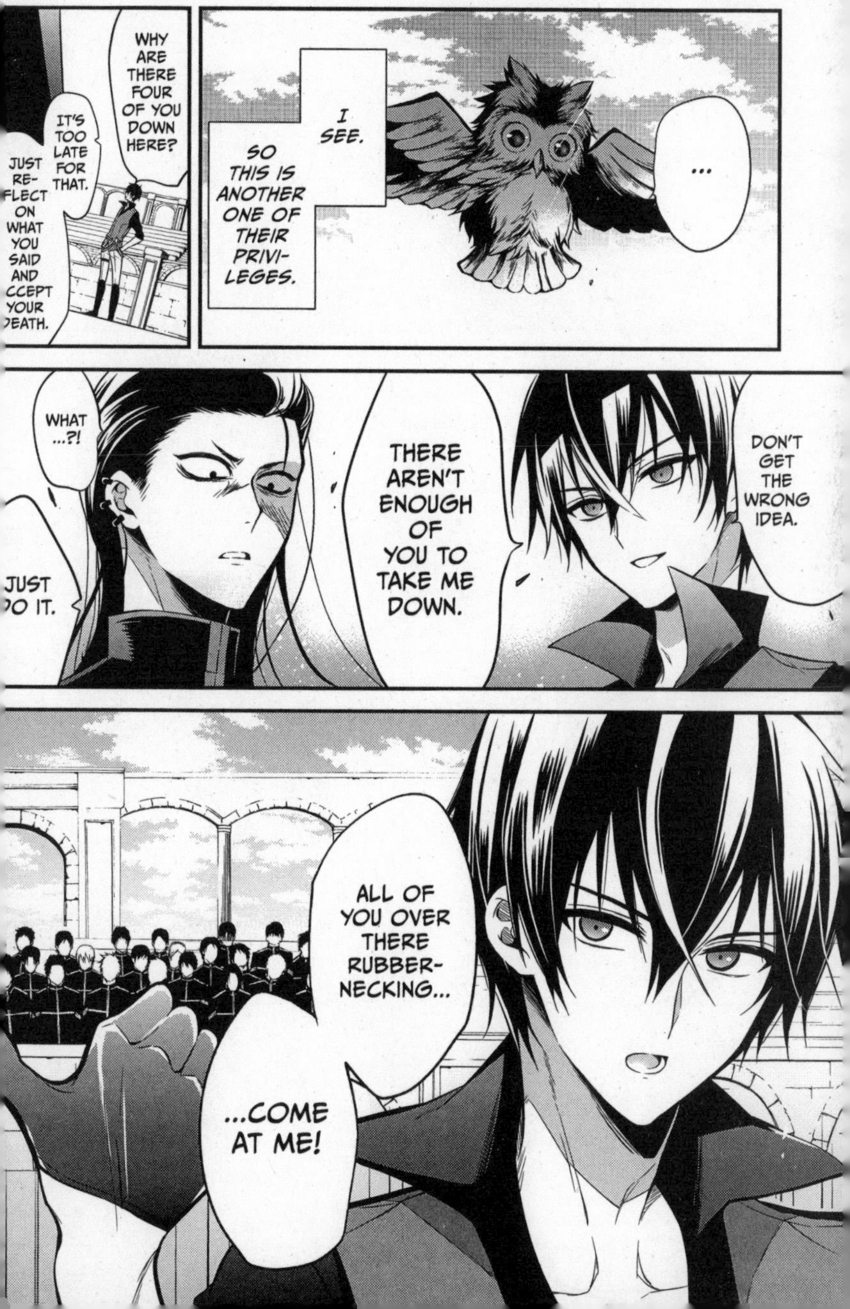
...
I SEE.
SO THIS IS ANOTHER ONE OF THEIR PRIVILEGES.
WHY ARE THERE FOUR OF YOU DOWN HERE?
IT'S TOO LATE FOR THAT.
JUST RE-FLECT ON WHAT YOU SAID AND CCEPT YOUR EATH.
DON'T GET THE WRONG IDEA.
THERE AREN'T ENOUGH OF YOU TO TAKE ME DOWN.
WHAT ...?!
JUST O IT.
ALL OF YOU OVER THERE RUBBER-NECKING...
...COME AT ME!

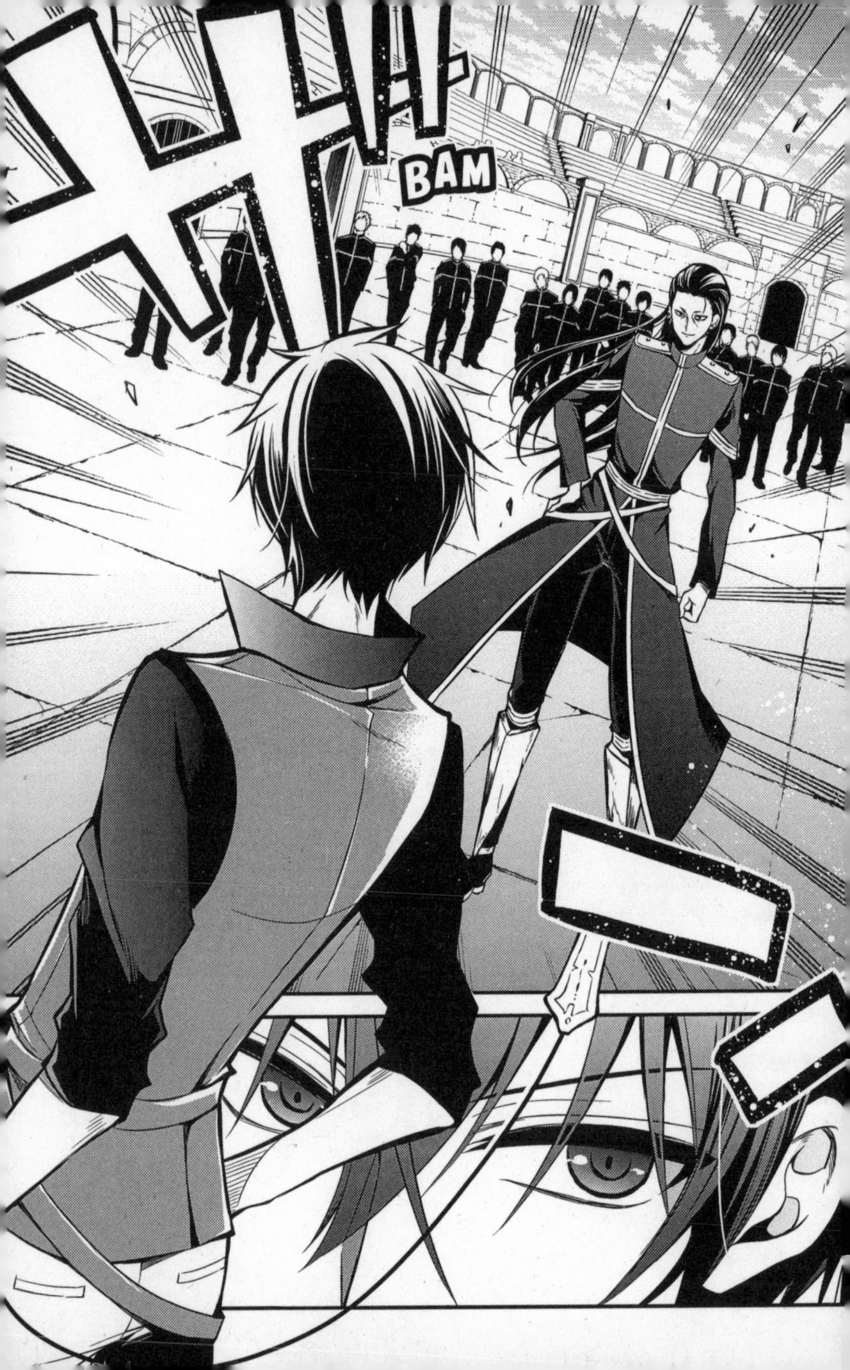
BAM

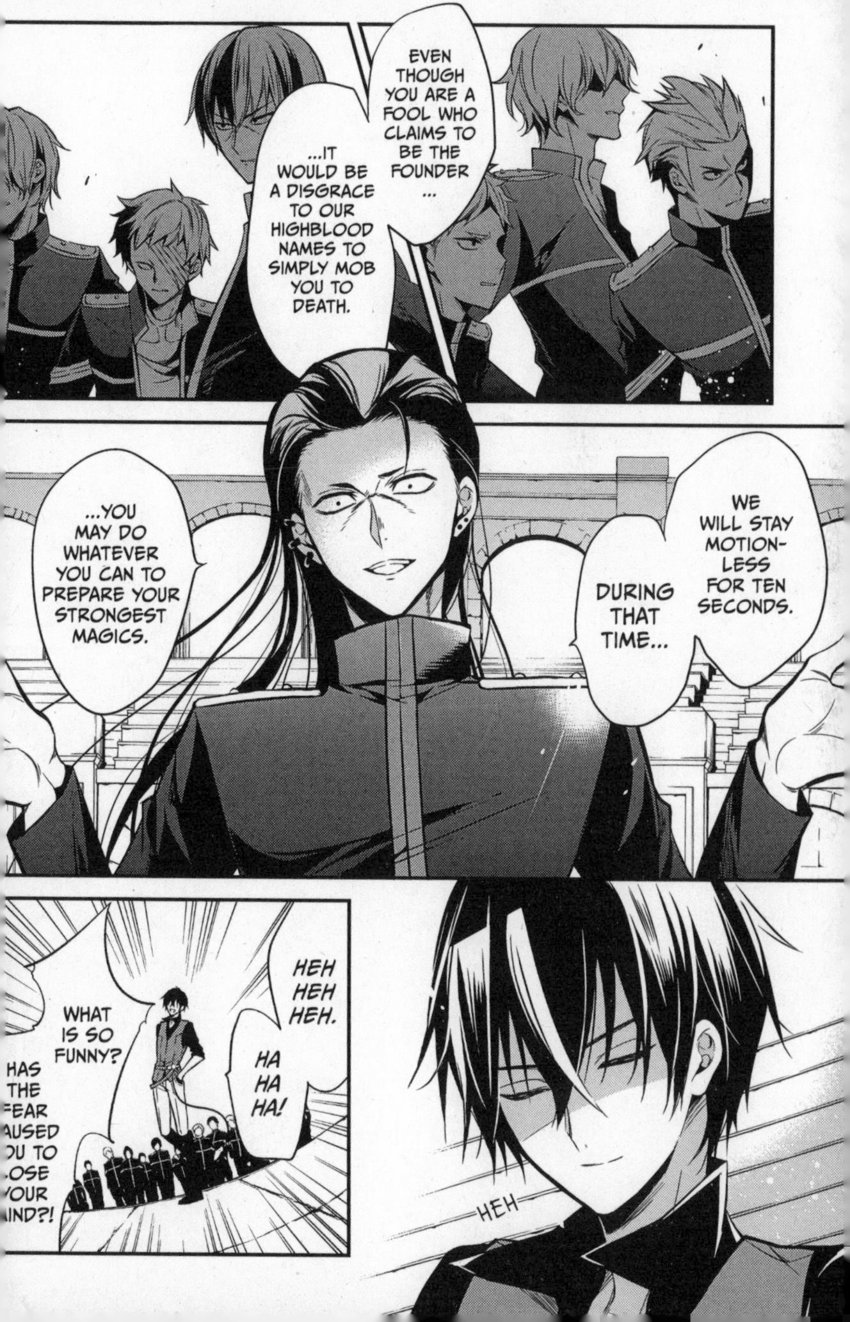
EVEN THOUGH YOU ARE A FOOL WHO CLAIMS TO BE THE FOUNDER ...
...IT WOULD BE A DISGRACE TO OUR HIGHBLOOD NAMES TO SIMPLY MOB YOU TO DEATH.
WE WILL STAY MOTION-LESS FOR TEN SECONDS.
DURING THAT TIME...
...YOU MAY DO WHATEVER YOU CAN TO PREPARE YOUR STRONGEST MAGICS.
HEH
HEH HEH HEH.
HA HA HA!
WHAT IS SO FUNNY?
HAS THE FEAR AUSED OU TO OSE YOUR IND?!

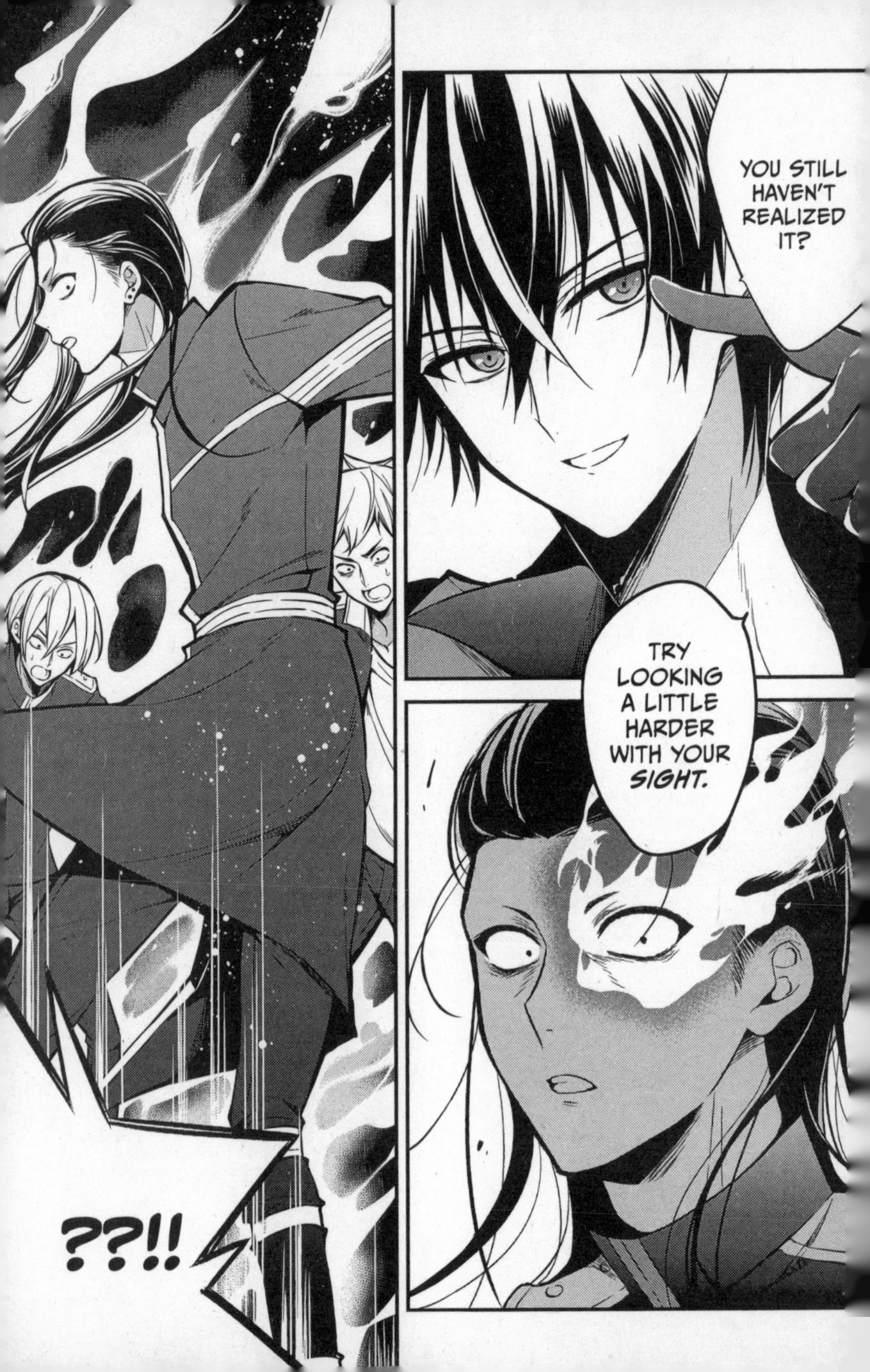
YOU STILL HAVEN'T REALIZED IT?
TRY LOOKING A LITTLE HARDER WITH YOUR *SIGHT.*
!
??!!

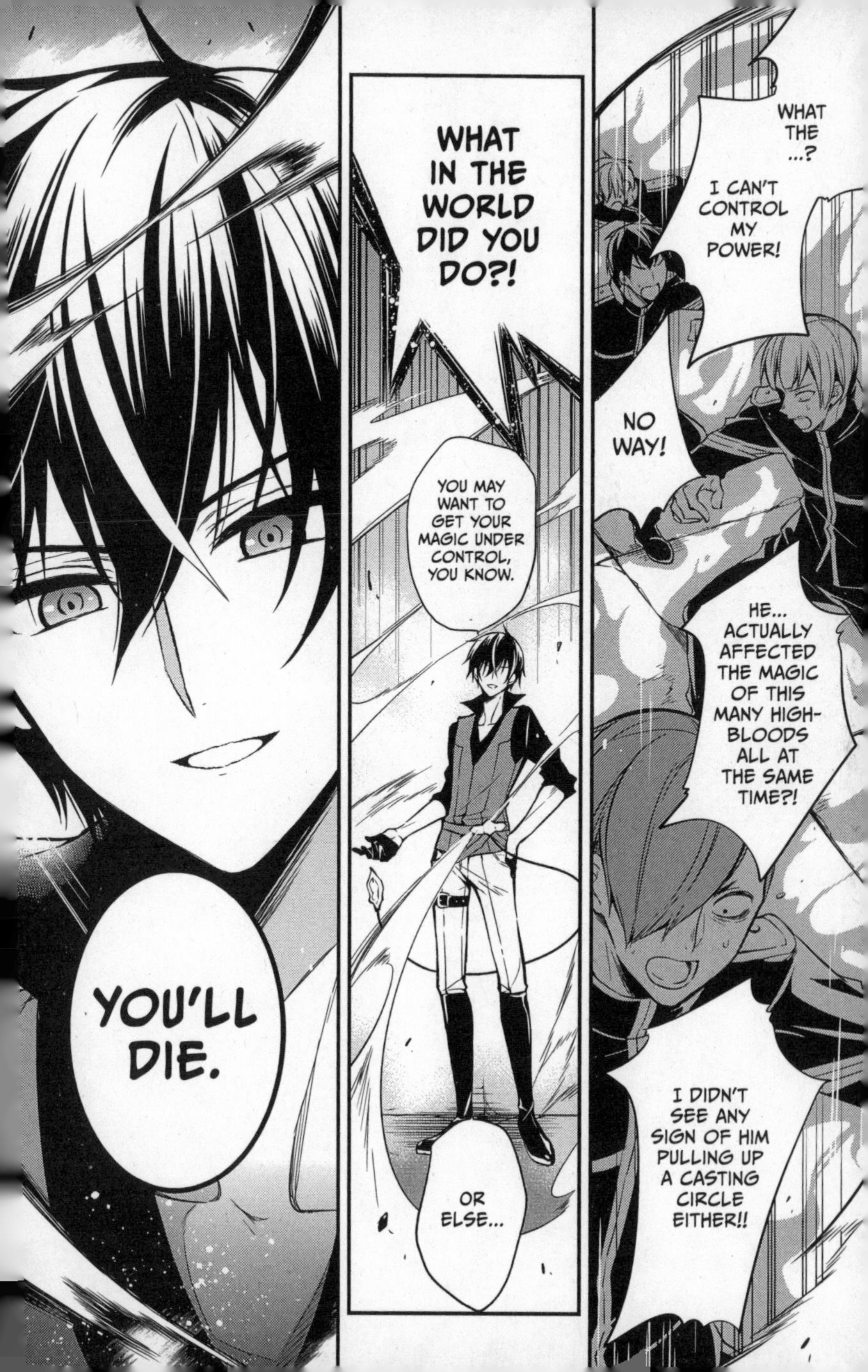
WHAT THE ...?
I CAN'T CONTROL MY POWER!
NO WAY!
HE... ACTUALLY AFFECTED THE MAGIC OF THIS MANY HIGH-BLOODS ALL AT THE SAME TIME?!
I DIDN'T SEE ANY SIGN OF HIM PULLING UP A CASTING CIRCLE EITHER!!
WHAT IN THE WORLD DID YOU DO?!
YOU MAY WANT TO GET YOUR MAGIC UNDER CONTROL, YOU KNOW.
OR ELSE...
YOU'LL DIE.

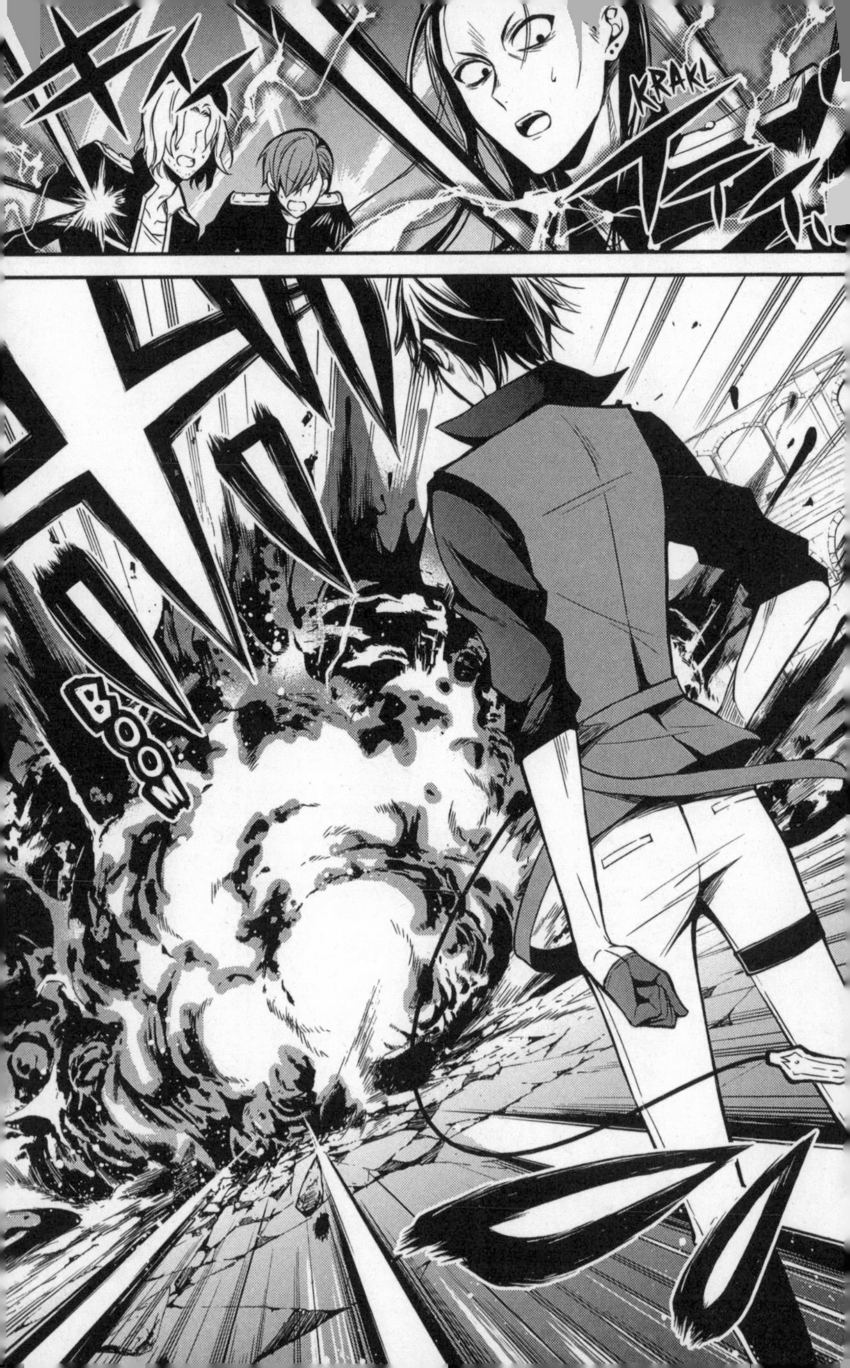
KRAKL
BOOM

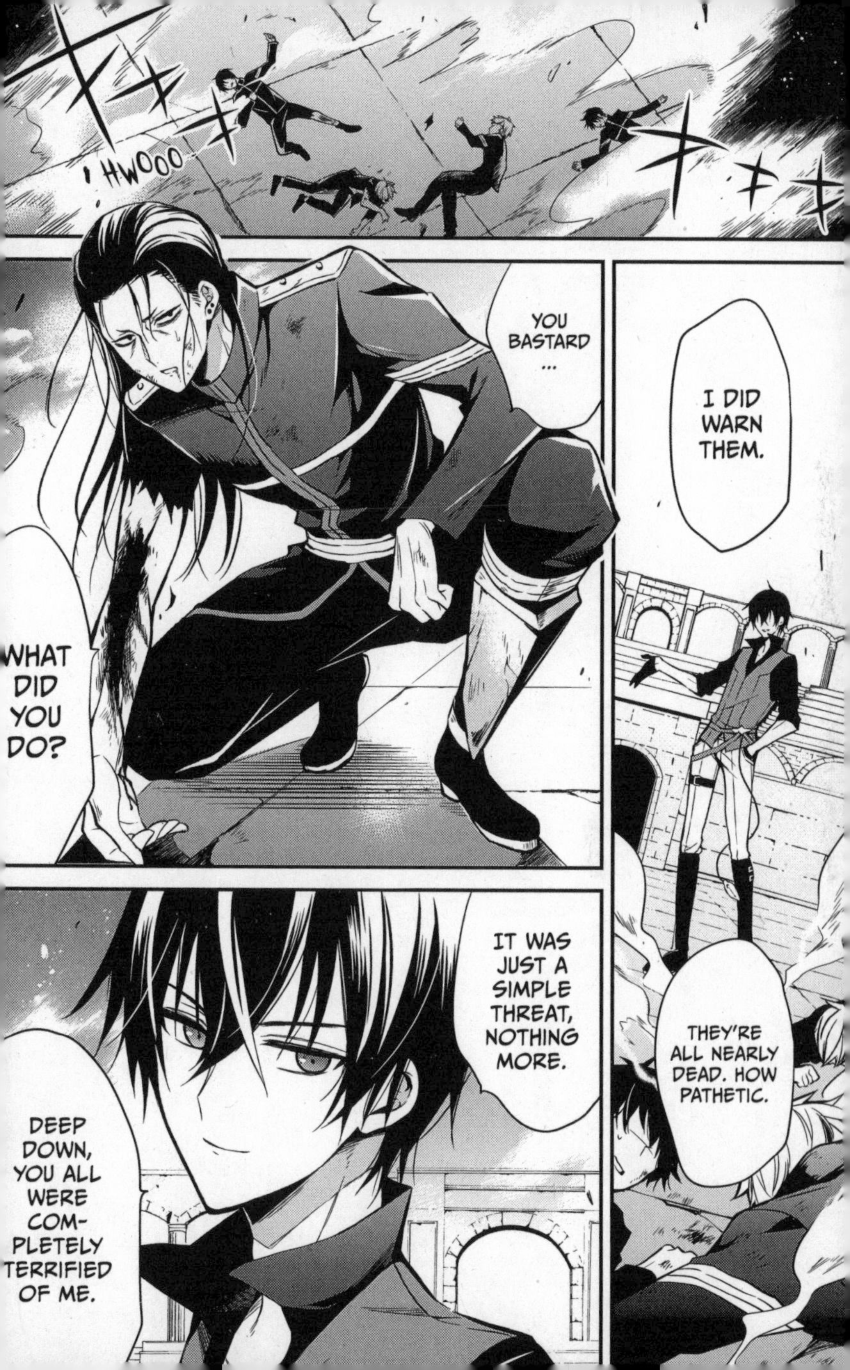
HWOOO
I DID WARN THEM.
THEY'RE ALL NEARLY DEAD. HOW PATHETIC.
YOU BASTARD...
WHAT DID YOU DO?
IT WAS JUST A SIMPLE THREAT, NOTHING MORE.
DEEP DOWN, YOU ALL WERE COM-PLETELY TERRIFIED OF ME.

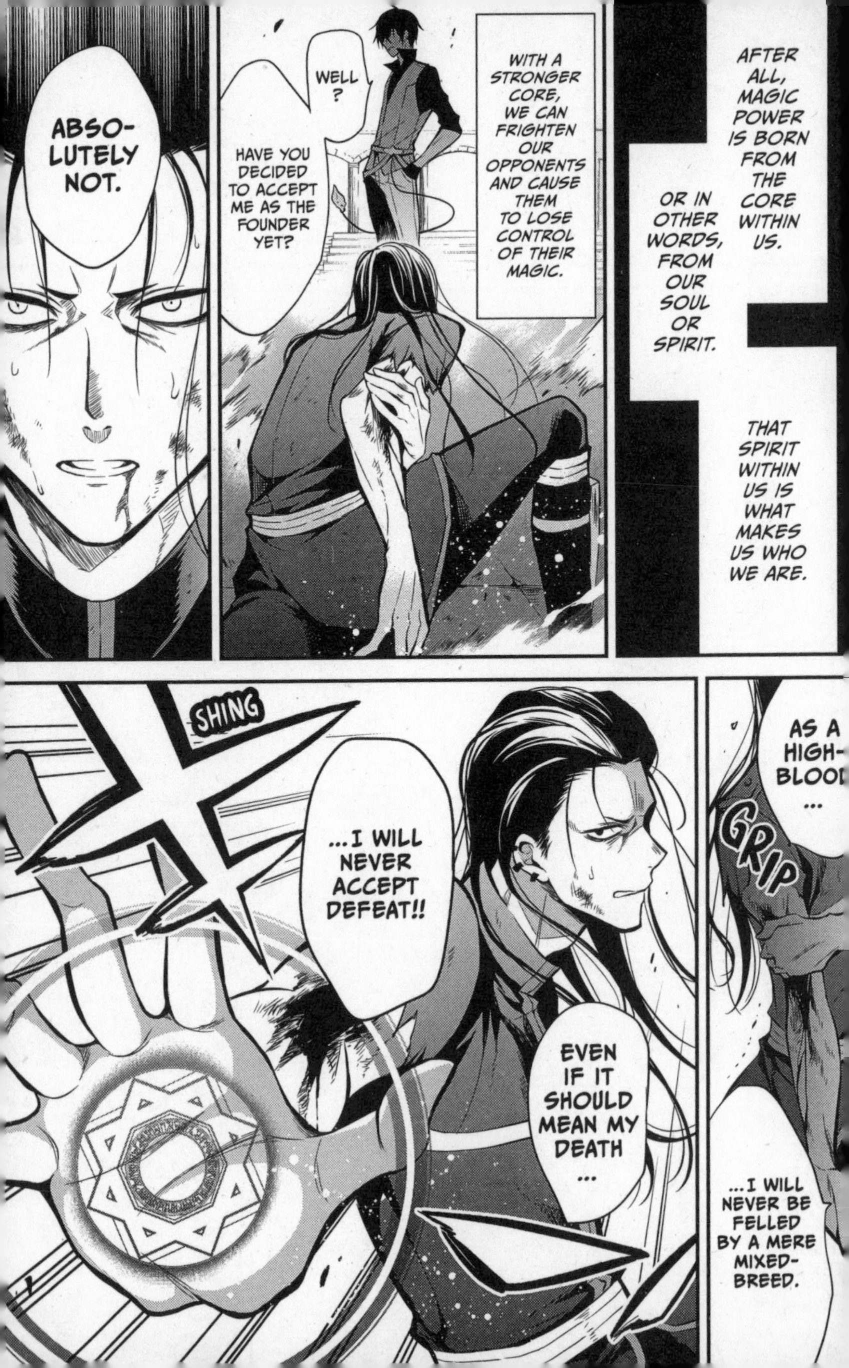
AFTER ALL, MAGIC POWER IS BORN FROM THE CORE WITHIN US.
OR IN OTHER WORDS, FROM OUR SOUL OR SPIRIT.
THAT SPIRIT WITHIN US IS WHAT MAKES US WHO WE ARE.
WITH A STRONGER CORE, WE CAN FRIGHTEN OUR OPPONENTS AND CAUSE THEM TO LOSE CONTROL OF THEIR MAGIC.
WELL?
HAVE YOU DECIDED TO ACCEPT ME AS THE FOUNDER YET?
ABSO-LUTELY NOT.
GRIP
...I WILL NEVER BE FELLED BY A MERE MIXED-BREED.
EVEN IF IT SHOULD MEAN MY DEATH...
...I WILL NEVER ACCEPT DEFEAT!!
SHING

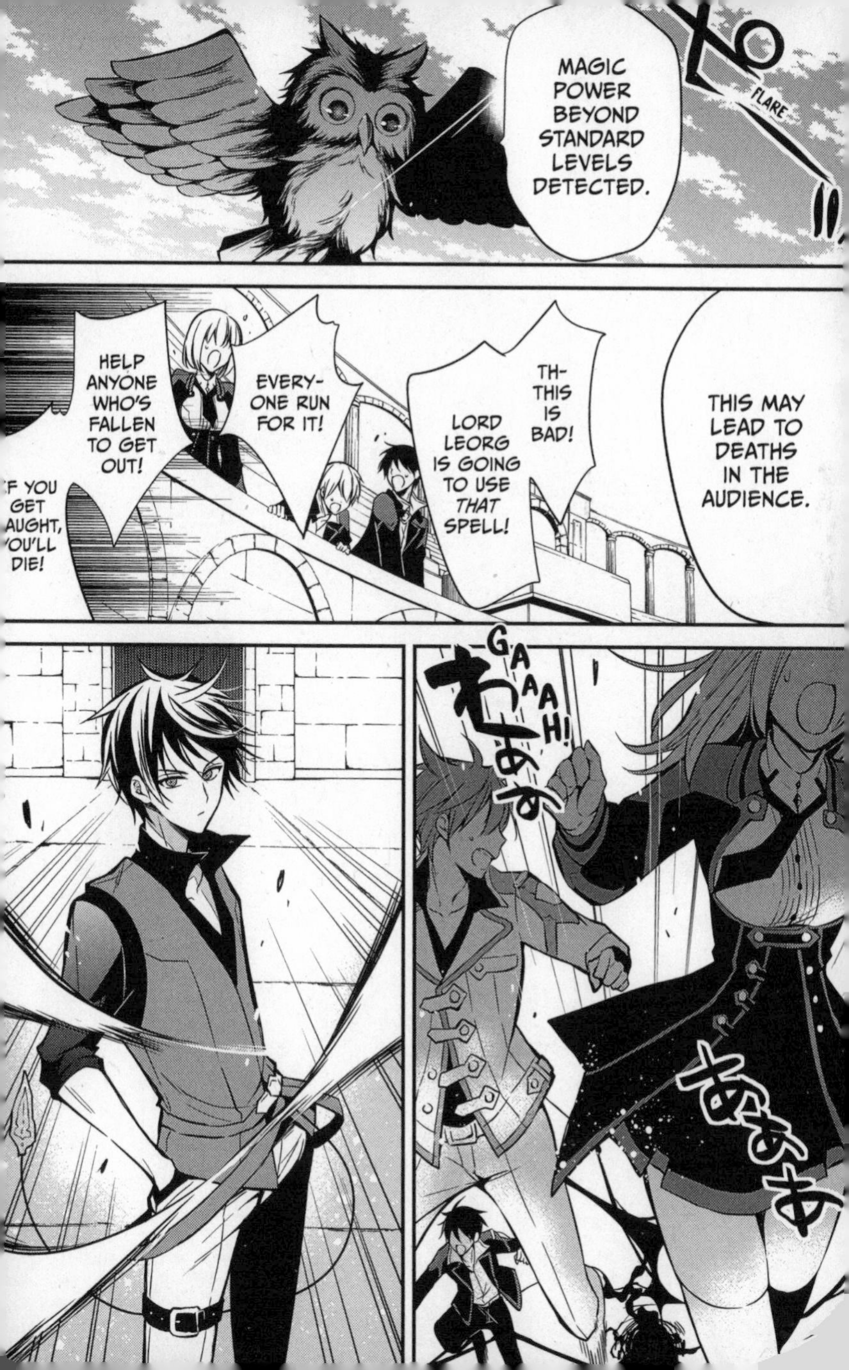
FLARE
MAGIC POWER BEYOND STANDARD LEVELS DETECTED.
THIS MAY LEAD TO DEATHS IN THE AUDIENCE.
TH- THIS IS BAD!
LORD LEORG IS GOING TO USE THAT SPELL!
EVERY- ONE RUN FOR IT!
HELP ANYONE WHO'S FALLEN TO GET OUT!
F YOU GET AUGHT, OU'LL DIE!
GAAAAH!
わああ
あああ

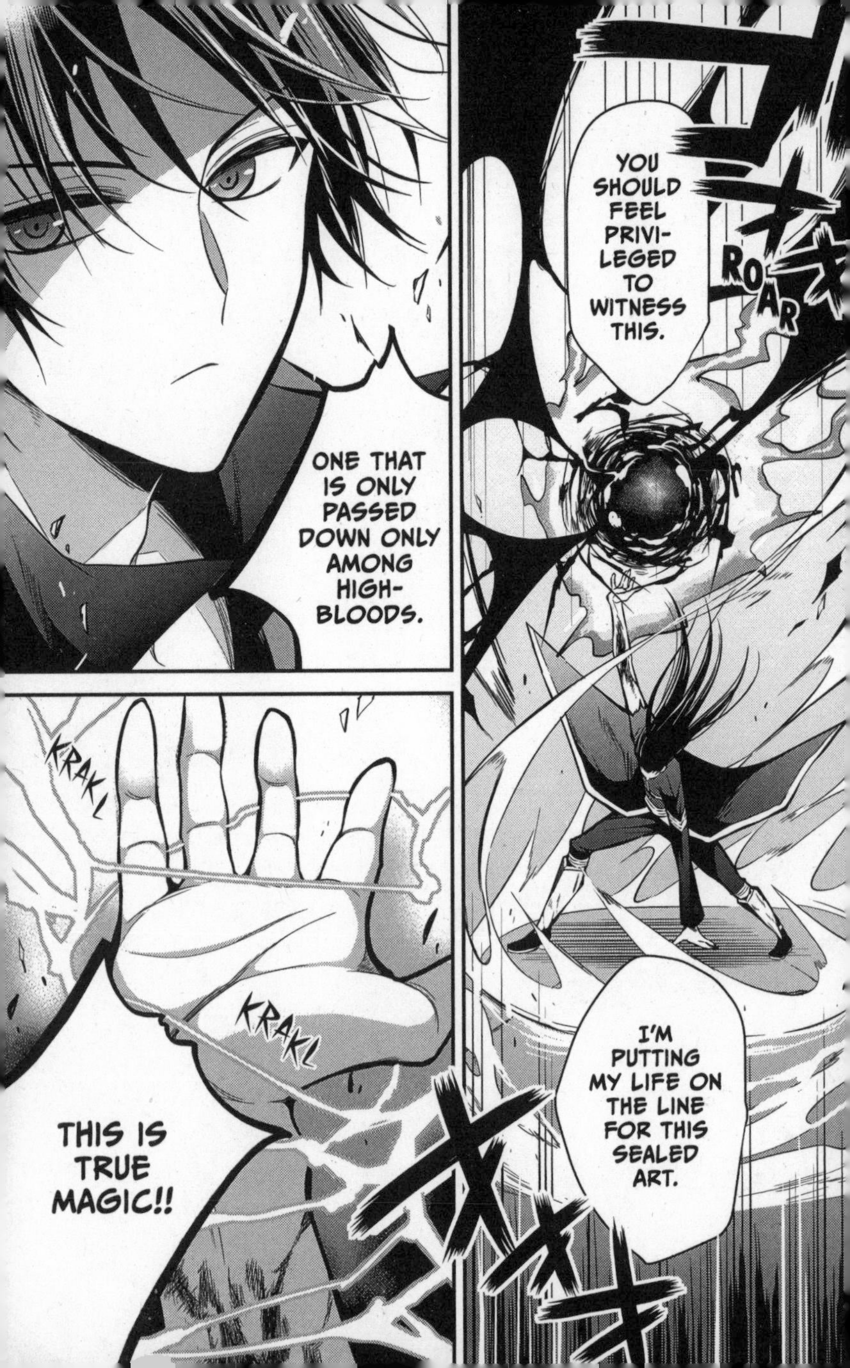
YOU SHOULD FEEL PRIVI-LEGED TO WITNESS THIS.
ROAR
I'M PUTTING MY LIFE ON THE LINE FOR THIS SEALED ART.
ONE THAT IS ONLY PASSED DOWN ONLY AMONG HIGH-BLOODS.
KRAKL
KRAKL
THIS IS TRUE MAGIC!!

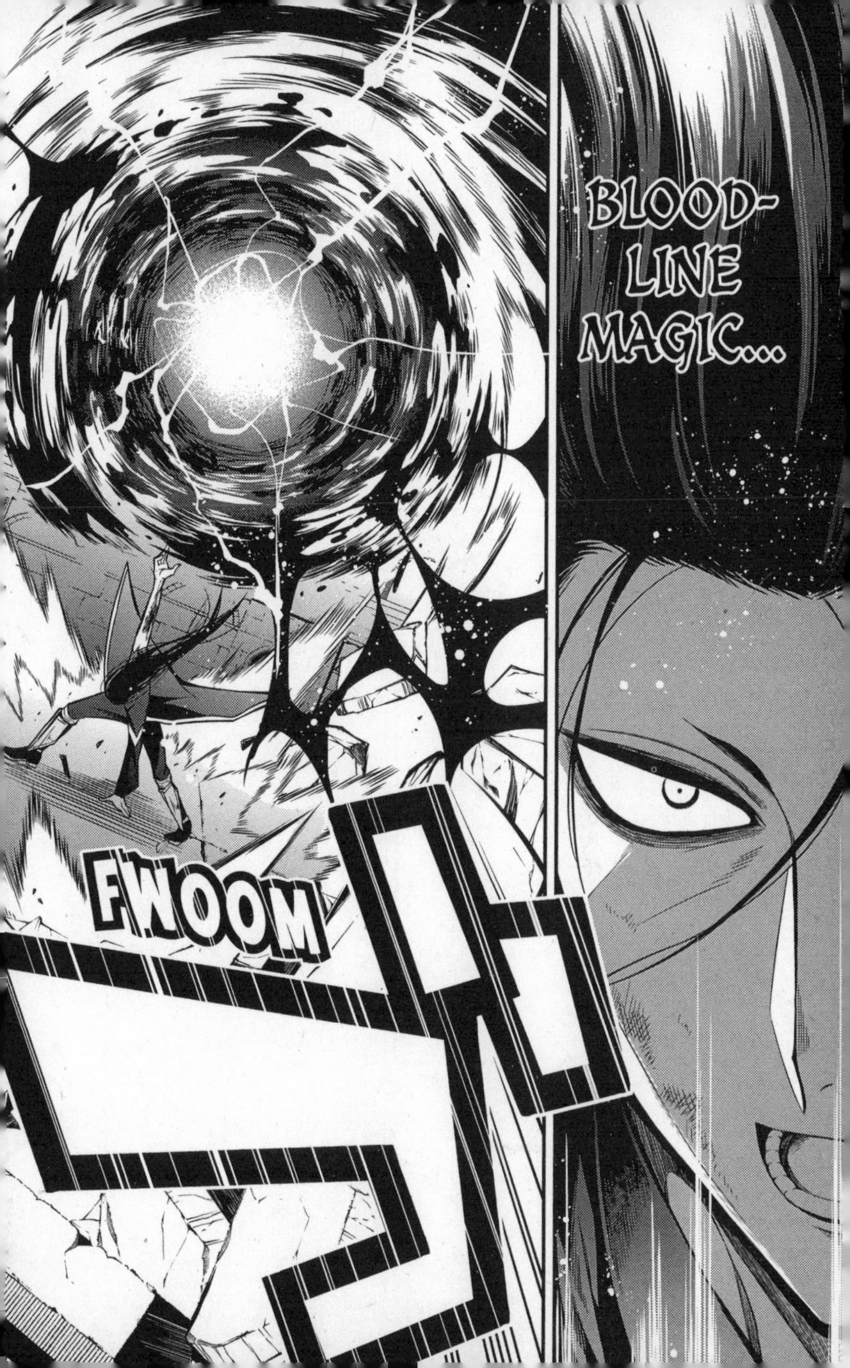
BLOOD-LINE MAGIC...
FWOOM

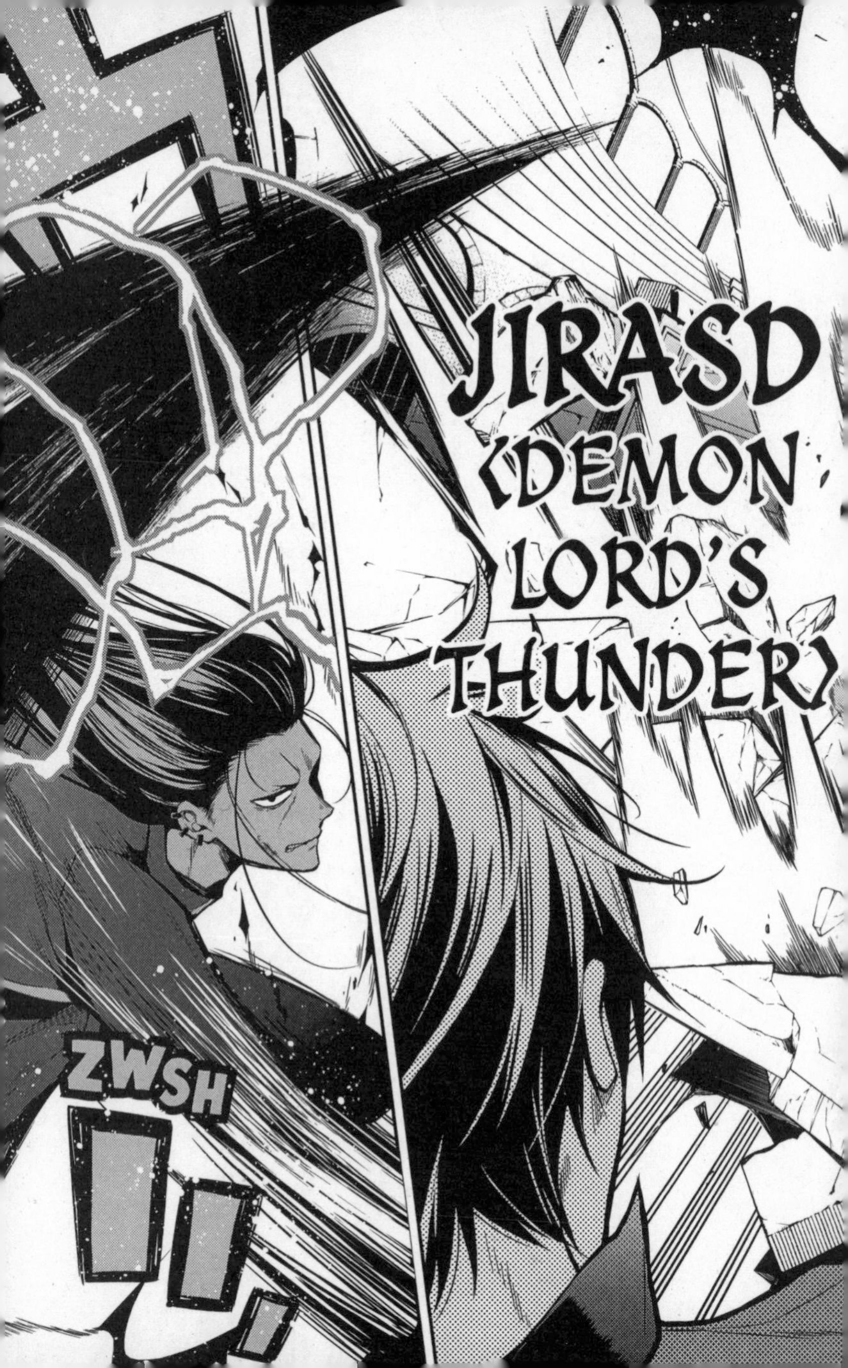
JIRASD (DEMON LORD'S THUNDER)
ZWSH

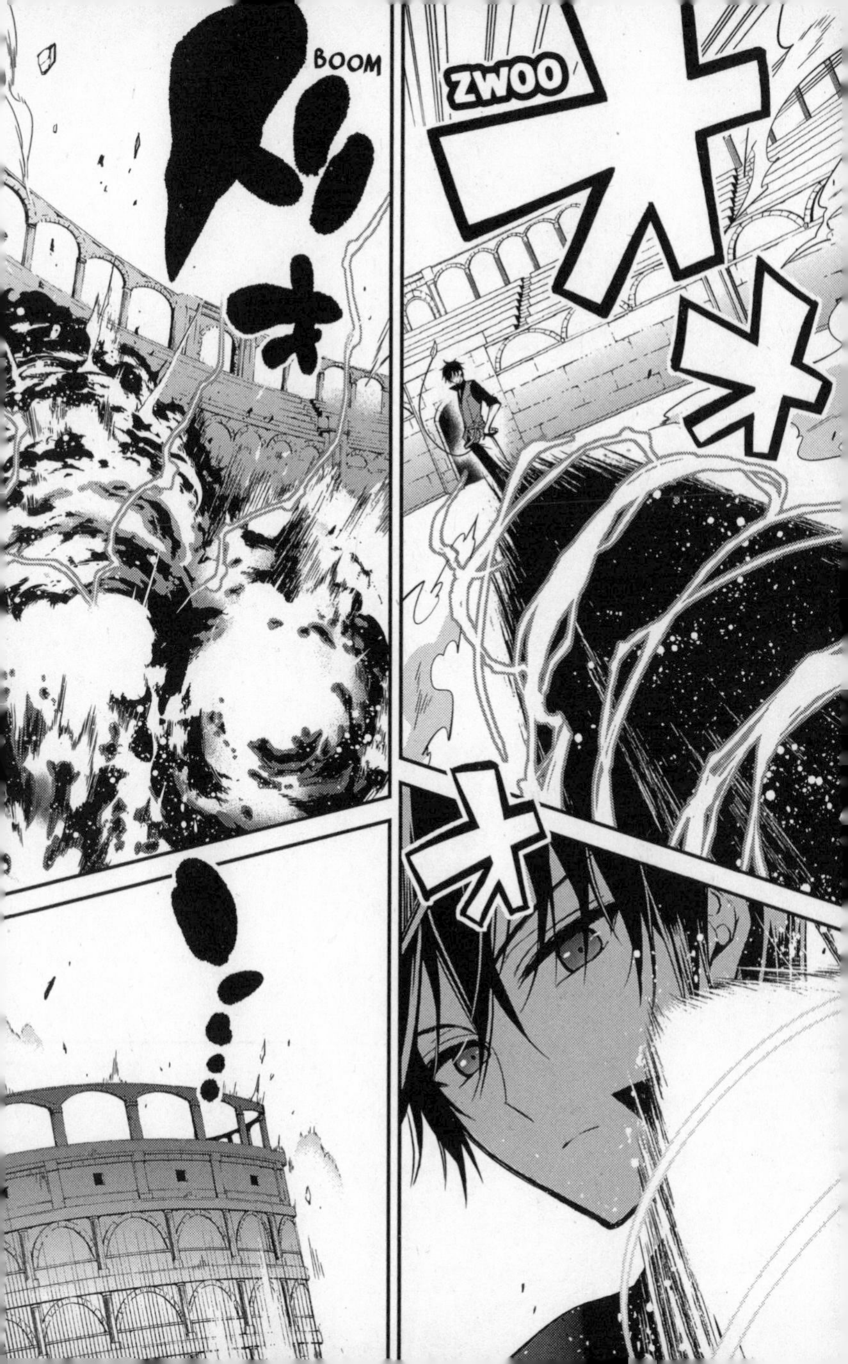
ZWOO
BOOM

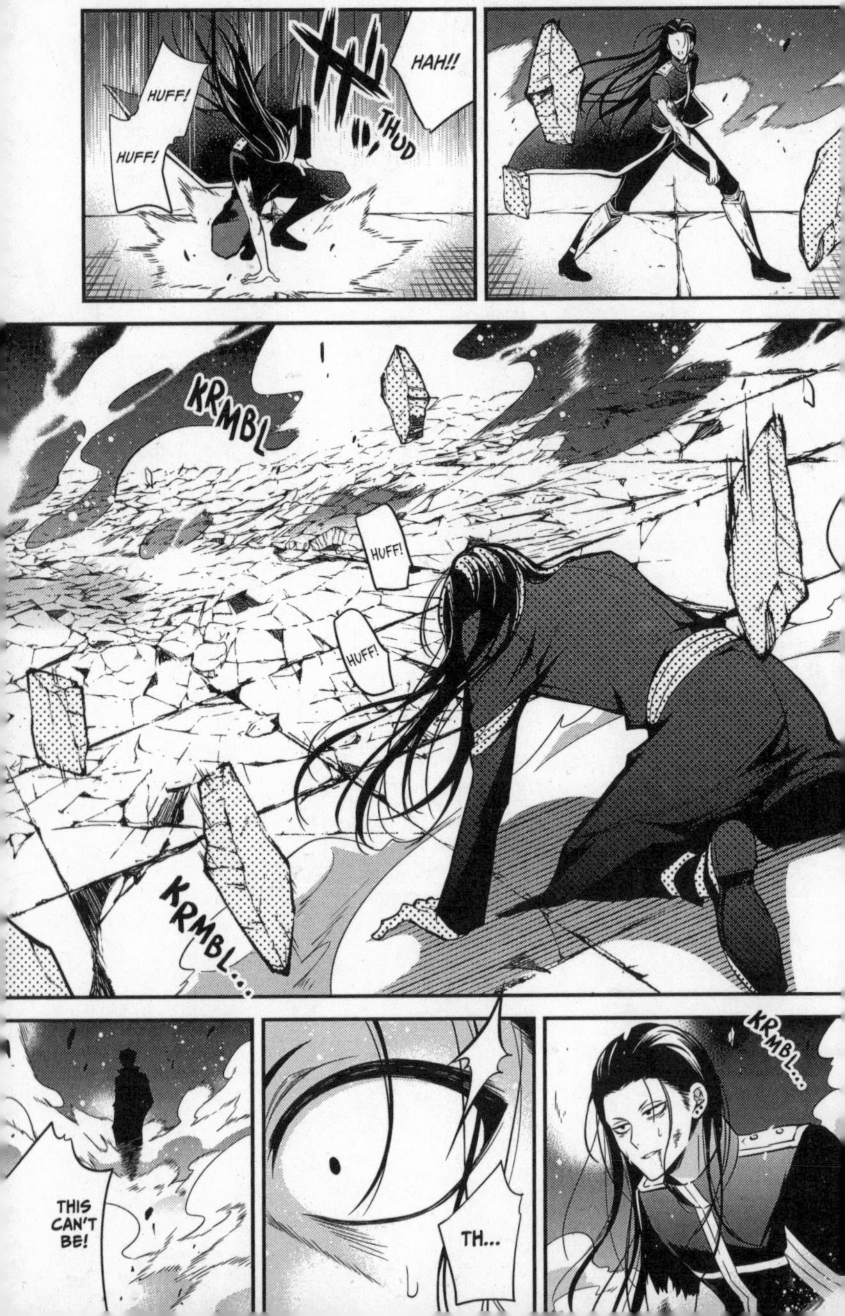
HAH!!
THUD
HUFF!
HUFF!
KRMBL
HUFF!
HUFF!
KRMBL...
KRMBL...
TH...
THIS CAN'T BE!

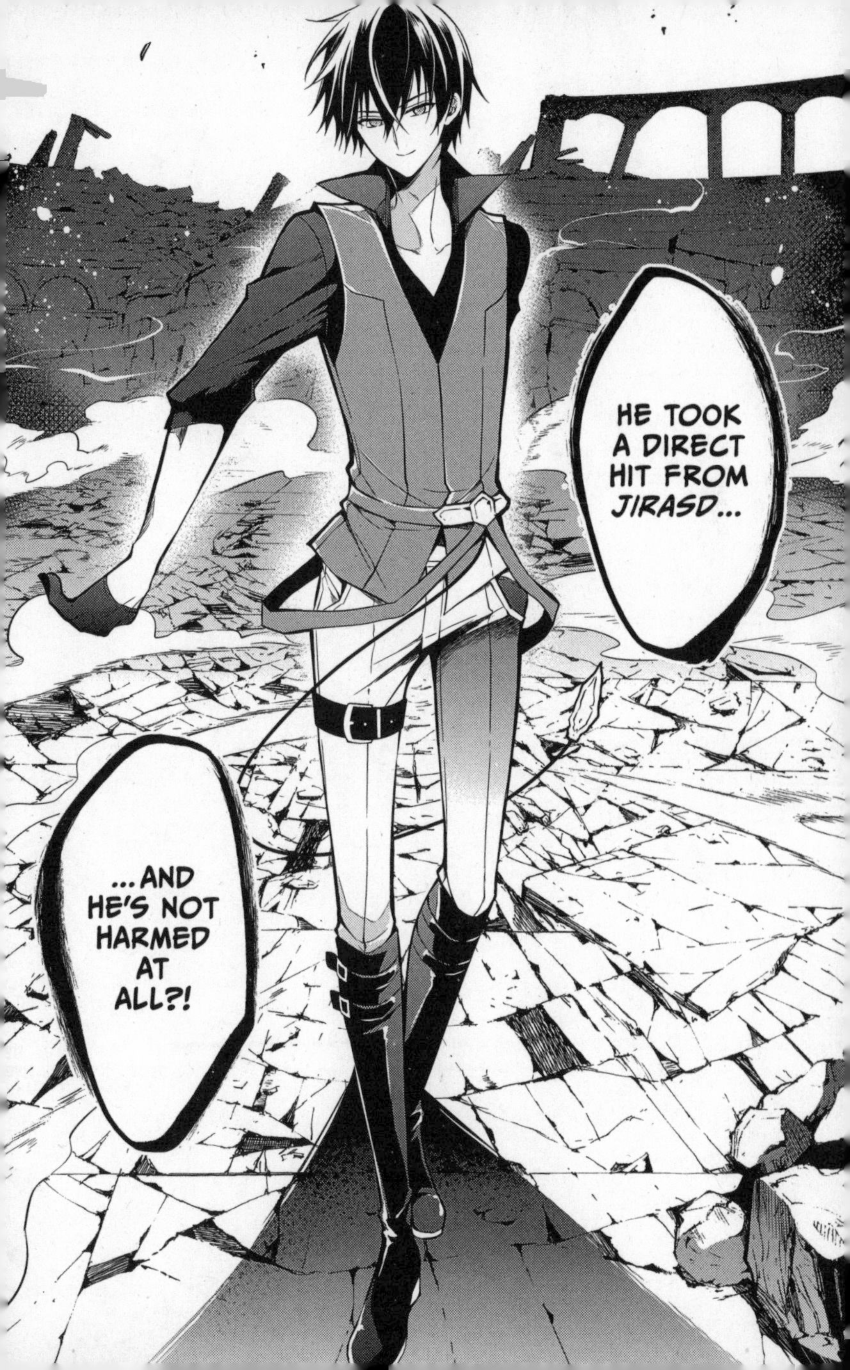
HE TOOK A DIRECT HIT FROM JIRASD...
...AND HE'S NOT HARMED AT ALL?!

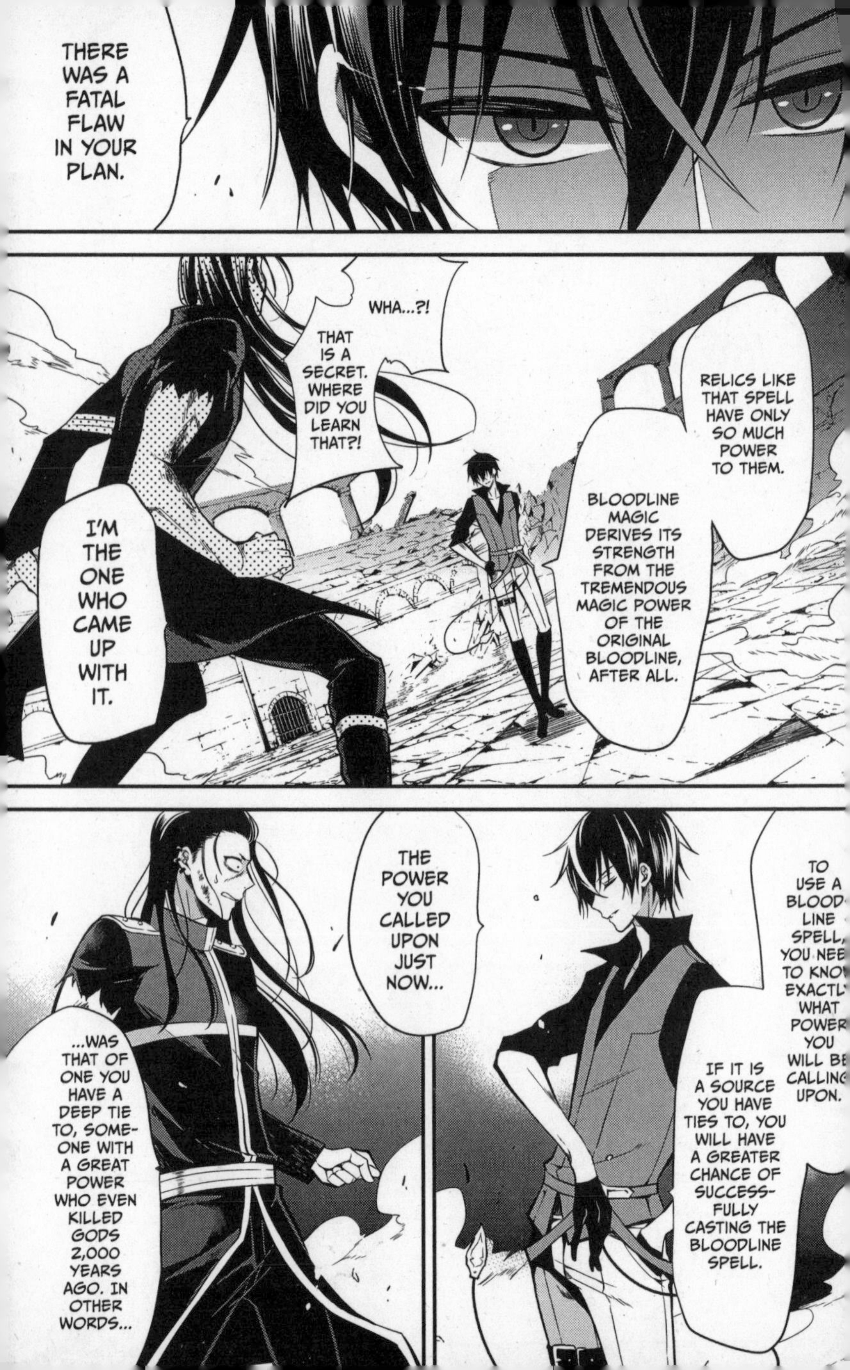
THERE WAS A FATAL FLAW IN YOUR PLAN.
RELICS LIKE THAT SPELL HAVE ONLY SO MUCH POWER TO THEM.
BLOODLINE MAGIC DERIVES ITS STRENGTH FROM THE TREMENDOUS MAGIC POWER OF THE ORIGINAL BLOODLINE, AFTER ALL.
WHA...?!
THAT IS A SECRET. WHERE DID YOU LEARN THAT?!
I'M THE ONE WHO CAME UP WITH IT.
TO USE A BLOOD- LINE SPELL, YOU NEE TO KNOW EXACTL WHAT POWER YOU WILL BE CALLING UPON.
IF IT IS A SOURCE YOU HAVE TIES TO, YOU WILL HAVE A GREATER CHANCE OF SUCCESS- FULLY CASTING THE BLOODLINE SPELL.
THE POWER YOU CALLED UPON JUST NOW...
...WAS THAT OF ONE YOU HAVE A DEEP TIE TO, SOME- ONE WITH A GREAT POWER WHO EVEN KILLED GODS 2,000 YEARS AGO. IN OTHER WORDS...

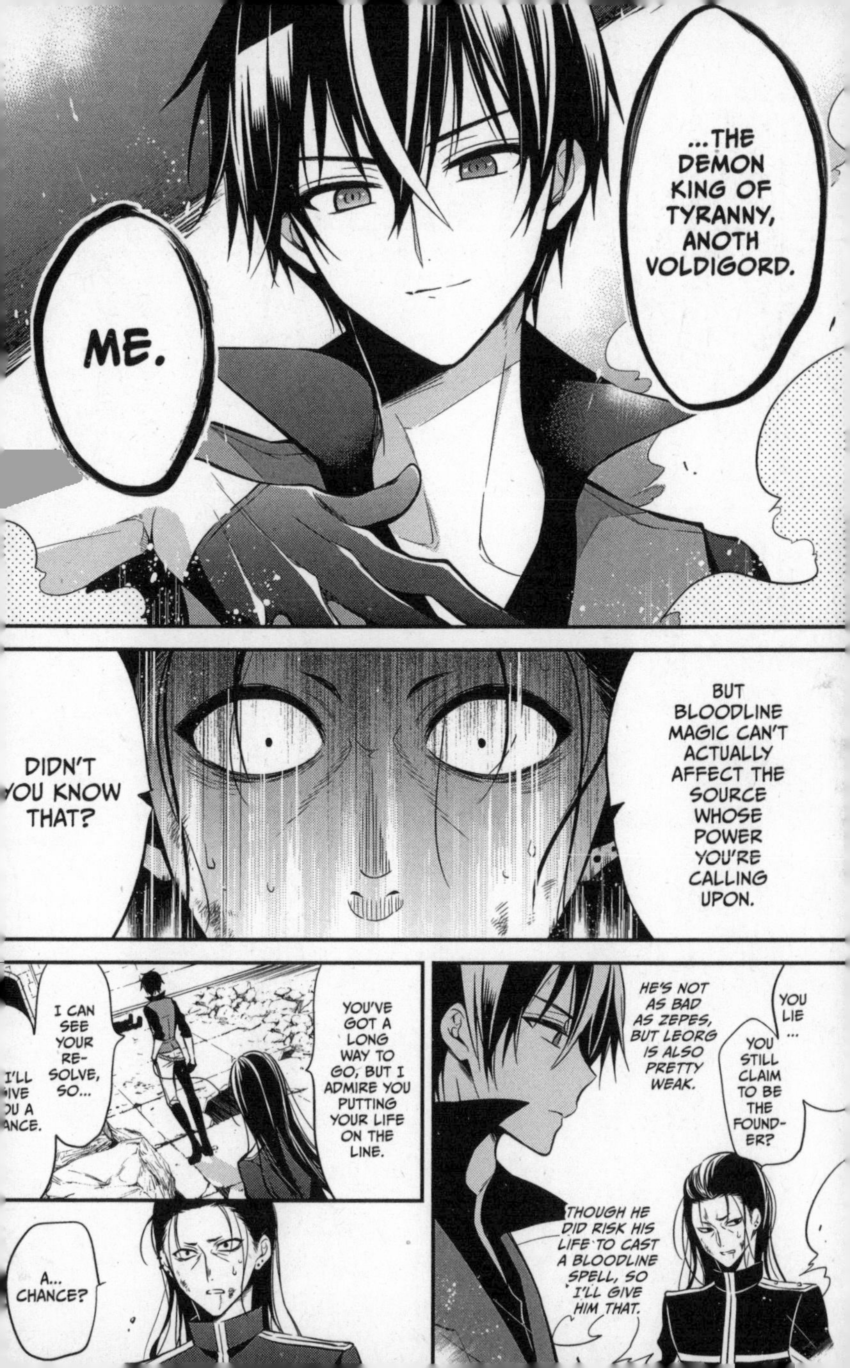
...THE DEMON KING OF TYRANNY, ANOTH VOLDIGORD.
ME.
BUT BLOODLINE MAGIC CAN'T ACTUALLY AFFECT THE SOURCE WHOSE POWER YOU'RE CALLING UPON.
DIDN'T YOU KNOW THAT?
YOU LIE ...
YOU STILL CLAIM TO BE THE FOUND-ER?
HE'S NOT AS BAD AS ZEPES, BUT LEORG IS ALSO PRETTY WEAK.
THOUGH HE DID RISK HIS LIFE TO CAST A BLOODLINE SPELL, SO I'LL GIVE HIM THAT.
YOU'VE GOT A LONG WAY TO GO, BUT I ADMIRE YOU PUTTING YOUR LIFE ON THE LINE.
I CAN SEE YOUR RE-SOLVE, SO...
I'LL IVE OU A ANCE.
A... CHANCE?

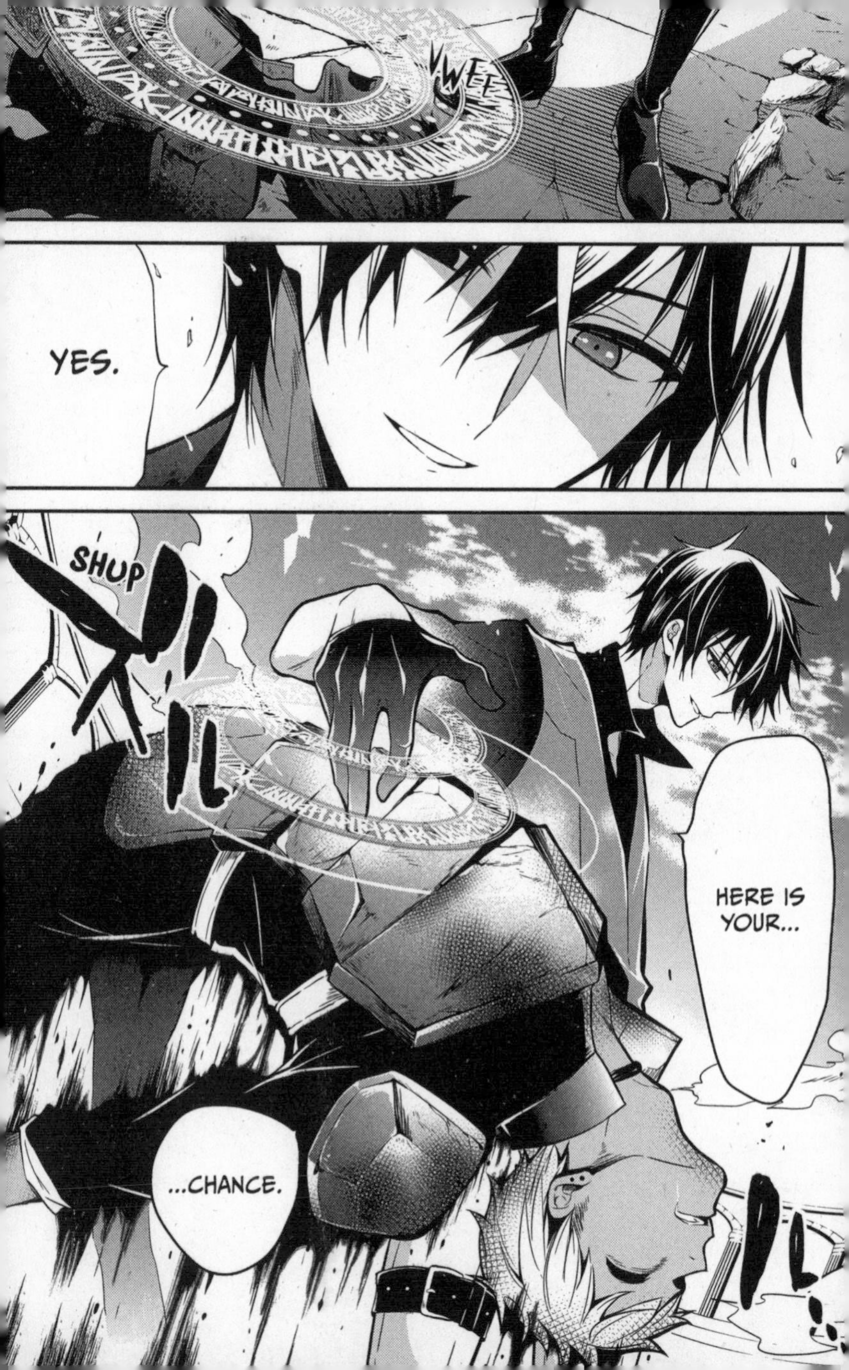
VWEE
YES.
SHUP
HERE IS YOUR...
...CHANCE.

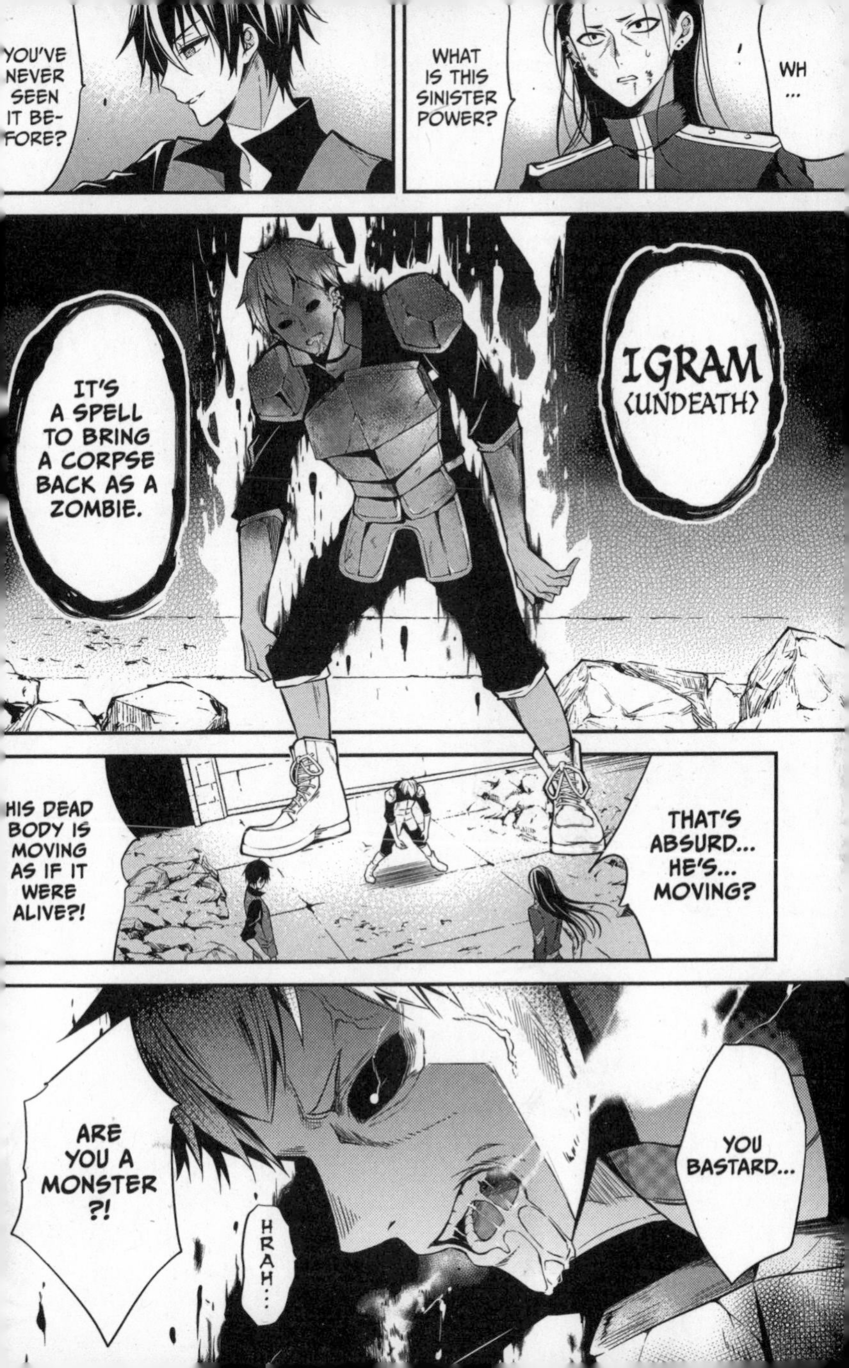

WH ...
WHAT IS THIS SINISTER POWER?
YOU'VE NEVER SEEN IT BEFORE?
IGRAM 〈UNDEATH〉
IT'S A SPELL TO BRING A CORPSE BACK AS A ZOMBIE.
THAT'S ABSURD... HE'S... MOVING?
HIS DEAD BODY IS MOVING AS IF IT WERE ALIVE?!
YOU BASTARD...
HRAH...
ARE YOU A MONSTER ?!

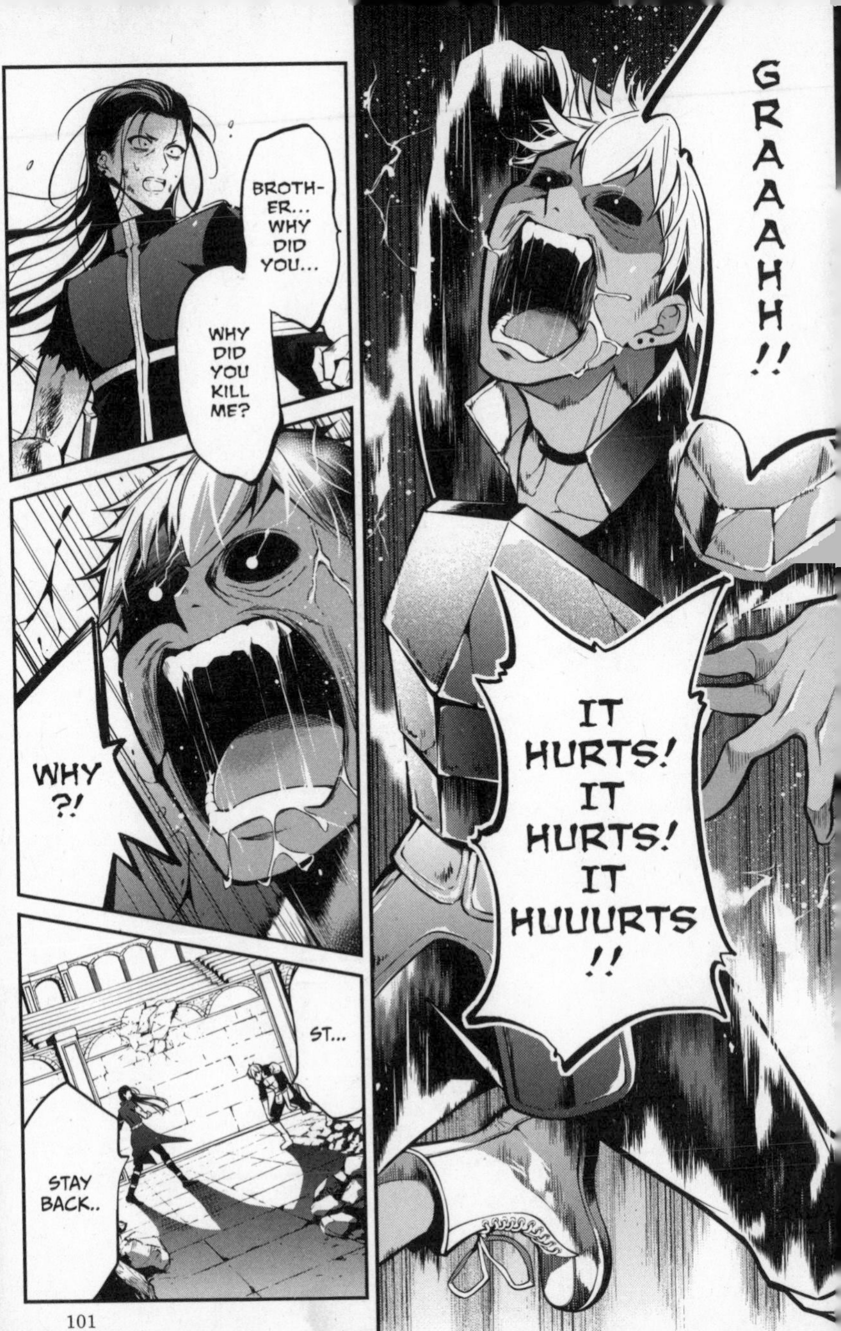
GRAAAHH!!
IT HURTS! IT HURTS! IT HUUURTS!!
BROTHER... WHY DID YOU...
WHY DID YOU KILL ME?
WHY?!
ST...
STAY BACK..

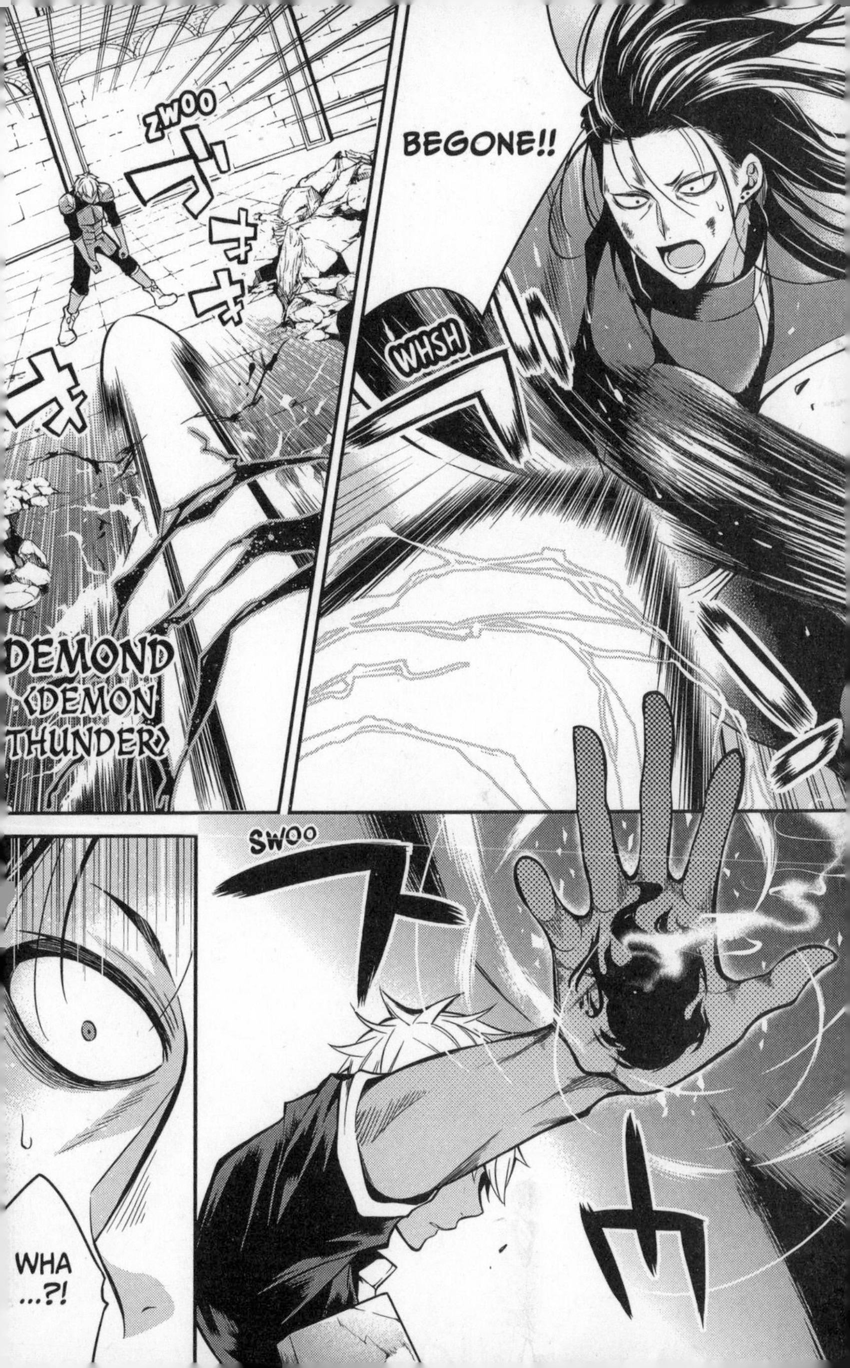
BEGONE!!
WHSH
ZWOO
DEMOND
(DEMON
THUNDER)
SWOO
WHA
...?!

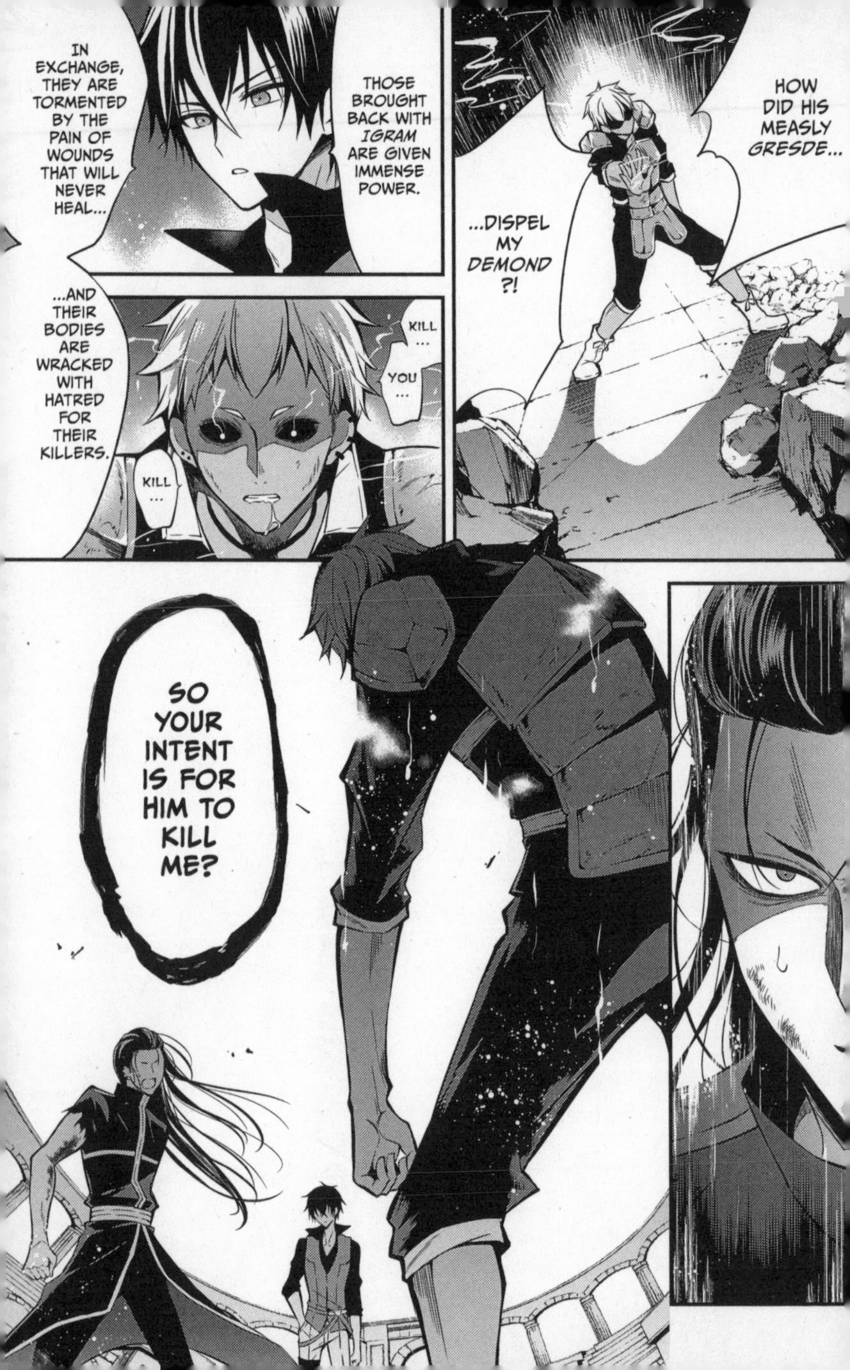
HOW DID HIS MEASLY GRESDE...
...DISPEL MY DEMOND?!
THOSE BROUGHT BACK WITH IGRAM ARE GIVEN IMMENSE POWER.
IN EXCHANGE, THEY ARE TORMENTED BY THE PAIN OF WOUNDS THAT WILL NEVER HEAL...
KILL...
YOU...
...AND THEIR BODIES ARE WRACKED WITH HATRED FOR THEIR KILLERS.
KILL...
SO YOUR INTENT IS FOR HIM TO KILL ME?

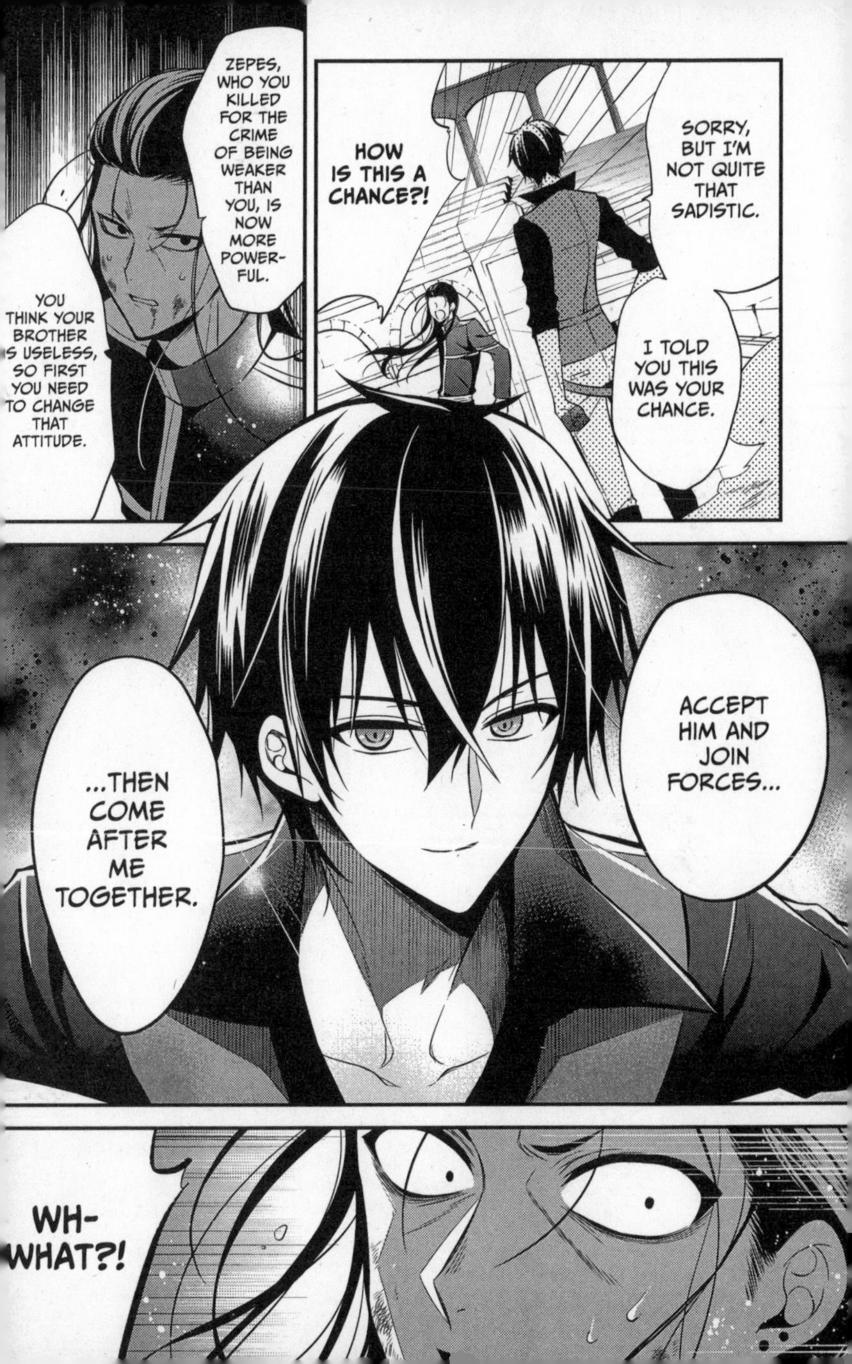
SORRY, BUT I'M NOT QUITE THAT SADISTIC.
HOW IS THIS A CHANCE?!
I TOLD YOU THIS WAS YOUR CHANCE.
ZEPES, WHO YOU KILLED FOR THE CRIME OF BEING WEAKER THAN YOU, IS NOW MORE POWER-FUL.
YOU THINK YOUR BROTHER IS USELESS, SO FIRST YOU NEED TO CHANGE THAT ATTITUDE.
ACCEPT HIM AND JOIN FORCES...
...THEN COME AFTER ME TOGETHER.
WH- WHAT?!

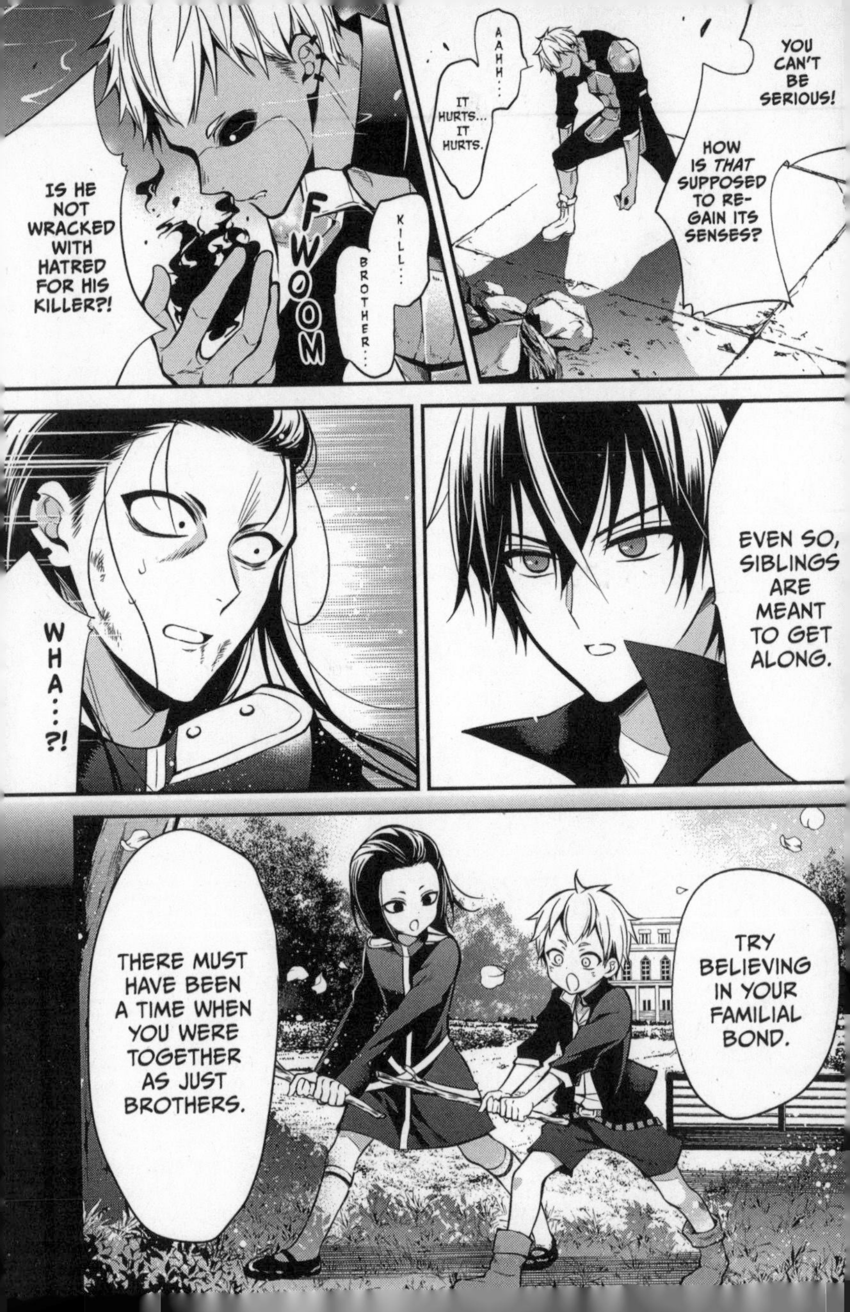
YOU CAN'T BE SERIOUS!
HOW IS *THAT* SUPPOSED TO RE-GAIN ITS SENSES?
AAHH...
IT HURTS... IT HURTS.
KILL... BROTHER...
FWOOM
IS HE NOT WRACKED WITH HATRED FOR HIS KILLER?!
EVEN SO, SIBLINGS ARE MEANT TO GET ALONG.
WHA...?!
TRY BELIEVING IN YOUR FAMILIAL BOND.
THERE MUST HAVE BEEN A TIME WHEN YOU WERE TOGETHER AS JUST BROTHERS.

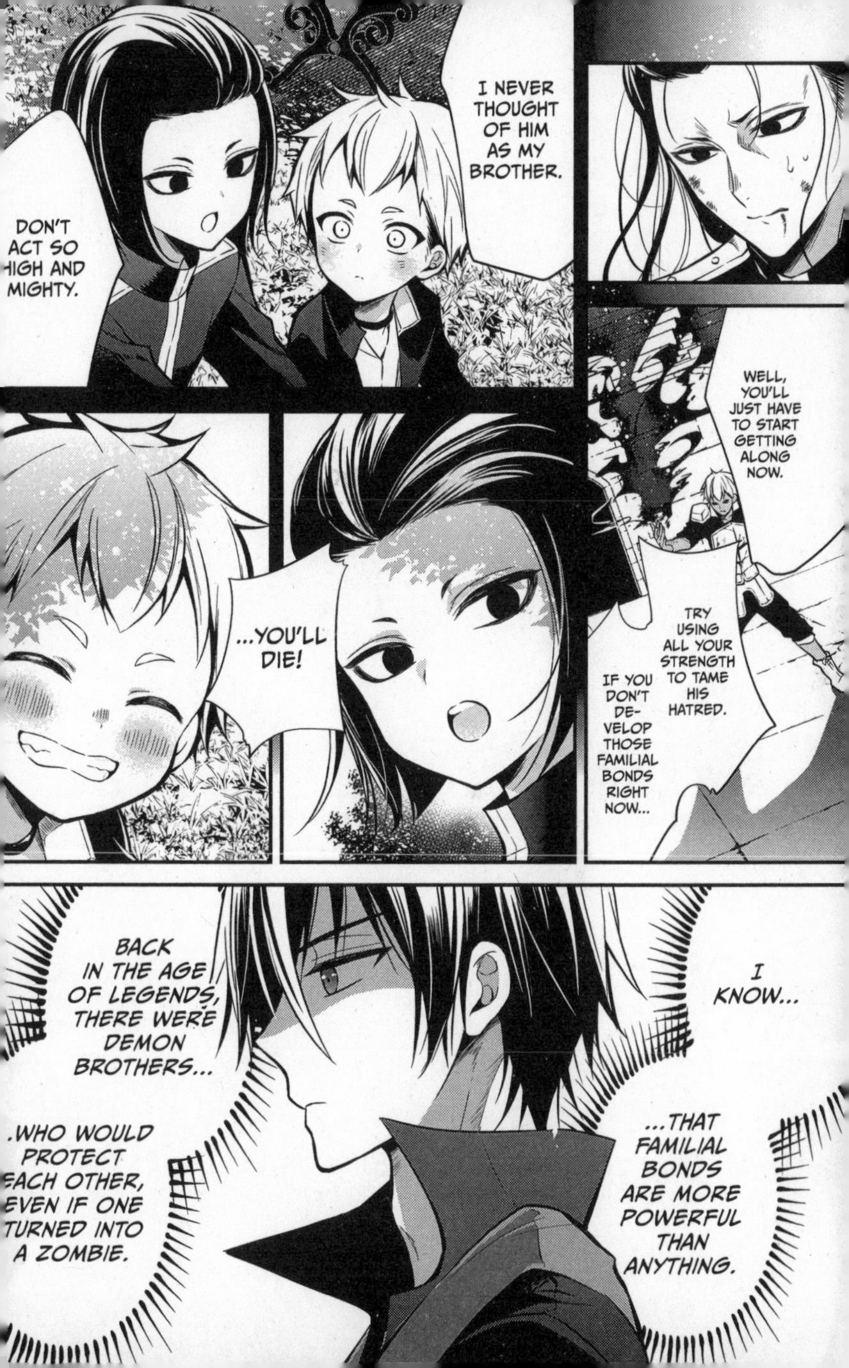
I NEVER THOUGHT OF HIM AS MY BROTHER.
DON'T ACT SO HIGH AND MIGHTY.
WELL, YOU'LL JUST HAVE TO START GETTING ALONG NOW.
TRY USING ALL YOUR STRENGTH TO TAME HIS HATRED.
IF YOU DON'T DE-VELOP THOSE FAMILIAL BONDS RIGHT NOW...
...YOU'LL DIE!
I KNOW...
...THAT FAMILIAL BONDS ARE MORE POWERFUL THAN ANYTHING.
BACK IN THE AGE OF LEGENDS, THERE WERE DEMON BROTHERS...
.WHO WOULD PROTECT EACH OTHER, EVEN IF ONE TURNED INTO A ZOMBIE.

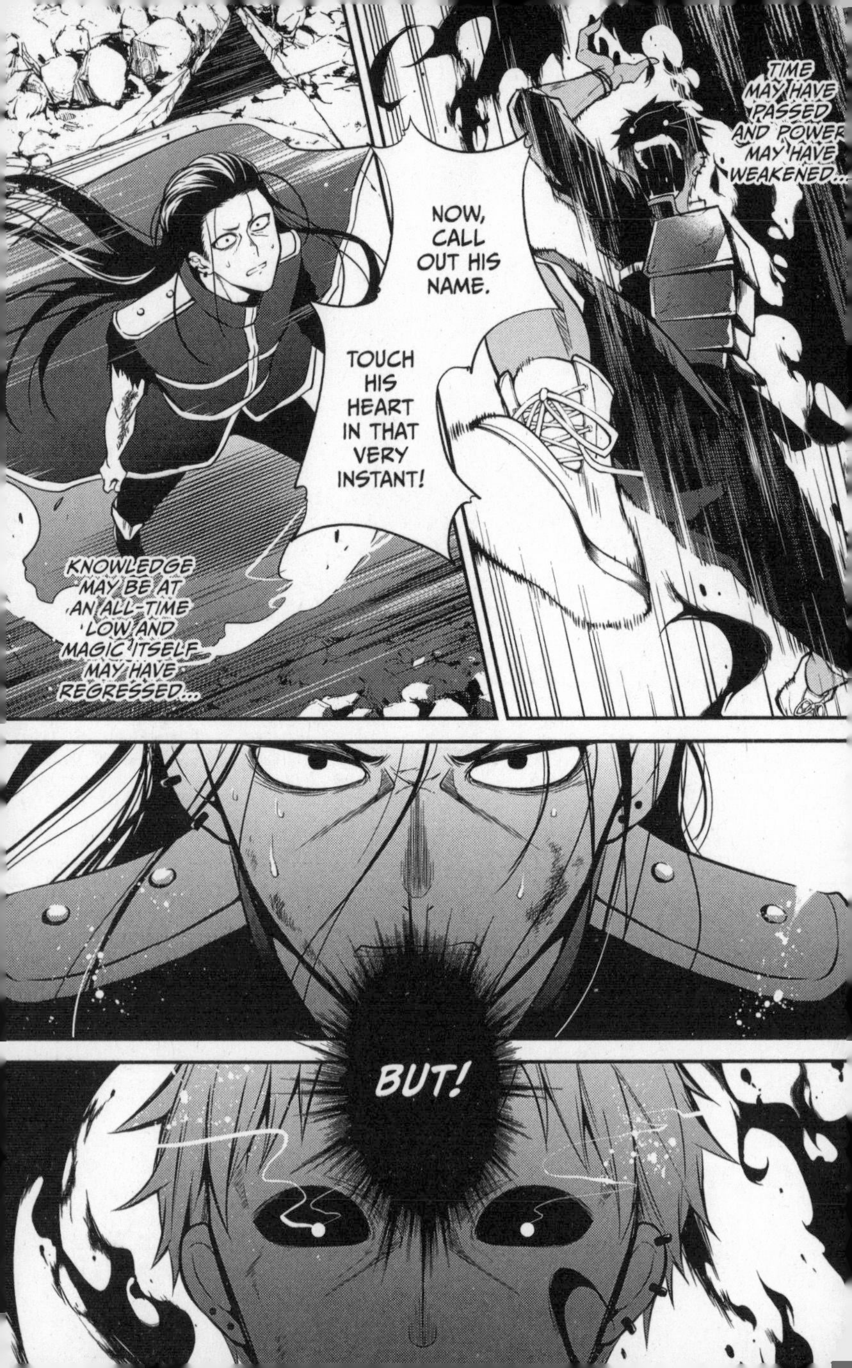
TIME MAY HAVE PASSED AND POWER MAY HAVE WEAKENED...
NOW, CALL OUT HIS NAME.
TOUCH HIS HEART IN THAT VERY INSTANT!
KNOWLEDGE MAY BE AT AN ALL-TIME LOW AND MAGIC ITSELF MAY HAVE REGRESSED...
BUT!

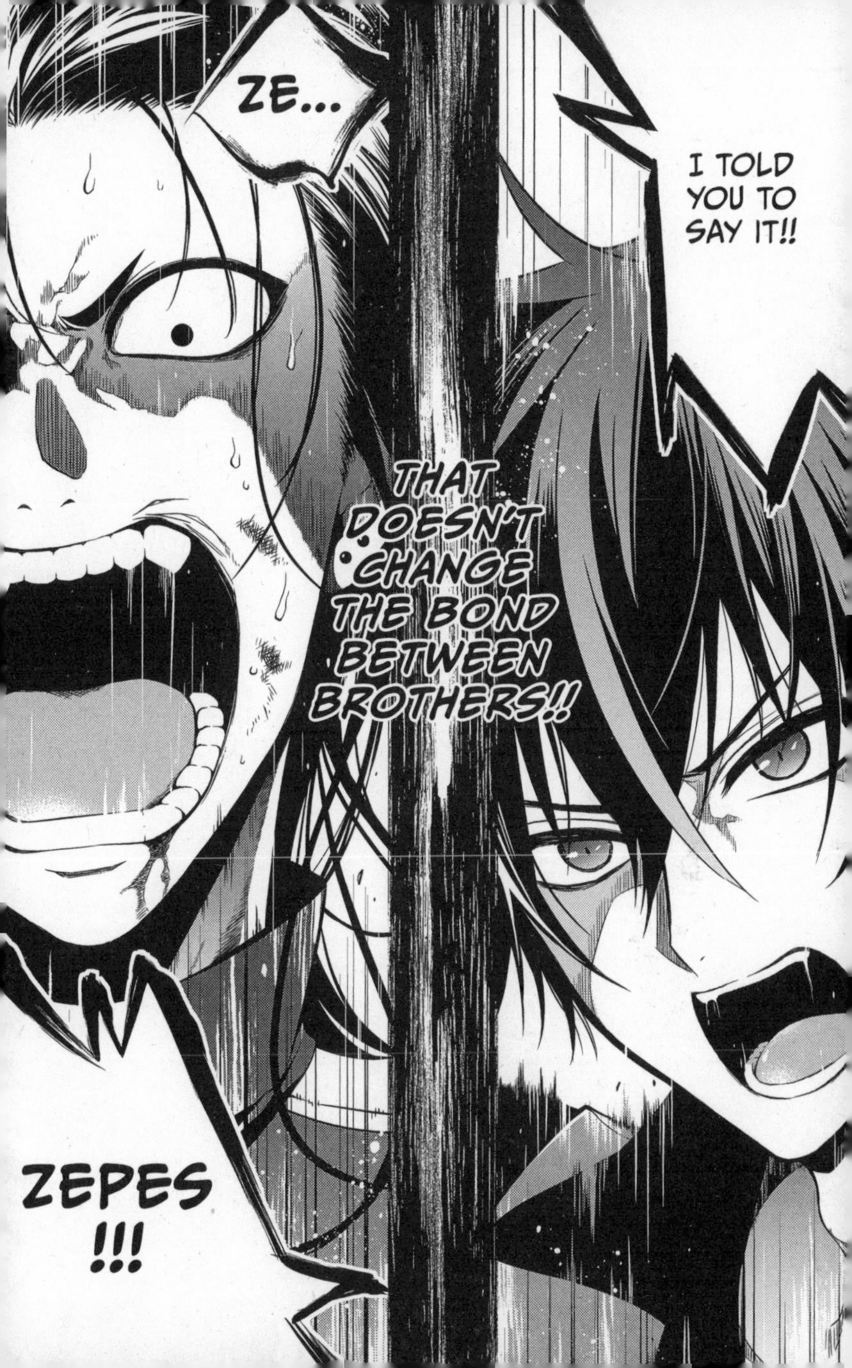
I TOLD YOU TO SAY IT!!
ZE...
THAT DOESN'T CHANGE THE BOND BETWEEN BROTHERS!!
ZEPES!!!

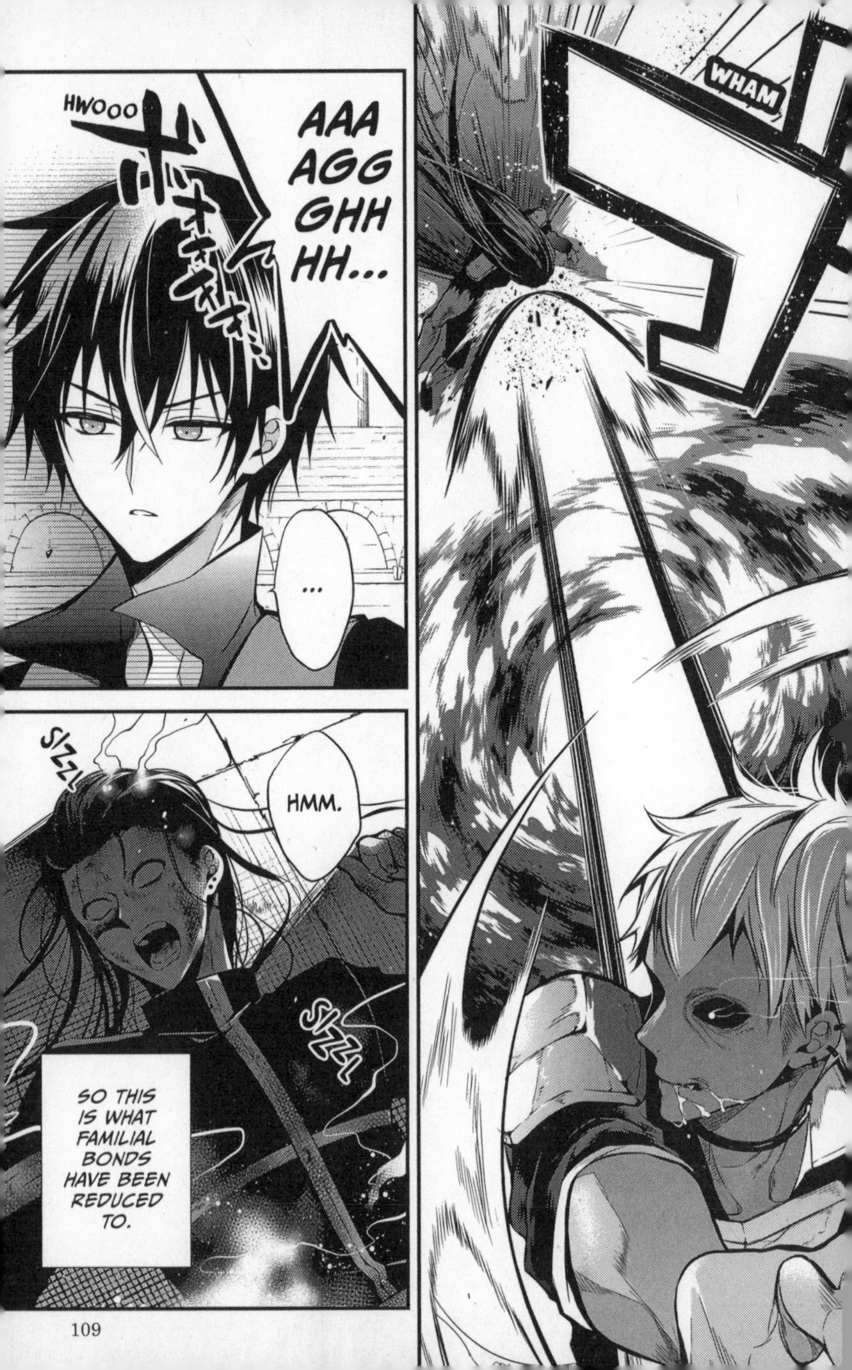
WHAM
HWOOO
AAAAGGGHHHH...
...
SIZZL
HMM.
SIZZL
SO THIS IS WHAT FAMILIAL BONDS HAVE BEEN REDUCED TO.

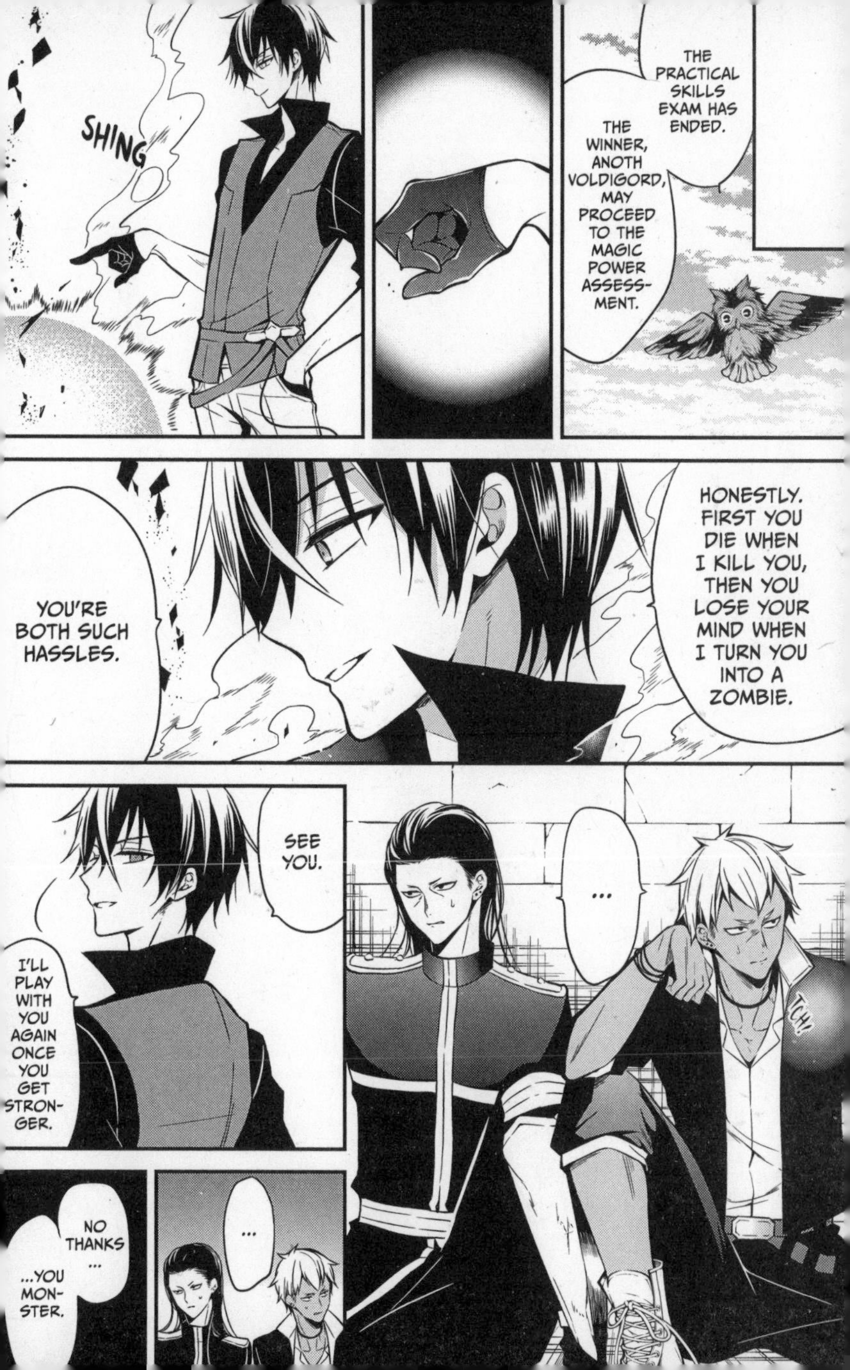
THE PRACTICAL SKILLS EXAM HAS ENDED.
THE WINNER, ANOTH VOLDIGORD, MAY PROCEED TO THE MAGIC POWER ASSESS-MENT.
SHING
HONESTLY. FIRST YOU DIE WHEN I KILL YOU, THEN YOU LOSE YOUR MIND WHEN I TURN YOU INTO A ZOMBIE.
YOU'RE BOTH SUCH HASSLES.
...
TCH!
SEE YOU.
I'LL PLAY WITH YOU AGAIN ONCE YOU GET STRON-GER.
...
NO THANKS...
...YOU MON-STER.

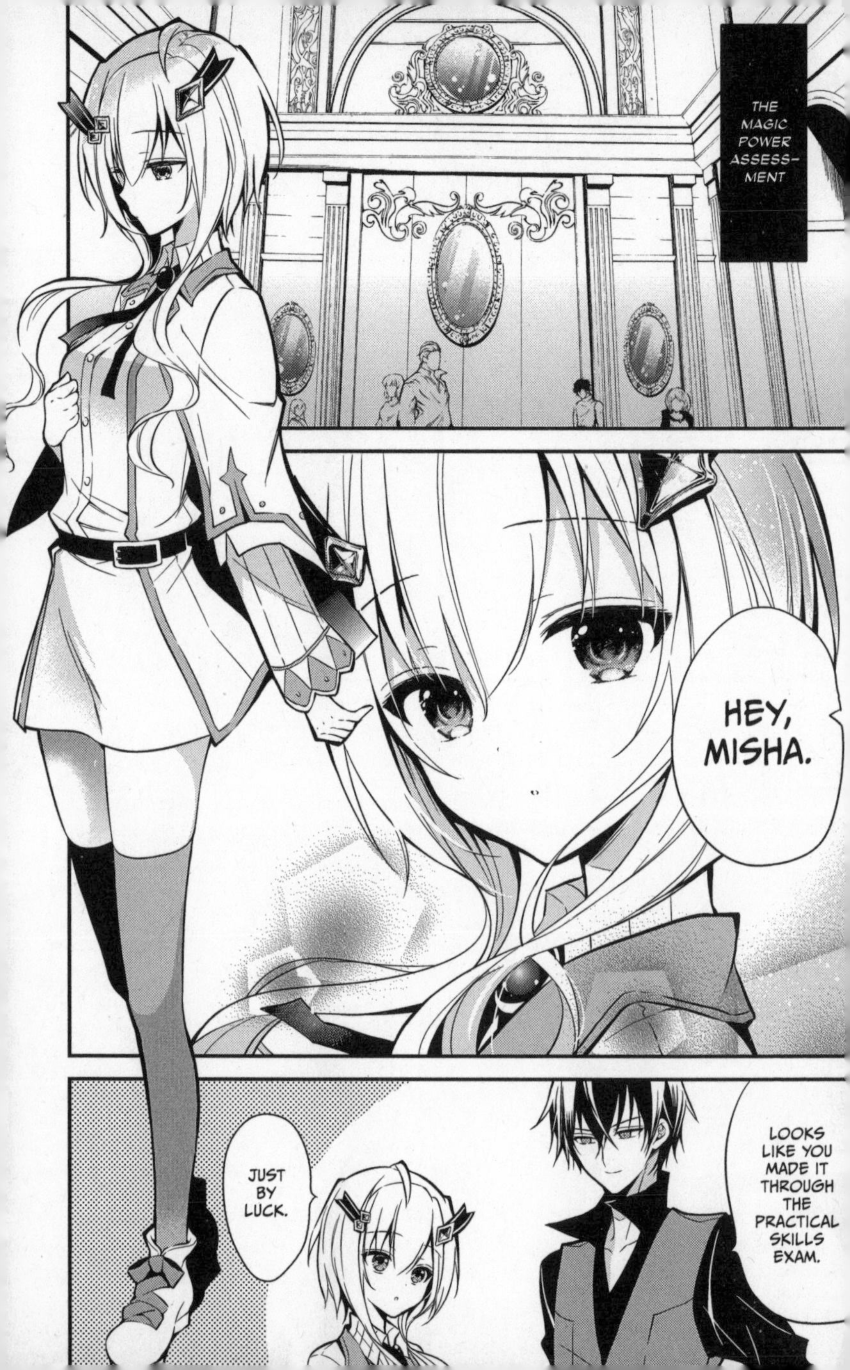
THE MAGIC POWER ASSESS-MENT
HEY, MISHA.
LOOKS LIKE YOU MADE IT THROUGH THE PRACTICAL SKILLS EXAM.
JUST BY LUCK.

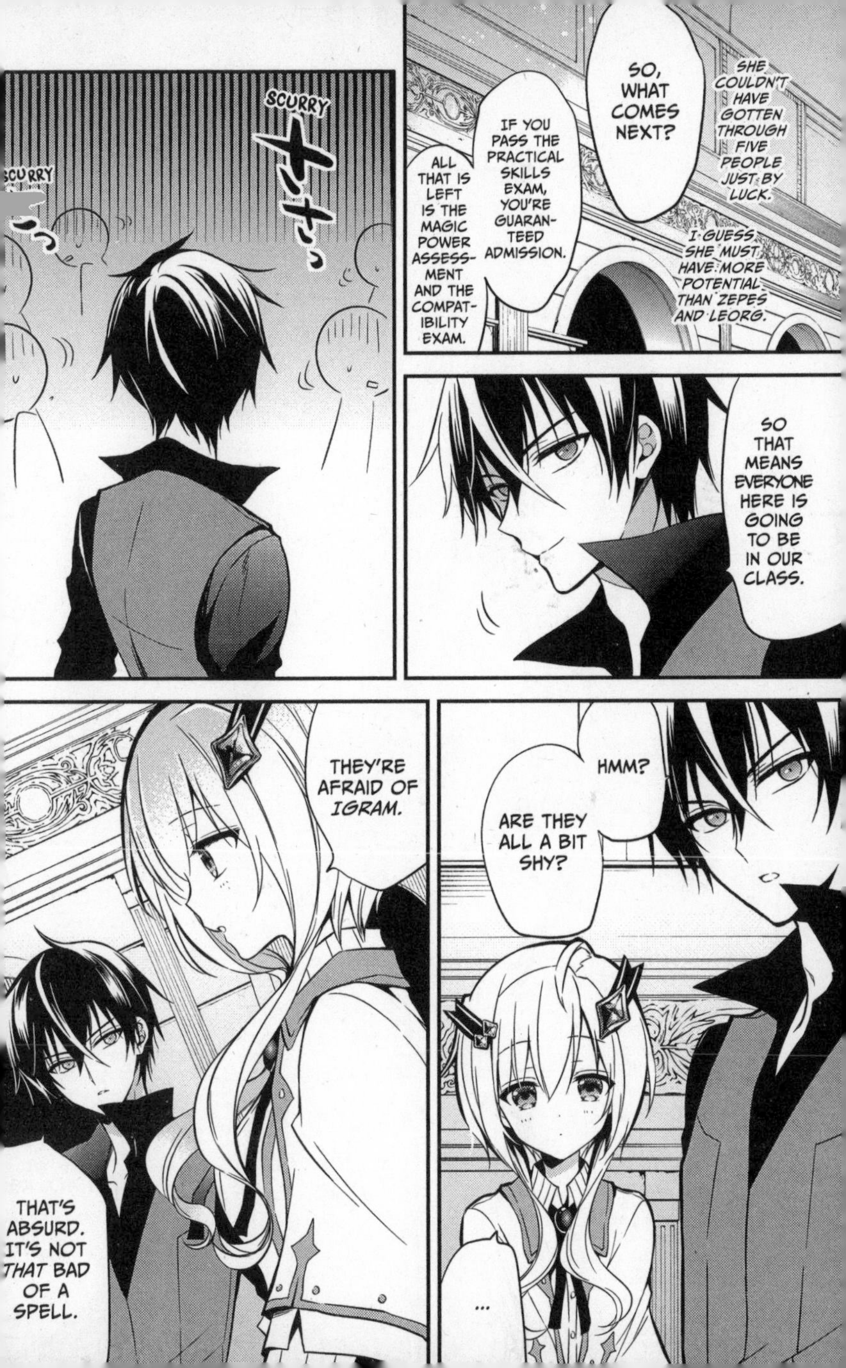
SHE COULDN'T HAVE GOTTEN THROUGH FIVE PEOPLE JUST BY LUCK.
I GUESS SHE MUST HAVE MORE POTENTIAL THAN ZEPES AND LEORG.
SO, WHAT COMES NEXT?
IF YOU PASS THE PRACTICAL SKILLS EXAM, YOU'RE GUARANTEED ADMISSION.
ALL THAT IS LEFT IS THE MAGIC POWER ASSESSMENT AND THE COMPATIBILITY EXAM.
SO THAT MEANS EVERYONE HERE IS GOING TO BE IN OUR CLASS.
SCURRY
SCURRY
HMM?
ARE THEY ALL A BIT SHY?
...
THEY'RE AFRAID OF *IGRAM*.
THAT'S ABSURD. IT'S NOT *THAT* BAD OF A SPELL.

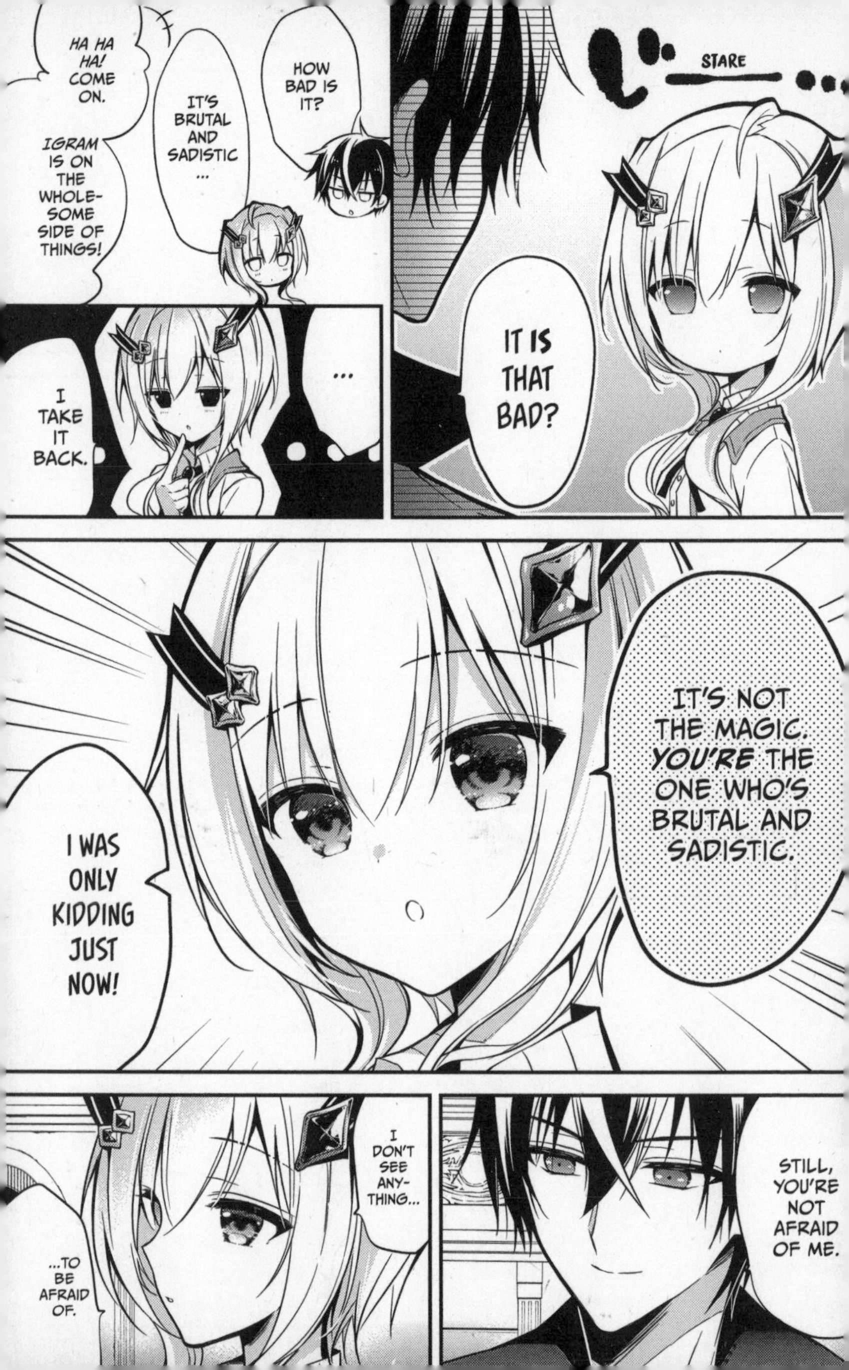
STARE
IT IS THAT BAD?
HOW BAD IS IT?
IT'S BRUTAL AND SADISTIC...
HA HA HA! COME ON.
IGRAM IS ON THE WHOLESOME SIDE OF THINGS!
...
I TAKE IT BACK.
IT'S NOT THE MAGIC. *YOU'RE* THE ONE WHO'S BRUTAL AND SADISTIC.
I WAS ONLY KIDDING JUST NOW!
STILL, YOU'RE NOT AFRAID OF ME.
I DON'T SEE ANYTHING...
...TO BE AFRAID OF.

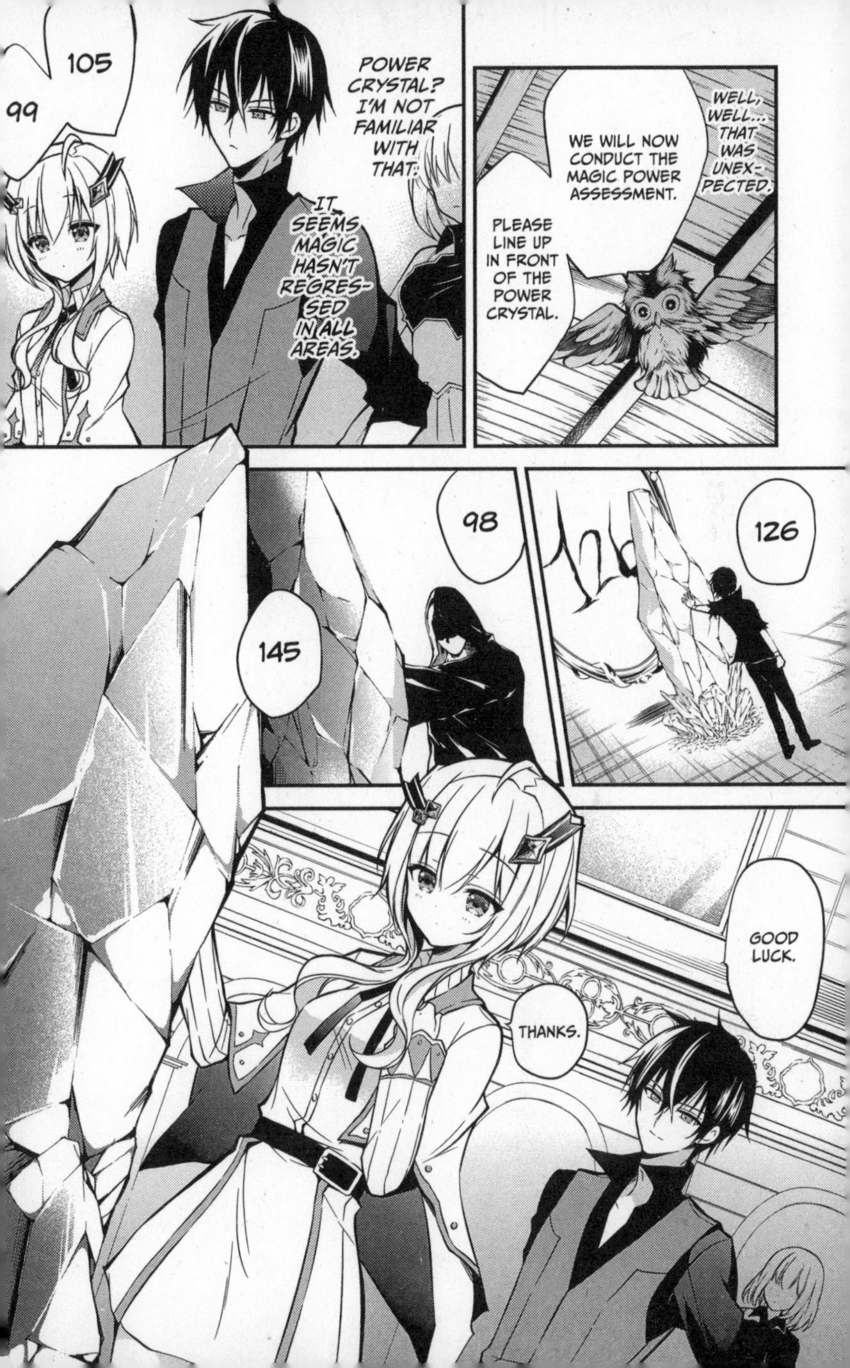
WELL, WELL... THAT WAS UNEXPECTED.
WE WILL NOW CONDUCT THE MAGIC POWER ASSESSMENT.
PLEASE LINE UP IN FRONT OF THE POWER CRYSTAL.
POWER CRYSTAL? I'M NOT FAMILIAR WITH THAT.
IT SEEMS MAGIC HASN'T REGRES-SED IN ALL AREAS.
105
99
126
98
145
GOOD LUCK.
THANKS.

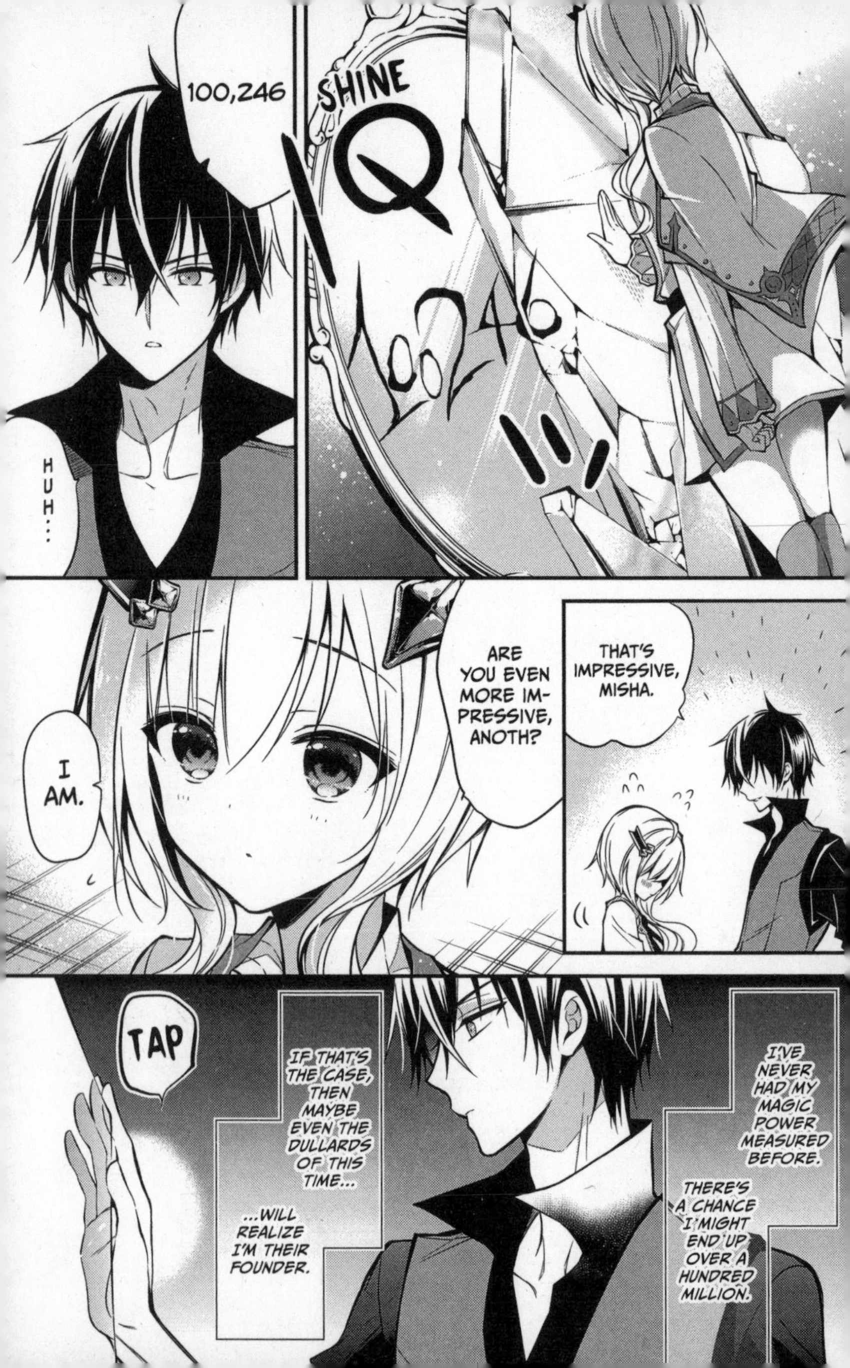
SHINE
100246
100,246
HUH...
THAT'S IMPRESSIVE, MISHA.
ARE YOU EVEN MORE IM-PRESSIVE, ANOTH?
I AM.
I'VE NEVER HAD MY MAGIC POWER MEASURED BEFORE.
THERE'S A CHANCE I MIGHT END UP OVER A HUNDRED MILLION.
IF THAT'S THE CASE, THEN MAYBE EVEN THE DULLARDS OF THIS TIME...
...WILL REALIZE I'M THEIR FOUNDER.
TAP

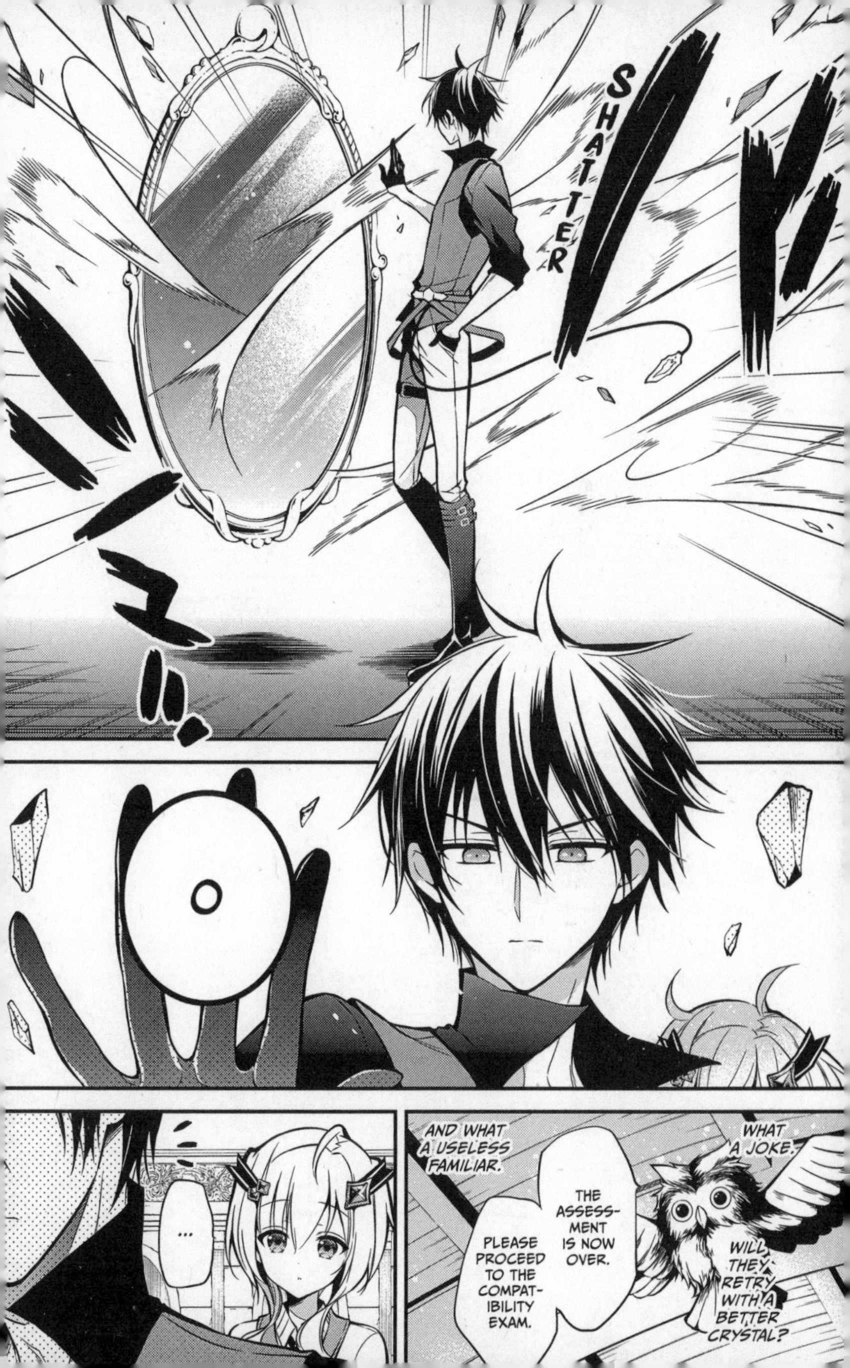
SHATTER
WHAT A JOKE.
AND WHAT A USELESS FAMILIAR.
WILL THEY RETRY WITH A BETTER CRYSTAL?
THE ASSESSMENT IS NOW OVER.
PLEASE PROCEED TO THE COMPATIBILITY EXAM.
...

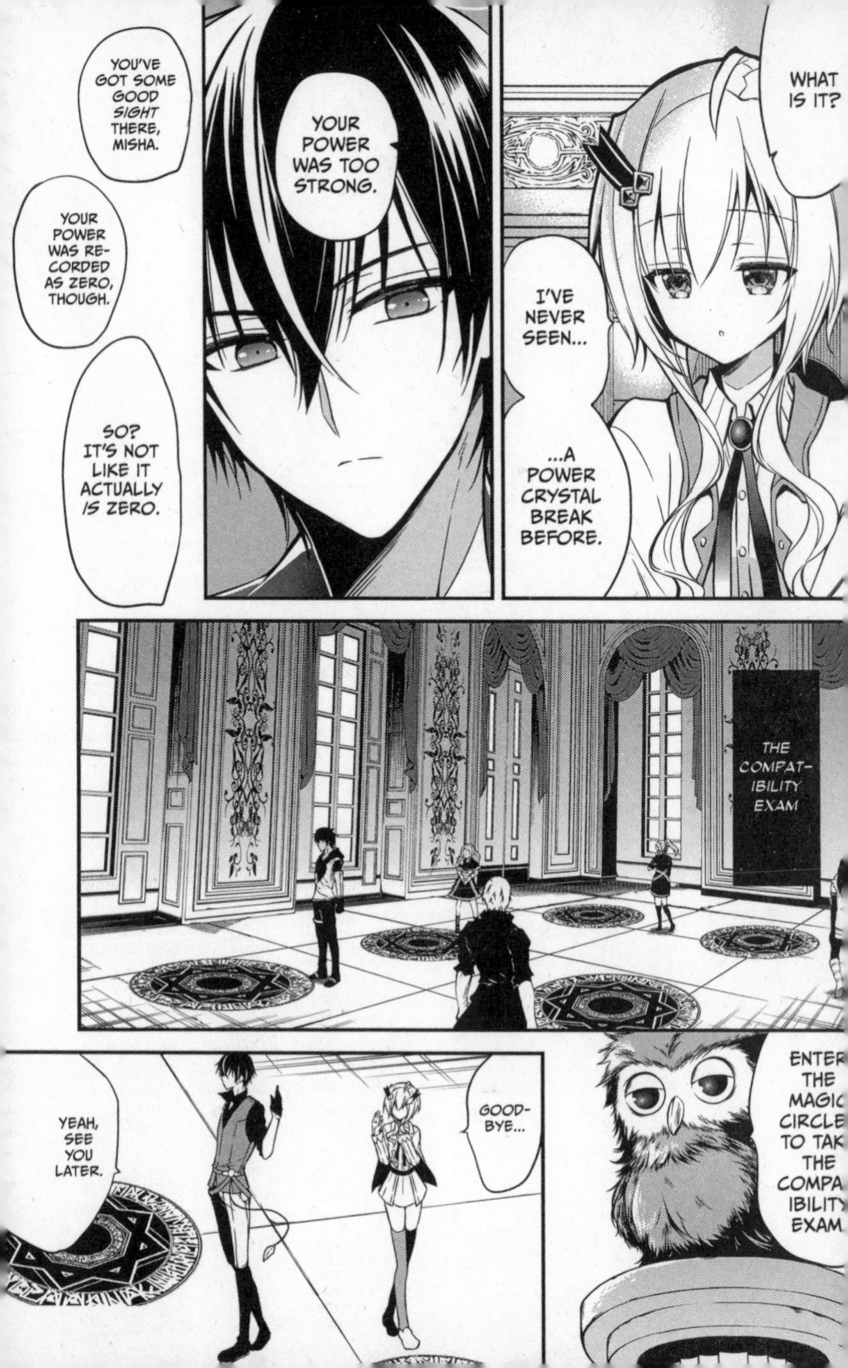
WHAT IS IT?
I'VE NEVER SEEN...
...A POWER CRYSTAL BREAK BEFORE.
YOUR POWER WAS TOO STRONG.
YOU'VE GOT SOME GOOD SIGHT THERE, MISHA.
YOUR POWER WAS RE-CORDED AS ZERO, THOUGH.
SO? IT'S NOT LIKE IT ACTUALLY IS ZERO.
THE COMPAT-IBILITY EXAM
ENTER THE MAGIC CIRCLE TO TAK THE COMPA IBILITY EXAM
... GOOD-BYE...
YEAH, SEE YOU LATER.

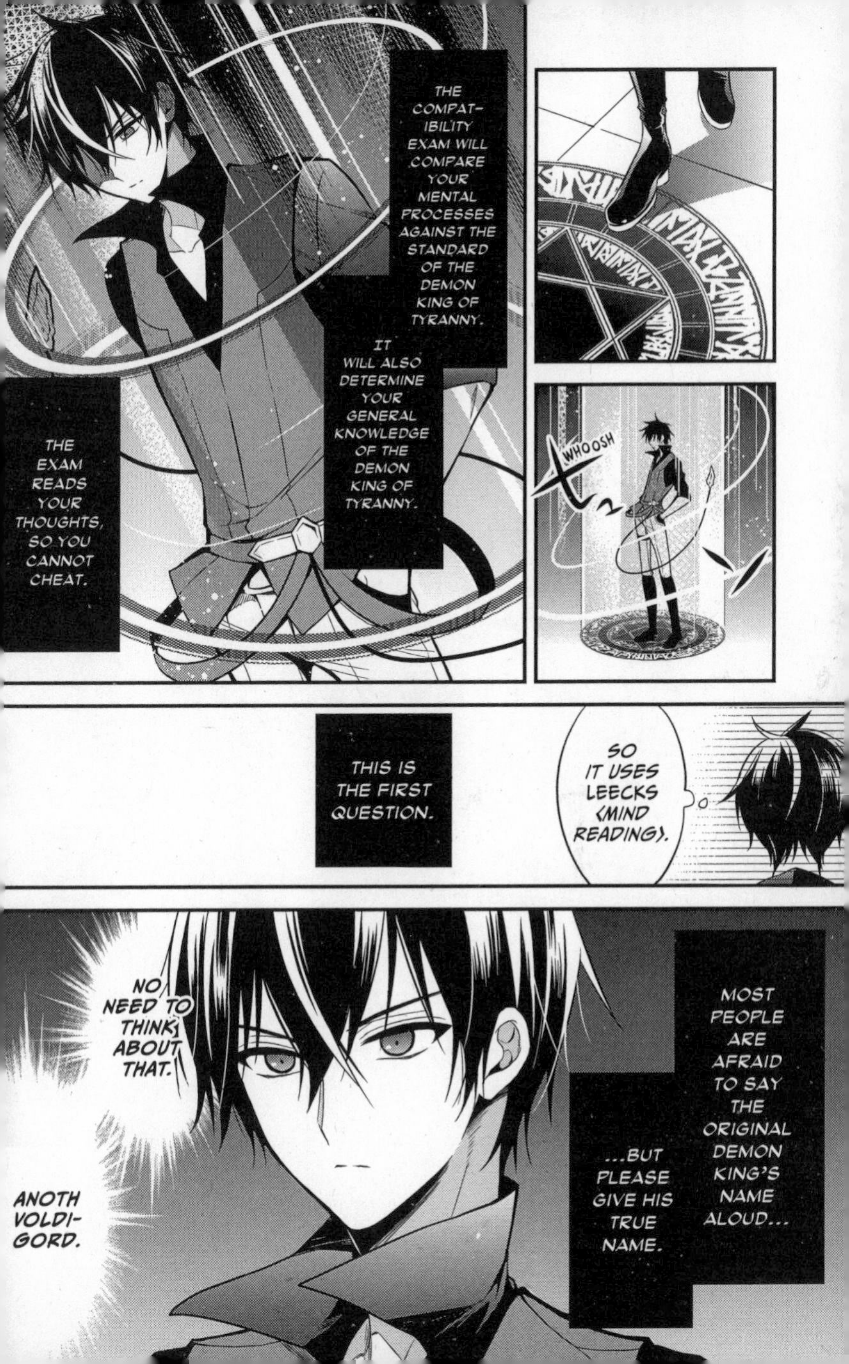
WHOOSH
THE COMPATIBILITY EXAM WILL COMPARE YOUR MENTAL PROCESSES AGAINST THE STANDARD OF THE DEMON KING OF TYRANNY.
IT WILL ALSO DETERMINE YOUR GENERAL KNOWLEDGE OF THE DEMON KING OF TYRANNY.
THE EXAM READS YOUR THOUGHTS, SO YOU CANNOT CHEAT.
SO IT USES LEECKS <MIND READING>.
THIS IS THE FIRST QUESTION.
MOST PEOPLE ARE AFRAID TO SAY THE ORIGINAL DEMON KING'S NAME ALOUD...
...BUT PLEASE GIVE HIS TRUE NAME.
NO NEED TO THINK ABOUT THAT.
ANOTH VOLDIGORD.

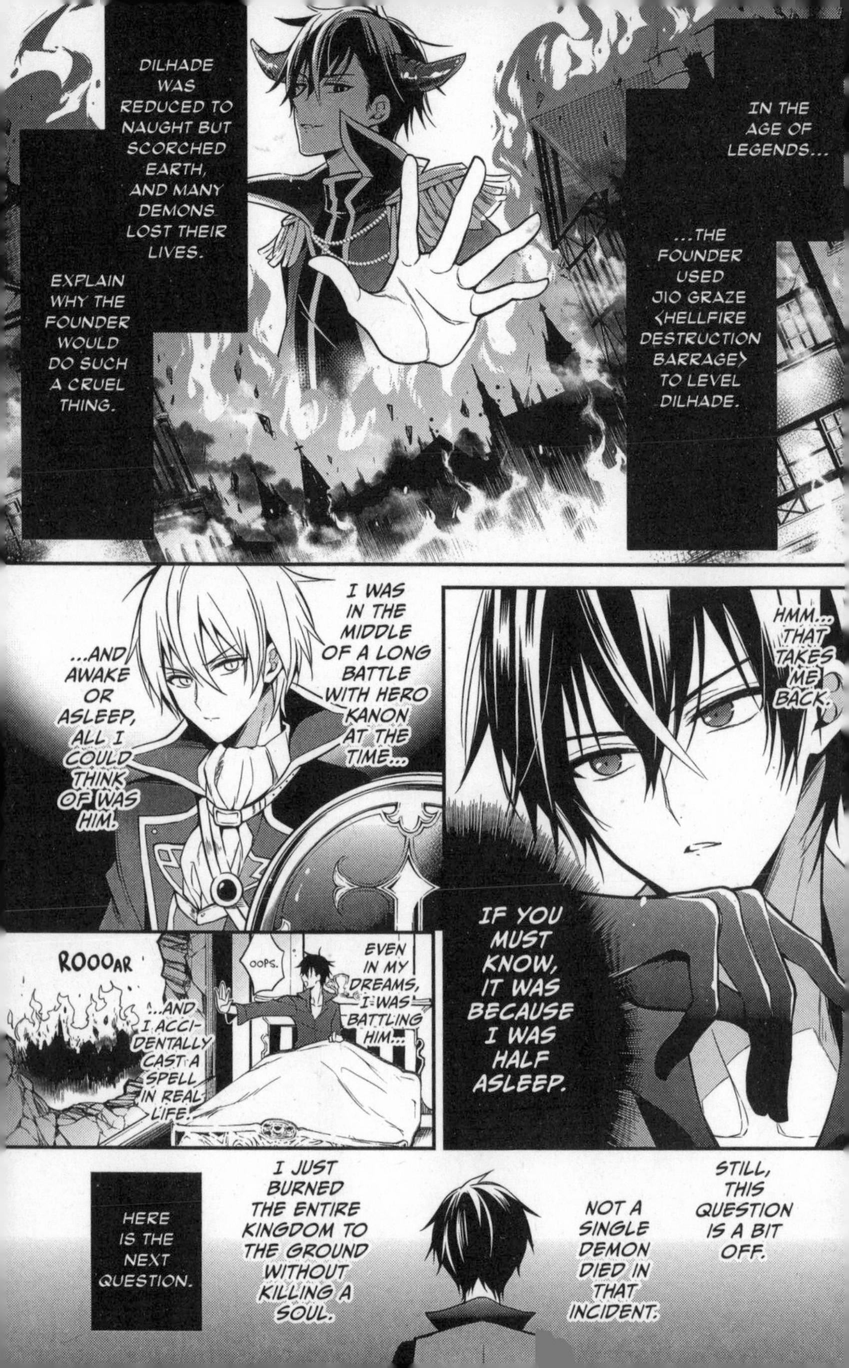
IN THE AGE OF LEGENDS...
...THE FOUNDER USED JIO GRAZE <HELLFIRE DESTRUCTION BARRAGE> TO LEVEL DILHADE.
DILHADE WAS REDUCED TO NAUGHT BUT SCORCHED EARTH, AND MANY DEMONS LOST THEIR LIVES.
EXPLAIN WHY THE FOUNDER WOULD DO SUCH A CRUEL THING.
HMM... THAT TAKES ME BACK.
IF YOU MUST KNOW, IT WAS BECAUSE I WAS HALF ASLEEP.
I WAS IN THE MIDDLE OF A LONG BATTLE WITH HERO KANON AT THE TIME...
...AND AWAKE OR ASLEEP, ALL I COULD THINK OF WAS HIM.
EVEN IN MY DREAMS, I WAS BATTLING HIM...
OOPS.
...AND I ACCIDENTALLY CAST A SPELL IN REAL LIFE.
ROOOAR
STILL, THIS QUESTION IS A BIT OFF.
NOT A SINGLE DEMON DIED IN THAT INCIDENT.
I JUST BURNED THE ENTIRE KINGDOM TO THE GROUND WITHOUT KILLING A SOUL.
HERE IS THE NEXT QUESTION.

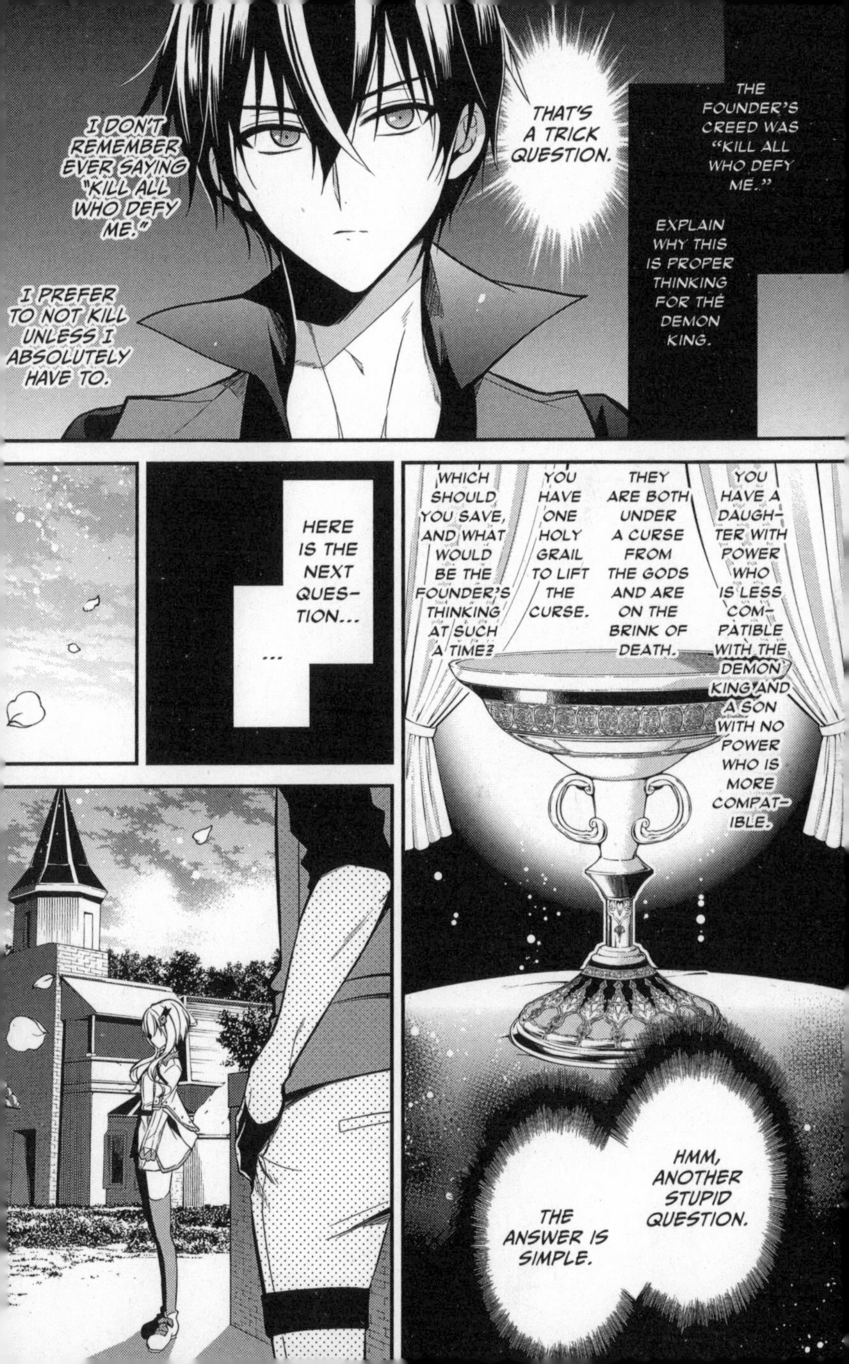
THE FOUNDER'S CREED WAS "KILL ALL WHO DEFY ME."
EXPLAIN WHY THIS IS PROPER THINKING FOR THE DEMON KING.
THAT'S A TRICK QUESTION.
I DON'T REMEMBER EVER SAYING "KILL ALL WHO DEFY ME."
I PREFER TO NOT KILL UNLESS I ABSOLUTELY HAVE TO.
YOU HAVE A DAUGHTER WITH POWER WHO IS LESS COMPATIBLE WITH THE DEMON KING AND A SON WITH NO POWER WHO IS MORE COMPATIBLE.
THEY ARE BOTH UNDER A CURSE FROM THE GODS AND ARE ON THE BRINK OF DEATH.
YOU HAVE ONE HOLY GRAIL TO LIFT THE CURSE.
WHICH SHOULD YOU SAVE, AND WHAT WOULD BE THE FOUNDER'S THINKING AT SUCH A TIME?
HMM, ANOTHER STUPID QUESTION.
THE ANSWER IS SIMPLE.
HERE IS THE NEXT QUESTION...
...

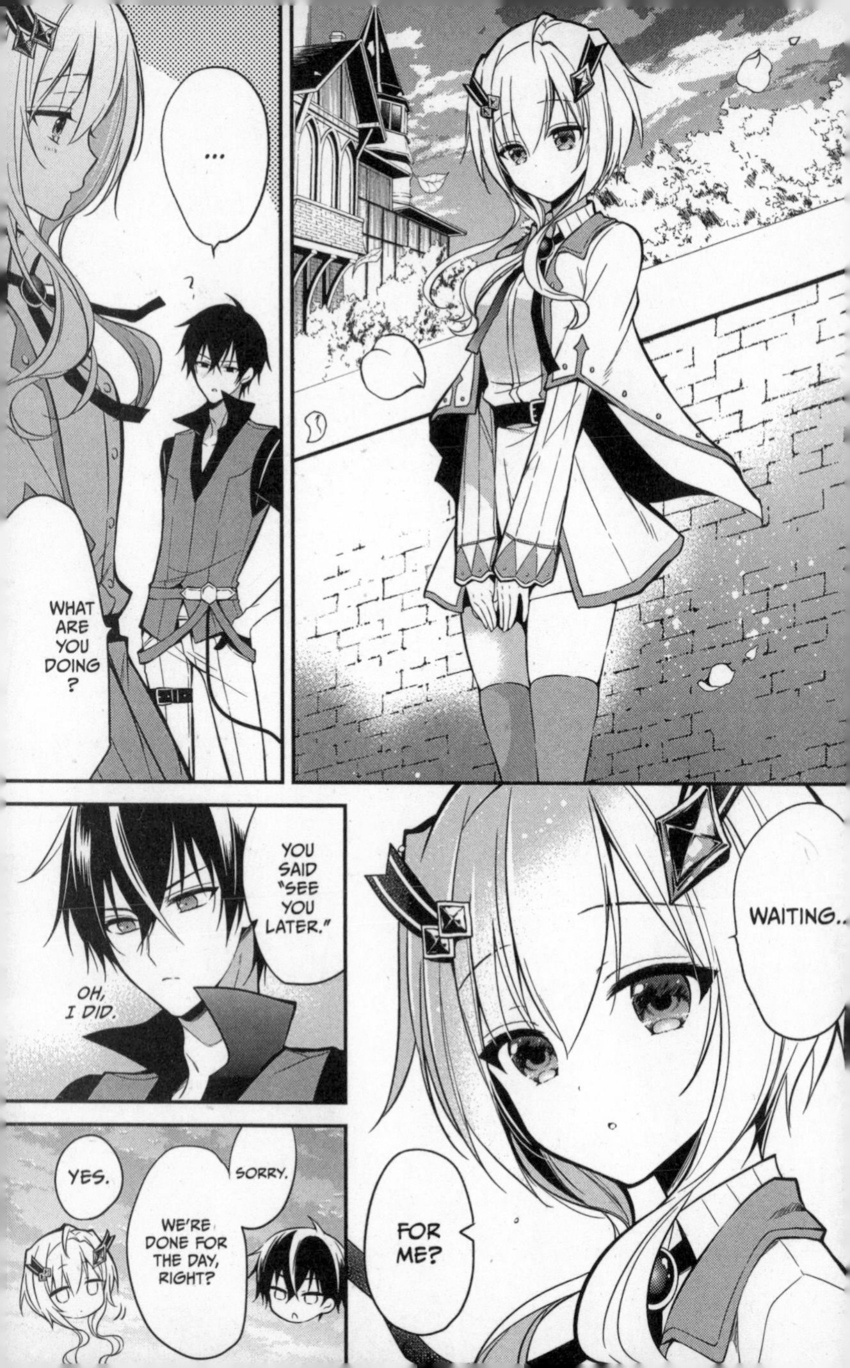
...
?
WHAT ARE YOU DOING?
WAITING...
FOR ME?
YOU SAID "SEE YOU LATER."
OH, I DID.
SORRY.
WE'RE DONE FOR THE DAY, RIGHT?
YES.

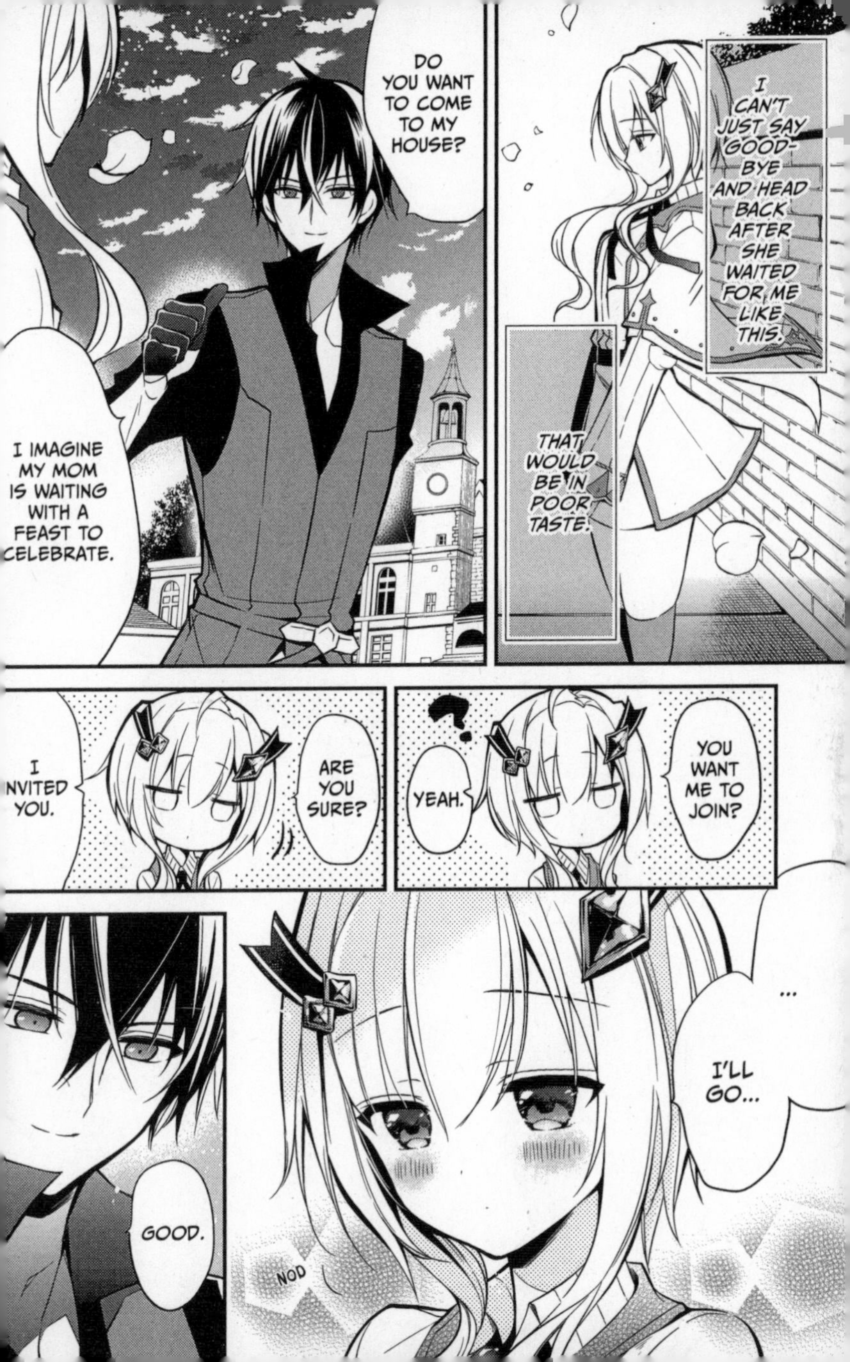

I CAN'T JUST SAY GOOD-BYE AND HEAD BACK AFTER SHE WAITED FOR ME LIKE THIS.
THAT WOULD BE IN POOR TASTE.
DO YOU WANT TO COME TO MY HOUSE?
I IMAGINE MY MOM IS WAITING WITH A FEAST TO CELEBRATE.
YOU WANT ME TO JOIN?
YEAH.
ARE YOU SURE?
I NVITED YOU.
...
I'LL GO...
NOD
GOOD.

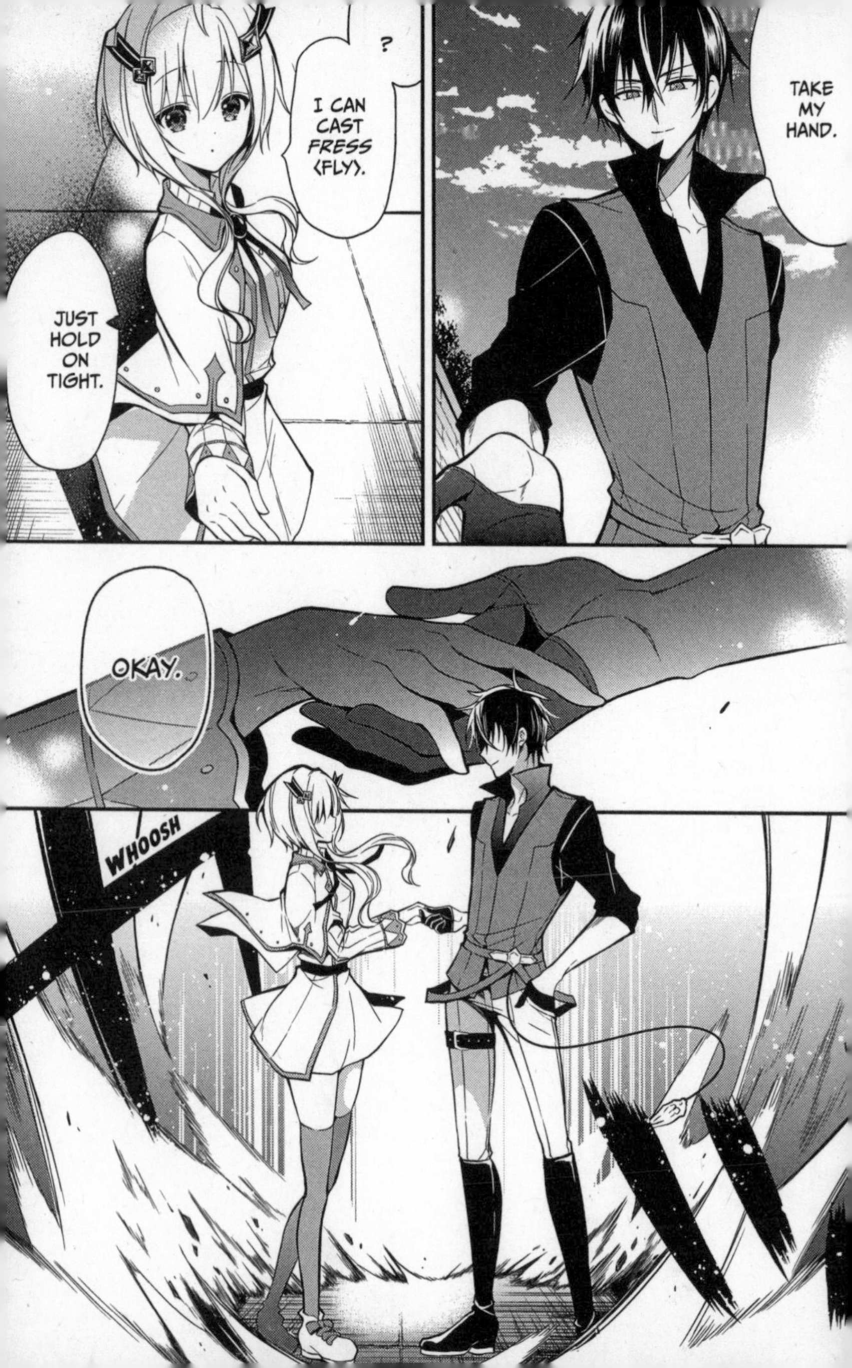
TAKE MY HAND.
?
I CAN CAST FRESS <FLY>.
JUST HOLD ON TIGHT.
OKAY.
WHOOSH

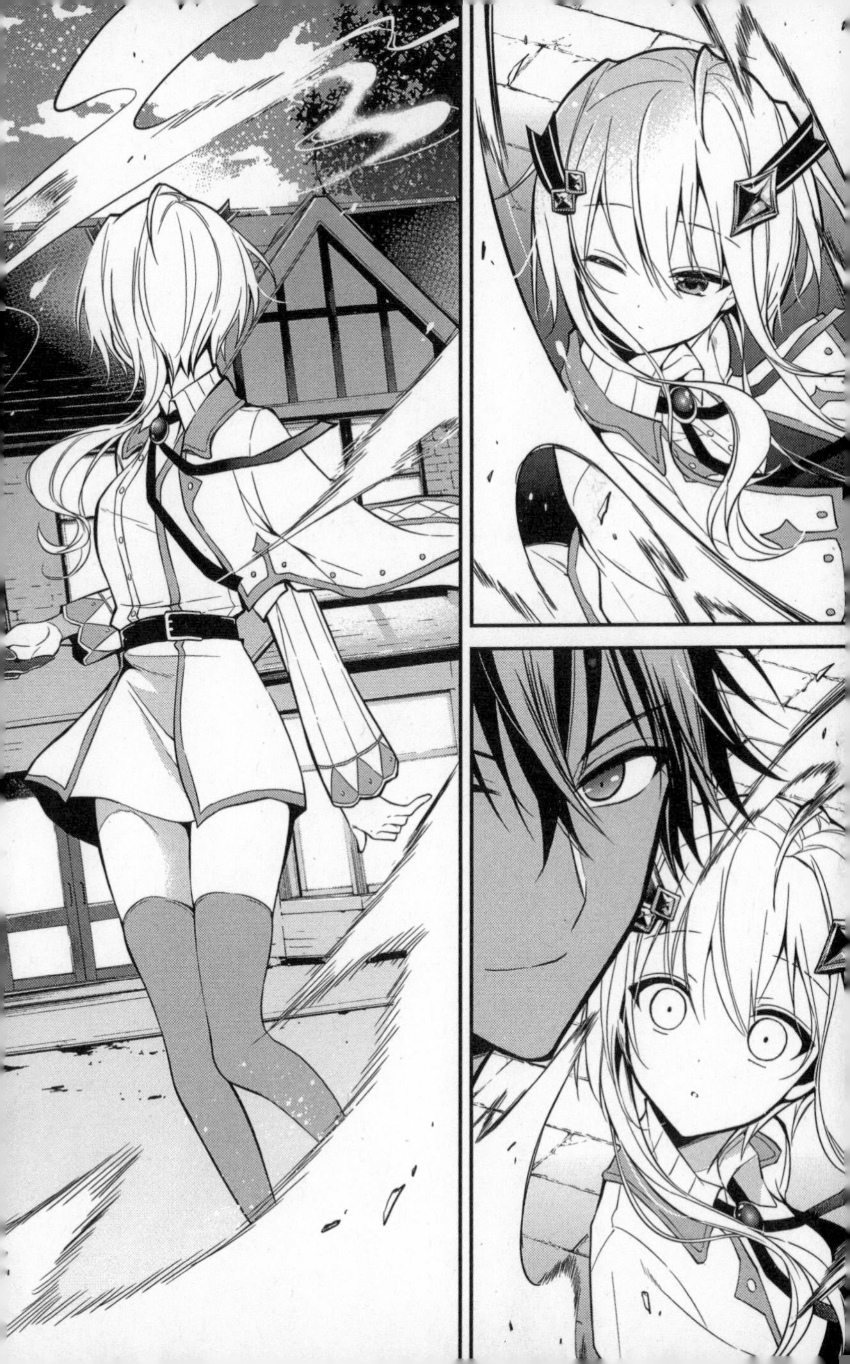

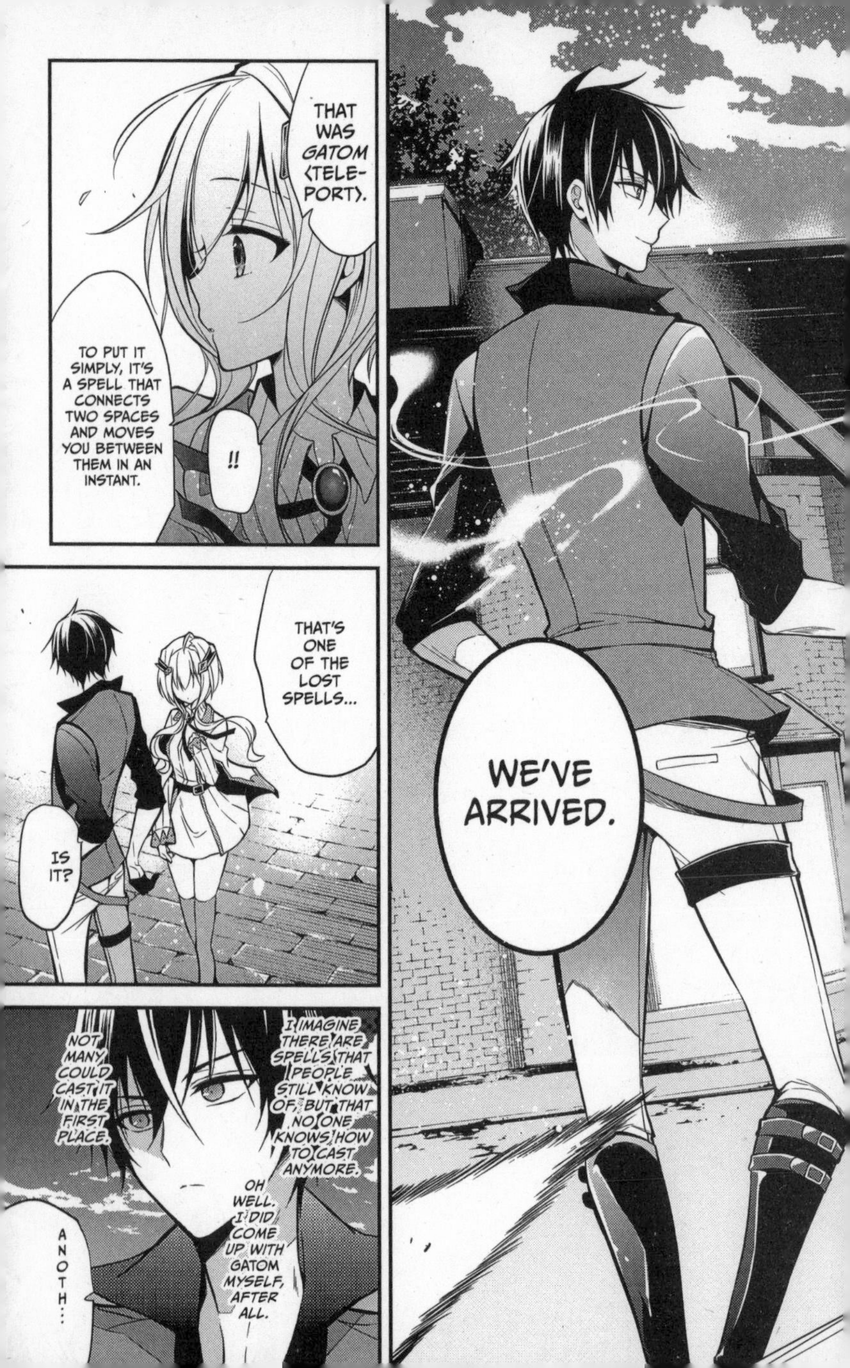
WE'VE ARRIVED.
THAT WAS GATOM ⟨TELEPORT⟩.
!!
TO PUT IT SIMPLY, IT'S A SPELL THAT CONNECTS TWO SPACES AND MOVES YOU BETWEEN THEM IN AN INSTANT.
THAT'S ONE OF THE LOST SPELLS...
IS IT?
I IMAGINE THERE ARE SPELLS THAT PEOPLE STILL KNOW OF, BUT THAT NO ONE KNOWS HOW TO CAST ANYMORE.
NOT MANY COULD CAST IT IN THE FIRST PLACE.
OH WELL. I DID COME UP WITH GATOM MYSELF, AFTER ALL.
ANOTH...

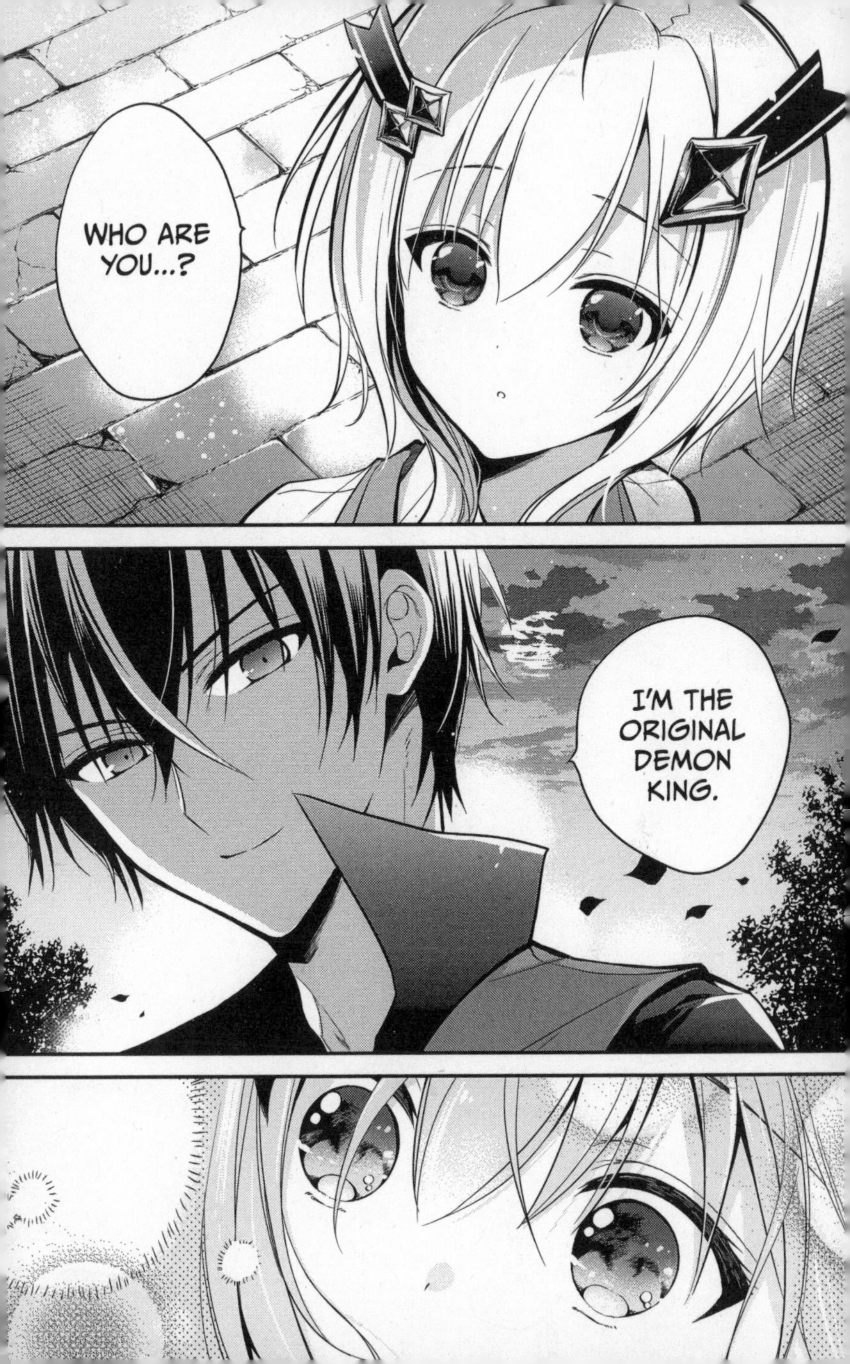
WHO ARE YOU...?
I'M THE ORIGINAL DEMON KING.

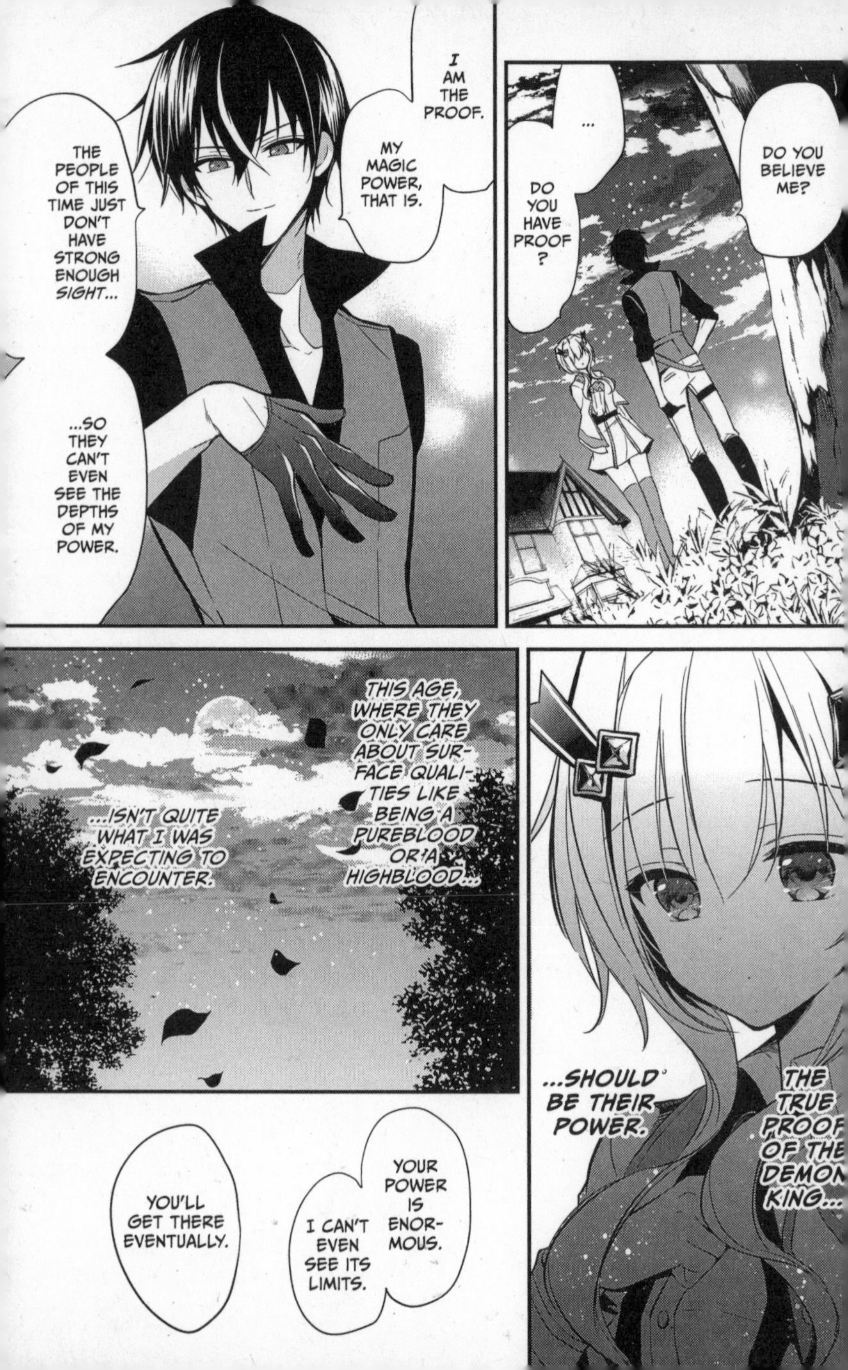
DO YOU BELIEVE ME?
...
DO YOU HAVE PROOF?
I AM THE PROOF.
MY MAGIC POWER, THAT IS.
THE PEOPLE OF THIS TIME JUST DON'T HAVE STRONG ENOUGH SIGHT...
...SO THEY CAN'T EVEN SEE THE DEPTHS OF MY POWER.
THE TRUE PROOF OF THE DEMON KING...
...SHOULD BE THEIR POWER.
THIS AGE, WHERE THEY ONLY CARE ABOUT SURFACE QUALITIES LIKE BEING A PUREBLOOD OR A HIGHBLOOD...
...ISN'T QUITE WHAT I WAS EXPECTING TO ENCOUNTER.
YOUR POWER IS ENORMOUS.
I CAN'T EVEN SEE ITS LIMITS.
YOU'LL GET THERE EVENTUALLY.

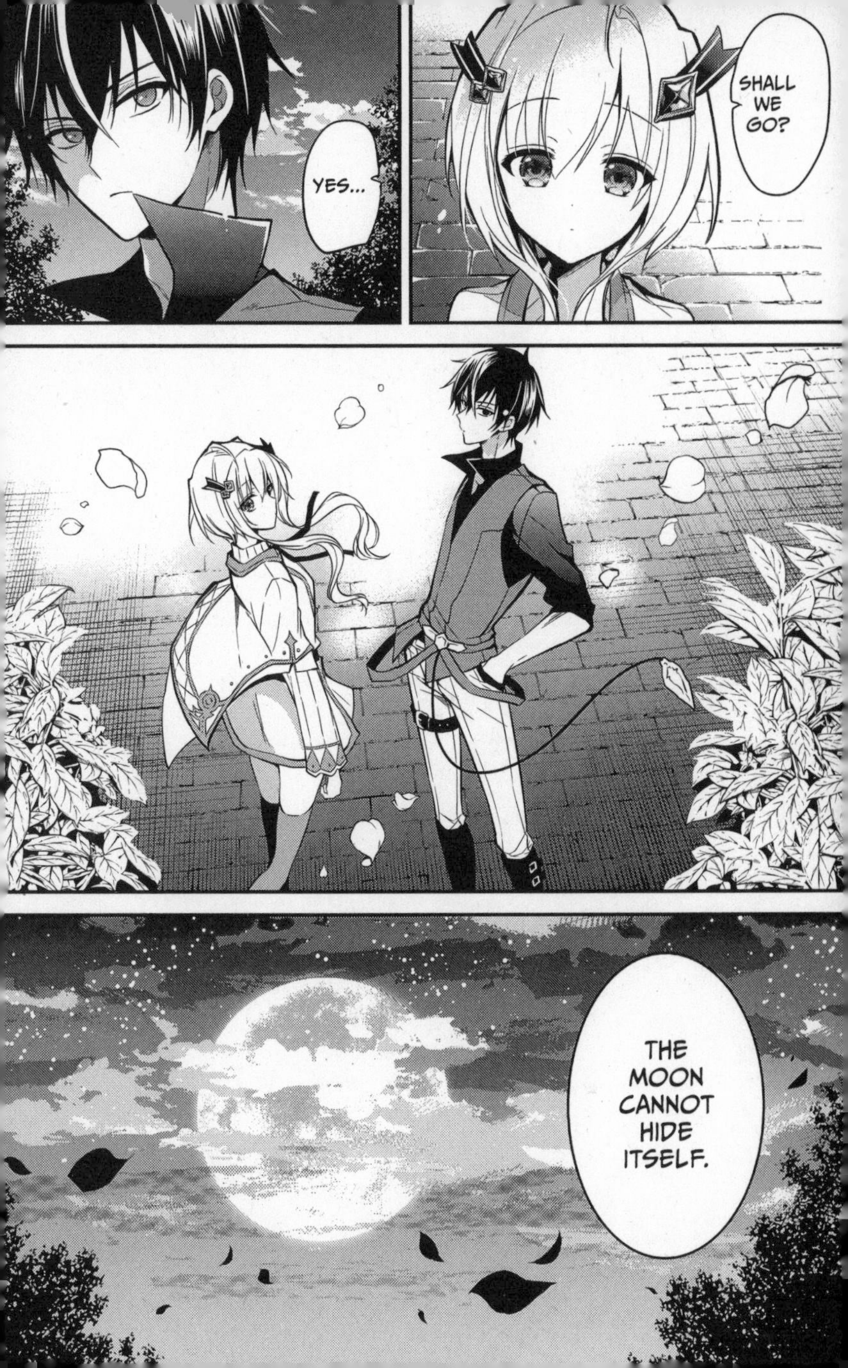
SHALL WE GO?
YES...
THE MOON CANNOT HIDE ITSELF.

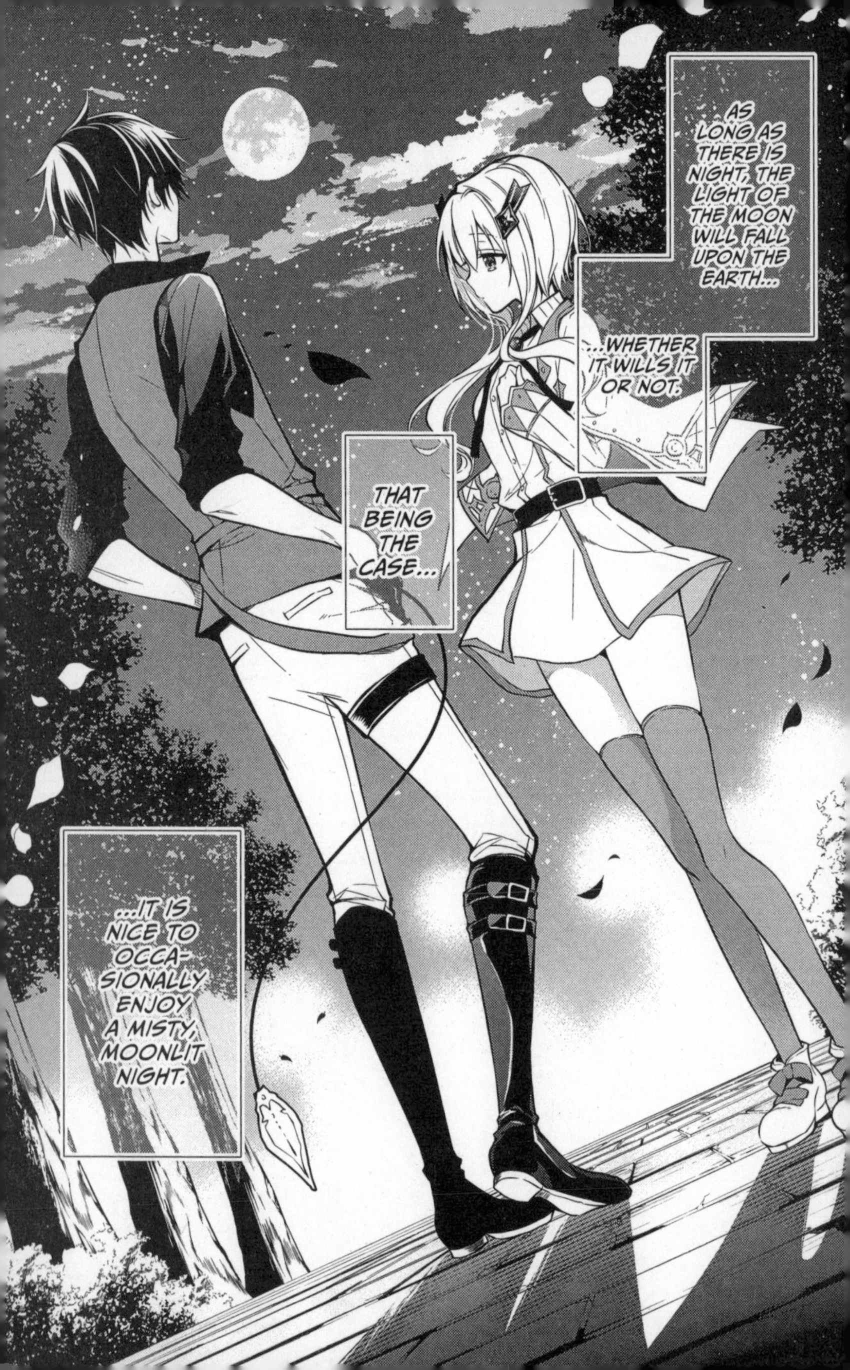
AS LONG AS THERE IS NIGHT, THE LIGHT OF THE MOON WILL FALL UPON THE EARTH...
...WHETHER IT WILLS IT OR NOT.
THAT BEING THE CASE...
...IT IS NICE TO OCCA-SIONALLY ENJOY A MISTY, MOONLIT NIGHT.

The Misfit of Demon King Academy

HISTORY'S STRONGEST DEMON KING REINCARNATES AND GOES TO SCHOOL WITH HIS DESCENDANTS

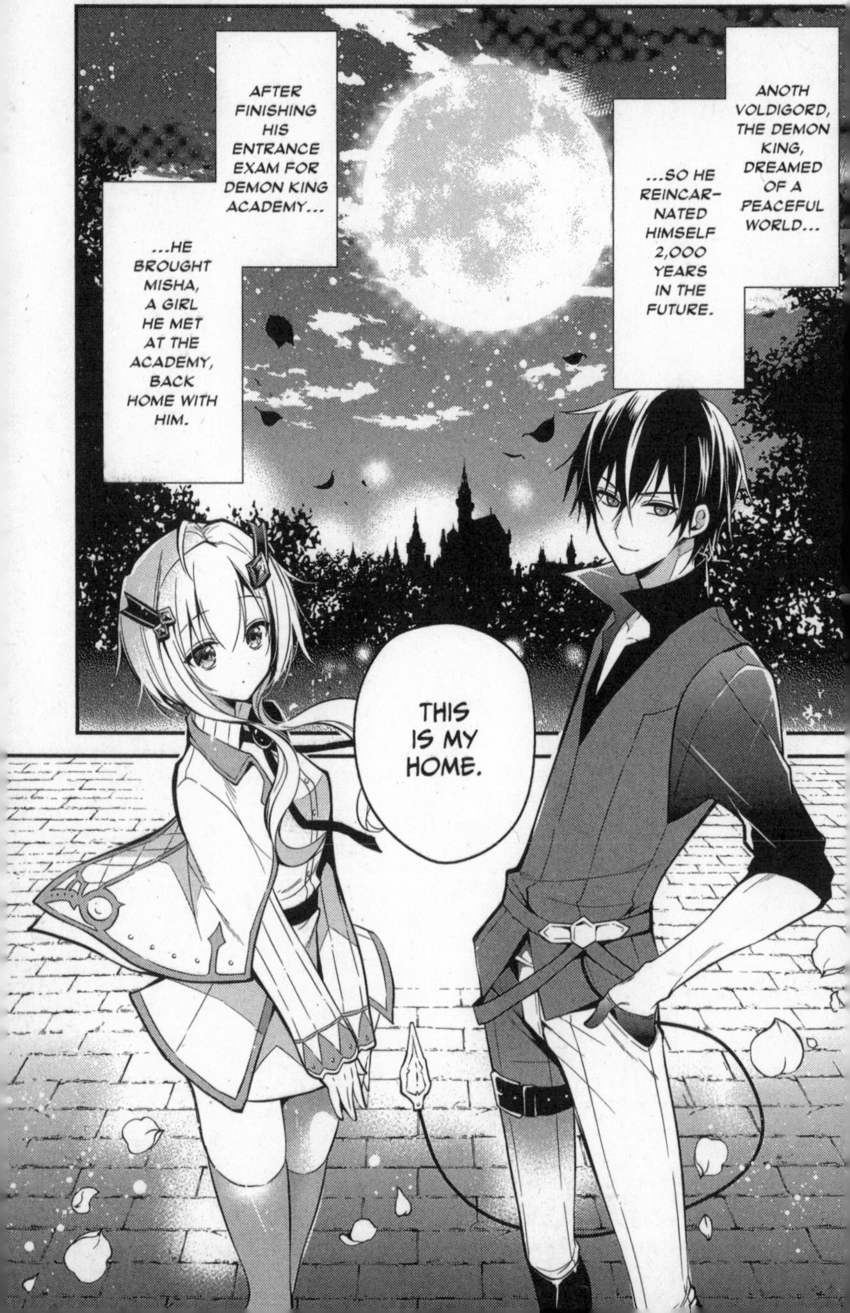
ANOTH VOLDIGORD, THE DEMON KING, DREAMED OF A PEACEFUL WORLD...
...SO HE REINCAR-NATED HIMSELF 2,000 YEARS IN THE FUTURE.
AFTER FINISHING HIS ENTRANCE EXAM FOR DEMON KING ACADEMY...
...HE BROUGHT MISHA, A GIRL HE MET AT THE ACADEMY, BACK HOME WITH HIM.
THIS IS MY HOME.

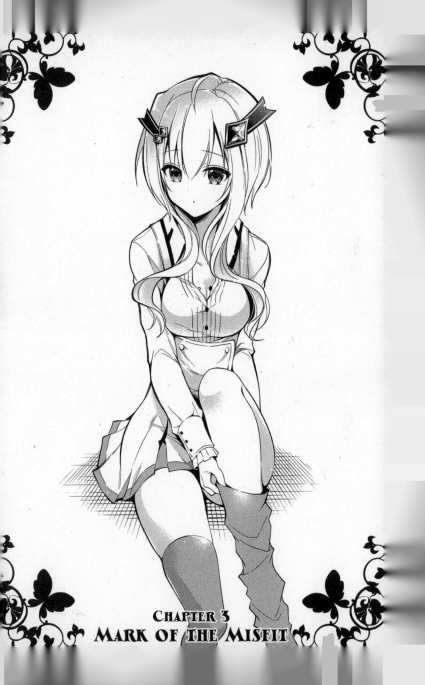

CHAPTER 3
MARK OF THE MISFIT

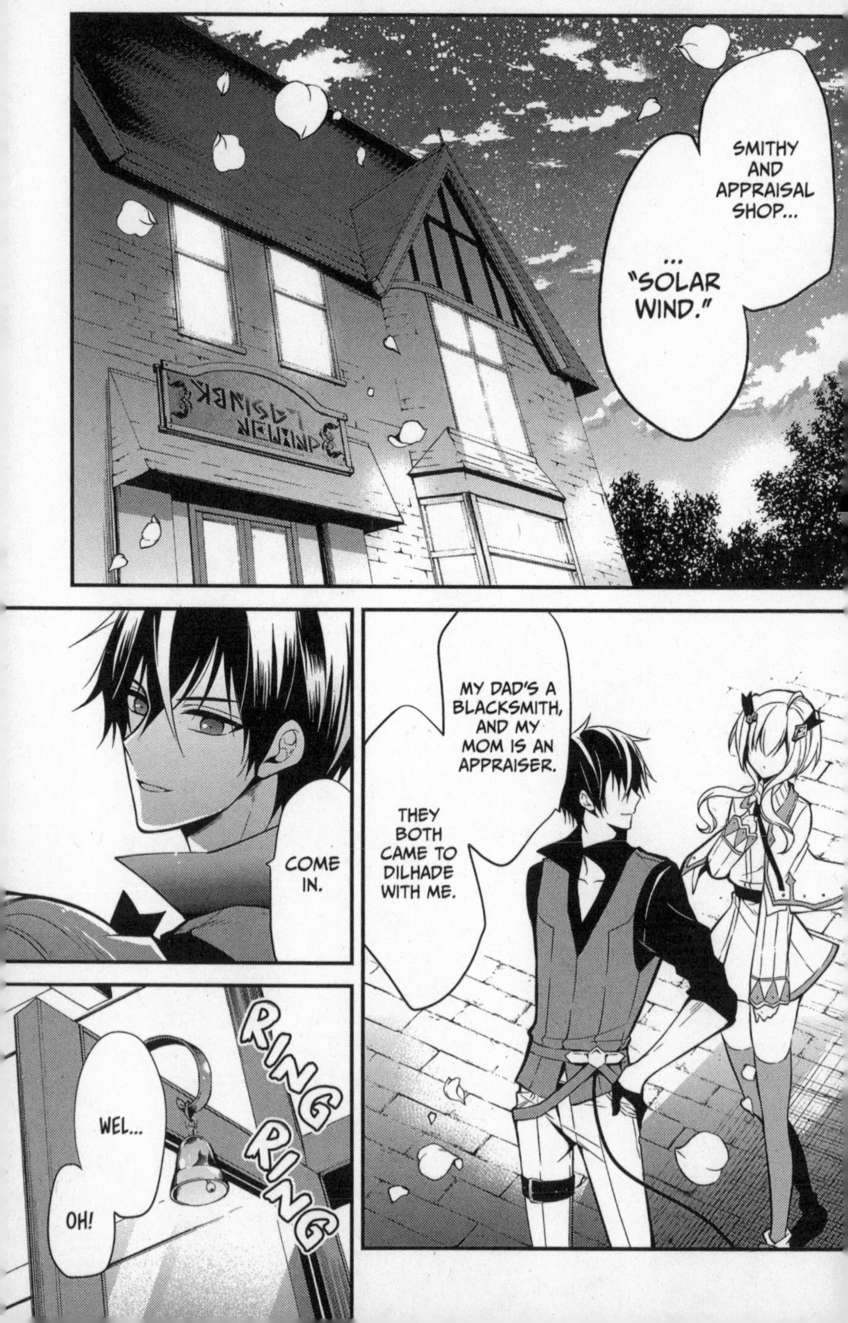
SMITHY AND APPRAISAL SHOP...
... "SOLAR WIND."
MY DAD'S A BLACKSMITH, AND MY MOM IS AN APPRAISER.
THEY BOTH CAME TO DILHADE WITH ME.
COME IN.
RING RING
WEL...
OH!

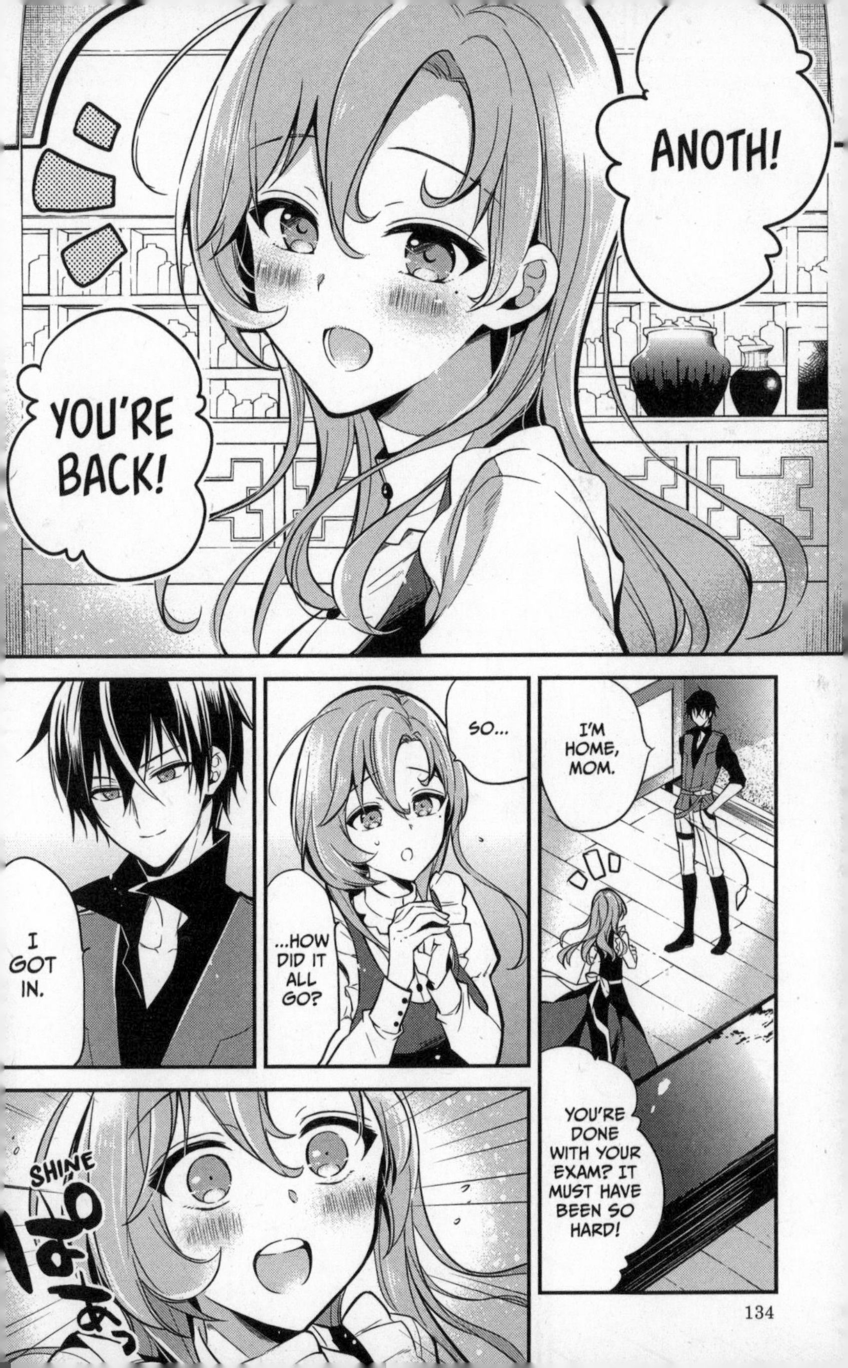
ANOTH!
YOU'RE BACK!
I'M HOME, MOM.
YOU'RE DONE WITH YOUR EXAM? IT MUST HAVE BEEN SO HARD!
SO...
...HOW DID IT ALL GO?
I GOT IN.
SHINE

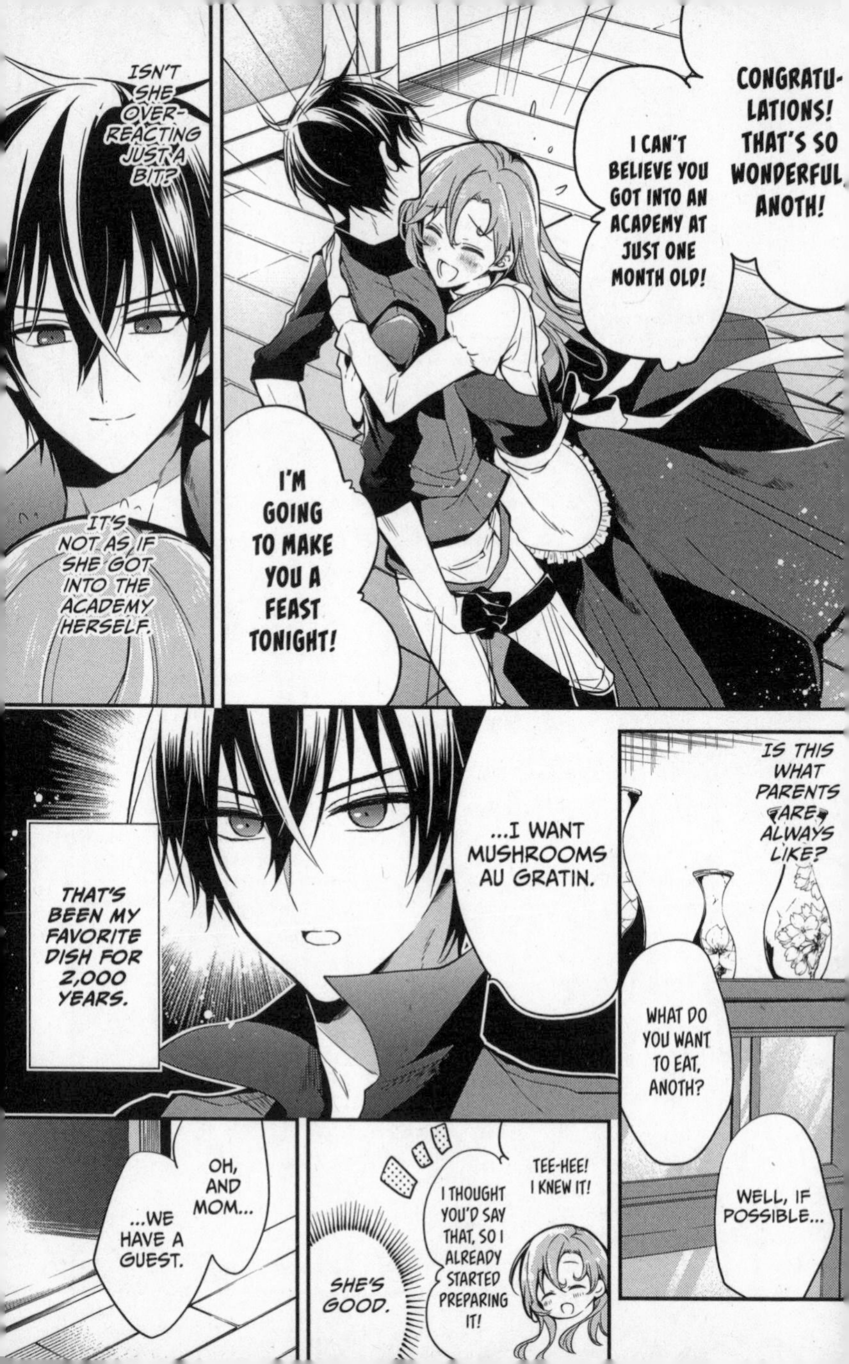
CONGRATULATIONS! THAT'S SO WONDERFUL, ANOTH!
I CAN'T BELIEVE YOU GOT INTO AN ACADEMY AT JUST ONE MONTH OLD!
I'M GOING TO MAKE YOU A FEAST TONIGHT!
ISN'T SHE OVER-REACTING JUST A BIT?
IT'S NOT AS IF SHE GOT INTO THE ACADEMY HERSELF.
IS THIS WHAT PARENTS ARE ALWAYS LIKE?
WHAT DO YOU WANT TO EAT, ANOTH?
WELL, IF POSSIBLE...
...I WANT MUSHROOMS AU GRATIN.
THAT'S BEEN MY FAVORITE DISH FOR 2,000 YEARS.
TEE-HEE! I KNEW IT!
I THOUGHT YOU'D SAY THAT, SO I ALREADY STARTED PREPARING IT!
SHE'S GOOD.
OH, AND MOM...
...WE HAVE A GUEST.

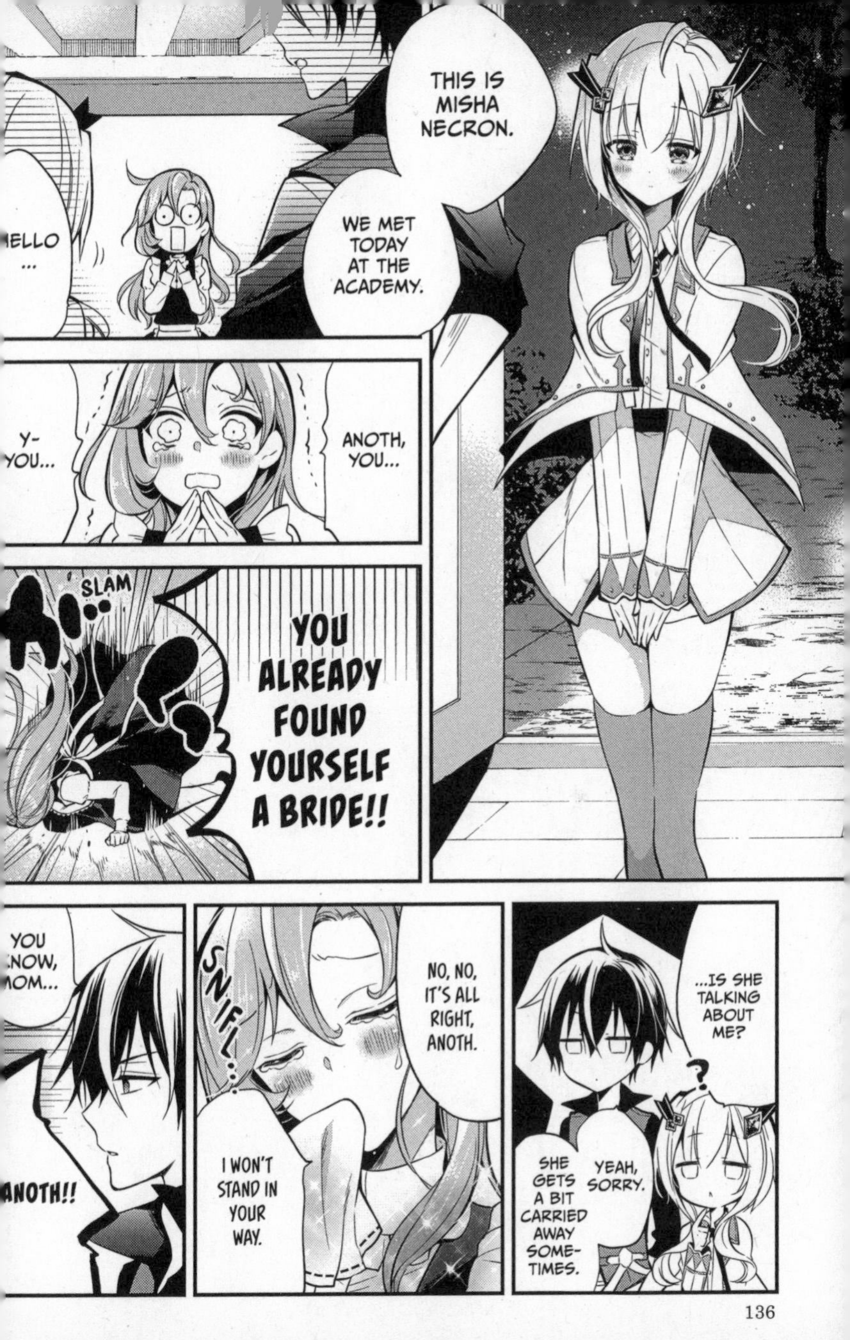
THIS IS MISHA NECRON.
WE MET TODAY AT THE ACADEMY.
ELLO ...
ANOTH, YOU...
Y- YOU...
YOU ALREADY FOUND YOURSELF A BRIDE!!
SLAM
...IS SHE TALKING ABOUT ME?
?
YEAH, SORRY.
SHE GETS A BIT CARRIED AWAY SOME-TIMES.
NO, NO, IT'S ALL RIGHT, ANOTH.
SNIFL...
I WON'T STAND IN YOUR WAY.
YOU NOW, OM...
NOTH!!

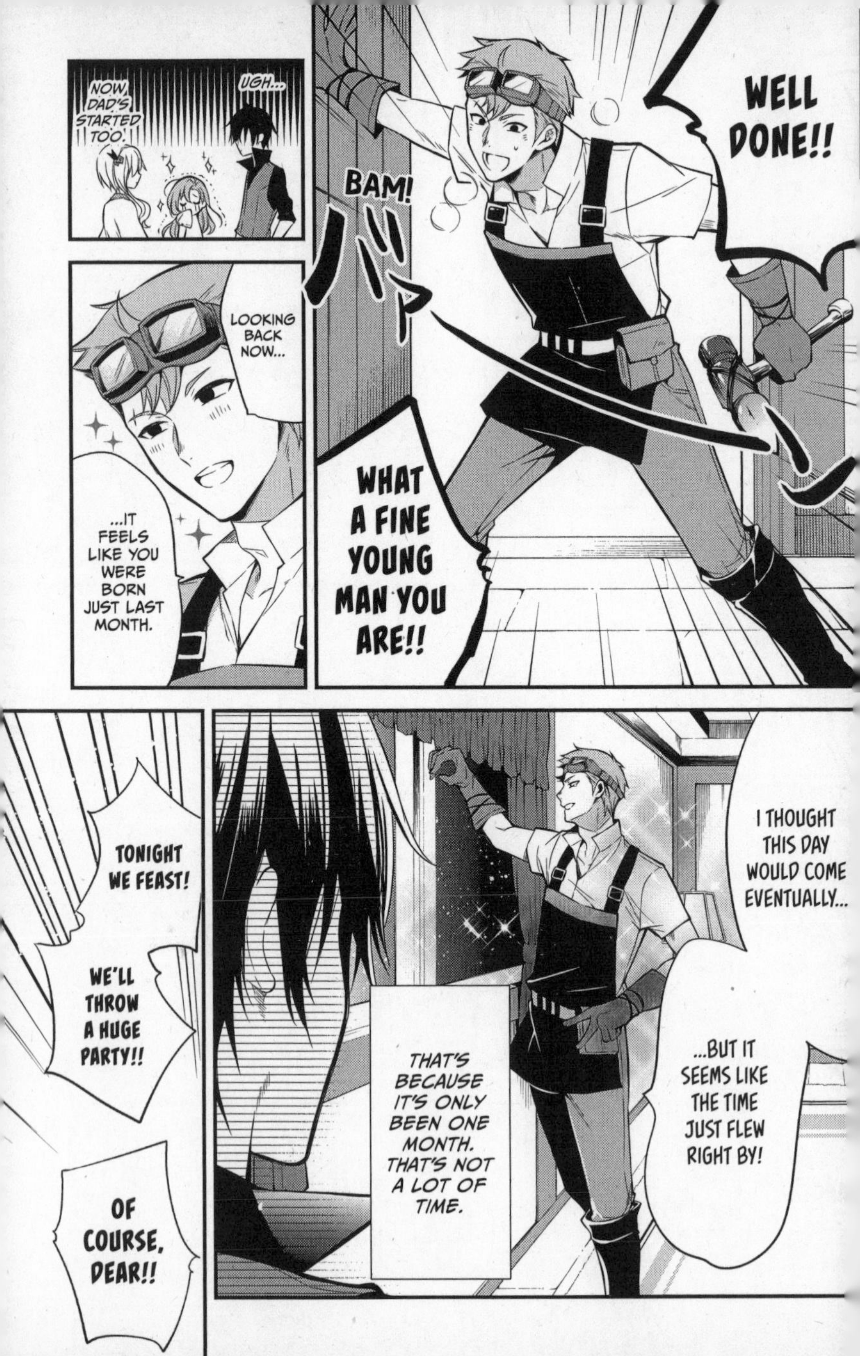
WELL DONE!!
BAM!
WHAT A FINE YOUNG MAN YOU ARE!!
UGH...
NOW DAD'S STARTED TOO.
LOOKING BACK NOW...
...IT FEELS LIKE YOU WERE BORN JUST LAST MONTH.
I THOUGHT THIS DAY WOULD COME EVENTUALLY...
...BUT IT SEEMS LIKE THE TIME JUST FLEW RIGHT BY!
THAT'S BECAUSE IT'S ONLY BEEN ONE MONTH. THAT'S NOT A LOT OF TIME.
TONIGHT WE FEAST!
WE'LL THROW A HUGE PARTY!!
OF COURSE, DEAR!!

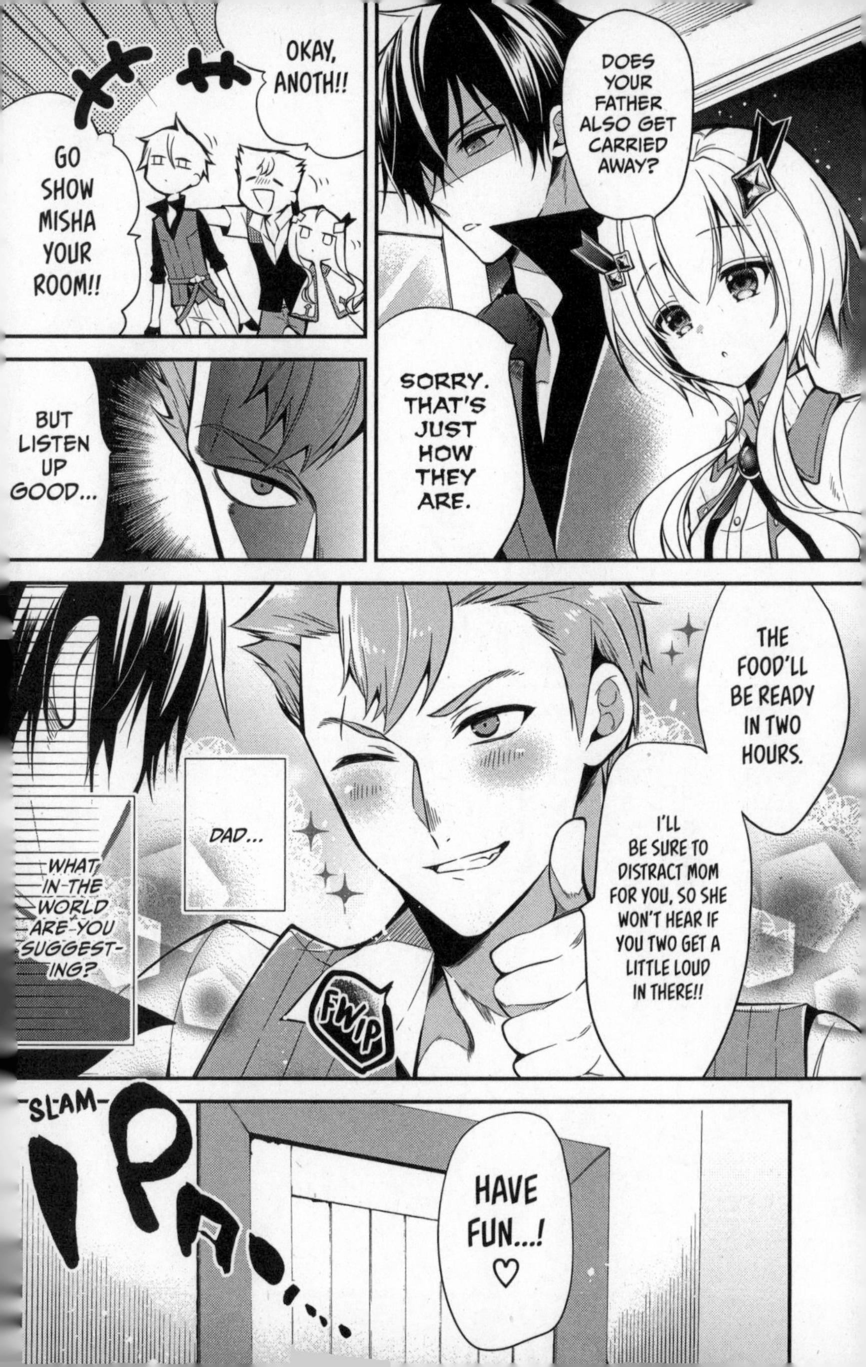
DOES YOUR FATHER ALSO GET CARRIED AWAY?
SORRY. THAT'S JUST HOW THEY ARE.
OKAY, ANOTH!!
GO SHOW MISHA YOUR ROOM!!
BUT LISTEN UP GOOD...
THE FOOD'LL BE READY IN TWO HOURS.
I'LL BE SURE TO DISTRACT MOM FOR YOU, SO SHE WON'T HEAR IF YOU TWO GET A LITTLE LOUD IN THERE!!
FWIP
DAD...
WHAT IN THE WORLD ARE YOU SUGGESTING?
HAVE FUN...! ♡
SLAM

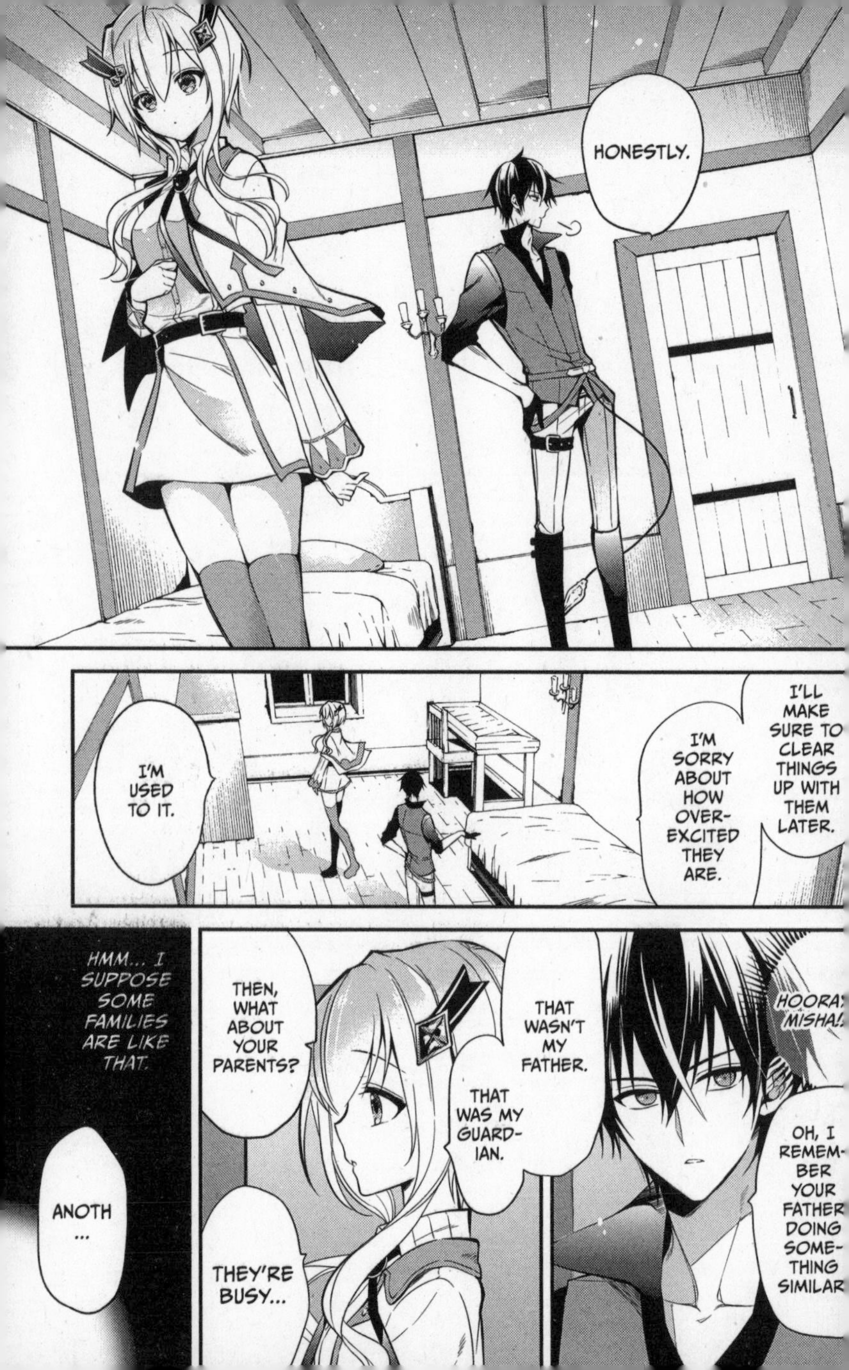
HONESTLY.
I'LL MAKE SURE TO CLEAR THINGS UP WITH THEM LATER.
I'M SORRY ABOUT HOW OVER-EXCITED THEY ARE.
I'M USED TO IT.
HOORA MISHA!
OH, I REMEMBER YOUR FATHER DOING SOMETHING SIMILAR
THAT WASN'T MY FATHER.
THAT WAS MY GUARDIAN.
THEN, WHAT ABOUT YOUR PARENTS?
THEY'RE BUSY...
HMM... I SUPPOSE SOME FAMILIES ARE LIKE THAT.
ANOTH ...

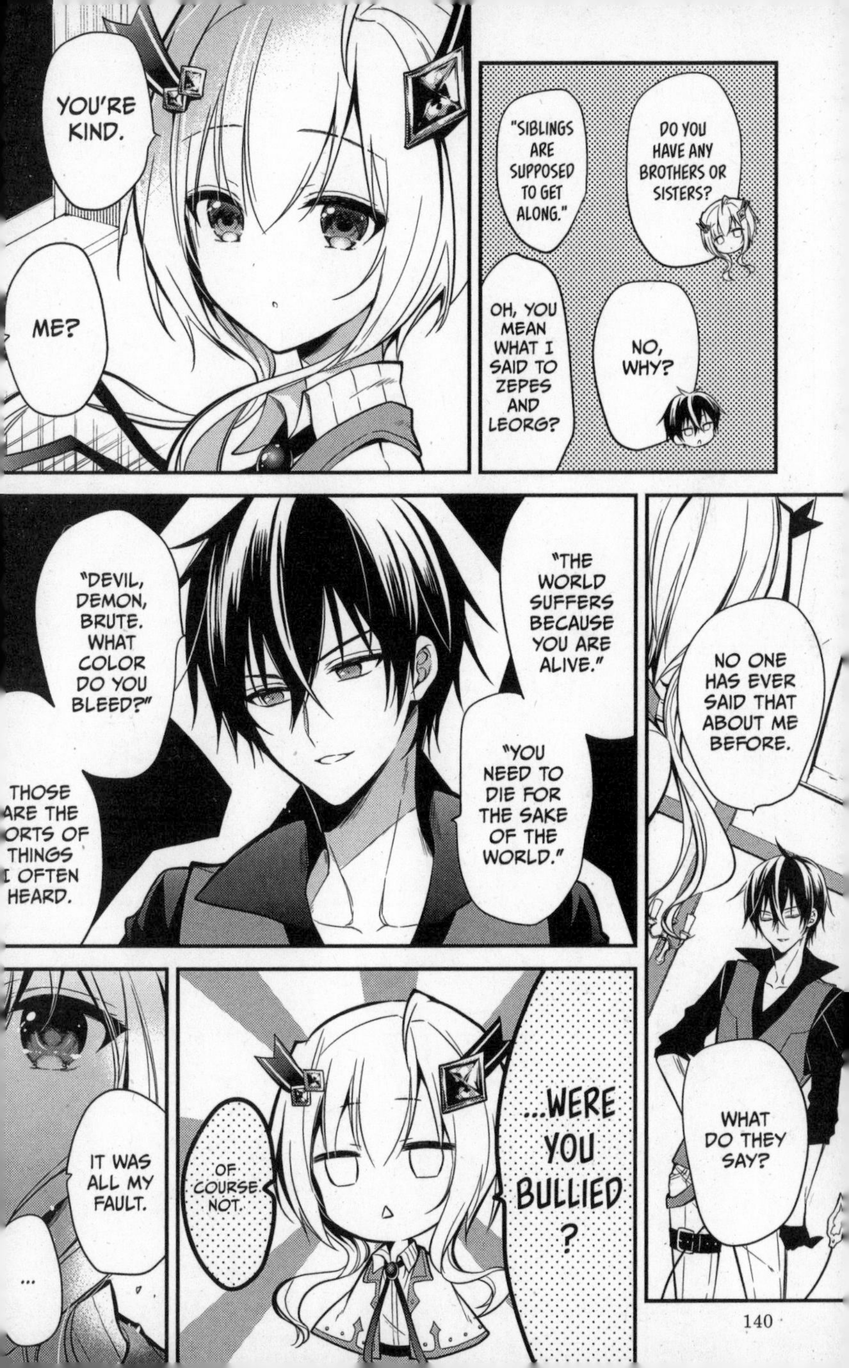
DO YOU HAVE ANY BROTHERS OR SISTERS?
NO, WHY?
"SIBLINGS ARE SUPPOSED TO GET ALONG."
OH, YOU MEAN WHAT I SAID TO ZEPES AND LEORG?
YOU'RE KIND.
ME?
NO ONE HAS EVER SAID THAT ABOUT ME BEFORE.
WHAT DO THEY SAY?
"THE WORLD SUFFERS BECAUSE YOU ARE ALIVE."
"YOU NEED TO DIE FOR THE SAKE OF THE WORLD."
"DEVIL, DEMON, BRUTE. WHAT COLOR DO YOU BLEED?"
THOSE ARE THE ORTS OF THINGS I OFTEN HEARD.
...WERE YOU BULLIED?
OF COURSE NOT.
IT WAS ALL MY FAULT.
...

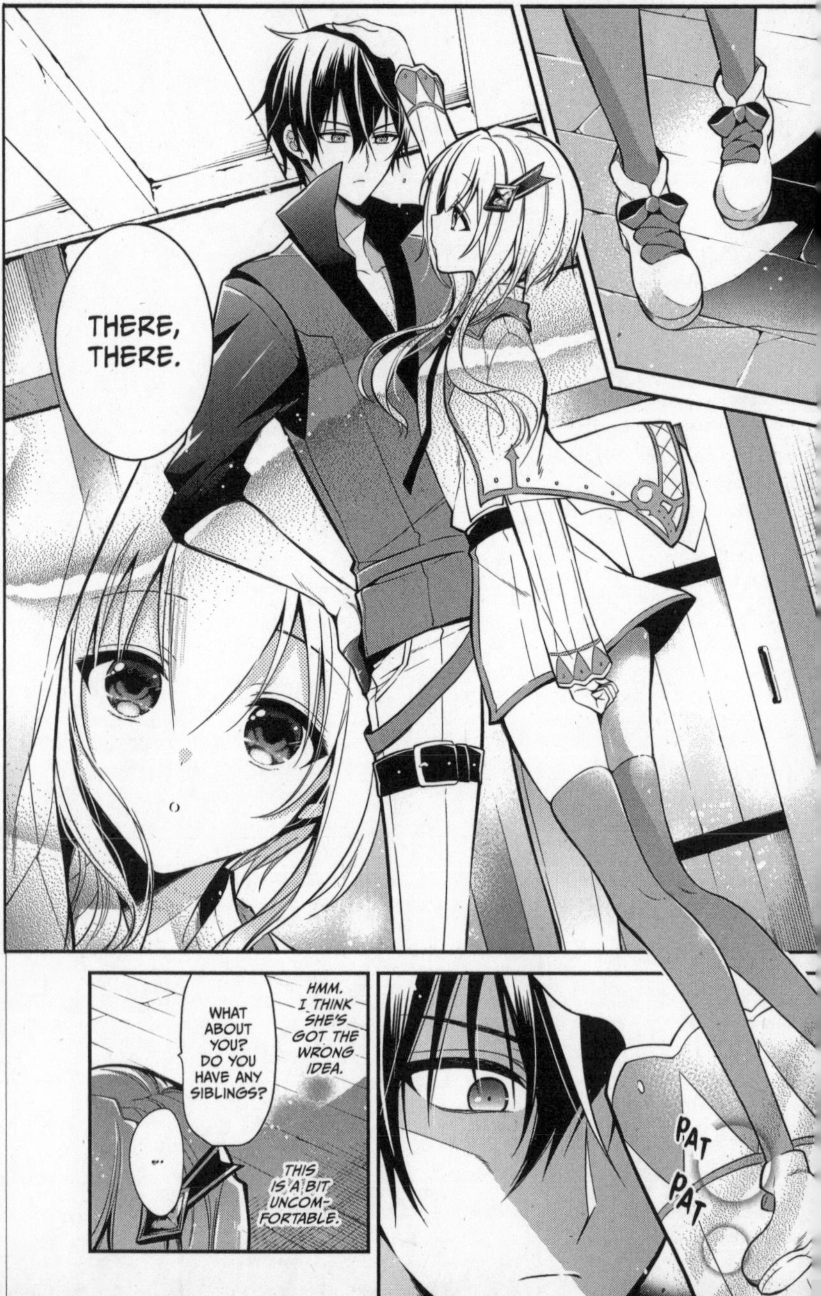
THERE, THERE.
PAT PAT
HMM. I THINK SHE'S GOT THE WRONG IDEA.
WHAT ABOUT YOU? DO YOU HAVE ANY SIBLINGS?
THIS IS A BIT UNCOM-FORTABLE.
...

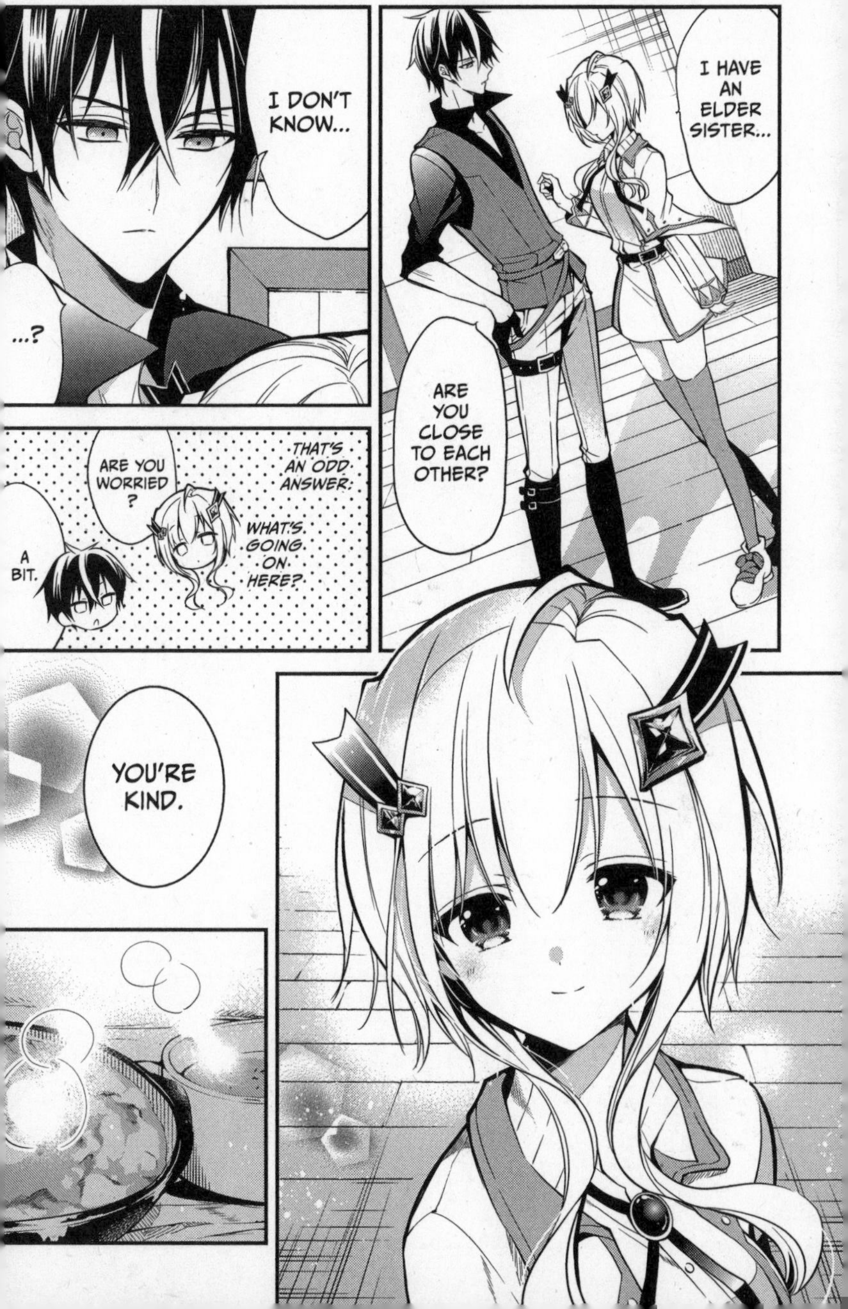
I HAVE AN ELDER SISTER...
ARE YOU CLOSE TO EACH OTHER?
I DON'T KNOW...
...?
THAT'S AN ODD ANSWER.
ARE YOU WORRIED?
WHAT'S GOING ON HERE?
A BIT.
YOU'RE KIND.

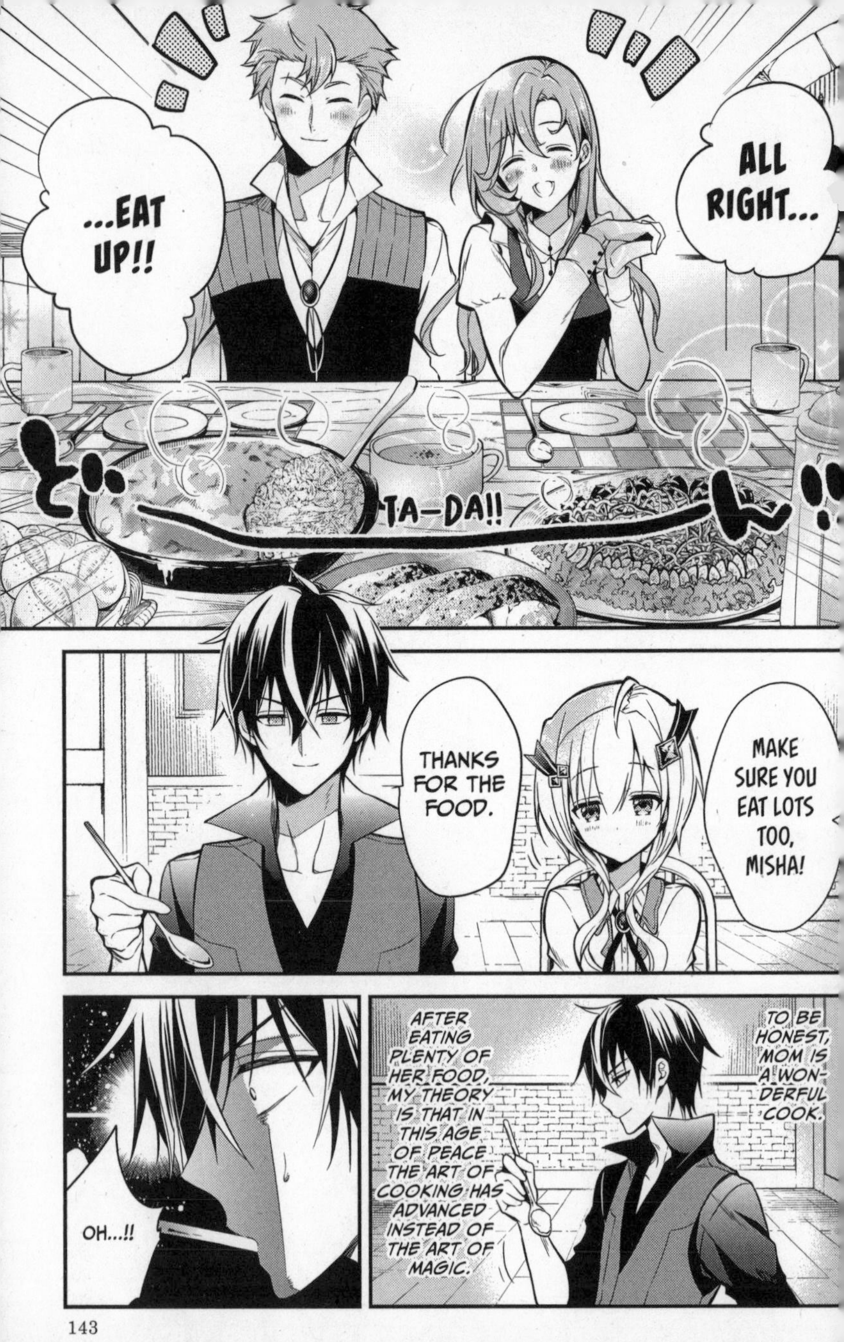
ALL RIGHT...
...EAT UP!!
TA-DA!!
MAKE SURE YOU EAT LOTS TOO, MISHA!
THANKS FOR THE FOOD.
TO BE HONEST, MOM IS A WON-DERFUL COOK.
AFTER EATING PLENTY OF HER FOOD, MY THEORY IS THAT IN THIS AGE OF PEACE THE ART OF COOKING HAS ADVANCED INSTEAD OF THE ART OF MAGIC.
OH...!!

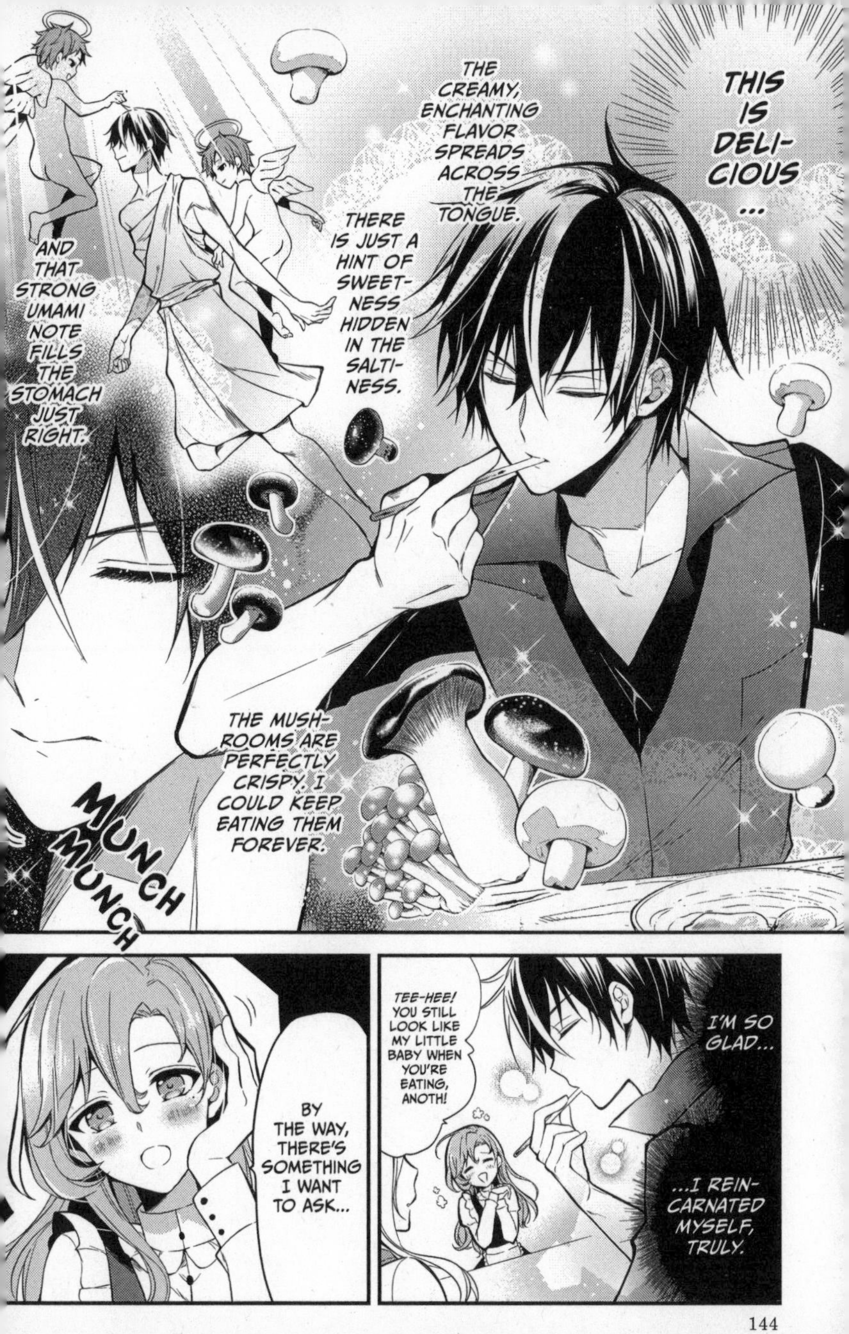
THIS IS DELI-CIOUS...
THE CREAMY, ENCHANTING FLAVOR SPREADS ACROSS THE TONGUE.
THERE IS JUST A HINT OF SWEET-NESS HIDDEN IN THE SALTI-NESS.
AND THAT STRONG UMAMI NOTE FILLS THE STOMACH JUST RIGHT.
THE MUSH-ROOMS ARE PERFECTLY CRISPY. I COULD KEEP EATING THEM FOREVER.
MUNCH MUNCH
I'M SO GLAD...
TEE-HEE! YOU STILL LOOK LIKE MY LITTLE BABY WHEN YOU'RE EATING, ANOTH!
...I REIN-CARNATED MYSELF, TRULY.
BY THE WAY, THERE'S SOMETHING I WANT TO ASK...

KOFF

MISHA, WHAT MADE YOU FALL IN LOVE WITH ANOTH?

SPIT

SNAP

...MOM'S GRATIN IS TRULY POWER- FUL.

TO MAKE ME, THE DEMON KING, LOSE MY COOL LIKE THAT...

I LET MY GUARD DOWN.

A-ARE YOU ALL RIGHT, ANOTH?!

Y-YEAH...

CLENCH

...

SO, WHAT IS IT?

PERHAPS MOM IS THE ONLY PERSON IN THIS AGE...

...WHO COULD STAND AGAINST ME.

I GUESS IT'S HOW KIND HE IS...

SMILE

SMILE

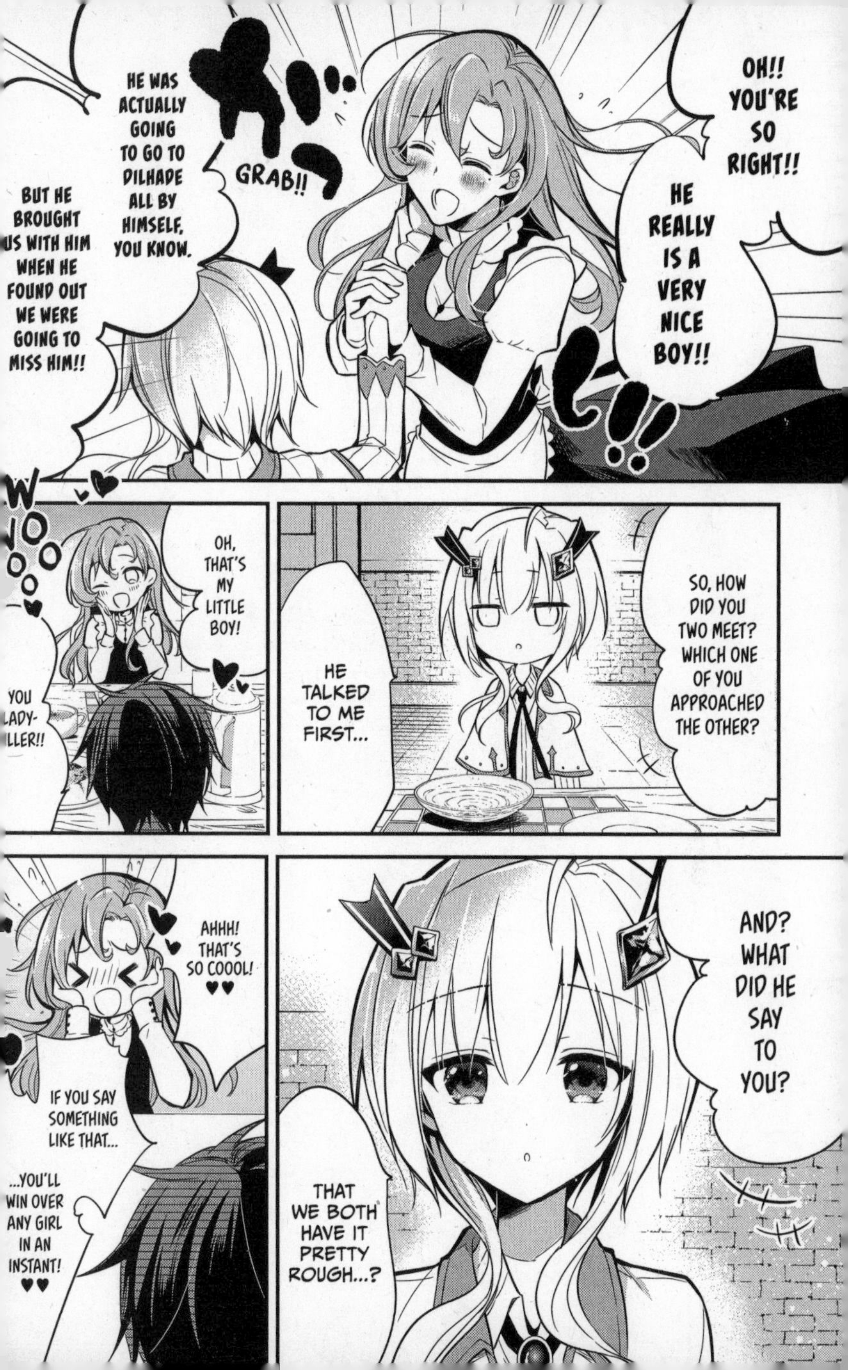
OH!! YOU'RE SO RIGHT!!
HE REALLY IS A VERY NICE BOY!!
GRAB!!
HE WAS ACTUALLY GOING TO GO TO DILHADE ALL BY HIMSELF, YOU KNOW.
BUT HE BROUGHT US WITH HIM WHEN HE FOUND OUT WE WERE GOING TO MISS HIM!!
SO, HOW DID YOU TWO MEET? WHICH ONE OF YOU APPROACHED THE OTHER?
HE TALKED TO ME FIRST...
WOOOOO
OH, THAT'S MY LITTLE BOY!
YOU LADY- LLER!!
AND? WHAT DID HE SAY TO YOU?
THAT WE BOTH HAVE IT PRETTY ROUGH...?
AHHH! THAT'S SO COOOL! ♥♥
IF YOU SAY SOMETHING LIKE THAT...
...YOU'LL WIN OVER ANY GIRL IN AN INSTANT! ♥♥

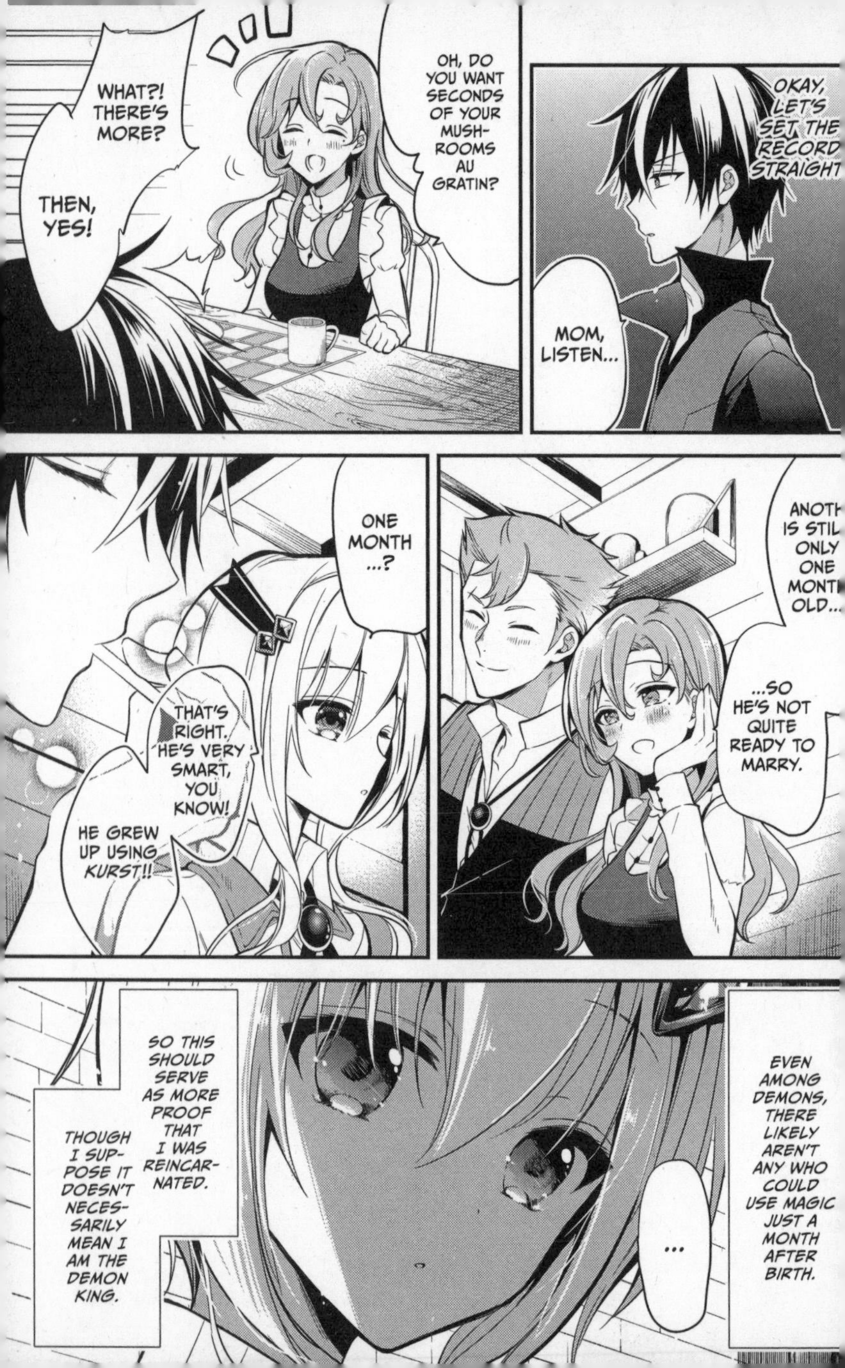
OKAY, LET'S SET THE RECORD STRAIGHT
MOM, LISTEN...
OH, DO YOU WANT SECONDS OF YOUR MUSHROOMS AU GRATIN?
WHAT?! THERE'S MORE?
THEN, YES!
ANOTH IS STIL ONLY ONE MONT OLD...
...SO HE'S NOT QUITE READY TO MARRY.
ONE MONTH ...?
THAT'S RIGHT. HE'S VERY SMART, YOU KNOW!
HE GREW UP USING KURST!!
EVEN AMONG DEMONS, THERE LIKELY AREN'T ANY WHO COULD USE MAGIC JUST A MONTH AFTER BIRTH.
...
SO THIS SHOULD SERVE AS MORE PROOF THAT I WAS REINCARNATED.
THOUGH I SUPPOSE IT DOESN'T NECESSARILY MEAN I AM THE DEMON KING.

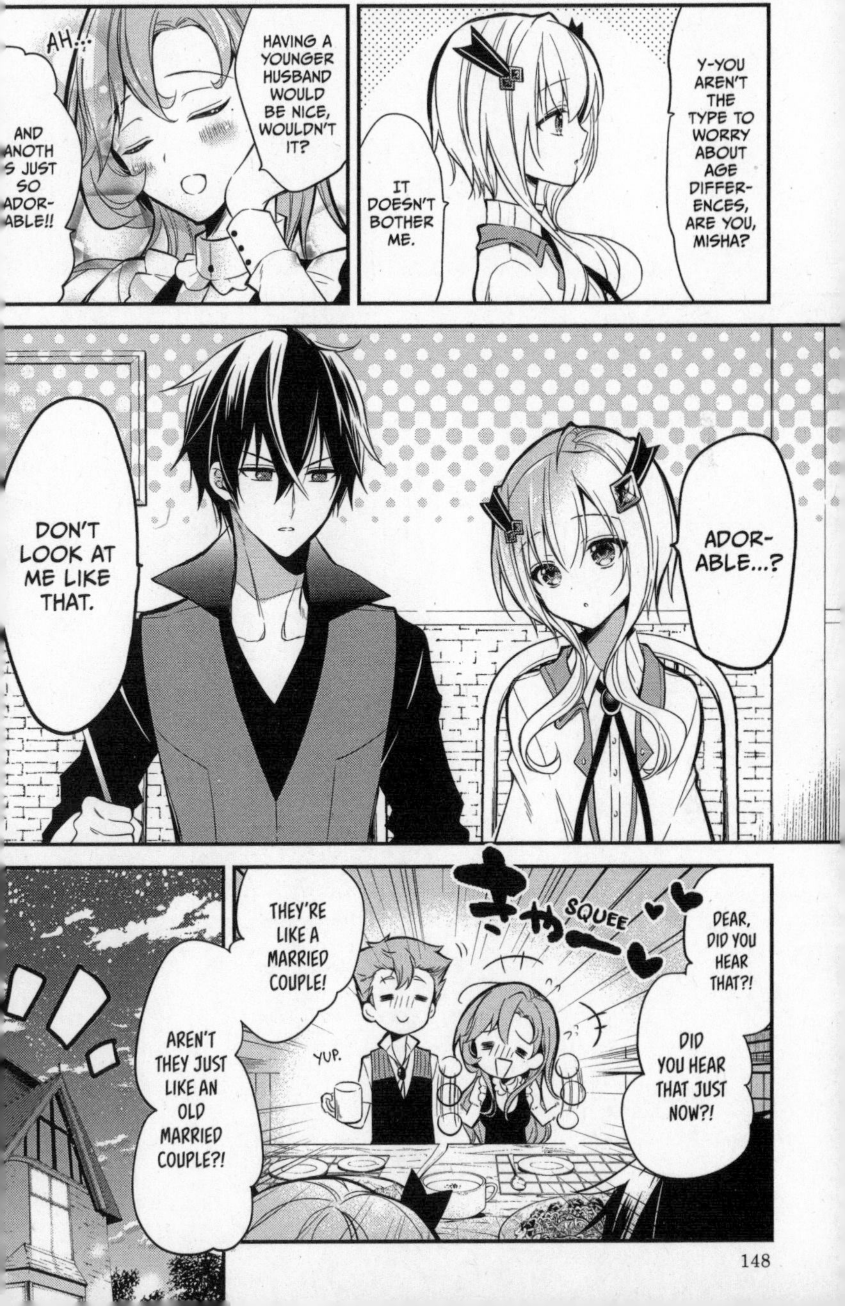
Y-YOU AREN'T THE TYPE TO WORRY ABOUT AGE DIFFERENCES, ARE YOU, MISHA?
IT DOESN'T BOTHER ME.
HAVING A YOUNGER HUSBAND WOULD BE NICE, WOULDN'T IT?
AH...
AND ANOTH S JUST SO ADORABLE!!
ADORABLE...?
DON'T LOOK AT ME LIKE THAT.
SQUEE
DEAR, DID YOU HEAR THAT?!
DID YOU HEAR THAT JUST NOW?!
THEY'RE LIKE A MARRIED COUPLE!
YUP.
AREN'T THEY JUST LIKE AN OLD MARRIED COUPLE?!
!!

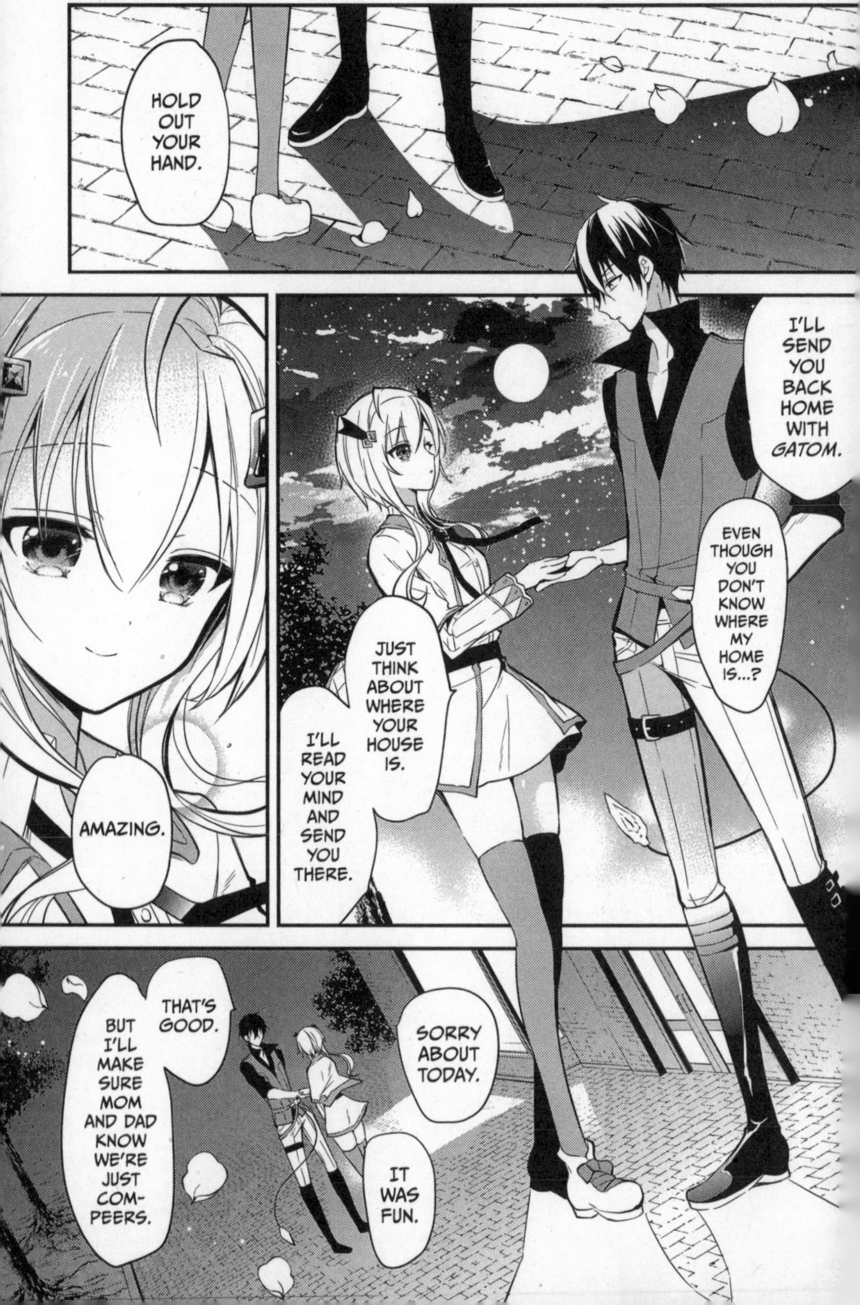
HOLD OUT YOUR HAND.
I'LL SEND YOU BACK HOME WITH *GATOM*.
EVEN THOUGH YOU DON'T KNOW WHERE MY HOME IS...?
JUST THINK ABOUT WHERE YOUR HOUSE IS.
I'LL READ YOUR MIND AND SEND YOU THERE.
AMAZING.
SORRY ABOUT TODAY.
IT WAS FUN.
THAT'S GOOD.
BUT I'LL MAKE SURE MOM AND DAD KNOW WE'RE JUST COM-PEERS.

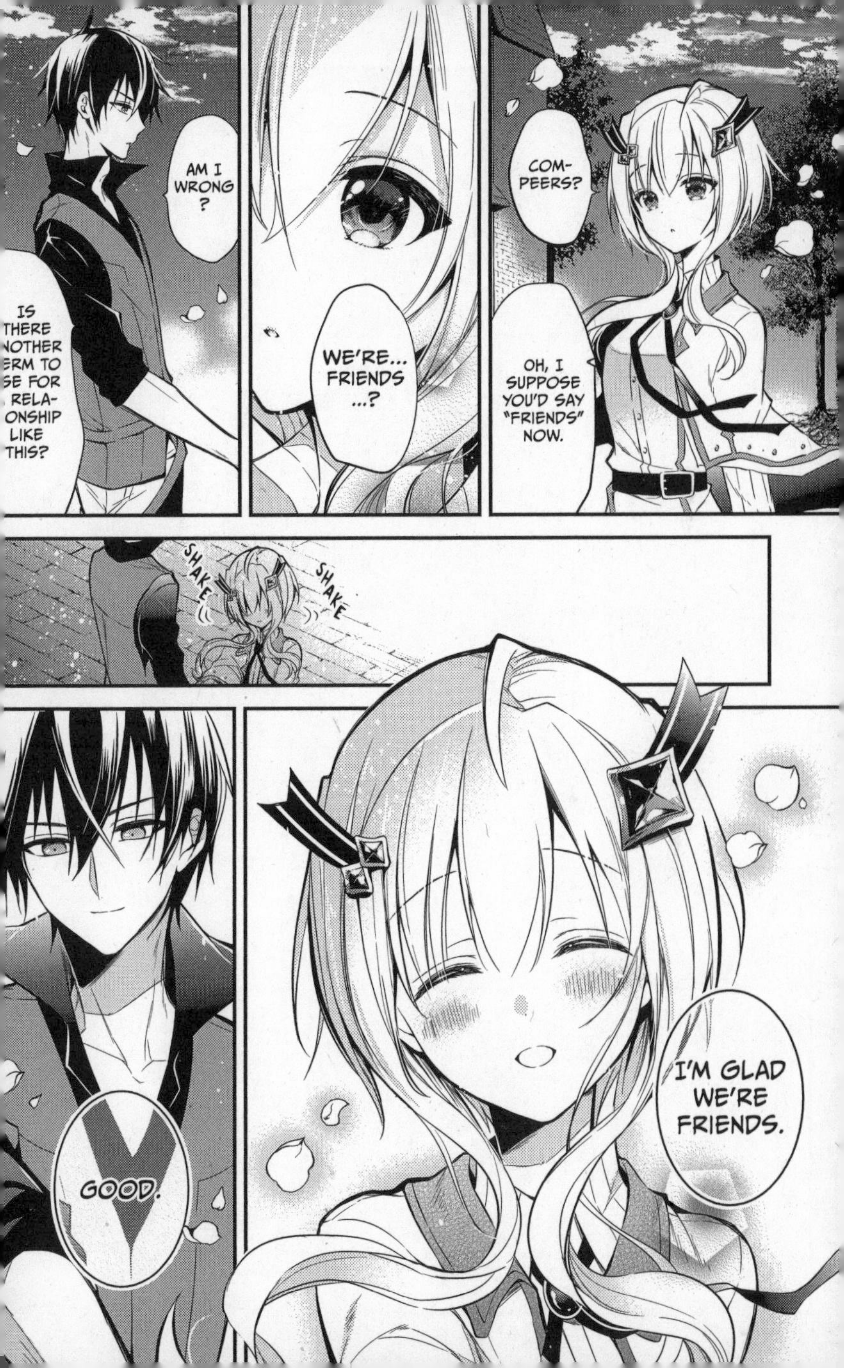
COM-PEERS?
OH, I SUPPOSE YOU'D SAY "FRIENDS" NOW.
WE'RE... FRIENDS ...?
AM I WRONG ?
IS THERE NOTHER ERM TO SE FOR RELA- ONSHIP LIKE THIS?
SHAKE
SHAKE
I'M GLAD WE'RE FRIENDS.
GOOD.

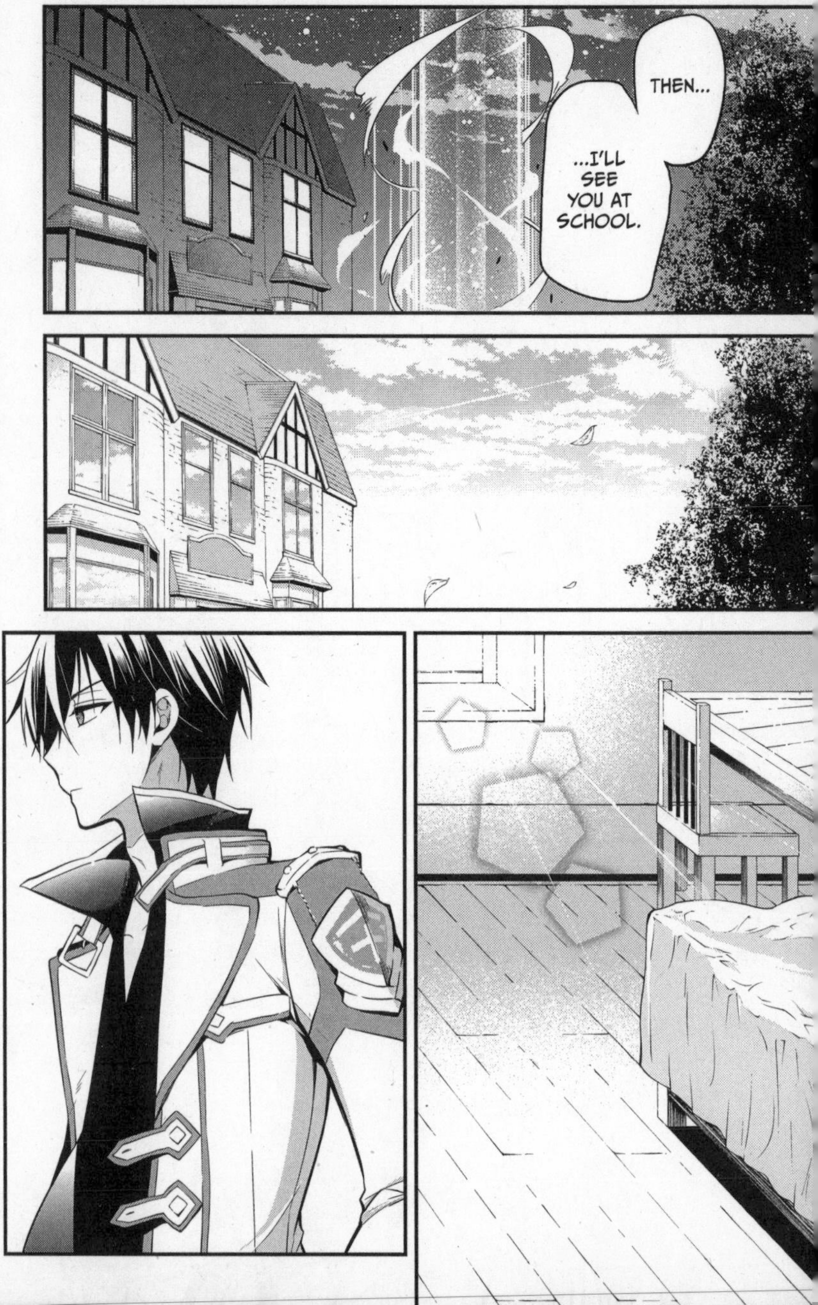
THEN...
...I'LL SEE YOU AT SCHOOL.

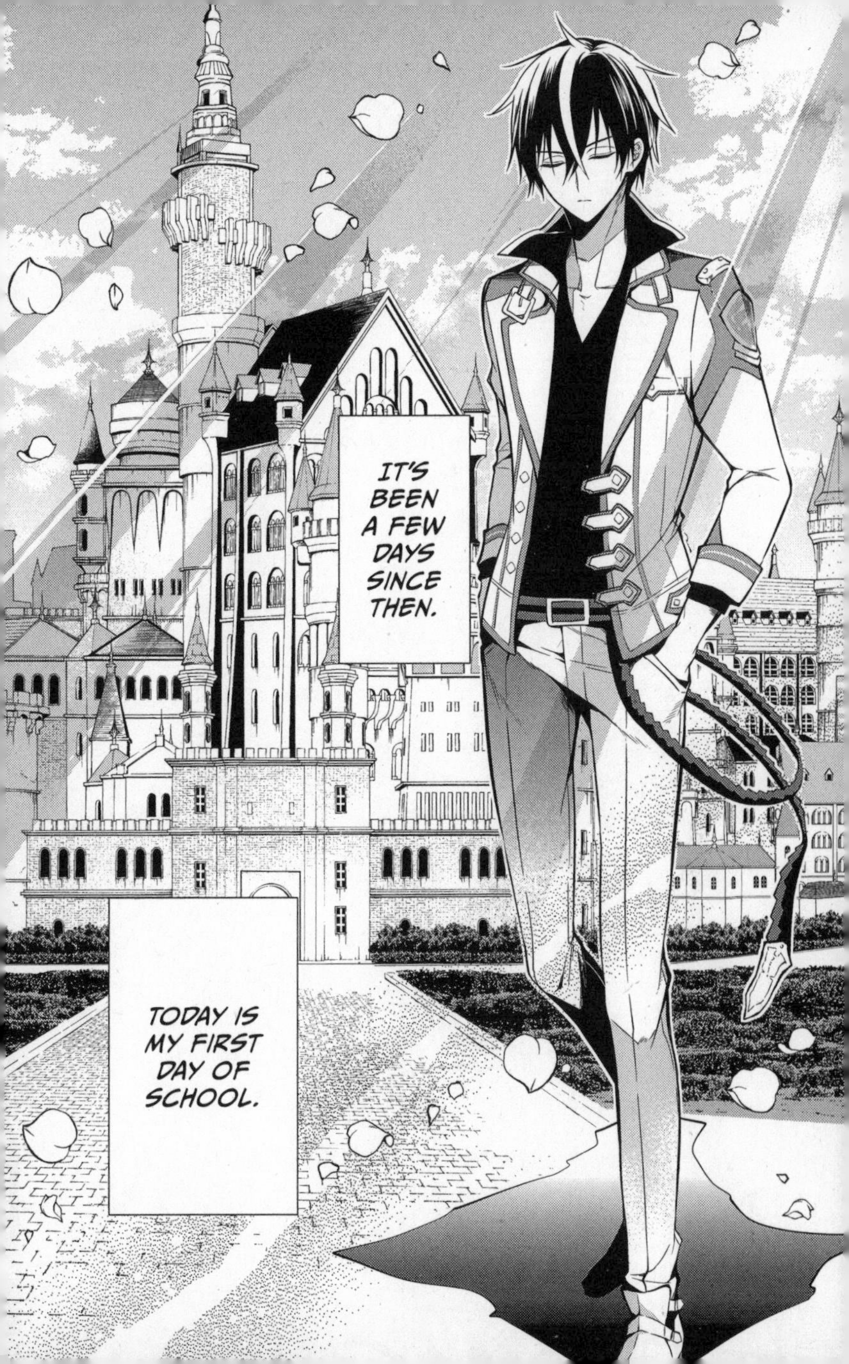
IT'S BEEN A FEW DAYS SINCE THEN.
TODAY IS MY FIRST DAY OF SCHOOL.

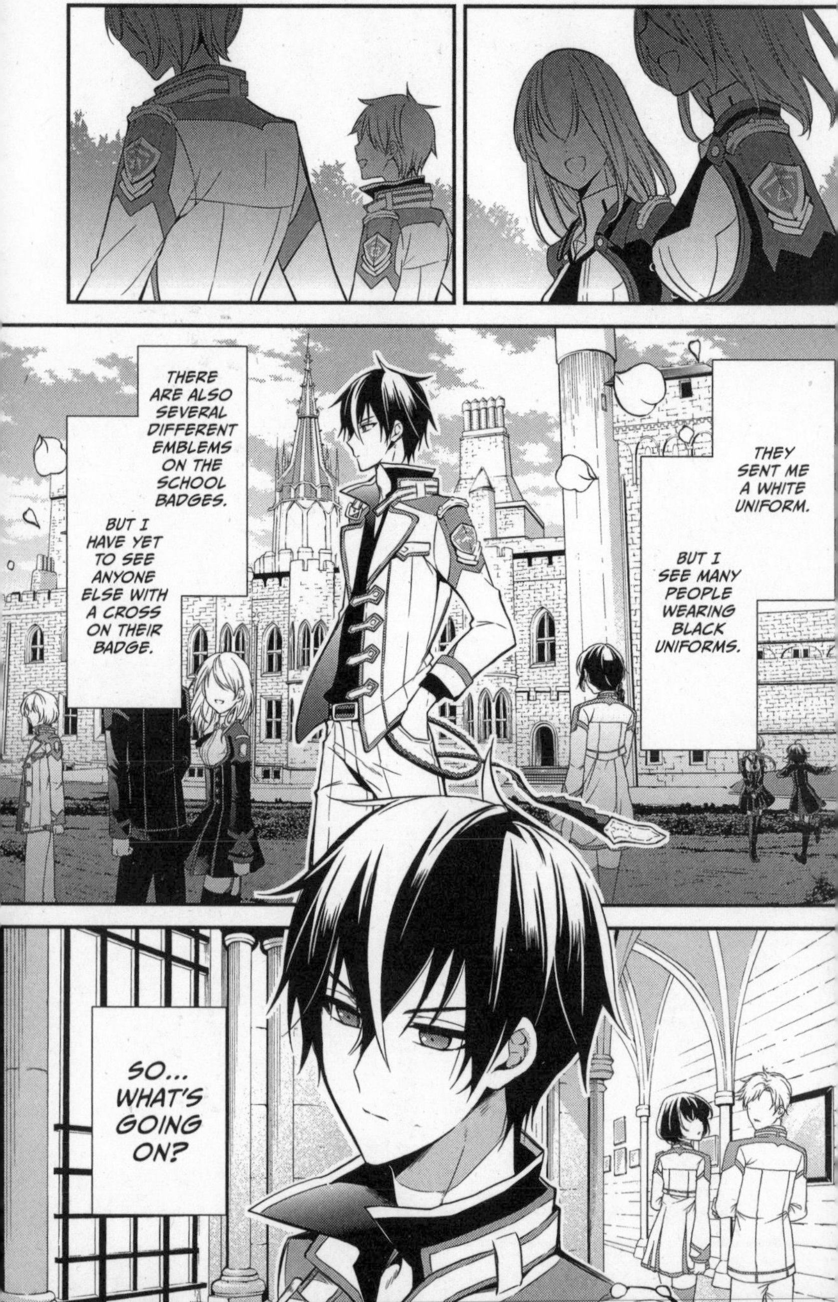
THEY SENT ME A WHITE UNIFORM.
BUT I SEE MANY PEOPLE WEARING BLACK UNIFORMS.
THERE ARE ALSO SEVERAL DIFFERENT EMBLEMS ON THE SCHOOL BADGES.
BUT I HAVE YET TO SEE ANYONE ELSE WITH A CROSS ON THEIR BADGE.
SO... WHAT'S GOING ON?

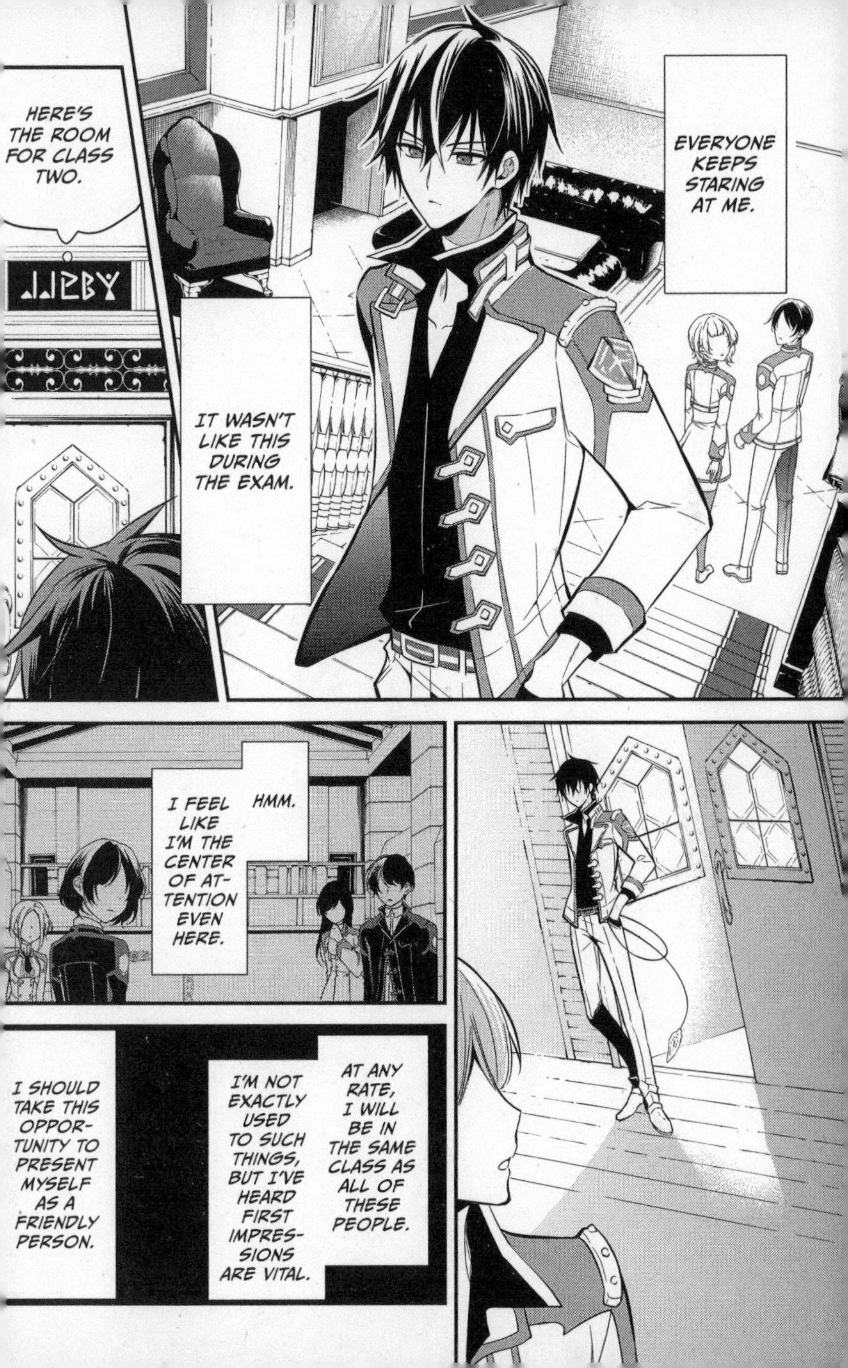
EVERYONE KEEPS STARING AT ME.
IT WASN'T LIKE THIS DURING THE EXAM.
HERE'S THE ROOM FOR CLASS TWO.
HMM.
I FEEL LIKE I'M THE CENTER OF ATTENTION EVEN HERE.
AT ANY RATE, I WILL BE IN THE SAME CLASS AS ALL OF THESE PEOPLE.
I'M NOT EXACTLY USED TO SUCH THINGS, BUT I'VE HEARD FIRST IMPRESSIONS ARE VITAL.
I SHOULD TAKE THIS OPPORTUNITY TO PRESENT MYSELF AS A FRIENDLY PERSON.

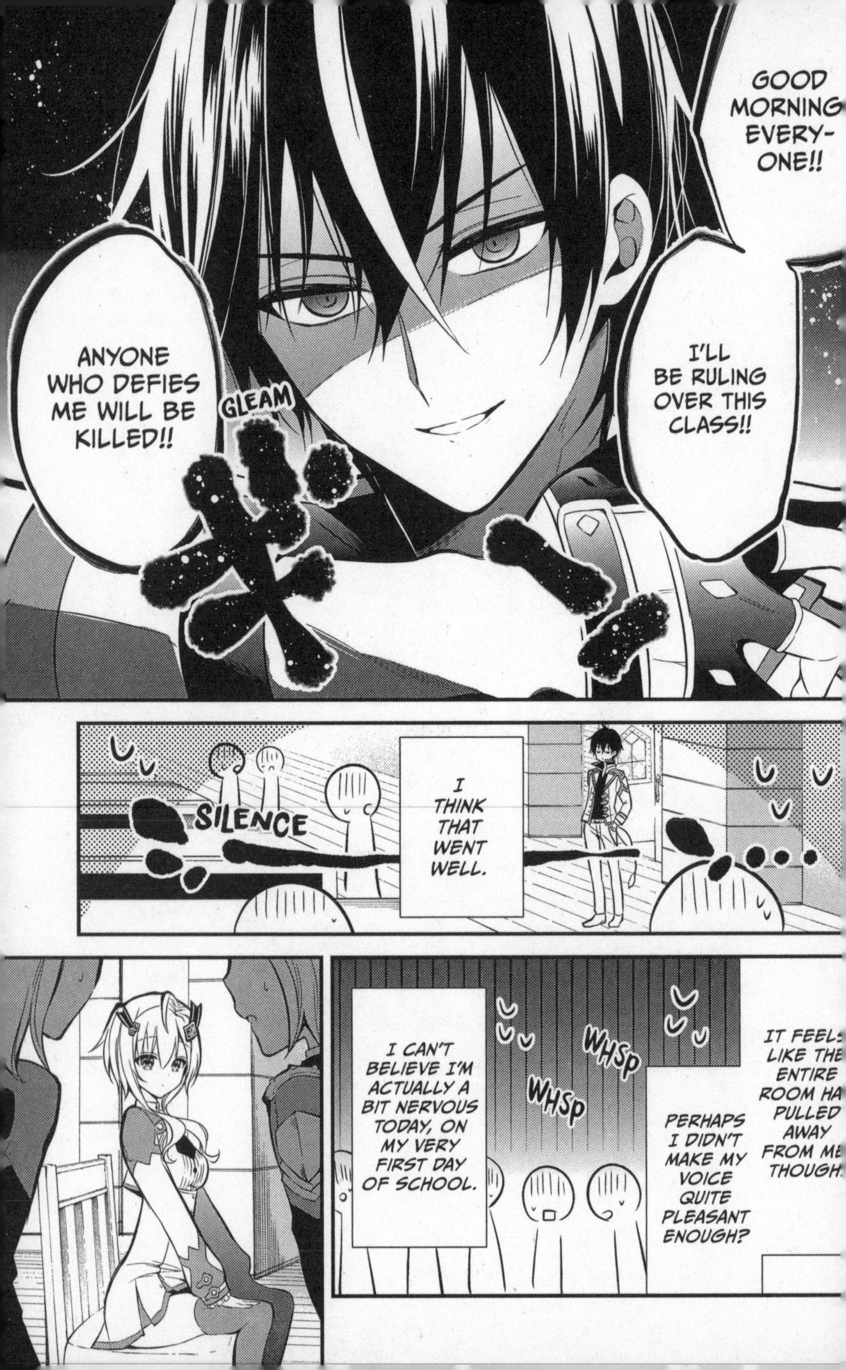
GOOD MORNING EVERY-ONE!!
I'LL BE RULING OVER THIS CLASS!!
ANYONE WHO DEFIES ME WILL BE KILLED!!
GLEAM
...
I THINK THAT WENT WELL.
SILENCE
IT FEELS LIKE THE ENTIRE ROOM HA PULLED AWAY FROM ME THOUGH
PERHAPS I DIDN'T MAKE MY VOICE QUITE PLEASANT ENOUGH?
WHSP
WHSP
I CAN'T BELIEVE I'M ACTUALLY A BIT NERVOUS TODAY, ON MY VERY FIRST DAY OF SCHOOL.

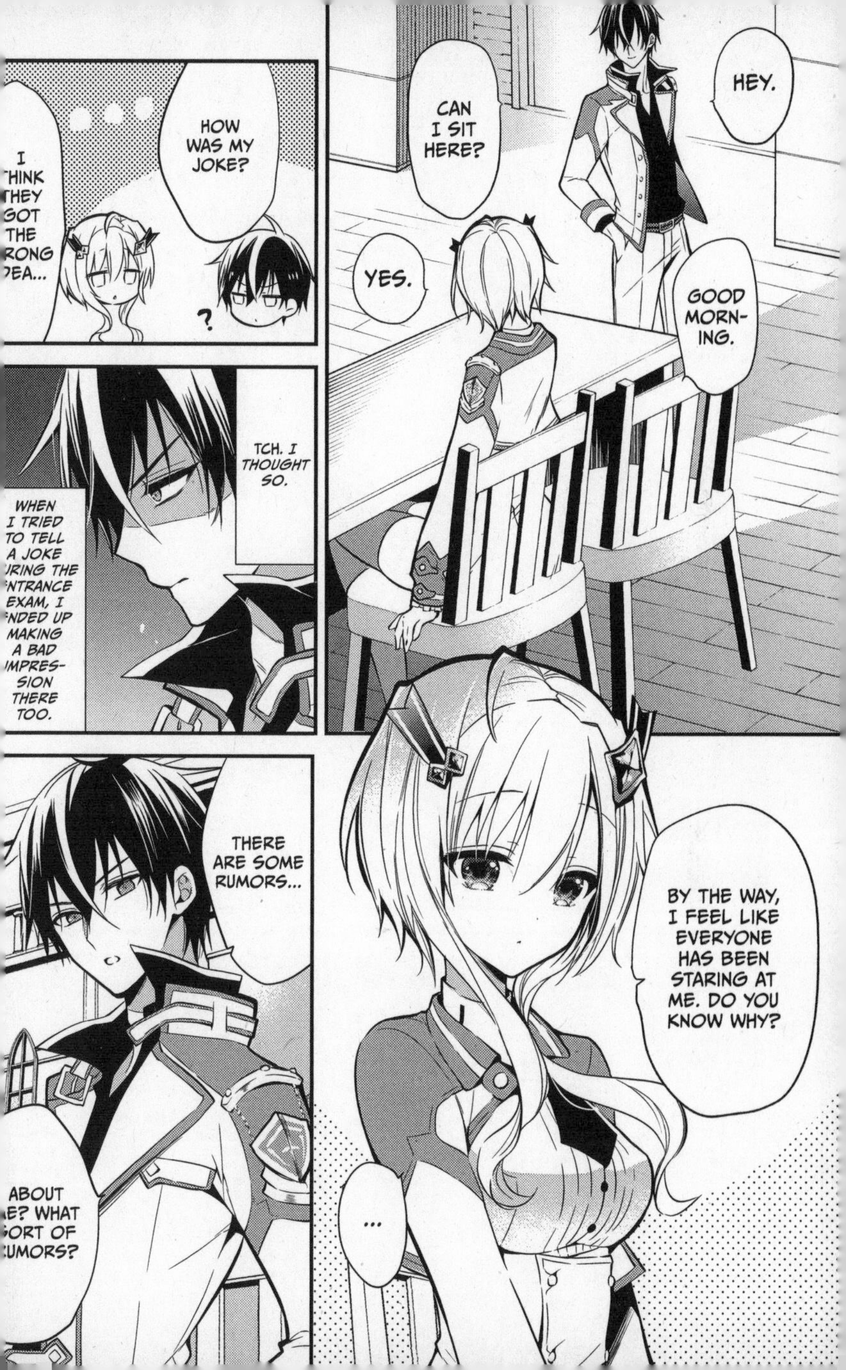
HEY.
GOOD MORN-ING.
CAN I SIT HERE?
YES.
HOW WAS MY JOKE?
I HINK HEY GOT THE RONG DEA...
TCH. I THOUGHT SO.
WHEN I TRIED TO TELL A JOKE URING THE NTRANCE EXAM, I NDED UP MAKING A BAD MPRES-SION THERE TOO.
BY THE WAY, I FEEL LIKE EVERYONE HAS BEEN STARING AT ME. DO YOU KNOW WHY?
...
THERE ARE SOME RUMORS...
ABOUT E? WHAT ORT OF UMORS?

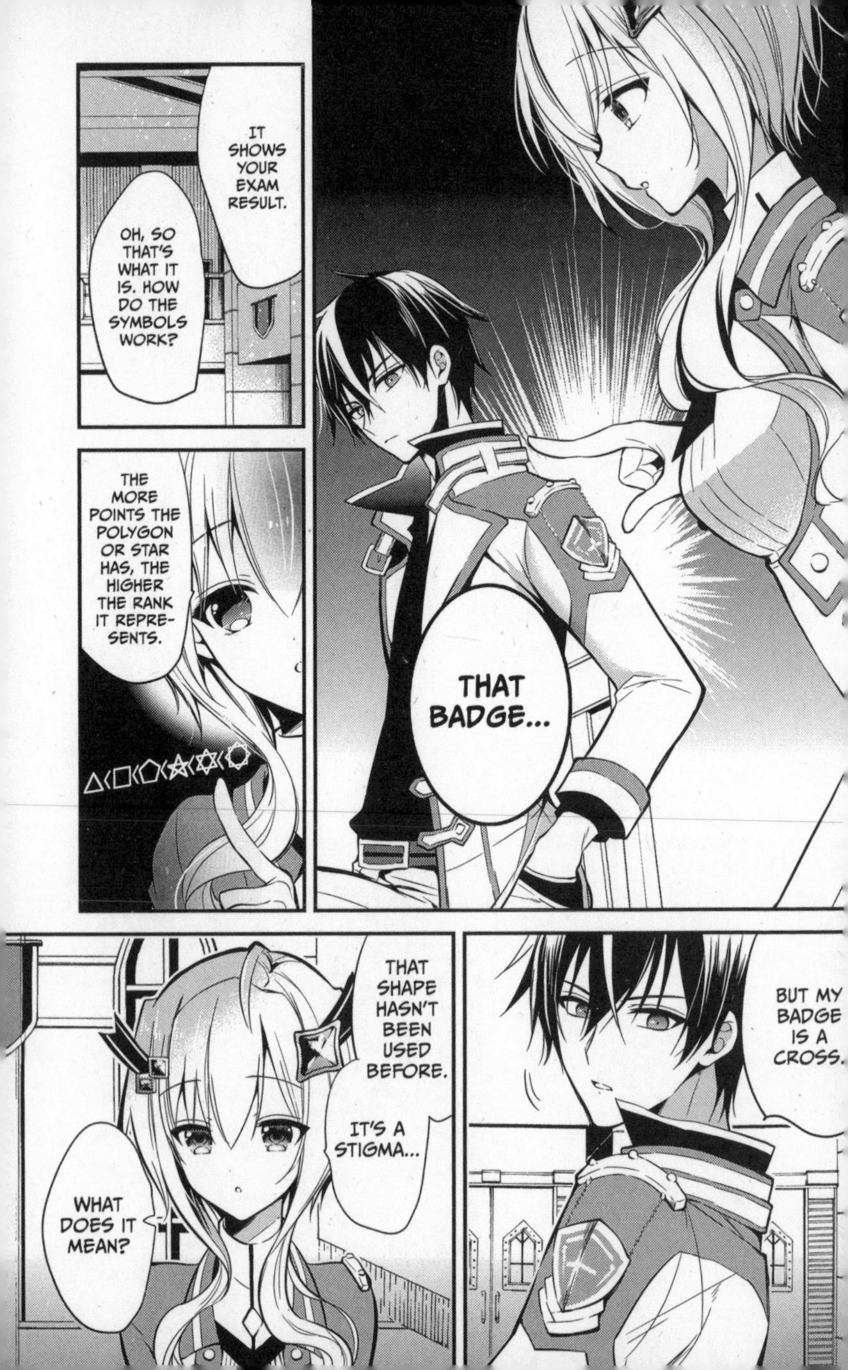
THAT BADGE...
IT SHOWS YOUR EXAM RESULT.
OH, SO THAT'S WHAT IT IS. HOW DO THE SYMBOLS WORK?
THE MORE POINTS THE POLYGON OR STAR HAS, THE HIGHER THE RANK IT REPRESENTS.
BUT MY BADGE IS A CROSS.
THAT SHAPE HASN'T BEEN USED BEFORE.
IT'S A STIGMA...
WHAT DOES IT MEAN?

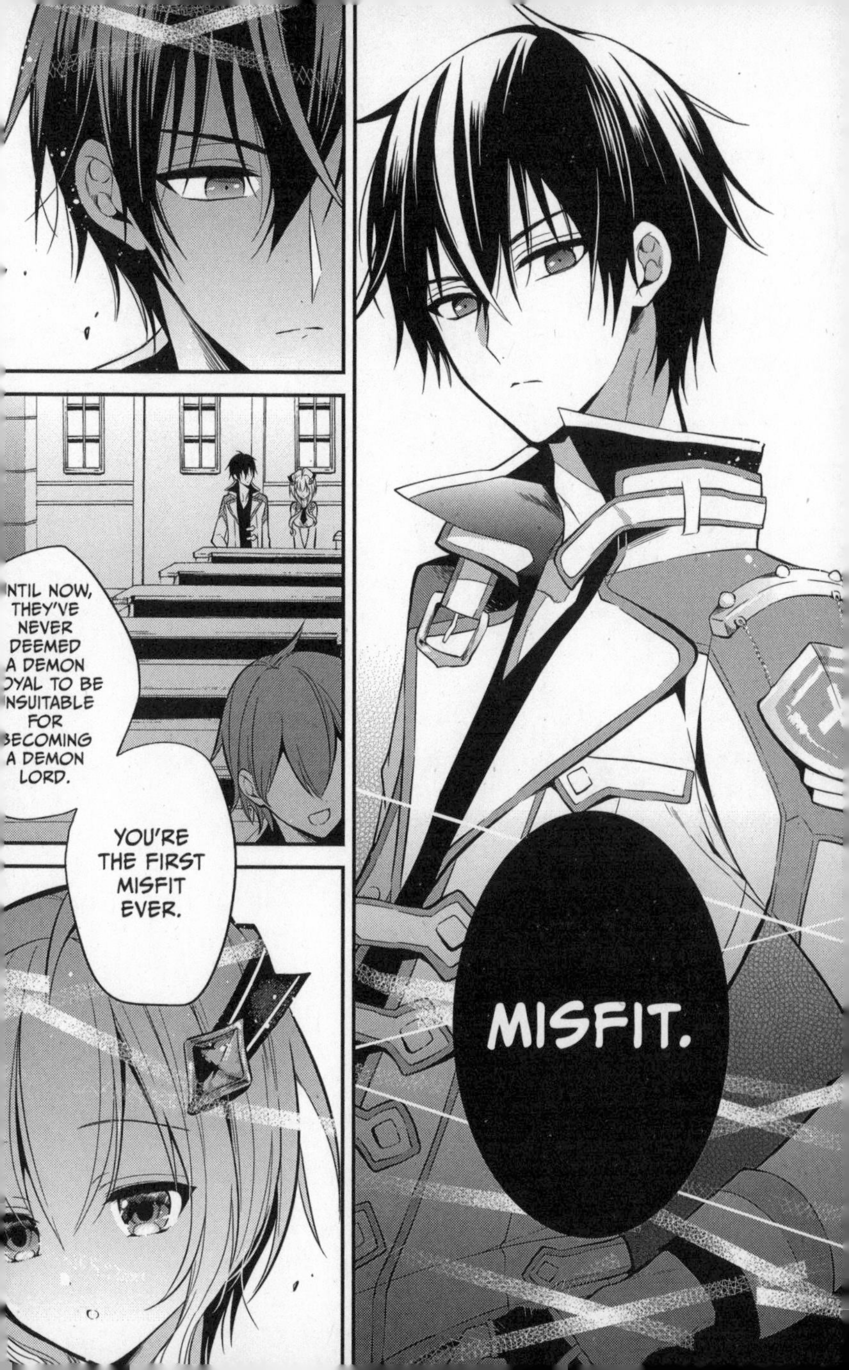
MISFIT.
NTIL NOW, THEY'VE NEVER DEEMED A DEMON OYAL TO BE NSUITABLE FOR ECOMING A DEMON LORD.
YOU'RE THE FIRST MISFIT EVER.

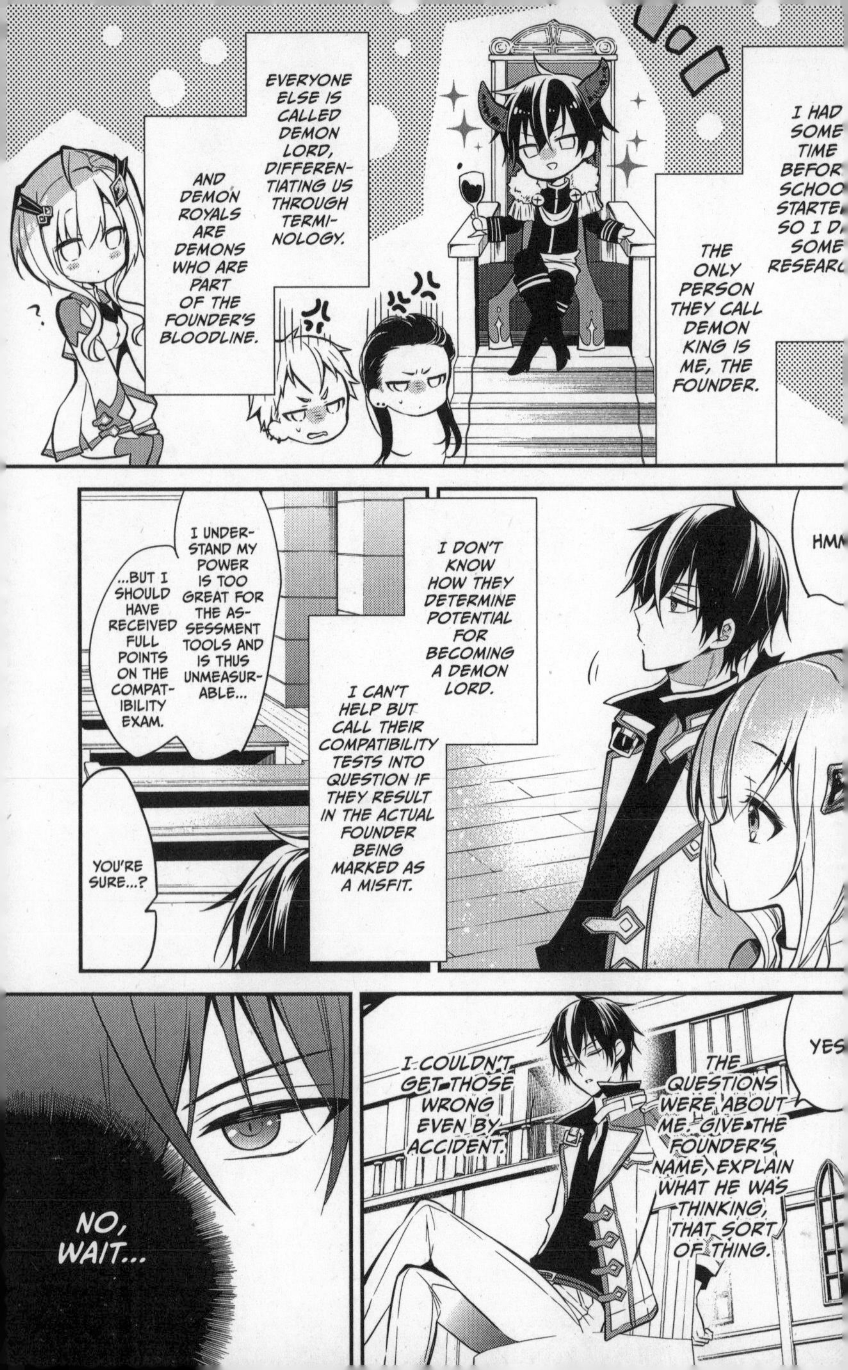
I HAD SOME TIME BEFOR SCHOO STARTE SO I D SOME RESEAR
THE ONLY PERSON THEY CALL DEMON KING IS ME, THE FOUNDER.
EVERYONE ELSE IS CALLED DEMON LORD, DIFFEREN-TIATING US THROUGH TERMI-NOLOGY.
AND DEMON ROYALS ARE DEMONS WHO ARE PART OF THE FOUNDER'S BLOODLINE.
HMM
I UNDER-STAND MY POWER IS TOO GREAT FOR THE AS-SESSMENT TOOLS AND IS THUS UNMEASUR-ABLE...
...BUT I SHOULD HAVE RECEIVED FULL POINTS ON THE COMPAT-IBILITY EXAM.
I DON'T KNOW HOW THEY DETERMINE POTENTIAL FOR BECOMING A DEMON LORD.
I CAN'T HELP BUT CALL THEIR COMPATIBILITY TESTS INTO QUESTION IF THEY RESULT IN THE ACTUAL FOUNDER BEING MARKED AS A MISFIT.
YOU'RE SURE...?
YES
THE QUESTIONS WERE ABOUT ME. GIVE THE FOUNDER'S NAME, EXPLAIN WHAT HE WAS THINKING, THAT SORT OF THING.
I COULDN'T GET THOSE WRONG EVEN BY ACCIDENT.
NO, WAIT...

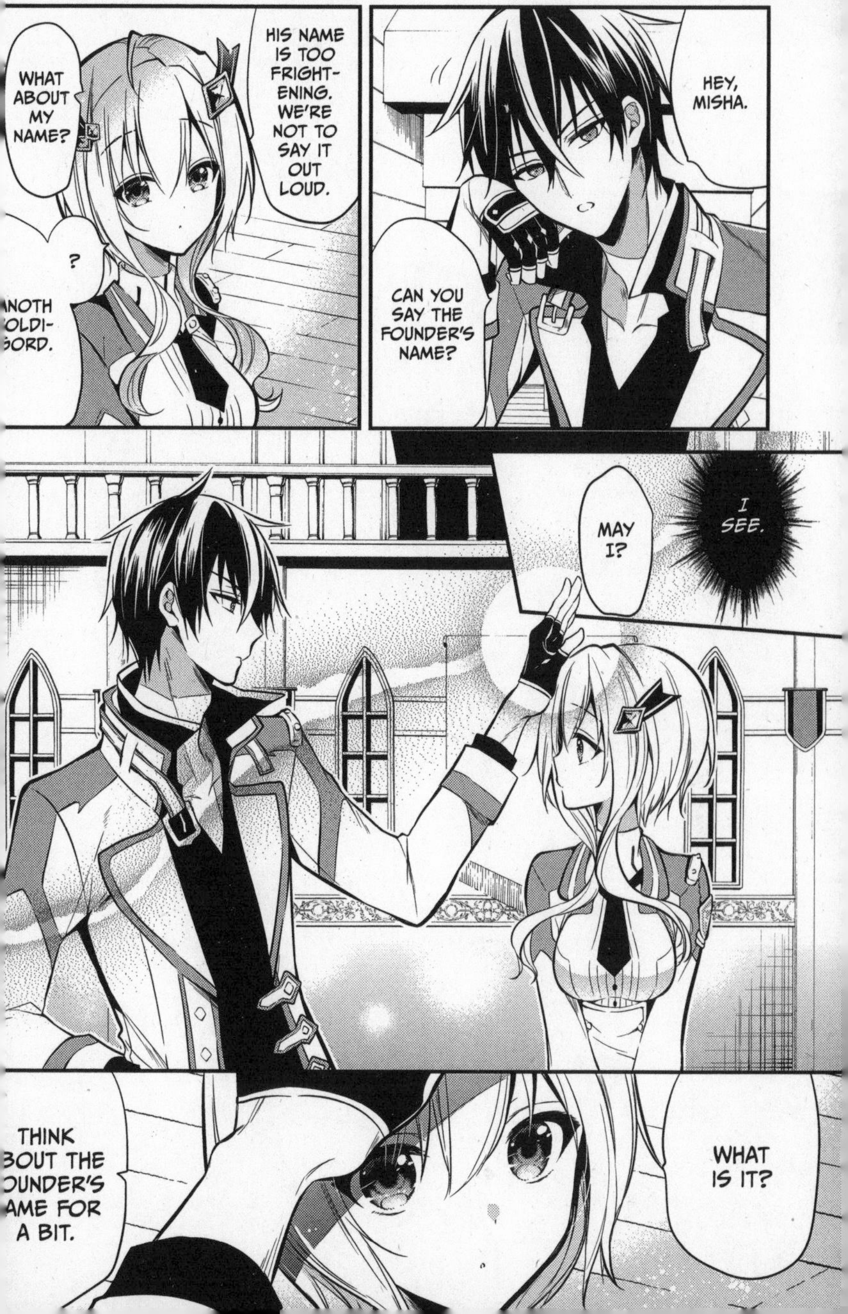
HEY, MISHA.
CAN YOU SAY THE FOUNDER'S NAME?
HIS NAME IS TOO FRIGHT-ENING. WE'RE NOT TO SAY IT OUT LOUD.
WHAT ABOUT MY NAME?
?
NOTH OLDI- ORD.
I SEE.
MAY I?
WHAT IS IT?
THINK BOUT THE OUNDER'S AME FOR A BIT.

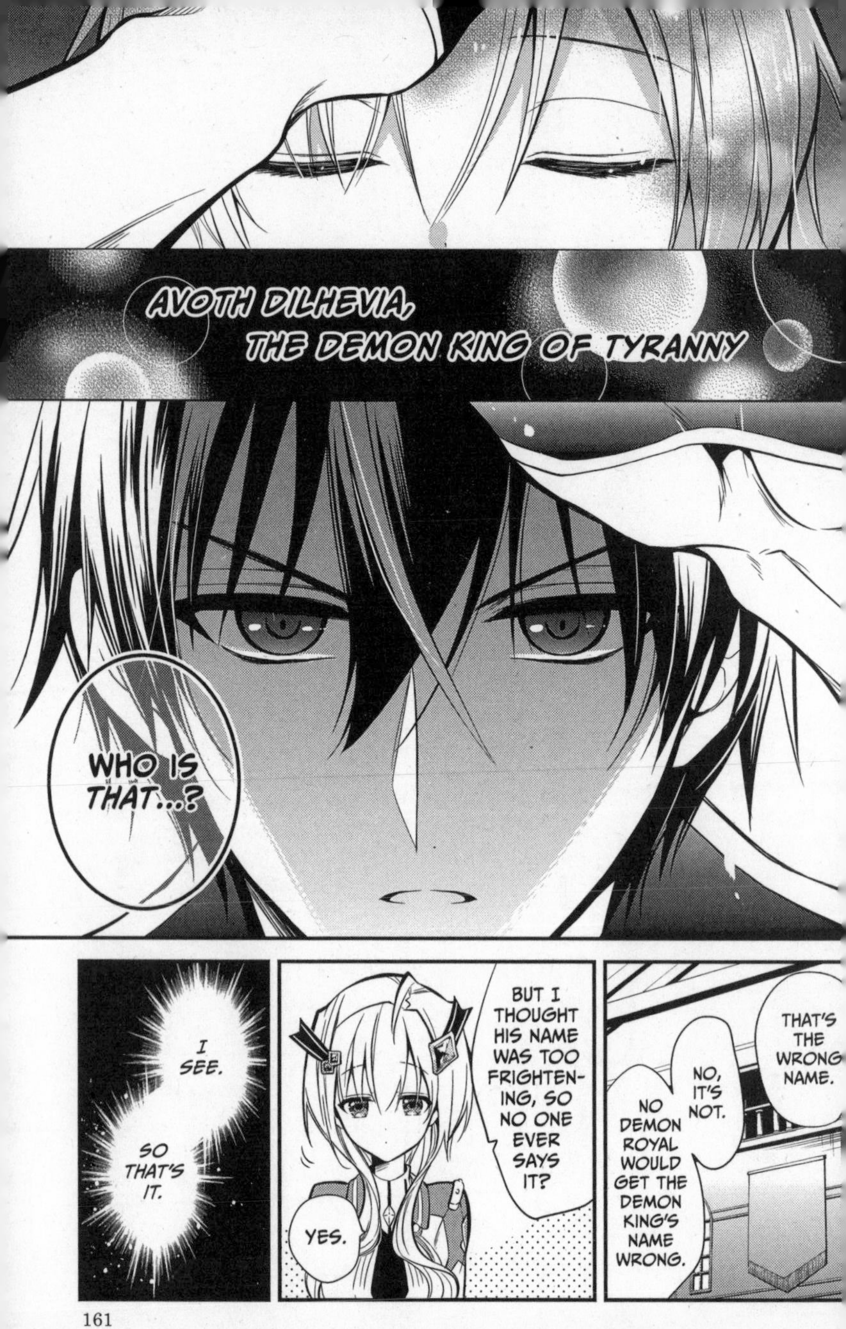
AVOTH DILHEVIA, THE DEMON KING OF TYRANNY
WHO IS THAT...?
THAT'S THE WRONG NAME.
NO, IT'S NOT.
NO DEMON ROYAL WOULD GET THE DEMON KING'S NAME WRONG.
BUT I THOUGHT HIS NAME WAS TOO FRIGHTEN-ING, SO NO ONE EVER SAYS IT?
YES.
I SEE.
SO THAT'S IT.

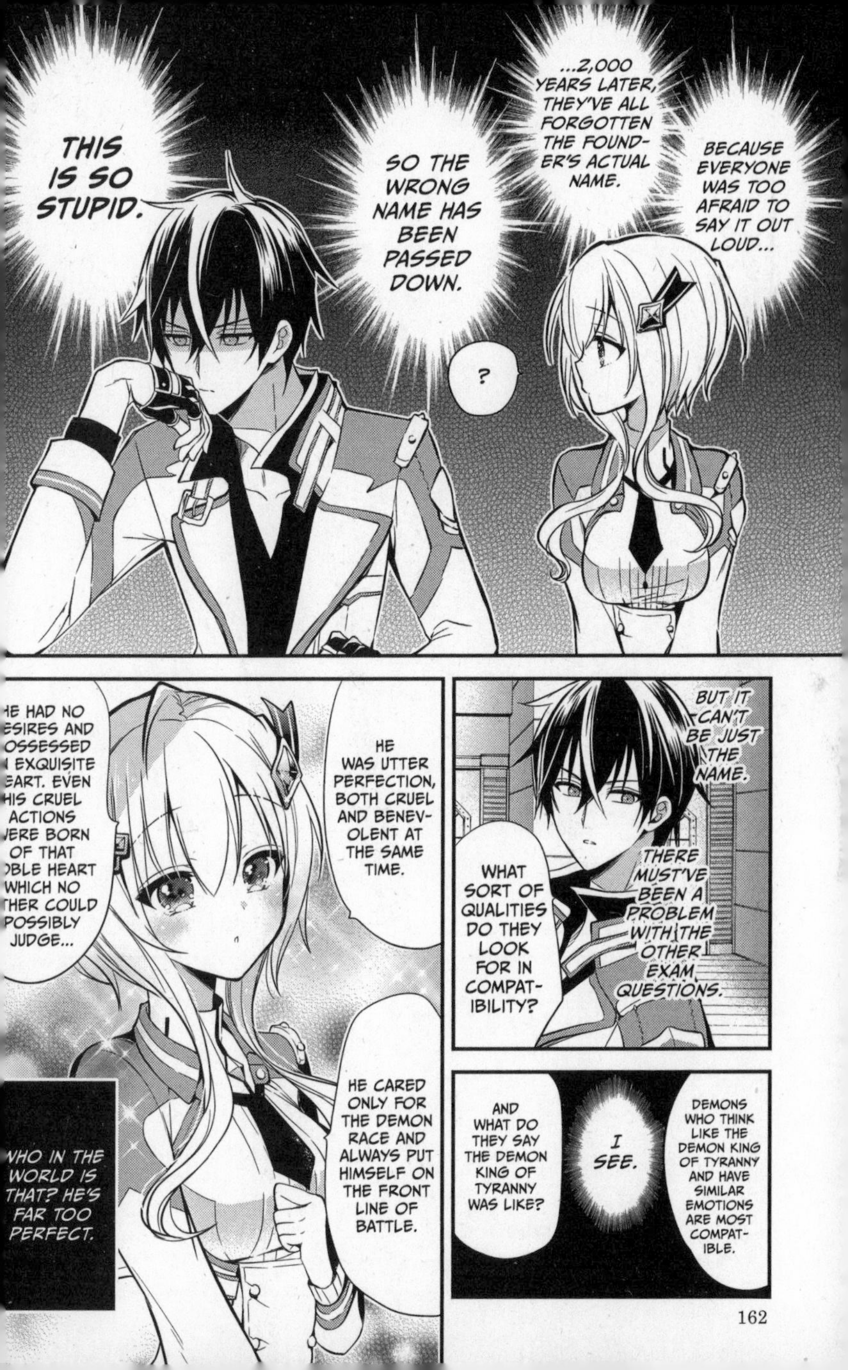
BECAUSE EVERYONE WAS TOO AFRAID TO SAY IT OUT LOUD...
...2,000 YEARS LATER, THEY'VE ALL FORGOTTEN THE FOUNDER'S ACTUAL NAME.
SO THE WRONG NAME HAS BEEN PASSED DOWN.
?
THIS IS SO STUPID.
BUT IT CAN'T BE JUST THE NAME.
THERE MUST'VE BEEN A PROBLEM WITH THE OTHER EXAM QUESTIONS.
WHAT SORT OF QUALITIES DO THEY LOOK FOR IN COMPATIBILITY?
DEMONS WHO THINK LIKE THE DEMON KING OF TYRANNY AND HAVE SIMILAR EMOTIONS ARE MOST COMPATIBLE.
I SEE.
AND WHAT DO THEY SAY THE DEMON KING OF TYRANNY WAS LIKE?
HE WAS UTTER PERFECTION, BOTH CRUEL AND BENEVOLENT AT THE SAME TIME.
HE HAD NO ESIRES AND OSSESSED N EXQUISITE EART. EVEN HIS CRUEL ACTIONS ERE BORN OF THAT OBLE HEART WHICH NO THER COULD POSSIBLY JUDGE...
HE CARED ONLY FOR THE DEMON RACE AND ALWAYS PUT HIMSELF ON THE FRONT LINE OF BATTLE.
WHO IN THE WORLD IS THAT? HE'S FAR TOO PERFECT.

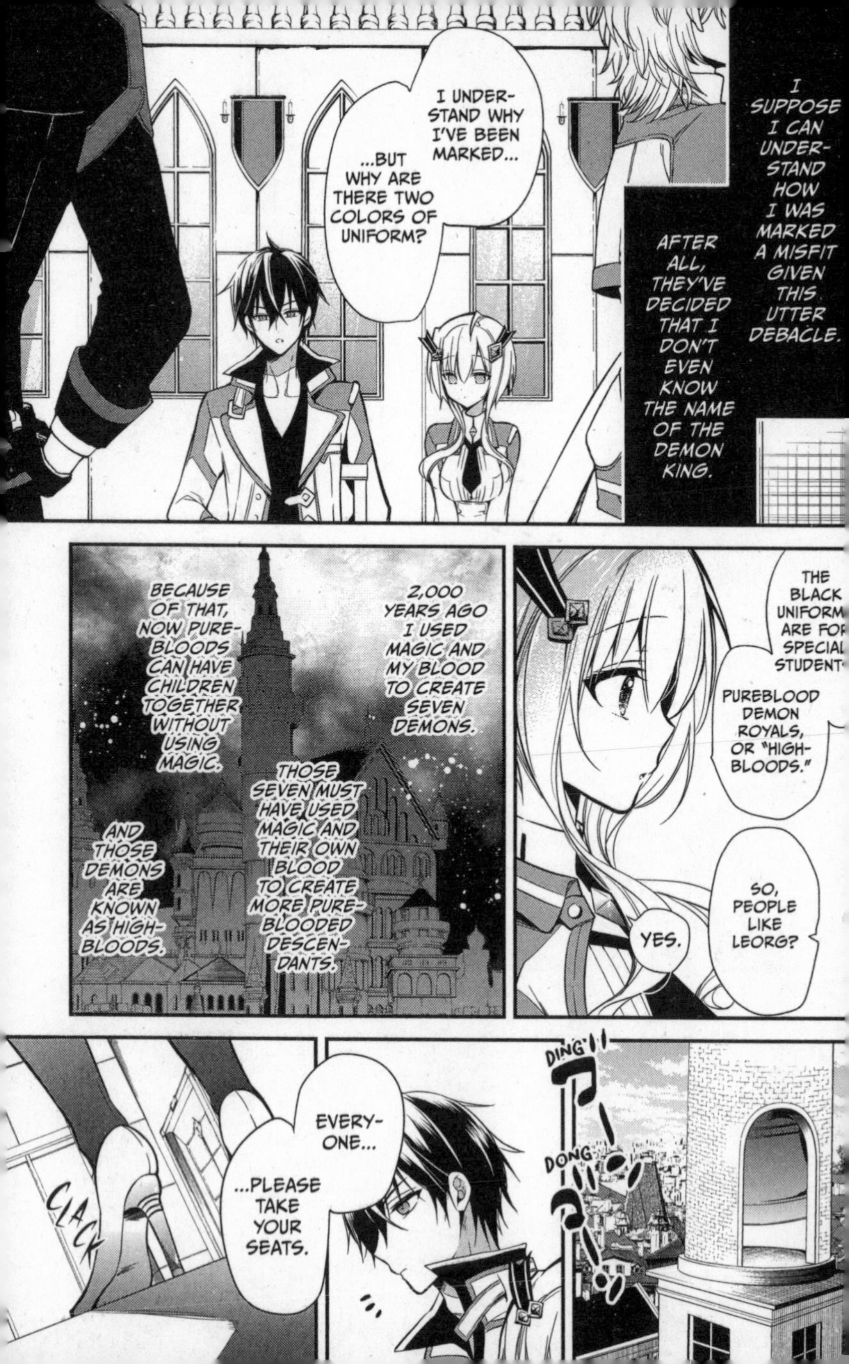
I SUPPOSE I CAN UNDERSTAND HOW I WAS MARKED A MISFIT GIVEN THIS UTTER DEBACLE.
AFTER ALL, THEY'VE DECIDED THAT I DON'T EVEN KNOW THE NAME OF THE DEMON KING.
I UNDERSTAND WHY I'VE BEEN MARKED...
...BUT WHY ARE THERE TWO COLORS OF UNIFORM?
THE BLACK UNIFORM ARE FOR SPECIAL STUDENT
PUREBLOOD DEMON ROYALS, OR "HIGH-BLOODS."
SO, PEOPLE LIKE LEORG?
YES.
2,000 YEARS AGO I USED MAGIC AND MY BLOOD TO CREATE SEVEN DEMONS.
THOSE SEVEN MUST HAVE USED MAGIC AND THEIR OWN BLOOD TO CREATE MORE PURE-BLOODED DESCENDANTS.
AND THOSE DEMONS ARE KNOWN AS HIGH-BLOODS.
BECAUSE OF THAT, NOW PURE-BLOODS CAN HAVE CHILDREN TOGETHER WITHOUT USING MAGIC.
DING
DONG
EVERYONE...
...PLEASE TAKE YOUR SEATS.
CLACK

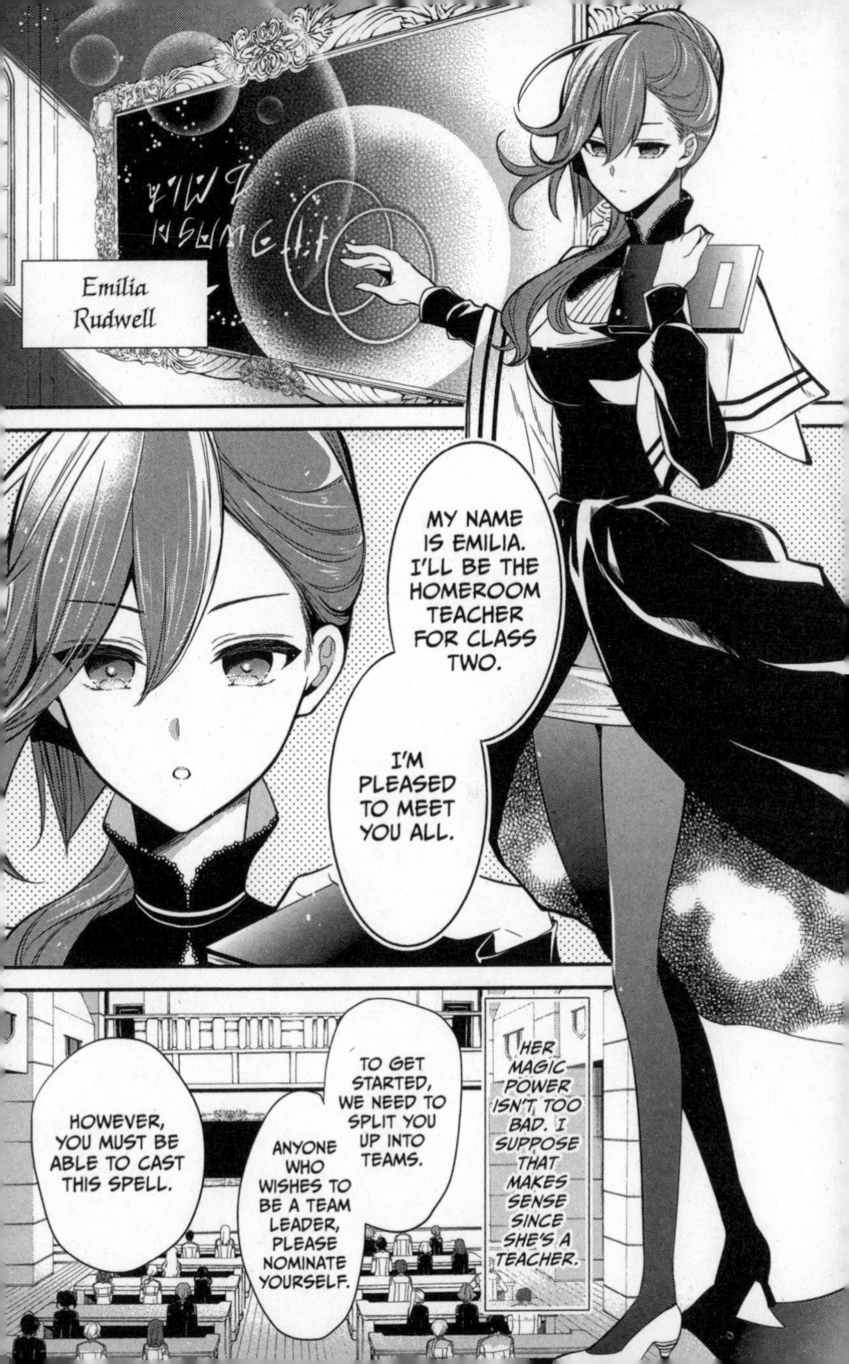
Emilia Rudwell
MY NAME IS EMILIA. I'LL BE THE HOMEROOM TEACHER FOR CLASS TWO.
I'M PLEASED TO MEET YOU ALL.
HER MAGIC POWER ISN'T TOO BAD. I SUPPOSE THAT MAKES SENSE SINCE SHE'S A TEACHER.
TO GET STARTED, WE NEED TO SPLIT YOU UP INTO TEAMS.
ANYONE WHO WISHES TO BE A TEAM LEADER, PLEASE NOMINATE YOURSELF.
HOWEVER, YOU MUST BE ABLE TO CAST THIS SPELL.

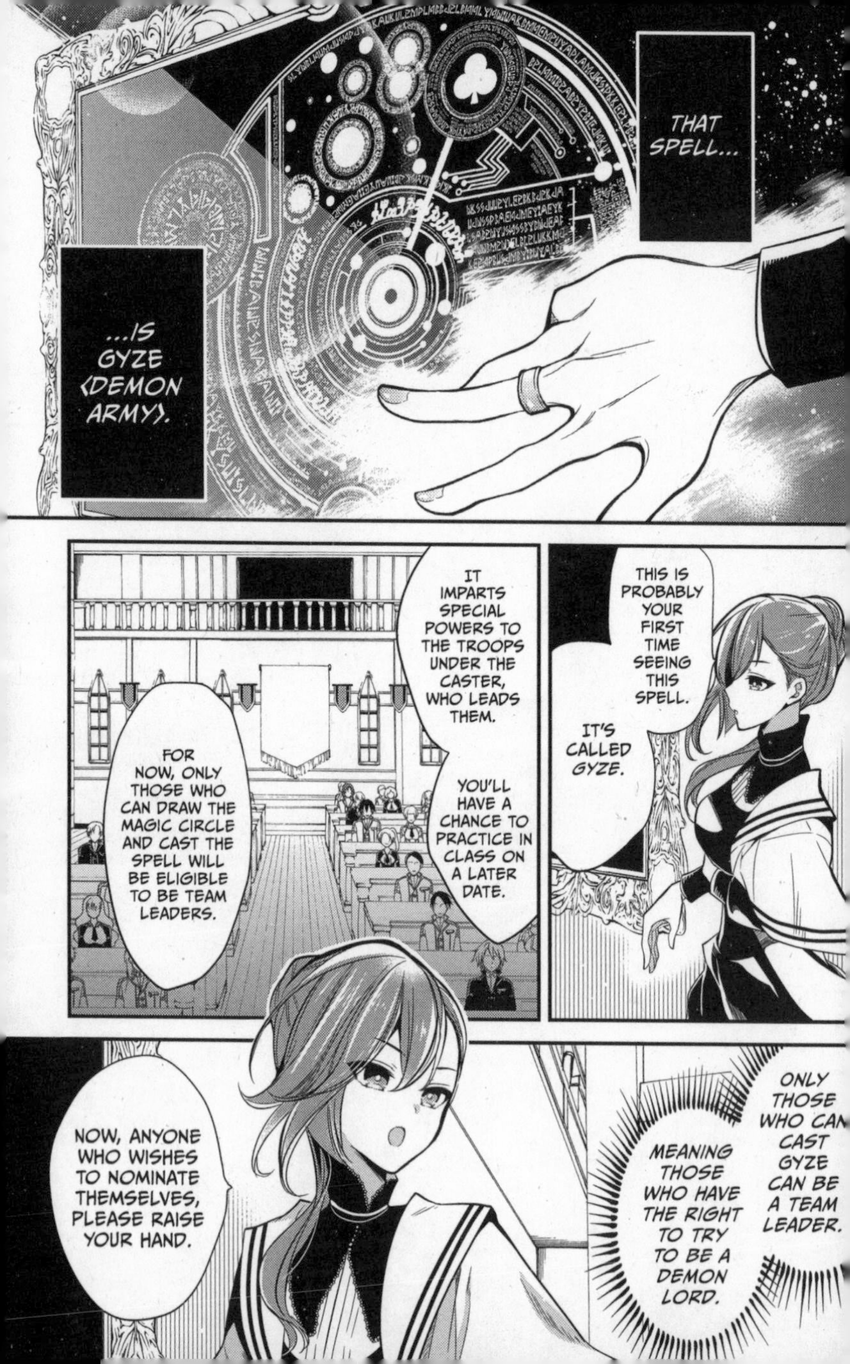
THAT SPELL...
...IS GYZE <DEMON ARMY>.
THIS IS PROBABLY YOUR FIRST TIME SEEING THIS SPELL.
IT'S CALLED GYZE.
IT IMPARTS SPECIAL POWERS TO THE TROOPS UNDER THE CASTER, WHO LEADS THEM.
YOU'LL HAVE A CHANCE TO PRACTICE IN CLASS ON A LATER DATE.
FOR NOW, ONLY THOSE WHO CAN DRAW THE MAGIC CIRCLE AND CAST THE SPELL WILL BE ELIGIBLE TO BE TEAM LEADERS.
ONLY THOSE WHO CAN CAST GYZE CAN BE A TEAM LEADER.
MEANING THOSE WHO HAVE THE RIGHT TO TRY TO BE A DEMON LORD.
NOW, ANYONE WHO WISHES TO NOMINATE THEMSELVES, PLEASE RAISE YOUR HAND.

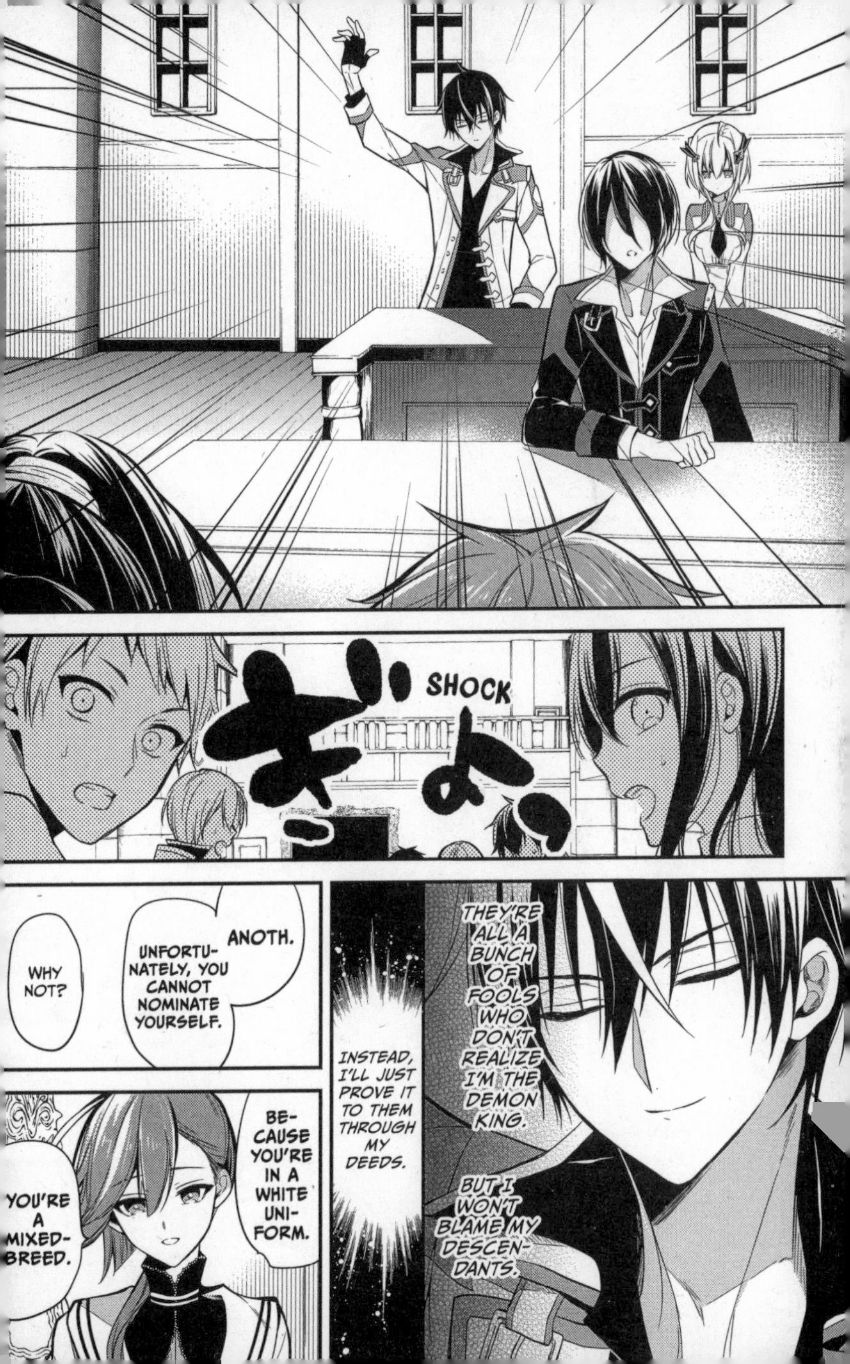
SHOCK
THEY'RE ALL A BUNCH OF FOOLS WHO DON'T REALIZE I'M THE DEMON KING.
BUT I WON'T BLAME MY DESCEN-DANTS.
INSTEAD, I'LL JUST PROVE IT TO THEM THROUGH MY DEEDS.
ANOTH. UNFORTU-NATELY, YOU CANNOT NOMINATE YOURSELF.
WHY NOT?
BE-CAUSE YOU'RE IN A WHITE UNI-FORM.
YOU'RE A MIXED-BREED.

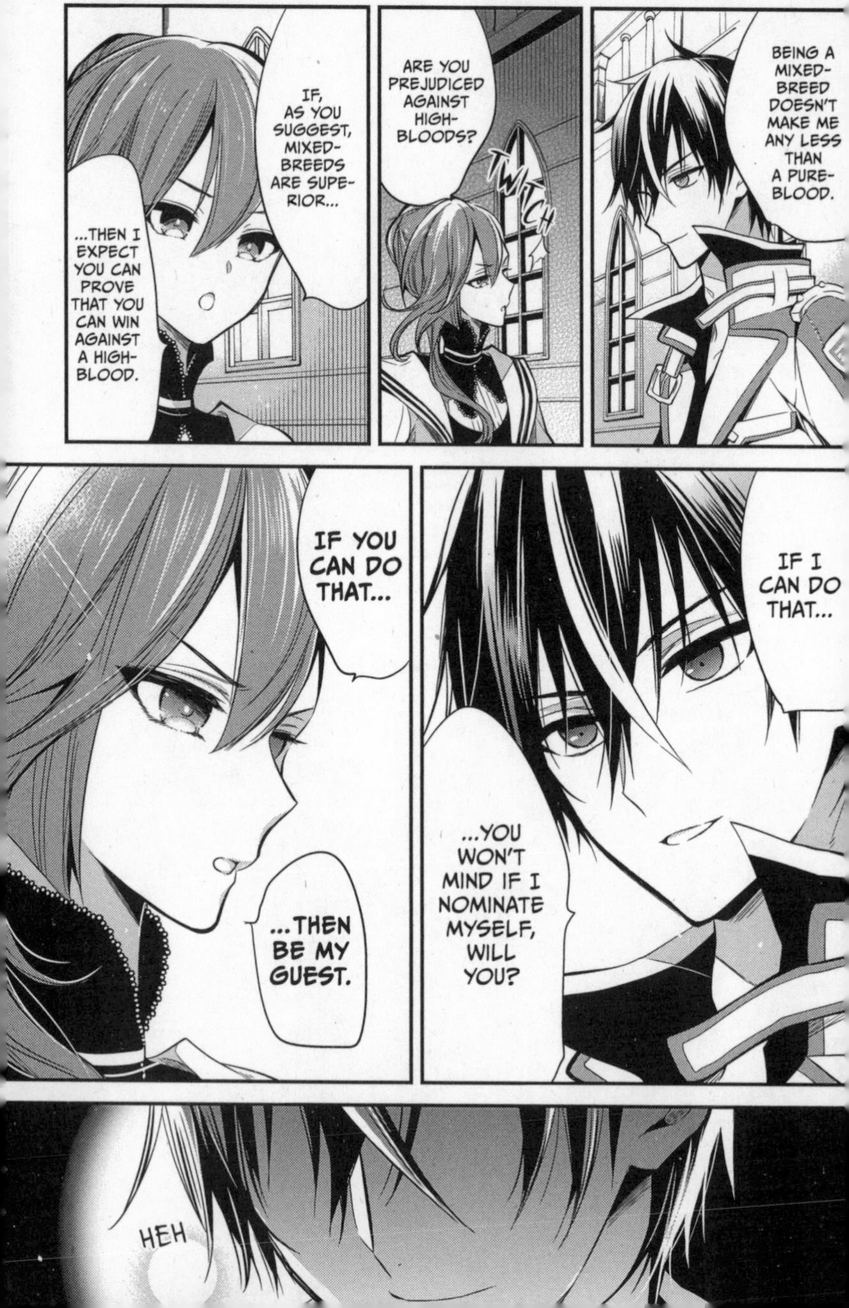
BEING A MIXED-BREED DOESN'T MAKE ME ANY LESS THAN A PURE-BLOOD.
ARE YOU PREJUDICED AGAINST HIGH-BLOODS?
TWITCH
IF, AS YOU SUGGEST, MIXED-BREEDS ARE SUPERIOR...
...THEN I EXPECT YOU CAN PROVE THAT YOU CAN WIN AGAINST A HIGH-BLOOD.
IF I CAN DO THAT...
...YOU WON'T MIND IF I NOMINATE MYSELF, WILL YOU?
IF YOU CAN DO THAT...
...THEN BE MY GUEST.
HEH

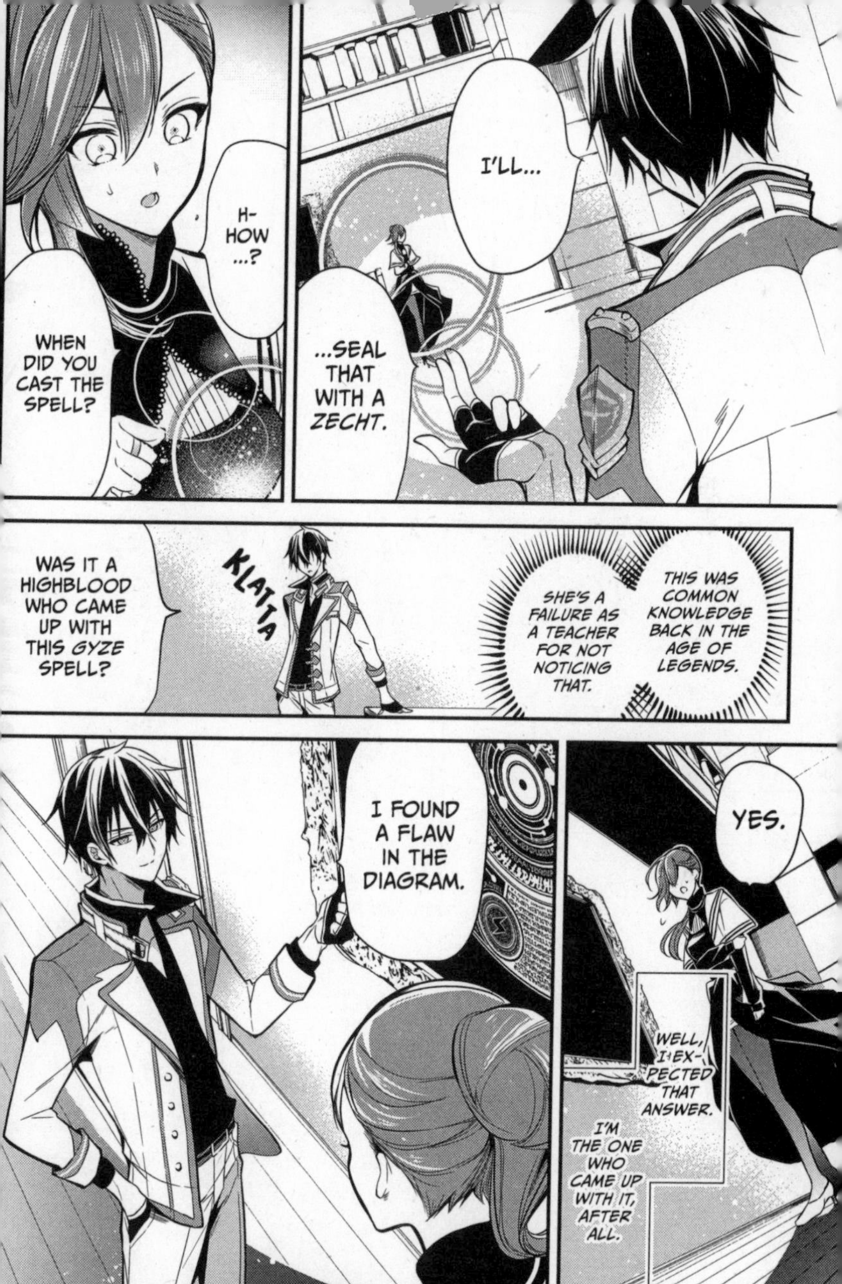
I'LL...
...SEAL THAT WITH A ZECHT.
H-HOW...?
WHEN DID YOU CAST THE SPELL?
THIS WAS COMMON KNOWLEDGE BACK IN THE AGE OF LEGENDS.
SHE'S A FAILURE AS A TEACHER FOR NOT NOTICING THAT.
KLATTA
WAS IT A HIGHBLOOD WHO CAME UP WITH THIS GYZE SPELL?
YES.
WELL, I EXPECTED THAT ANSWER.
I'M THE ONE WHO CAME UP WITH IT, AFTER ALL.
I FOUND A FLAW IN THE DIAGRAM.

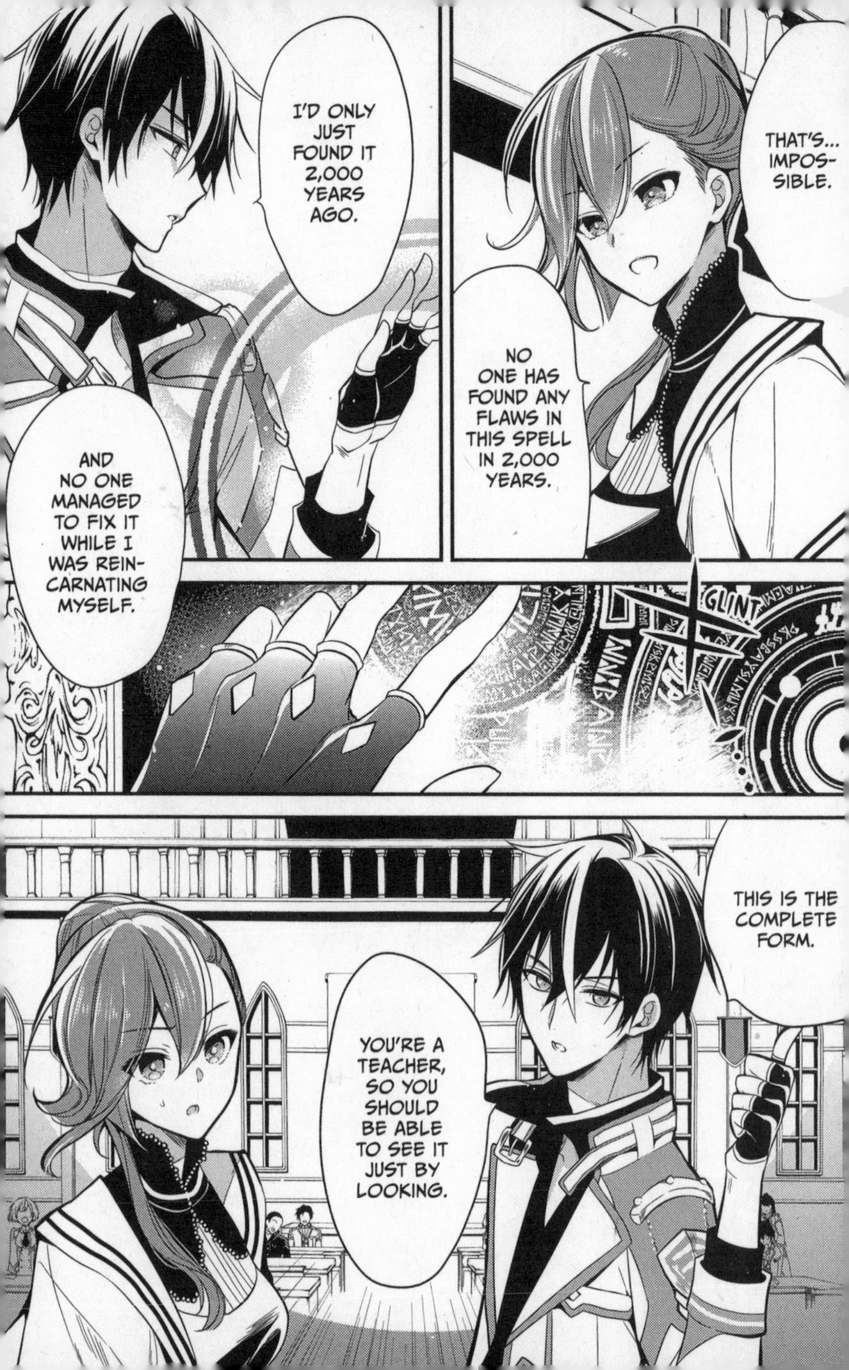
THAT'S... IMPOSSIBLE.
NO ONE HAS FOUND ANY FLAWS IN THIS SPELL IN 2,000 YEARS.
I'D ONLY JUST FOUND IT 2,000 YEARS AGO.
AND NO ONE MANAGED TO FIX IT WHILE I WAS REINCARNATING MYSELF.
GLINT
THIS IS THE COMPLETE FORM.
YOU'RE A TEACHER, SO YOU SHOULD BE ABLE TO SEE IT JUST BY LOOKING.

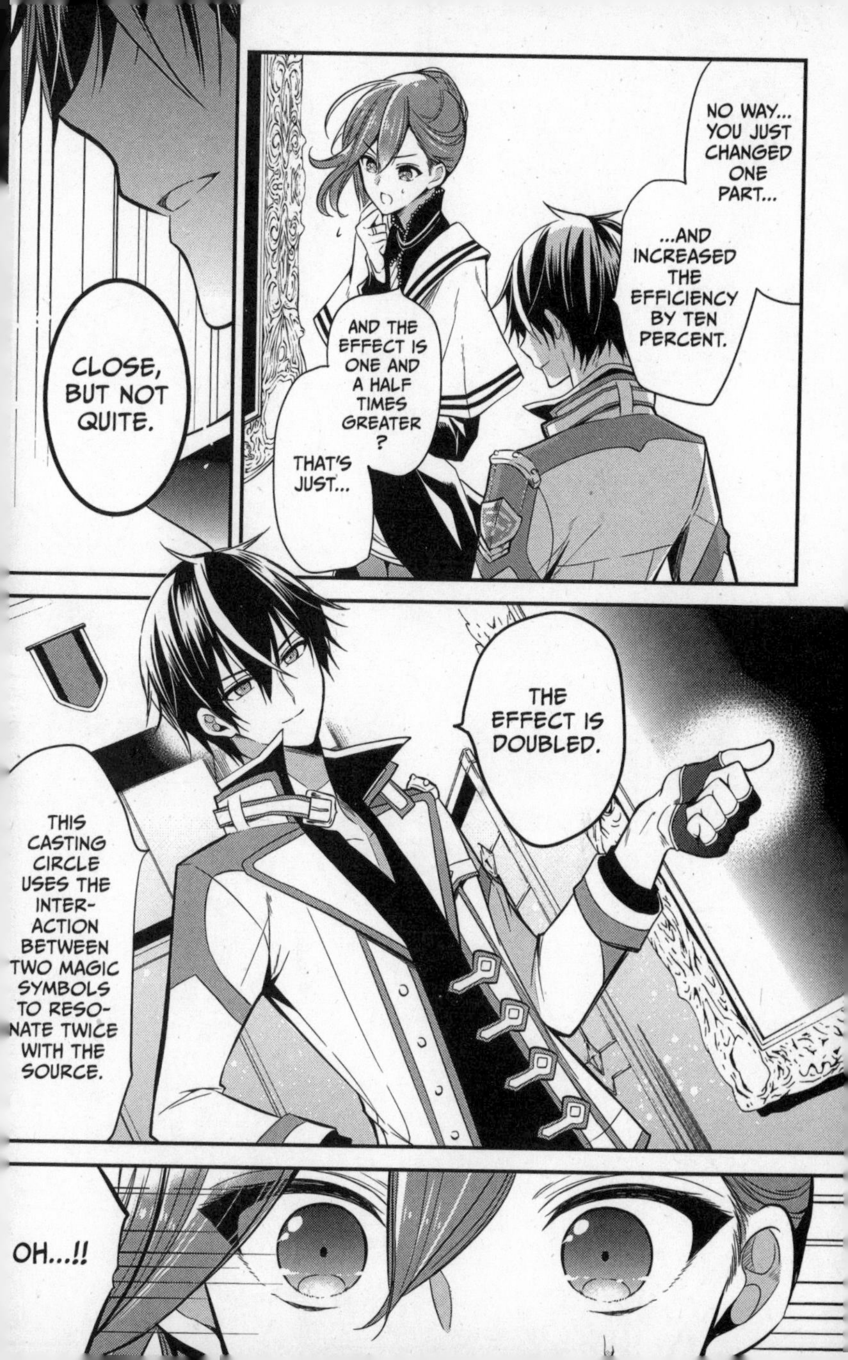
NO WAY... YOU JUST CHANGED ONE PART...
...AND INCREASED THE EFFICIENCY BY TEN PERCENT.
AND THE EFFECT IS ONE AND A HALF TIMES GREATER?
THAT'S JUST...
CLOSE, BUT NOT QUITE.
THE EFFECT IS DOUBLED.
THIS CASTING CIRCLE USES THE INTER-ACTION BETWEEN TWO MAGIC SYMBOLS TO RESO-NATE TWICE WITH THE SOURCE.
OH...!!

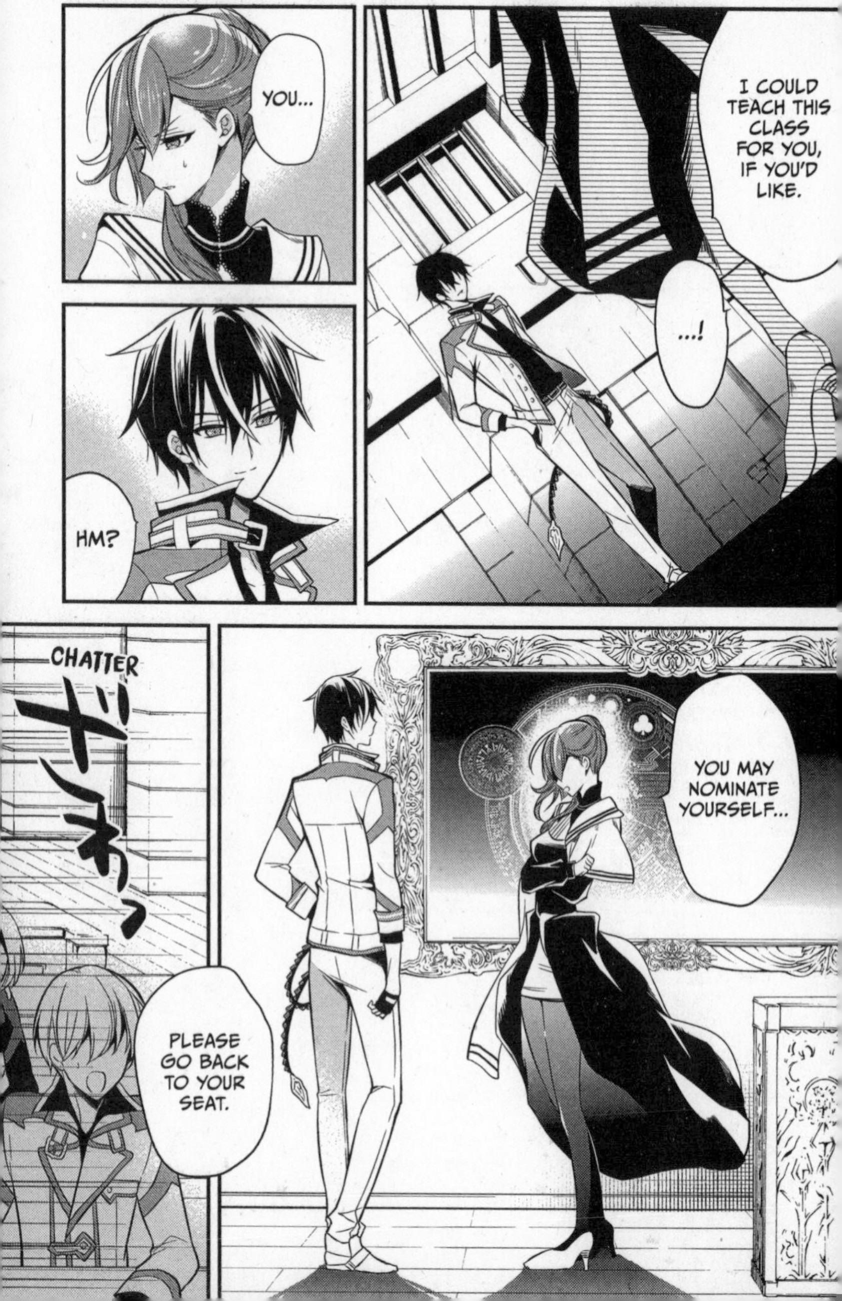
I COULD TEACH THIS CLASS FOR YOU, IF YOU'D LIKE.
...!
YOU...
HM?
YOU MAY NOMINATE YOURSELF...
PLEASE GO BACK TO YOUR SEAT.
CHATTER

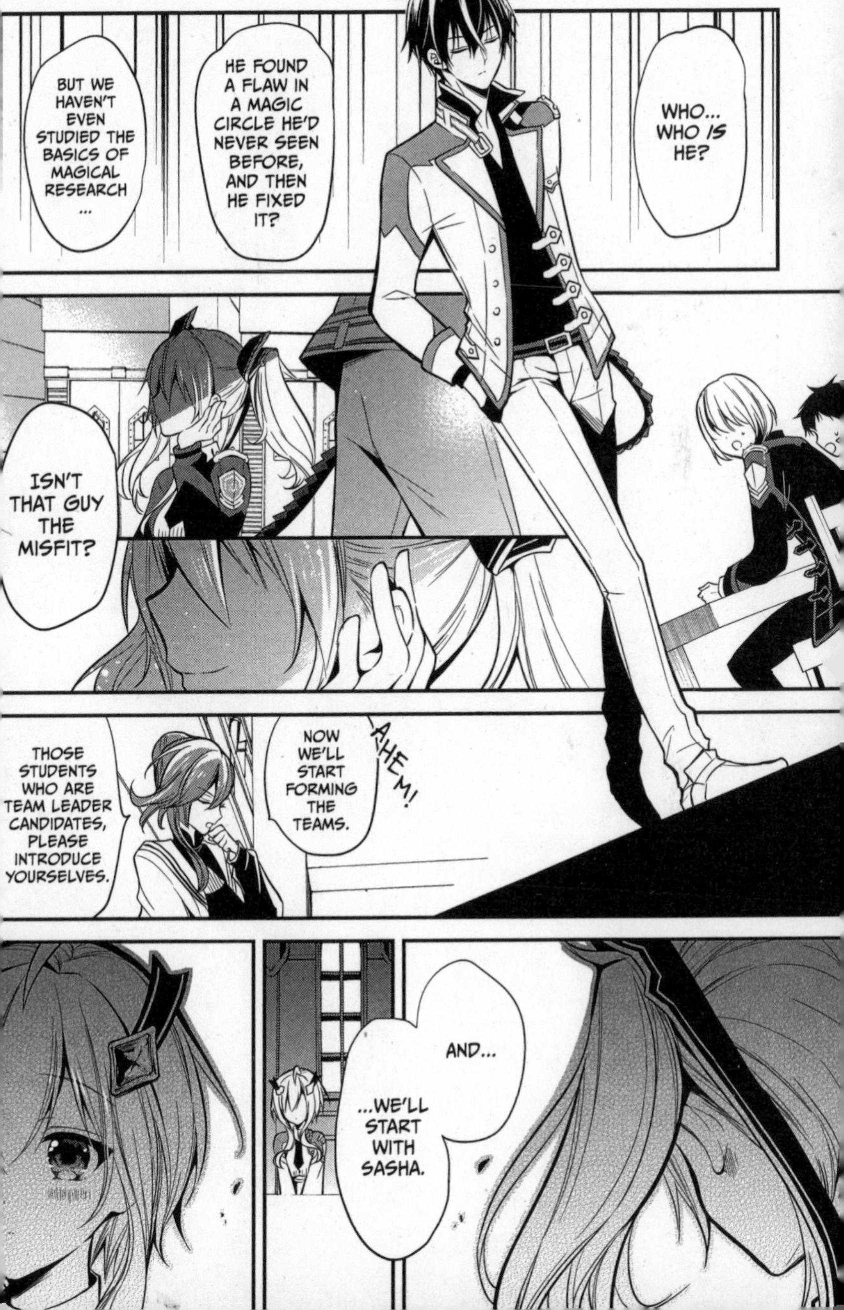
WHO... WHO *IS* HE?
HE FOUND A FLAW IN A MAGIC CIRCLE HE'D NEVER SEEN BEFORE, AND THEN HE FIXED IT?
BUT WE HAVEN'T EVEN STUDIED THE BASICS OF MAGICAL RESEARCH ...
ISN'T THAT GUY THE MISFIT?
AHEM!
NOW WE'LL START FORMING THE TEAMS.
THOSE STUDENTS WHO ARE TEAM LEADER CANDIDATES, PLEASE INTRODUCE YOURSELVES.
AND...
...WE'LL START WITH SASHA.

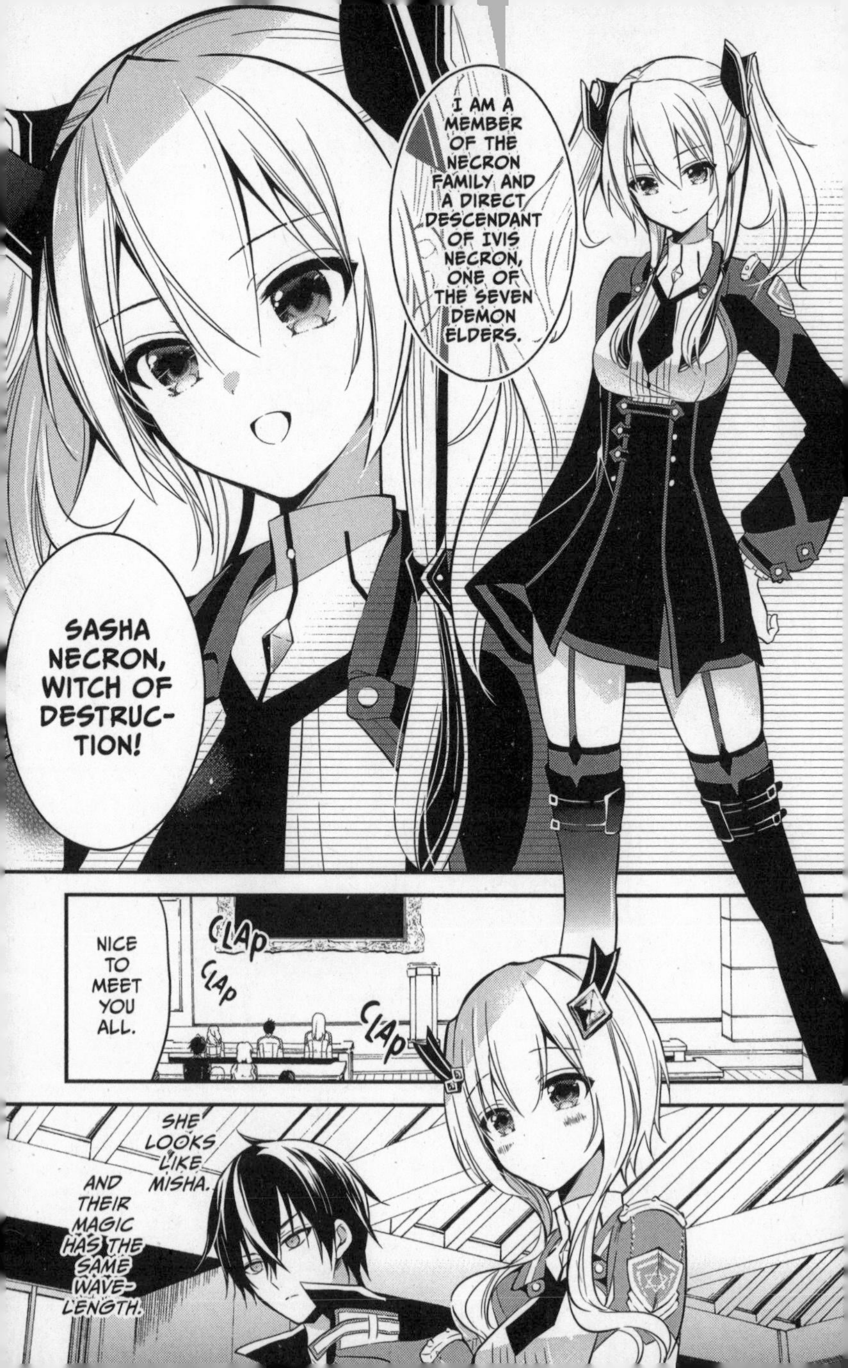
I AM A MEMBER OF THE NECRON FAMILY AND A DIRECT DESCENDANT OF IVIS NECRON, ONE OF THE SEVEN DEMON ELDERS.
SASHA NECRON, WITCH OF DESTRUC-TION!
CLAP
CLAP
CLAP
NICE TO MEET YOU ALL.
SHE LOOKS LIKE MISHA.
AND THEIR MAGIC HAS THE SAME WAVE-LENGTH.

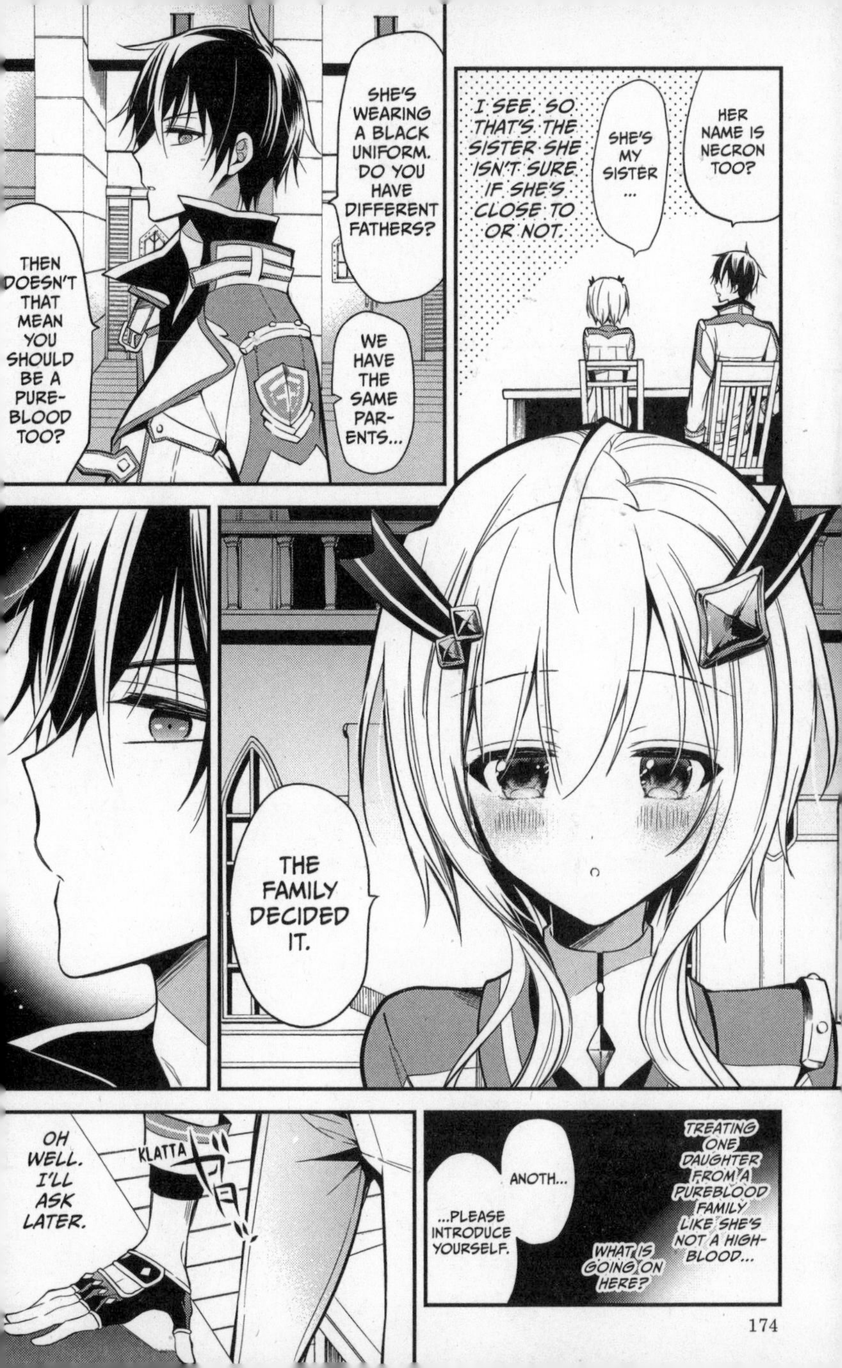
HER NAME IS NECRON TOO?
SHE'S MY SISTER ...
I SEE. SO THAT'S THE SISTER SHE ISN'T SURE IF SHE'S CLOSE TO OR NOT.
SHE'S WEARING A BLACK UNIFORM. DO YOU HAVE DIFFERENT FATHERS?
WE HAVE THE SAME PAR-ENTS...
THEN DOESN'T THAT MEAN YOU SHOULD BE A PURE-BLOOD TOO?
THE FAMILY DECIDED IT.
TREATING ONE DAUGHTER FROM A PUREBLOOD FAMILY LIKE SHE'S NOT A HIGH-BLOOD...
WHAT IS GOING ON HERE?
ANOTH...
...PLEASE INTRODUCE YOURSELF.
KLATTA
OH WELL. I'LL ASK LATER.

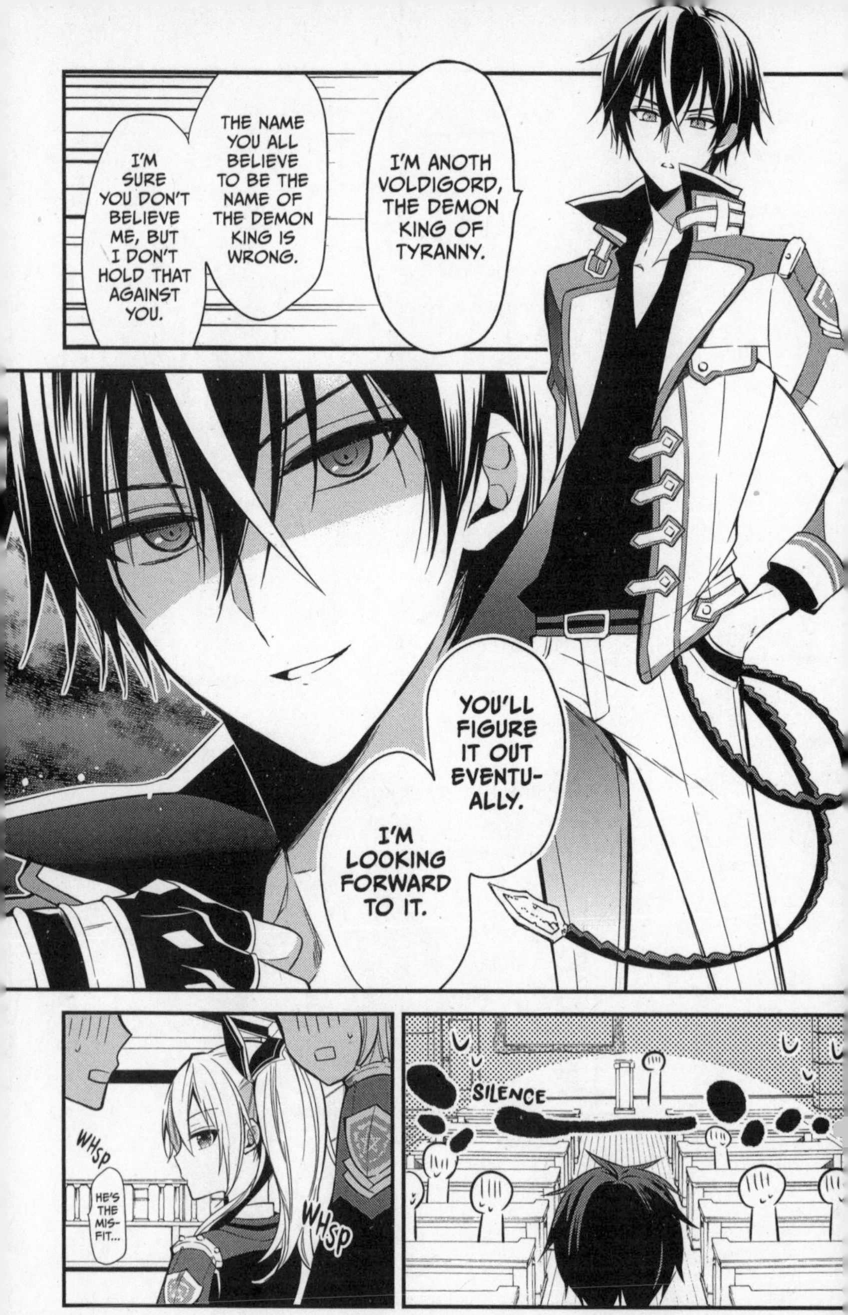
I'M ANOTH VOLDIGORD, THE DEMON KING OF TYRANNY.
THE NAME YOU ALL BELIEVE TO BE THE NAME OF THE DEMON KING IS WRONG.
I'M SURE YOU DON'T BELIEVE ME, BUT I DON'T HOLD THAT AGAINST YOU.
YOU'LL FIGURE IT OUT EVENTU-ALLY.
I'M LOOKING FORWARD TO IT.
SILENCE
WHSP
WHSP
HE'S THE MIS-FIT...

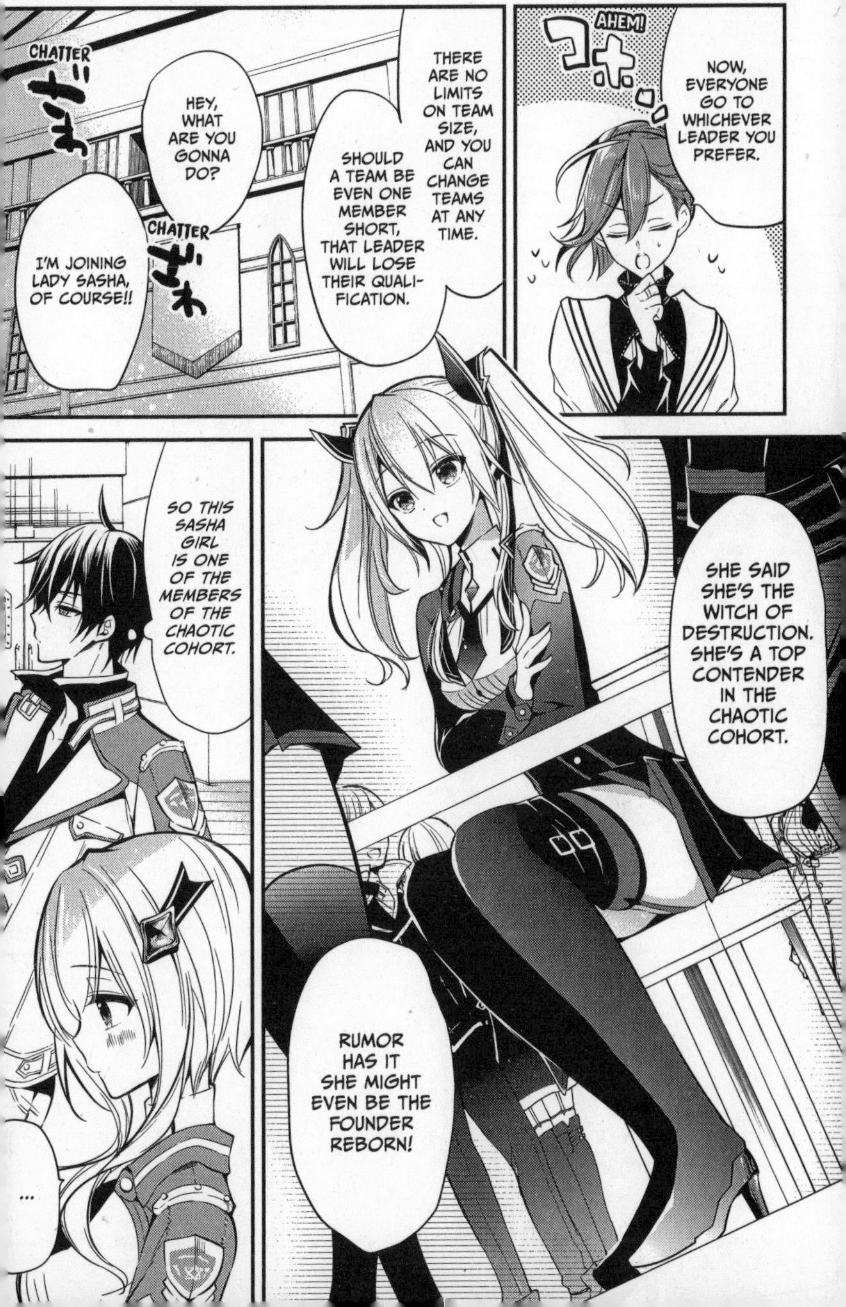
AHEM!
NOW, EVERYONE GO TO WHICHEVER LEADER YOU PREFER.
THERE ARE NO LIMITS ON TEAM SIZE, AND YOU CAN CHANGE TEAMS AT ANY TIME.
SHOULD A TEAM BE EVEN ONE MEMBER SHORT, THAT LEADER WILL LOSE THEIR QUALI-FICATION.
HEY, WHAT ARE YOU GONNA DO?
CHATTER
CHATTER
I'M JOINING LADY SASHA, OF COURSE!!
SHE SAID SHE'S THE WITCH OF DESTRUCTION. SHE'S A TOP CONTENDER IN THE CHAOTIC COHORT.
RUMOR HAS IT SHE MIGHT EVEN BE THE FOUNDER REBORN!
SO THIS SASHA GIRL IS ONE OF THE MEMBERS OF THE CHAOTIC COHORT.
...

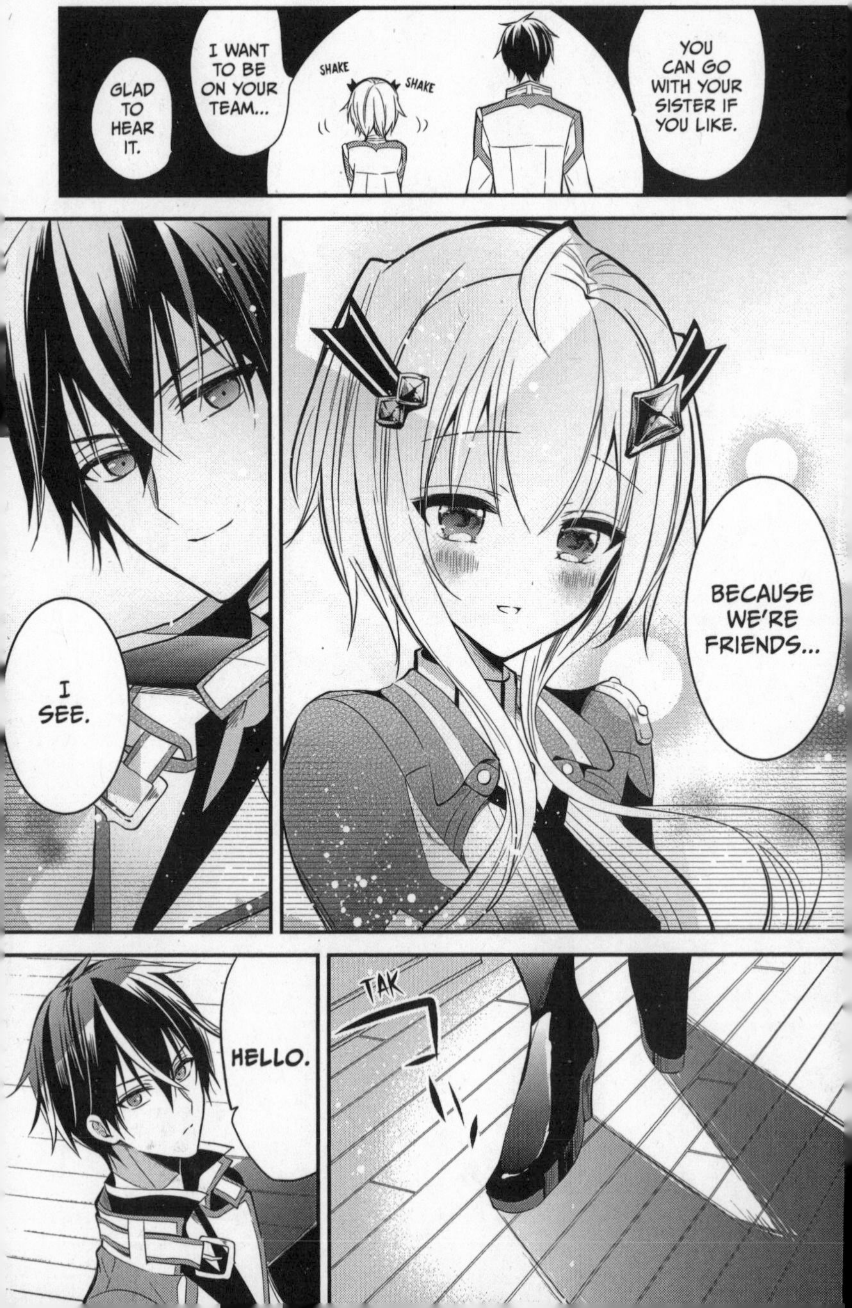
YOU CAN GO WITH YOUR SISTER IF YOU LIKE.
SHAKE
SHAKE
I WANT TO BE ON YOUR TEAM...
GLAD TO HEAR IT.
BECAUSE WE'RE FRIENDS...
I SEE.
TAK
HELLO.

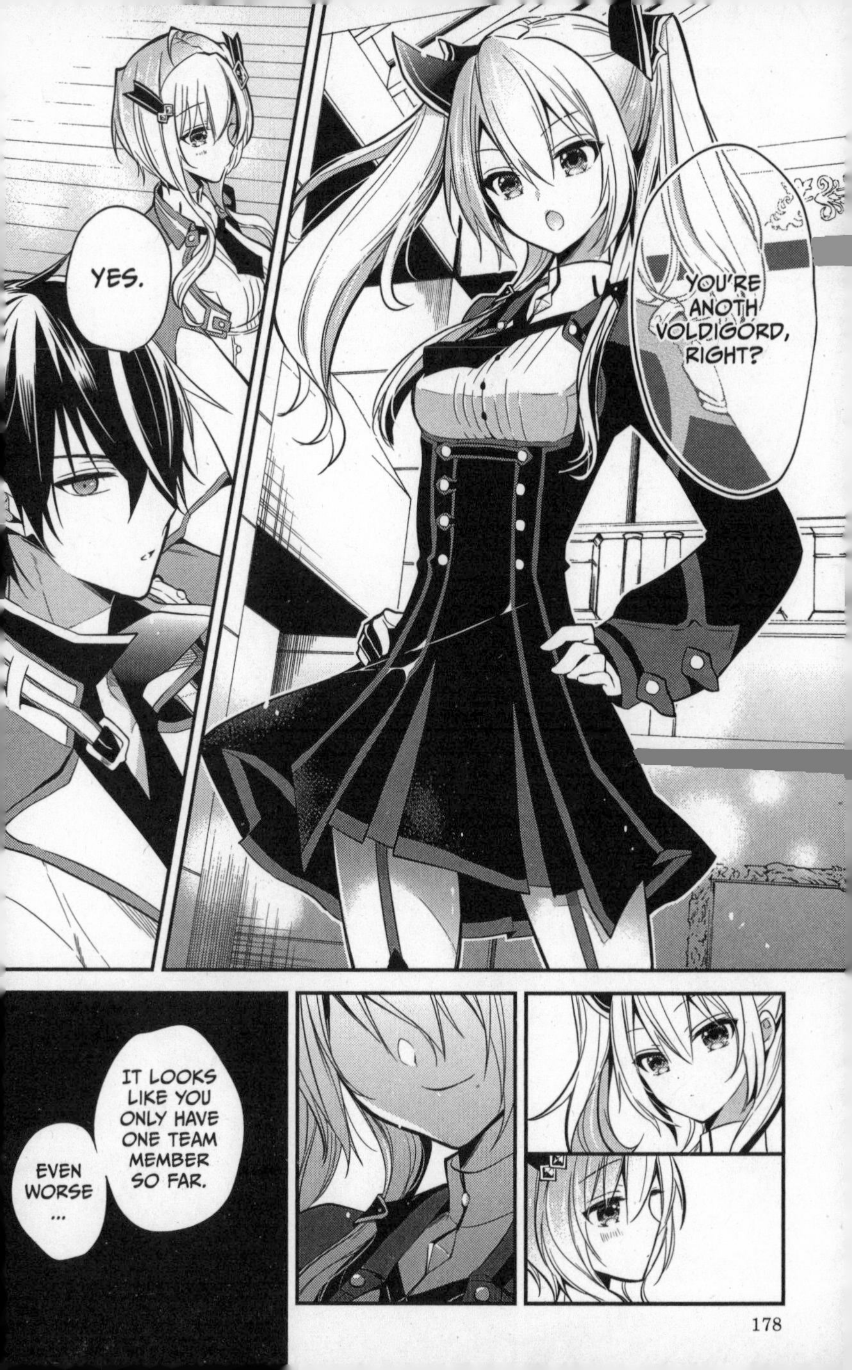
YOU'RE ANOTH VOLDIGORD, RIGHT?
YES.
IT LOOKS LIKE YOU ONLY HAVE ONE TEAM MEMBER SO FAR.
EVEN WORSE ...

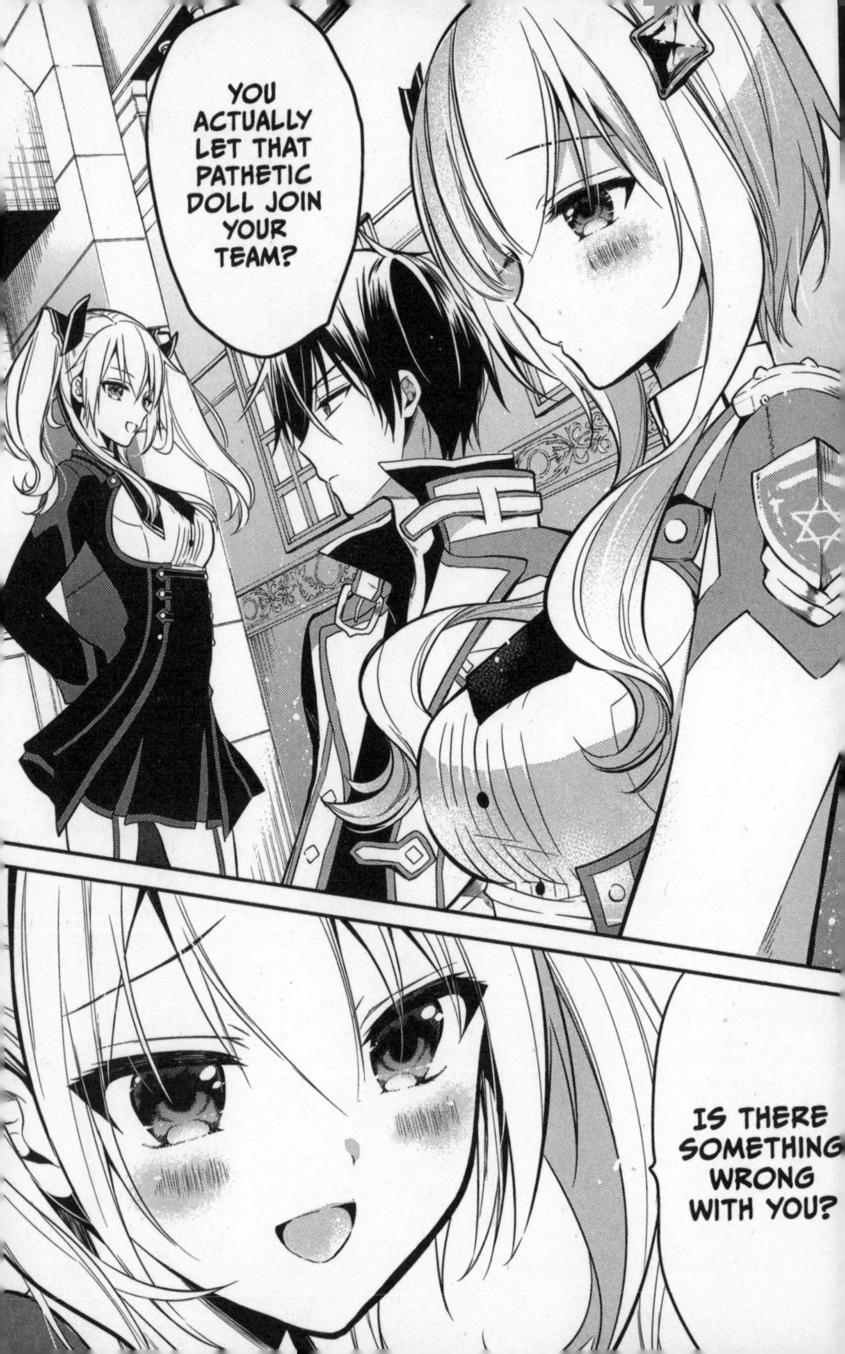
YOU ACTUALLY LET THAT PATHETIC DOLL JOIN YOUR TEAM?
IS THERE SOMETHING WRONG WITH YOU?

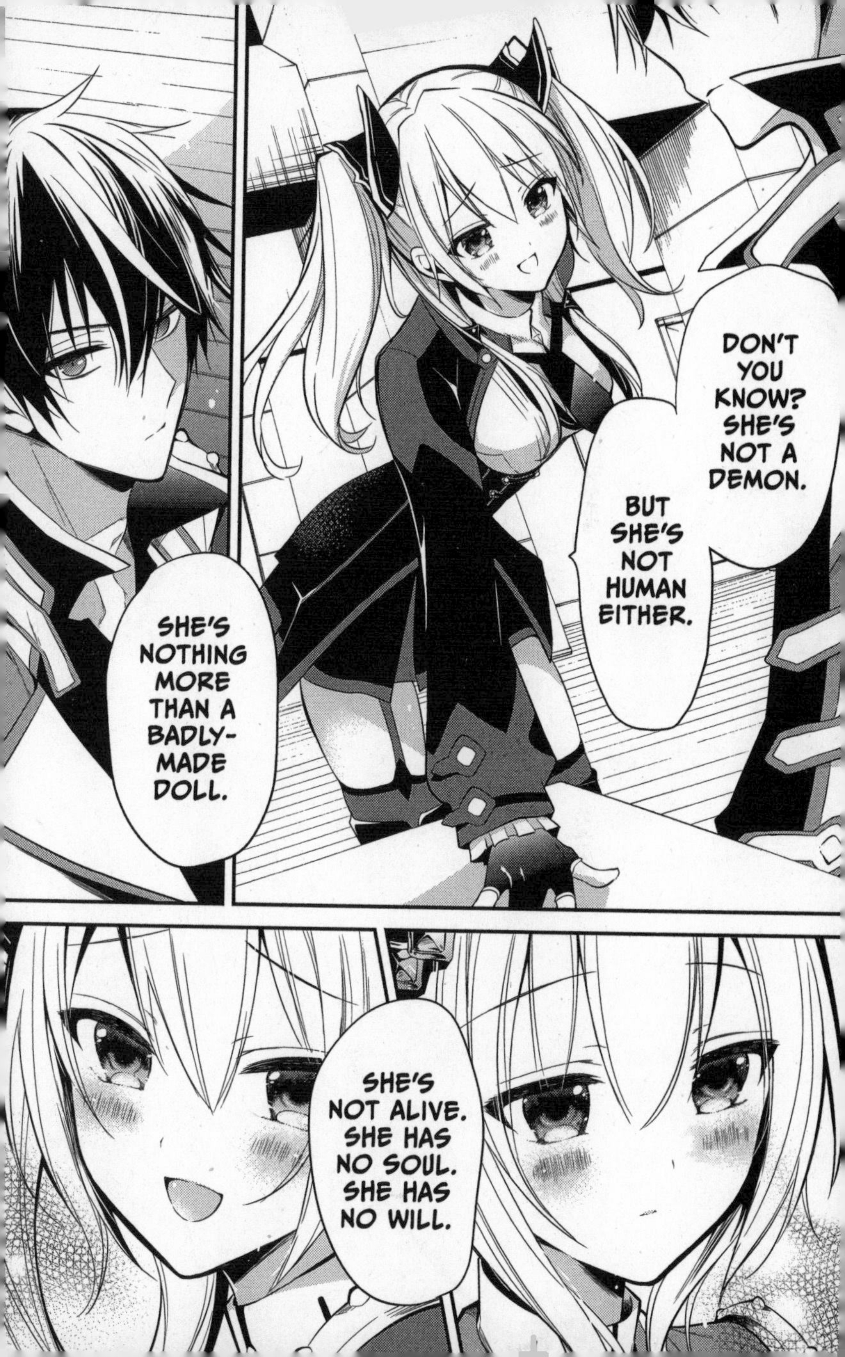
DON'T YOU KNOW? SHE'S NOT A DEMON.
BUT SHE'S NOT HUMAN EITHER.
SHE'S NOTHING MORE THAN A BADLY-MADE DOLL.
SHE'S NOT ALIVE. SHE HAS NO SOUL. SHE HAS NO WILL.

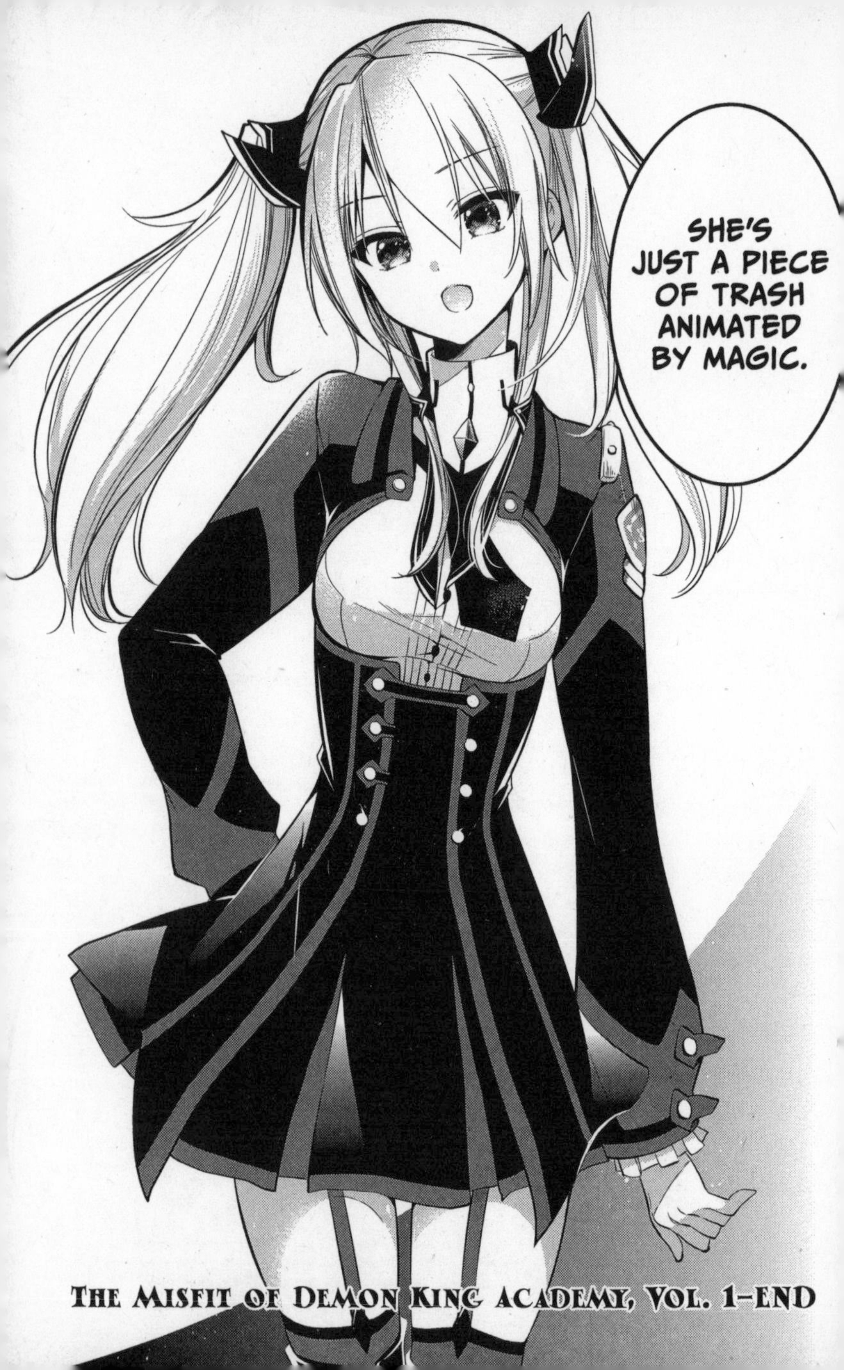
SHE'S JUST A PIECE OF TRASH ANIMATED BY MAGIC.
THE MISFIT OF DEMON KING ACADEMY, VOL. 1—END

The Misfit of
Demon King Academy

HISTORY'S STRONGEST DEMON KING REINCARNATES
AND GOES TO SCHOOL WITH HIS DESCENDANTS

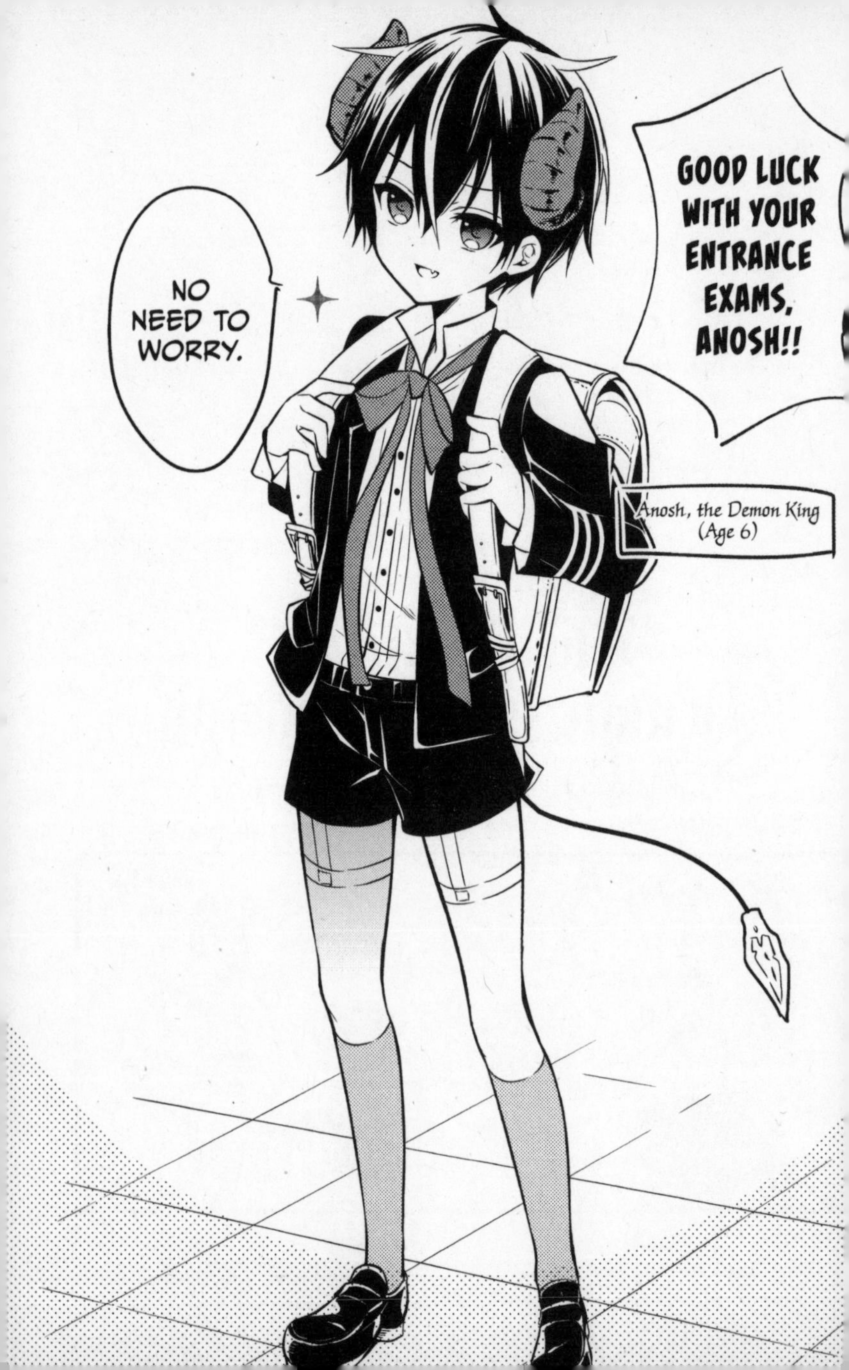
GOOD LUCK WITH YOUR ENTRANCE EXAMS, ANOSH!!
NO NEED TO WORRY.
Anosh, the Demon King (Age 6)

The Misfit of Demon King Academy

HISTORY'S STRONGEST DEMON KING REINCARNATES AND GOES TO SCHOOL WITH HIS DESCENDANTS

PLEASED TO MEET YOU, MISHA.
WHEN DID THIS PLACE BECOME A KINDERGARTEN?

The Misfit of Demon King Academy

HISTORY'S STRONGEST DEMON KING REINCARNATES AND GOES TO SCHOOL WITH HIS DESCENDANTS

Please turn to page 191
to read the bonus short story
"The Serious Way to
Resolve a Misunderstanding,"
written by SHU!

to meet her gaze.

"Anoth...?"

As Misha taught me, I brought my face close to Mom's and said, in all seriousness, "Trust me. You are mistaken in so many ways. There is no problem here. I'm serious."

"Really? Y-yes, of course! You're actually serious this time, aren't you?"

"Exactly. Do you understand now?"

"Yes, I'm so sorry, Anoth. You were serious, but I didn't trust you! I've come to my senses now! You aren't fooling around. You're serious!"

Mom jumped up to her feet and left the room with Dad. They were both smiling.

"Stay as long as you like, Misha!"

The door closed quietly.

"Hmm. Was that right, Misha?"

"Not quite."

THE END

She stood and stepped in front of me. "Try to get closer to her, if possible."

"I see. And then?"

She looked me straight in the eyes. "Like this. Don't use your Sight."

"Oh. I understand."

Taking her advice, I brought my face even closer to hers and met her eyes. "So, like thi—"

The door opened with a bang, and Mom walked in, her face all smiles.

"I'm home, Anoth! Are you all right? You weren't lonely, were...you...?" Her smile faded quickly, and she gasped, as if realizing something. "Y-you said you could watch the shop by yourself...all by yourself... Is this what you meant by watching the shop...?!"

Behind Mom, who was busy falling to her knees, was none other than Dad, with a dazed expression on his face. "On the bed...staring into each other's eyes...clothes mussed, breathing heavily..."

That last part was all in his imagination.

"Dad, look closer," I said, using the serious expression I had just learned from Misha. "We would hardly be breathing heavily from just this. And our clothes are fine."

"Wha...?! Y-you..." He was clearly in shock.

Misha tilted her head. "We what?"

"You're...experienced...?! You mean, you've already progressed beyond that stage?!"

I slowly rose to my feet and and went to Mom's side. She was muttering things like, "It's all right, Isabella. It's all right. Premarital sex... No, it has to be some mistake. Just a mistake..."

"Mom." She was still slumped on the floor, so I knelt down

walked in and sat on my desk chair. "Where are your parents?"

As I settled on the bed I said, "Unfortunately, they're out. I'm home alone today."

Then I remembered something and let out a short chuckle.

"Is something funny?"

"This is absolutely perfect. Mom asked me if I was worried about watching the shop on my own. I asked her why in the world I would be and told her about how I once stayed behind in my castle to face an entire human army on my own. But it was as if she didn't even hear my words."

Misha tilted her head. "Maybe you should have just said it normally?"

"Why? Are you saying I couldn't convince her because I didn't say it the right way?"

She froze. She looked like she wanted to nod, but she couldn't bring herself to do it out of the desire to be nice to me. "Hypothetically, yes."

"Hmm. Well, that is a possibility. Still, her misunderstanding is a problem for me. How am I to get her to actually listen to what I say?"

"You have to be serious," she said bluntly.

"I *was* serious. I suppose she did not catch on to that, though. What should I do?"

"...Look her right in the eyes."

"Look her in the eyes with my Sight?" I opened my eyes wide and focused my Sight on Misha with every bit of seriousness I could muster. "Like this?"

She stared back at me in silence, perhaps unsure how to answer. She looked as if she wanted to say that my face was frightening. "Too much."

"I'm still not quite used to the ways of this age, I suppose. Could you show me an example?"

Oh. She wasn't used to having friends, so she hesitated outside the door. How adorable.

"No need to fear. Even if you were to make some blunder far beyond anything I could imagine, I'm not so callous that I would end our friendship over that."

At that, Misha gave a faint smile. "I'm glad."

"Oh, that's right. I need to return this to you before I forget."

I pulled up a casting circle and reached into it to retrieve a silver brooch. It featured the design of an owl. Misha had showed it to Mom and Dad the other day when they asked her what sorts of accessories were popular in Midhayes. Dad was supposed to return it to her before she left, but apparently he had completely forgotten.

"Thank you."

"I should be thanking you. Dad said they found it very helpful."

"I'm glad." She sounded relieved. "I'll see you."

"You're leaving already?"

"I just came to get the brooch."

"If you don't have anything you need to do, you should stay and hang out. I was starting to get bored here by myself."

She blinked twice. "What about the books?"

"Just a way to pass the time. They're nothing to prioritize over a friend."

She thought about this for a moment and then answered, "I'll stay."

"Shall we go up to my room?"

She nodded and followed me. We went up to the second floor and entered my room.

"Go ahead and sit wherever you like."

After looking around my sparsely furnished room, Misha

be their last, would choose such a form of entertainment. I imagine that none of the authors of these stories had ever seen battle before.

Even as these thoughts ran through my head, I let my heart delight in the fictional tales. And then I heard footsteps outside.

It wasn't Mom and Dad. It was just one person. I thought it might be a customer for the smithy or appraisal shop, but the person just stood outside the door silently, making no move to come in.

After looking through the door with my Sight, I lifted my hand and crooked my finger toward me. My magic power reacted, and the door opened.

Standing there, her eyes wide with surprise, was Misha.

"What is it? Do you have business with me? If so, you should come in."

After blinking several times, she nodded her head at me and came inside. "How did you know?"

"My Sight is strong."

She tilted her head in confusion. "Clairvoyance?"

"Yes." I waved my finger, and the nine books closed. Then I sent a bit of power their way, and they floated through the air to settle on the bookshelf. "Why were you standing in front of the door?"

"...I was nervous."

"Nervous? Of what?"

She hung her head and softly said, "I wasn't sure what to say to you."

"Really? You worry over the strangest things."

"I'm not used to this," she said in a detached voice.

"What are you talking about?"

"Friends."

The Misfit of Demon King Academy

HISTORY'S STRONGEST DEMON KING REINCARNATES AND GOES TO SCHOOL WITH HIS DESCENDANTS

Bonus Short Story

The Serious Way to Resolve a Misunderstanding
by SHU

Nine books floated in the air.

In the storefront part of our house, I sank into a chair. I snapped my fingers, which glowed with the pale light of magic as the pages of the nine books started to flip, and I followed them with my magical Sight.

All of the books were novels. Mom and Dad bought them for me to pass the time while I waited until school started, but for some reason, they were actually interesting. They were all about demons fighting each other. Maybe that was what was popular in Dilhade.

Two thousand years ago there weren't a lot of stories, and the popular ones were all about love or the daily life of simple townsfolk. That was what the demons of old longed for.

Apparently, in the present day, all of the stories were heroic adventures wherein blood was washed away with yet more blood. Even so, they were oddly meek. Though the demons in the stories were at war, many of them were still somehow soft.

It had to be because Dilhade was at peace. No one in the middle of a war, always wondering if the next moment might

The Misfit of Demon King Academy

HISTORY'S STRONGEST DEMON KING REINCARNATES AND GOES TO SCHOOL WITH HIS DESCENDANTS

SHU (Story)

While I was reading this amazing adaptation, I realized something: Kaya sensei keeps making changes to fulfill all of my selfish little requests (I'm so sorry about that...), but this manga was already amazing to begin with. I'm 120% satisfied. If you read the original novel along with this adaptation, you'll learn more about this world and the characters, and that will make you enjoy the manga that much more. So please, check it out sometime.

KAYAHARUKA (Art)

The original story was very interesting, and all of the characters are extremely appealing. I love it all. And the relationships between the characters just keep getting more and more interesting! I'll do my best to convey the appeal of the original story, so please enjoy!

YOSHINORI SHIZUMA (Character Design)

Manga adaptations can depict a lot of little details that the illustrations in a novel just can't get across, so I'm looking forward to all of Anoth's escapades in the future. Do check out the novel as well!

The Misfit of Demon King Academy

1

ORIGINAL STORY BY SHU
ART BY KAYAHARUKA
CHARACTER DESIGN BY YOSHINORI SHIZUMA

Translation: Leighann Harvey
Lettering: Phil Christie
Cover Design: Andrea Miller
Editor: Leyla Aker

THE MISFIT OF DEMON KING ACADEMY Volume 1
© SHU 2018
© 2018 Kayaharuka/SQUARE ENIX CO., LTD.
Licensed by KADOKAWA CORPORATION
First published in Japan in 2018 by SQUARE ENIX CO., LTD.
English translation rights arranged with
SQUARE ENIX CO., LTD. and SQUARE ENIX INC.
English translation © 2020 by SQUARE ENIX CO., LTD.

All rights reserved. Published in the United States by Square Enix Manga/Books,
an imprint of the Book Publishing Division of SQUARE ENIX, INC.

SQUARE ENIX and the SQUARE ENIX logo are registered trademarks
or trademarks of Square Enix Holdings Co., Ltd.

ISBN: 978-1-64609-042-6

Library of Congress Cataloging-in-Publication data is on file with the publisher.

Printed in the U.S.A.
First printing, April 2020
10 9 8 7 6 5 4 3 2 1

WITHDRAWN

SQUARE ENIX
MANGA & BOOKS
www.square-enix-books.com